Nuclear Minds

Nuclear Minds

*Cold War Psychological Science and
the Bombings of Hiroshima and Nagasaki*

RAN ZWIGENBERG

THE UNIVERSITY OF CHICAGO PRESS   CHICAGO AND LONDON

The University of Chicago Press, Chicago 60637
The University of Chicago Press, Ltd., London
© 2023 by The University of Chicago
All rights reserved. No part of this book may be used or reproduced in any manner
whatsoever without written permission, except in the case of brief quotations in critical
articles and reviews. For more information, contact the University of Chicago Press,
1427 E. 60th St., Chicago, IL 60637.
Published 2023
Printed in the United States of America

32 31 30 29 28 27 26 25 24 23   1 2 3 4 5

ISBN-13: 978-0-226-82591-5 (cloth)
ISBN-13: 978-0-226-82676-9 (paper)
ISBN-13: 978-0-226-82675-2 (e-book)
DOI: https://doi.org/10.7208/chicago/9780226826752.001.0001

Library of Congress Cataloging-in-Publication Data

Names: Zwigenberg, Ran, 1976–author.
Title: Nuclear minds : Cold War psychological science and the bombings of
     Hiroshima and Nagasaki / Ran Zwigenberg.
Description: Chicago : The University of Chicago Press, 2023. |
     Includes bibliographical references and index.
Identifiers: LCCN 2022049592 | ISBN 9780226825915 (cloth) |
     ISBN 9780226826769 (paperback) | ISBN 9780226826752 (ebook)
     Subjects: LCSH: Nuclear warfare—Psychological aspects. | Atomic bomb
     victims—Japan—Hiroshima-shi. | Cold War.
Classification: LCC U263 .Z88 2023 | DDC 355.02/17019—dc23/eng/20230117
LC record available at https://lccn.loc.gov/2022049592

♾ This paper meets the requirements of ANSI/NISO Z39.48-1992 (Permanence of Paper).

FOR CHIKAKO

Contents

Note on Language   ix

Introduction   1

PART 1.   Bombing Minds

CHAPTER 1.   American Psychological Sciences and the Road to Hiroshima and Nagasaki   27

CHAPTER 2.   Bombing "the Japanese Mind": Alexander Leighton's Hiroshima   50

CHAPTER 3.   Healing a Sick World: The Nuclear Age on the Analyst's Couch   74

CHAPTER 4.   Nuclear Trauma and Panic in the United States   92

PART 2.   Researching Minds, Healing Minds

CHAPTER 5.   Y. Scott Matsumoto, the ABCC, and A-Bomb Social Work   121

CHAPTER 6.   Konuma Masuho and the Psychiatry of the Bomb   157

CHAPTER 7.   Kubo Yoshitoshi and the Psychology of Peace   189

CHAPTER 8.   Social Workers, Nuclear Sociology, and the Road to PTSD   222

Conclusion 248

Acknowledgments 257

Notes 261

Index 301

Note on Language

This book uses the standard Japanese, Chinese, and Korean format of family name before given name. In cases of scholars writing primarily in English, the family name is placed last, as it is in the names of Western scholars. Macrons are used throughout, except in names of people and places that are used widely in English, such as Tokyo or Osaka.

Introduction

"This book does not judge its subjects. They are not stupid, smart, brave, or cowardly; they are human. Their decisions were influenced by many factors, which, often, they were not conscious of. The historian . . . has no monopoly on the truth, but as long as he is honest in his work, and he is aware that not a few pieces are missing in the puzzle, his writing and exposés might be of some value." — Amiram Ezov[1]

Robert Lifton's Hiroshima

In April 1962, a young Jewish American psychiatrist named Robert Jay Lifton, then in Japan to conduct research on Japanese youth, went on a visit to Hiroshima. There he met a Japanese colleague by the name of Kubo Yoshitoshi, a psychology professor at Hiroshima University. The meeting was one of a series of meetings and visits that left a strong impression on Lifton and his wife, Betty Jean Lifton. Lifton recalled that in visiting the A-Bomb Museum and looking at the exhibits, "somehow seeing these pictures in Hiroshima was entirely different: one was there; it really happened; and the most profoundly disturbing thought — then and throughout our stay in Hiroshima — It might happen again, everywhere, with bombs a thousand times the strength of that first 'little' A-bomb." The visit left the two almost physically ill: "We left that part of the exhibit reeling . . . both of us anxious, fearful and depressed." As Lifton met more survivors, doctors, and activists, he began to contemplate staying in Hiroshima and conducting psychological research on its survivors. Lifton met with Kubo to learn about his research into the psychological state of *hibakusha* (A-bomb survivors). The meeting was not a success. In a letter to a friend, David Riesman, Lifton remarked: "I found our talk curiously unsatisfying, and it was hard to tell exactly what he was after in his studies." Lifton conceded that Kubo had made some "interesting points," and that foremost among them was the observation that "survivors of the A-bomb have no clear 'end' to their disaster experience, since they carried within them the constant fear that at any point . . . they could become sick and die." In addition, Kubo observed that "survivors appear to be reasonably calm on the surface, much like anyone else, even when discussing such things as bomb tests and war dangers. But under certain stimuli . . . they manifest great anxiety." Survivors, Kubo observed, "recall the A-bomb catastrophy [*sic*] and again imagine themselves involved in it."[2] Whatever survivors had experienced on 6 August 1945, it seems to have stayed with them for years after the event.

Although Lifton came out of the meetings rather disappointed, Kubo's observations propelled him to make a decision with profound consequences for his career, and for the history of trauma in Hiroshima and beyond.

> It was after leaving Kubo that I felt rather definite about going ahead. He seemed to have, whatever the limitations of his research, entered into a psychological-moral-historical sphere at the very center of mankind's critical dilemma, but for various reasons . . . he did not seem to have the perspective to deal with problems in this sphere (and in all fairness one must add that no one has a perspective of sufficiently heroic dimensions to really do justice to these matters). I felt that, while aware of my own limitations, my particular combination of moral concern, depth-psychological background, research experience, and knowledge and arrangements in Japan had brought me to a point where I could make a worthwhile effort at learning and communicating something about these ultimately unknowable and perhaps insolvable issues.

Lifton stayed in Hiroshima and conducted groundbreaking research, which resulted six years later in his book *Death in Life*.[3] In the following years, Lifton's Hiroshima research, together with his work and activism on behalf of Holocaust survivors and Vietnam veterans, eventually led him to be involved deeply with the creation of the category of post-traumatic stress disorder (PTSD). In all these cases, Lifton and his colleagues found survivors experiencing long-term damage very much along the lines described by Kubo in the 1962 meeting. The journey that had begun with the Hiroshima meeting led Lifton to sit on the committee that drafted the entry for PTSD for the American Psychiatric Association's (APA) *Diagnostic and Statistical Manual of Mental Disorders* (*DSM III*) in 1980. This

INTRODUCTION

development had profound effects far beyond the narrow field of psychiatry. From the mid-1980s onward, PTSD and trauma studies became ubiquitous in academic studies of the impact of war and disaster, as well as in society at large. In Japan, however, it was only in the 1990s, and thanks in part to Lifton's own influence and contacts with Japanese doctors, that PTSD research and psychiatric care were finally initiated in Hiroshima and Nagasaki in the 1990s and 2000s.[4]

The gap and delay in recognition between Japan and the West is mirrored in the scholarly literature about trauma. Lifton's work and contribution to the development of PTSD are well recognized.[5] Kubo's work, by comparison, and that of other Japanese researchers remains virtually unknown. It was this gap that first drew me into research on *hibakusha*. Lifton's research and stay in Hiroshima, as well as his involvement with and research on Holocaust survivors, became the subject of one chapter in my first book, *Hiroshima: The Rise of Global Memory Culture*.[6] In that chapter I also had a small section on Japanese researchers' contributions to research on the *hibakusha*, including Kubo's work. That particular section and the chapter as a whole are the genesis of this study. Even after completing that chapter, I felt compelled to go back to the topic and to the work done "on the ground" in Hiroshima and Nagasaki. Thus, I set out to explore the work of Kubo and his peers in order to examine the ways in which Japanese psychological sciences dealt with the suffering brought about by the atomic bomb.

However, I could only find a relatively small number of Japanese researchers who had tackled *hibakusha* psychology prior to the mid-1960s. In the years leading up to Lifton's visit, Hiroshima and Nagasaki *hibakusha* faced a dismal lack of care, and the multiple psychological effects of their experience in August 1945 were poorly understood. This was a picture very different from the contemporary experience of many Holocaust survivors, who, both in my own research and that of contemporaries, were the main group to whom *hibakusha* were compared. From the mid-1950s onward, a substantial body of medical, legal, and historical work developed around Holocaust trauma, which in turn led to adequate care and compensation for survivors.[7] Acknowledgment of the survivors' suffering, however, did not come easily. Victims of Nazi persecution had to fight a German campaign of denial and obstruction. Much of the subsequent research was therefore produced by sympathetic investigators and campaigners from the United States, Israel, and elsewhere, who set out in the late 1950s and 1960s to help survivors obtain care and compensation.[8] No such campaign was conducted on behalf of A-bomb survivors by the psychological sciences. Only a handful of Japanese doctors were working on the issue, and no compensation or specialized psychological care centers for mental injuries existed until relatively recently.[9] What then accounts for these very different histories?

The Holocaust and the nuclear destruction of Hiroshima and Nagasaki were events of a different order, producing vastly different reactions and postwar histories. It should not come as a surprise that the histories of psychiatry in the two cases are also different. As I have demonstrated elsewhere, however, the Holocaust and the atomic bomb were seen until the 1960s, and arguably even to the end of the Cold War, as comparable and interchangeable symbols of the worst that humans can do to other humans.[10] Furthermore, following Lifton (and especially after the establishment of PTSD), psychiatrists and psychologists have routinely viewed both cases as medically comparable.[11] Yet the pre-*DSM III* reaction of contemporary psychiatrists was quite different. Examining the earlier histories of both cases brings the commonalities and differences into sharper focus, and allows us to better understand the role that denial of psychological suffering played in both cases. The point here is not to argue that Japanese and American doctors should have recognized PTSD in *hibakusha*, or to condemn their blindness in contrast to our "enlightened" present. Indeed, as Svenja Goltermann has noted, much of the use of PTSD in trauma studies ignores the fact that the category is a historical construct and was unavailable—or, in the case of trauma, understood very differently—before the 1960s.[12] My aim is not to "recover" PTSD but to examine how individuals and institutions operated and made sense of their historical circumstances, by comparing these two contemporary yet distinct responses to vast human tragedy.

In the Japanese case, most actors acknowledged the possibility of long-term psychological damage, but did not mount a coherent response. This "failure" can be understood as the result of a confluence of developments. The American campaign of denial and neglect of the A-bomb's long-term effects was important in this regard. But perhaps more important were the complex links between radiation damage and psychiatric effects, which were unknown at the time and remained unexplored for decades. These factors combined to make research difficult and led Kubo Yoshitoshi and his peers down a path very different from that of their Western colleagues who were then working with Holocaust survivors. This result, I argue, was not a simple case of denial in the sense of a cover-up. Although there was much blame to go around, especially on the side of the American medi-

INTRODUCTION

cal and nuclear establishments, it was the way science was deployed that made research difficult, and organizing care for *hibakusha* problematic. This was especially true with regard to problems of objectivity and causation inherent in trauma, where the event causing the trauma and the appearance of symptoms can be years apart. As Kubo's own trajectory demonstrates, when psychologists did organize politically, they were less interested in the trauma of individuals and more in the ills of society at large—and, likewise, less in healing survivors than in working for peace and the prevention of war.

Indeed, until now, American denial and suppression were the main reasons given by Japanese researchers for lack of recognition. Researchers attributed the neglect of *hibakusha* mental health chiefly to American censorship and the infamous "press code" that suppressed research and discussion of the A-bomb's malevolent impact.[13] However, the press code had been loosened considerably in 1949, and the occupation ended in 1952, and so the relative lack of research cannot be explained by censorship alone. Nakazawa Masao makes this exact point, incidentally, while defending Lifton's record in a scathing critique of the failure of Japanese psychology and psychiatry to tackle *hibakusha* mental health problems.[14] The reasons for the paucity of research, again, were more complex than any sort of "failure" on the side of Japanese researchers to diagnose PTSD (a category that simply did not exist before the 1980s) or an active suppression of research. In fact, though research into *hibakusha* psychological suffering was indeed scarce, psychologists and psychiatrists have been writing about and researching the impact of the nuclear age on the human psyche continuously since 1945. But Nakazawa was correct in pointing out that most of this research did not take place in Japan. As I quickly realized, though the "suppression" argument is too simplistic, the reality of American occupation and US scientific hegemony, as well as the global nature of research into war trauma, meant that Japanese researchers had little incentive to take such work. And even when they did take it, the research was highly constrained. Consequently, one could not tell the story of post-Hiroshima research as only a Japanese story. For better or for worse, Japanese researchers acted within a transnational context in which US researchers and, to a lesser degree, other Western researchers had a decisive impact on research into A-bomb trauma.

Lifton was by no means the first researcher to tackle *hibakusha* psychology. Though these early forays into the field remain woefully understudied, the survivors' mental state was surveyed by American military teams as early as November 1945. Mere weeks after the attack, the US

Strategic Bombing Survey (USSBS) conducted extensive surveys in Hiroshima and Nagasaki to determine the A-bomb's psychological effects and the way it impacted morale. This research was the beginning of global efforts by psychiatrists, psychologists, and the wider social sciences to tackle the complex ways in which our minds were affected by the advent of the nuclear age. USSBS findings were central to a new domestic civil defense effort and coincided with a general rise in the interest and status of the psychological sciences in North American society. In Japan, the massive American research apparatus, the employment opportunities it offered, and the heightened prestige of American social science led to a monumental shift in Japanese psychology and psychiatry, from German to North American models and methodologies. Thus, when Lifton and Kubo met, they were already enmeshed in a transpacific network of knowledge production about nuclear trauma. Such connections indirectly led them into seeing the mental damage of the A-bomb in very similar terms; yet at the same time they increasingly led them, and the greater community of researchers around them, away from each other.

Nuclear Minds: The Argument

Taking the Kubo-Lifton meeting as a point of departure, this manuscript surveys the reactions of the psychological sciences in Japan and in the United States to the A-bomb's impact, and examines how Cold War politics, American denial, and the difficulty of studying so-called "A-bomb disease" limited recognition of the mental hurt of those who were exposed to the bomb. This study examines the academic "echo systems" that Kubo and Lifton belonged to, and retraces the steps that led both researchers into that fateful meeting in April 1962. To a lesser extent, it then follows their divergent paths and the impact of the meeting. Specifically, this study examines the ways in which the psychological impact of the bomb on survivors was understood before the emergence of trauma studies and PTSD as a primary category in our understanding of the impact of war on individuals and societies. Like Lifton, I set out to ask why so few doctors tried to ameliorate *hibakusha* suffering before the 1990s. The question of denial, both as an ethical and a historical question, stands at the heart of this study. However, again, I do not seek to retroactively condemn doctors for their supposed "blindness" to trauma. Quite the contrary. It was not only doctors who "failed" to issue the right diagnosis, though some did

INTRODUCTION

minimize and deny suffering. The victims' experience, as well, did not necessarily conform to our contemporary expectations. One cannot force the subjective experiences and history of victims into "a straitjacket of retrospective diagnostic ascription."[15] Thus, this study aims, first, to understand the historical, cultural, and scientific contexts in which researchers and victims were acting; and second, to explore the way suffering was understood by the psychological sciences before the availability of PTSD as a category, and in different cultural contexts. In short, this study is a prehistory of PTSD with a specific focus on the psychological research done in a non-Western context, which integrates nuclear research and Japan into an emerging body of work on the history of trauma.

This study makes a number of interrelated arguments. First, I argue that trauma was not a significant concept in early psychological research into the impact of nuclear weapons. As Svenja Goltermann has argued in her work on German military veterans, "Trauma was an extremely marginal interpretive category" among mainstream psychiatrists in postwar Europe.[16] Psychological and psychiatric research on Hiroshima and Nagasaki, I argue, likewise rarely referred to trauma. Institutional and political constraints—most notably the psychological sciences' entanglement with Cold War science—led researchers to concentrate on short-term damage and somatic reactions, and even in some cases to a denial of victims' suffering. For American researchers, who mostly worked within the emerging military-academic complex, research on the A-bomb's impact was done largely as part of a wider effort to evaluate the possible use of nuclear weapons in future conflicts. Japanese doctors, for their part, either were following American methodologies and concerns, or, coming out of the German tradition, were suspicious of purely psychological symptoms and always on the lookout for better "scientific and objective" causes for their patients' symptoms. This trajectory was not exceptional at the time. The German and Japanese cases were part of a larger trend. As mentioned above, similar trajectories and constraints led doctors to deny the suffering of Holocaust survivors. In the nuclear case, problems with working on the still unknown impact of radiation further complicated the diagnostic picture.

A second argument I make in this book is that nuclear psychology was part of a wider field that dealt with the targeting of civilians during war. Much of the literature about trauma and war, especially that of the world wars, relates to military psychiatry and the experiences of soldiers in the field. With the possible exception of research into British reactions to the

Blitz, very little has been written, then or now, about the experience of civilians. However, a large body of scholarship evolved around researchers who sought to evaluate the efficiency of aerial bombing on enemy civilians, and the ways civil defense could protect civilians from the psychiatric consequences of war. World War II and the early Cold War saw an unprecedented mobilization of psychiatrists and psychologists in the service of military aims. An important group of researchers sought to help air forces in evaluating scientifically and objectively their drive to target enemy population centers. The A-bomb, like the terror bombing before it, was aimed at the enemy's "mind." Bombing was psychological warfare via napalm. It was meant not just to destroy infrastructure and human bodies, but also to shatter morale and the enemy's will to resist. What World War II air forces were attempting to do was to cause mental shock and the collapse of individuals and communities, creating a theory and praxis of applied trauma. This was, of course, only one of several justifications and explanations for the bombing campaign. And much of the theorizing was done ex post facto by postwar evaluators. Nonetheless, it had an important influence on the way that nuclear weapons and their impacts were viewed. Thus, even after the war psychological experts mostly concentrated on the group psychology rather than the individual, and relegated mental hurt to secondary experience. The A-bomb was seen as a psychological weapon, and researchers sought to understand its efficiency through psychological and scientific means, turning mystical ideas about fighting spirit and élan into measurable and reliable data in the service of Cold War militaries.

A third and related argument considers the nature of medical science practiced by mid-century researchers in the Cold War West. Whether they were German, Japanese, or American, postwar psychiatry and psychology saw a resurgence of the ideas of scientific objectivity and freedom from political constraints as the pinnacle of scientific praxis. In the early postwar period, reacting to the overt politicization of science by both the Nazi and the Soviet regimes, American and allied scientific institutions pushed an idea of science purportedly free from politics and government control. As Audra Wolfe has shown, this conceptualization of science was in itself a political choice, which was actively encouraged by the American government as a form of "propaganda of the deed."[17] In our context, I argue that this emphasis on objectivity and apolitical science had a stifling impact on *hibakusha* research. The difficulty in proving causation, and in diagnosing the impact of trauma on survivors' minds, made researchers wary of being "unobjective" and "too sympathetic" to survivors. Indeed, these were the

INTRODUCTION

very words that researchers who sought to block recognition of survivors' compensation used to criticize sympathizers.[18] This development was especially important in the West German and Japanese case. Postwar reconstruction in both countries was promoted in psychological terms, and being objective and rational was seen as an antidote to the ills of fascism. Furthermore, the strong tradition of scientific objectivity and influence of German medical science, in which most Japanese researchers had trained, reinforced this "return" to objectivity. As Miriam Kingsberg Kadia has noted in her work, the ideal of objectivity was the "epistemological unconscious that anchored the transwar generation" of Japanese social scientists.[19] And science, practiced the American way, was the tool that enabled researchers to reintegrate into the global scientific community.

This leads us to the fourth theme of this book, which concerns the lack of research on transcultural trauma in Hiroshima and Nagasaki. The category of trauma should not be employed uncritically, neither across historical periods nor across cultures. This is especially true for a category that Western researchers developed in a non-Western context in which emotional suffering was understood differently. Research on the A-bomb's psychological impact conspicuously lacked a transcultural dimension. Except in some analysis by Lifton and other Western scholars, no researcher, and especially no Japanese researcher, sought to examine the suffering unleashed by the bomb through a transcultural lens. Although transcultural psychiatry and psychology was a topic dealt with extensively by UNESCO and other international bodies at the time, Japanese scientists rarely broached the topic in relation to A-bomb disease.[20] The reason for this, I argue, was the uneven power relationship between American and Japanese researchers, and the desire of Japanese researchers to integrate into the American-dominated global scientific community, which drove them away from cultural difference, and into the use of "objective" and "universal" criteria. Researchers who were especially progressive sought to move away from the racially driven psychology of the wartime years. Antiracism was an important force in wartime and early postwar research, arguing for the essential compatibility of Japanese and Western minds. Significantly, this enabled a break from the wartime and earlier use of psychology in the service of colonialism, and the application of Western science on Japanese minds. But this trend, again, worked against any sustained engagement with the cultural aspects of nuclear trauma, as it eventually erased all difference. This is not to say that culture lacked an impact on the way survivors *experienced* the impact of the A- bomb. But the multiple biases of researchers and the way experiences were *recorded* left us with little with which to evaluate the nature of the phenomenon.

Although the general trajectory of research was to move away from the overt politicization of psychiatric science, the relationship between politics and medicine, I argue, had a dual and paradoxical impact on research. This fifth theme, psychological science and politics, is entangled with all other issues examined in this work. With the advent of the nuclear age, the human sciences sought to prevent the horrors that physics and chemistry had unleashed on humanity. No less of a figure than the world's top psychiatrist, George Brock Chisholm, the first head of the World Health Organization (WHO), told his colleagues in 1946 that "the world is sick," and called on the profession to help stir the ship of humanity back toward normality.[21] Psychologists and psychiatrists organized in the name of science, rationality, and peace, which they saw as one and the same. The A-bomb, and war and aggression in general, were analyzed in psychological terms, and the era saw large-scale mobilization of the professions in the service of peace. Yet this did not translate into any advocacy for survivors. Postwar science was generally conservative in nature, and most psychologists worked through and with governments. However, this early combination of advocacy and science, in the next generation, the Vietnam generation, was what led Lifton and others to bring together psychiatry and antiwar activism. Of particular importance was the Vietnam generation's focus on victims' suffering, which their predecessors had lacked. Here the politics of memory and the rising status of survivors, which I have examined elsewhere, were of critical importance. The prominence of Holocaust survivors made dismissing their claims unacceptable in the West, thereby bringing greater recognition to their suffering. Yet paradoxically, in Japan, the rising status of *hibakusha* as heroes of the antiwar movement led to a rejection of Lifton's work, and resistance to the notion of long-term trauma. Activists, as well as many survivors, were loath to "tar" *hibakusha,* who long suffered from discrimination, with the stigma of mental illness, and preferred to show them as having overcome their difficulties through the struggle for peace. Thus, counterintuitively and despite their intentions, by promoting survivors' activism, activists also promoted the denial of long-term suffering.

The final and sixth theme of this book concerns the gendered politics of care and research. Throughout the whole period covered by this book, the majority of researchers, in whichever research community we encounter, were mostly men. Both in Japan and the West, whether in relation to Ho-

INTRODUCTION

locaust or Hiroshima survivors, Blitz victims, or Vietnamese who were exposed to Agent Orange, most of those who did the research, participated in the conferences, and left correspondence were elite men. These male doctors mostly shared a military background and extensive connections with German psychological sciences, whether through training or through involvement with émigré colleagues. This Eurocentric and male-centric world was a reflection of the skewed nature of mid-twentieth century scientific education, which favored men, and of a larger gendered division of labor, in which men did research while women were responsible for care. This was true both for those who sympathized with survivors and fought for recognition, and for those who sought to deny compensation and care. While men debated symptoms and diagnosis, the day-to-day care of survivors who struggled with mental health issues was left with social workers and nurses, or with caregivers in the community, the majority of whom were women.

Throughout this work I have tried to give equal voice to these unsung heroines. However, unfortunately, this sixth theme represents one of the research challenges I was least able to tackle in this book. Lack of sources and secondary research, coupled with the impact of the worldwide coronavirus crisis, prevented me from doing the research needed to further uncover the story of those who cared for psychologically wounded survivors of nuclear trauma. Female care workers, unlike male researchers, left little records of their work, and until the 1980s and the forming of care workers' associations, the knowledge they possessed about *hibakusha* care was passed on orally or in the form of case files—which under Japan's strict privacy laws, especially in relation to mental health issues, are not accessible.

A related gap is the relative lack of victims' voices in this manuscript. Medical history is notoriously, though sometimes unavoidably, biased toward doctors and researchers. The patients and the way they experience disease is often a casualty of this bias. As mentioned earlier, tackling this bias head-on is especially important in a non-Western context, where victims have experienced nuclear trauma differently. However, lack of access to case files has meant that methodologically, I have had to evaluate survivors' psychological states in retrospect after a gap of decades. This is exactly the kind of ahistorical psychological analysis I had wished to avoid. One must work from historical sources forward, and not the other way around. However, this does not mean interviews are not useful in gauging general trends. And I have used oral history, especially with care workers. Whenever possible, I have strived to incorporate victims and care workers' voices and experience in this work. However, I leave it for other historians to tell the story in full.

Finally, a note on language and the historicity of terms used in this manuscript. As elaborated on below, the very word and definition of "trauma" is historically constructed through a complex interplay of subjective perceptions, cultural interpretations, and medical knowledge. The definitions and understanding of the word are specific to the time and place in which they are used. In general, I use the terminology that was employed by researchers and the words used by patients at the time. Survivors, I argue, were not "traumatized" by their A-bomb experience, as they did not use the language of trauma, and did not have a cultural understanding of what they had been through as trauma. This understanding only came much later. As late as 1987, a study of thirty-seven survivors at the outpatient clinic of Yoyogi Psychiatric Hospital in Tokyo did not mention trauma or PTSD in describing patients' symptoms.[22] This does not mean—and I cannot stress this enough—that survivors did not suffer, or that the A-bomb did not leave them with long-term mental damage. Far from it. In fact, one of the questions this book asks is when and how the term "trauma" (*torauma* or *kokoro no kizu*—wounds of the heart, in Japanese) came to be used in its current understanding to describe survivor experience, and why it took so long to be acknowledged. That said, throughout this book I do use the word "trauma" in analyzing and discussing the phenomenon from our vantage point, to help facilitate understanding of developments historically and across cultural contexts. The reader should keep in mind that trauma is an "elastic and ambiguous term," and is inherently subjective.[23] Thus, we need to be diligent and cautious in applying our Western and contemporary categories to different times and places.

A second and related issue of language is the use of the words "survivor" for victims, and "psychologists" or "psychiatrists" for researchers. As I have shown elsewhere, the word "survivor" also has its own history and, as with the word "trauma," I alternate here, according to context, between contemporary terms and current terms. As for the researchers who are the main focus of this book, in discussing most of the period before the 1980s I prefer to use the term "psychological experts" rather than disciplinary terms. This does not mean that these terms were not important. But most of the figures who impacted nuclear psychological research worked across disciplinary boundaries that were far looser before the 1960s, and some were trained in more than one field. Thus, Robert Lifton, for instance, calls

INTRODUCTION

the researchers who dealt with psychiatry and war as the "professions" in plural, and thought of them as encompassing a group much more broad than academically trained psychiatrists.[24] Sociologists, psychologists, anthropologists, and other figures throughout this book all made significant contributions to post-Hiroshima psychological research. My use of disciplinary terms, accordingly, reflects this historical reality.

Nuclear Trauma: A Very Short History and Histography

The concept of PTSD had an enormous influence on Western and, subsequently, global society. It altered our understanding of armed conflict and the price of war. "The discourse of trauma," Andreas Huyssen wrote, "radiates out from a multi-national, ever more ubiquitous Holocaust discourse, [and] is energized . . . by the intense interest in witness and survivor testimonies, and then merges with the discourses about AIDS, slavery, family violence and so on."[25] Similarly, I argue that the Holocaust was just one part of a much larger global constellation that brought PTSD to the fore. This is by no means the first time that the Eurocentric nature (and larger problems) of PTSD history are being critiqued. A spate of work has examined the emergence of PTSD critically, from mostly Marxist and postcolonial perspectives. Drawing on the work of Foucault and other theorists, scholars such as Gary Greenberg, Bruce Cohen, and others have decried the power of PTSD and the *DSM* system over the way we think about mental disease.[26] More specifically, writers such as Ethan Waters and, from a more theoretical angle, China Mills have criticized "global psychiatrization" and the way American-centered "psychiatric colonization" has dominated thinking among non-Western medical professionals, erasing the vast cultural diversity of human experience with what we call mental health.[27] Yet these critics supply us only with a cursory look at the way in which non-Westerners dealt with the categories of trauma and PTSD as they emerged, and the historical experience of Asian and other non-Western locales is hardly acknowledged by scholars.

This gap is rather curious, as trauma research was long connected to the study of the other. Early researchers of the phenomenon such as the British doctors Charles Myers, W. H. R, Rivers, and others—like Alexander Leighton, a central figure in this manuscript—researched non-Western people before World War I.[28] This involvement of the "shell shock doctors" with anthropology and colonialism remains underresearched. The connection between colonialism and the encounter of psychological experts with so-called "primitives" and that most modern disease, trauma, is not accidental. William McDougall, for instance, saw the cerebral, "more developed" parts of the soldiers' brains succumbing to the "older, more primitive" parts as the result of the shock of war; he also used the evolutionary metaphor of a tree, and "primitive" versus more developed "higher" branches.[29] Rivers, whose most famous patient was the poet Siegfried Sassoon, had a more positive take. Rivers was a trained anthropologist, and he studied the people of New Guinea and the Solomon Islands together with Myers and McDougall. In his lectures at the Maghull Military Hospital, he compared the medical experiences of "primitive and Western societies" to those of British military doctors.[30] Rivers used his anthropological experience to highlight the problem of suggestion, which he defined as "a process by which one mind acts upon another unwittingly," as a therapeutic tool. He argued that Melanesian people could teach the British something about the "place taken by suggestion both in the production and the treatment of the disease."[31] Such conflicting and complex attitudes to race and trauma had an important impact on the research done in and on Japan.

Recently, a number of emerging researchers have tried to fill these gaps in scholarship and globalize the history of psychiatry. The past decade has seen work on the history of psychiatry, including trauma, in the Middle East, in Africa, and at the WHO.[32] In the East Asian context, work in China, Taiwan, Japan, and other countries has sought to trace the emergence of modern psychiatry in those societies.[33] Specifically in regard to trauma, an upcoming volume edited by Mark S. Micale and Hans Pols, *Traumatic Pasts in Asia: History, Psychiatry and Trauma 1930 to the Present*, gathers an emerging group of scholars on the topic in order to examine the history of trauma in Asia.[34] Many scholars who are taking part in that volume, including this author, have been publishing groundbreaking work on the history of trauma in Taiwan, Japan, the Koreas, and beyond. Specifically in regard to Japan, the work of Janice Matsumura and Nakamura Eri on the Imperial Army is of special interest.[35] The history of trauma in Japan is still a relatively a young field with only a few dedicated monographs in Japanese on the topic. This is even more true of the study of nuclear trauma. Indeed, the historical lack of scientific research into *hibakusha* trauma is mirrored in the relative paucity of historical research on the topic. Almost all the work is done by psychologists who uncritically apply contemporary notions of PTSD to victims.[36] One significant exception is

INTRODUCTION

the work of the psychiatrist Nakazawa Masao. Nakazawa, who was also an activist and has played an important role in the introduction of trauma to Japan, is one of the few practitioners who are historically sensitive.[37]

There is a disconnect between the large body of work done by contemporary psychologists on *hibakusha* and historical work on the topic. On the other hand, quite a few works make connections between work on the psychology of Holocaust survivors and Japan.[38] With the exception of work on Okinawa, the much more politically thorny cases of Asian victims of Japan are left unexplored.[39] Another field in which connections are made, especially since Fukushima, is work on victims of nuclear accidents at Chernobyl and elsewhere. It is these exact connections on which I wish to expand. Another arena to which this book contributes, and which again has largely been disconnected from work on Hiroshima, is work on mostly American cultural responses to the nuclear age. Nuclear anxiety and its effect on global culture and politics have been topics of much academic interest in the last couple of decades. Work by Paul Boyer, Spencer Weart, and, more recently, Joseph Maco and others has done much to further our understanding of atomic anxiety.[40] Psychological warfare was an important part of this literature, most notably the work of Guy Oakes on "emotional management," practiced by the US government in its drive to control nuclear terror on the home front.[41] In a way more specifically tied to the history of medicine, Jackie Orr and Andrea Tone examined important aspects of the history of psychiatry during the nuclear age.[42] Two other fields of contribution are, of course, the history of Hiroshima and Nagasaki, and the history of PTSD in Japan and globally. This book, though global in scope, is first and foremost about Hiroshima and Nagasaki, and Japan. It is indebted to the work done on medical history in Japan, and especially psychiatry, by authors such as Susan Burns, Junko Kitanaka, Akihito Suzuki, and others, as well as the aforementioned Nakamura Eri and Janice Matsumura.[43] Work on the history of psychiatry in Israel and Germany, especially in regard to the Holocaust, is also important in this regard.

Finally, there is the history of PTSD itself. Ben Shepard, Allan Young, Didier Fassin, Richard Rechtman, Ruth Leys, and, more recently, Svenja Goltermann and others, have done much to further our understanding of the history of the phenomenon. The works of these historians provide us with multiple insights and an important context for our investigation. One crucial point on which practically all historians agree is the modern nature of the phenomenon. Historians of PTSD generally point to the mid-nineteenth century as the starting point of research into psychological trauma in the West (nonhistorians take trauma much further back in time). In East Asia, the impact of colonialism and transformations that came with modernization and Westernization (as it was understood at the time; the two terms, of course, are not synonyms) placed it on a similar time line.[44] As Paul Lerner and Mark Micale argued, "The expansion of the trauma concept . . . was simultaneously responsive to and constitutive of 'modernity.'"[45] The nineteenth century saw a profound paradigm shift in Western psychiatry, with doctors moving away from hereditary explanations to disease and giving more and more credence to psychogenic illness. This shift was a direct response to new modern technologies, the rise of the administrative state, new ideas of "self," and new relationships between man and society. This development was not only the result of big "systematic" changes, but also very much the result of a sustained effort by doctors to gain recognition for and understanding of their patients' suffering.

The shift to psychological trauma was not a linear and smooth process. Advocates of trauma faced stiff opposition both within and outside the nascent establishment of psychiatry. Indeed, trauma was never a matter for medical professionals alone. From its beginning, with reactions to train accidents and the carnage of modern warfare in the American Civil War and in Europe, diagnosis and medical development were entangled with politics, economics, and administrative issues. The diagnosis and praxis of psychological trauma was, and still is, an intensely political and contentious process. As Dagmar Herzog pointed out in relation to later debates, "Politics . . . literally moved the science forward," and it is through the dialectic of science and politics that trauma is examined here.[46] Rather than medical advances alone, it was changes in the politics of the profession toward a more radical and critical engagement with the impact of war that served to propel research on survivors and the acknowledgment of long-term trauma.[47]

Trauma was impacted by various kinds of politics, ranging from class to gender and to racial politics. As Allan Horwitz pointed out, trauma has a "heavily gendered history."[48] He was referring to the gendered spheres of research wherein the experience of combat was the main arena of trauma research for men, whereas the arena of sexual assault and related traumas was the one for women. One can add to this insight that the emergence of trauma as a distinct category was a move from the feminine and domestic world of hysteria and emotional angst to the masculine one of combat and work accidents. What researchers like John Eric Erichsen and Hermann

INTRODUCTION

Oppenheim had to explain was how seemingly normal male patients with no hereditary issues were experiencing feminine-hysteria-like symptoms following accidents. This again was also seen by some as a reversion to "primitive" modes of behavior, befitting of colonial people. Some scholars claimed that what were termed "railway spine" symptoms were due to physical damage to the spine or brain. The German neurologist Hermann Oppenheim, who was the first to develop "traumatic neurosis" as a distinct category, distinguished such mental damage from the more feminine "hysteria," and directly connected damage to what we will now call the traumatic event. Other scholars, notably Jean-Martin Charcot, insisted that such symptoms could be caused by hysteria, were not distinct, and were purely or mostly psychological in origin. Charcot emphasized the role of "extreme fear," and argued that memories of past shocks were not conscious but lingered in the patients' unconscious, a very new idea at the time. Early on, Sigmund Freud also entered this debate, arguing that the origins of all traumata originated in the sexual experiences and traumas of early childhood. Freud's significant contribution was the discarding of a hereditary basis altogether, and the location of trauma squarely in the psychological realm.[49]

The central problem for early researchers, and one that is still with us today, was the question to what extent trauma was a mental phenomenon. Paul Lerner and Mark Micale have seen the move from railway spine to traumatic neurosis as part of the "progressive mentalization of trauma concept," which culminated with the introduction of PTSD.[50] Though basically correct (and Lerner and Micale would surely acknowledge this), we should not be misled by the word "progress" in describing this history. Already in the late nineteenth century, the situation was far more complex. Oppenheim, for instance, argued for both somatic and psychogenic mechanisms, and Charcot still believed in the hereditary basis of disease. Generally speaking, debates within the small European community of trauma researchers did revolve around two basic questions. First, again, was the question of whether external physical or psychological shock was the cause of "traumatic neurosis." The second, related question was whether this was the cause of internal psychological causes or external causes—that is, whether men who succumbed to trauma were susceptible to disease, through hereditary or similar constitutional factors, and whether all men could be traumatized.

The understanding of "traumatic neurosis" changed considerably with the coming of World War I. Charles Myers's introduction of the concept of shell shock, and the entry of the "PIE principles" (proximity to the battle, immediacy of treatment, and expectancy of recovery, including return to duty) through the work of American Thomas Salmon propelled trauma, literally, to the front of military medicine. Trauma remained an important presence in public debates in the interwar years, and was closely connected with the struggles over pensions. This, again, did not mean a progressive acceptance of trauma. The German pension law of 1926 rejected the long-term impact of war neurosis, and the work of pioneers like Abraham Kardiner, who took such syndromes seriously, remained little known. On the other hand, with the rise of combat psychiatry in Anglo-American military psychiatry, there was increasing acceptance of traumatic neurosis as a valid medical phenomenon. During World War II, more and more doctors came to accept that everybody had a breaking point, and that succumbing to the pressures of battle had nothing to do with masculinity or valor (this was not the case in Germany, the Soviet Union, or Japan, a topic we will return to). On the other hand, PIE and military medicine as a whole were completely oriented toward preventing short-term damage. Doctors argued that all soldiers needed to recover was rest and social pressure to get back to the fight. Long-term damage remained understudied and mostly unrecognized.

It is not my intention here to write a full survey of the rise of trauma in the West. For our purposes it is sufficient to note that trauma was always entangled with the politics of war, race, and gender. This history is well known. Historians of trauma have done excellent and comprehensive research on these debates and the various nuances and historical contingencies that drove the history of trauma. However, there is a curious gap in the chronology presented in current histories. Most histories of trauma devote a significant amount of attention to developments in World War II, and then focus on the Vietnam War era. The mid-1940s to the mid-1960s are often left uncovered. Allan Young, author of perhaps the most groundbreaking work on PTSD history, wrote: "Interest in the war neuroses rapidly faded once the war was over."[51] Similarly, a recent history of PTSD argues that between *DSM I* (1952) and *DSM II* (1968), the field "lost interest in trauma."[52] These two decades are exactly when most of the work examined below happened. Such gaps are understandable, if one is to trace the history of PTSD and related terms through a narrow focus on institutional psychiatry and the progression of manuals such as the *DSM*, and through a mostly Western lens. Certainly, the bias of the field toward military psychiatry also explains some of this. This view is not

INTRODUCTION   19

necessarily wrong. With the war over, trauma, indeed, stopped being an
urgent issue. There were a couple of notable exceptions to this, research
on Holocaust survivors and prisoners of war being the most important.
Overall, historians of trauma tend not to dwell on the 1940s and 1950s as
significant decades in the history of trauma. Most scholars skip over them
and point to the late 1960s as the moment when the movement that eventually led to insertion of PTSD into the *DSM* in 1980 began. Hiroshima
and nuclear psychology do not feature prominently in that work. Lifton's
role and his connection with Hiroshima are mentioned, most prominently
in Ben Shepard's work, but the main research "genealogies," to use Ruth
Leys's apt term, concern military psychiatry, Holocaust research (a recent
development), and, to a lesser extent, work with victims of sexual violence
and industrial accidents.[53] It is one of the main tasks of this book to fill the
gap in trauma history and to explore the nuclear roots of the history that
led to PTSD.

This is not to belittle the important work done by Leys and other
historically-minded trauma scholars. Nuclear psychology was perhaps
overlooked; but thanks to the work of trauma historians and anthropologists, we now have a clear picture of the emergence of trauma as a historical concept. One cannot stress enough the importance of historicity
when talking about trauma. Much more than in the case of physical disease, the way a person interprets their symptoms has a critical impact on
the nature of psychiatric disease. Such interpretations are culturally and
historically determined. Consequentially, in this work, I employ a social
constructionist perspective to trauma and other psychiatric terms, which
follows the work of philosopher of science Ian Hacking. For Hacking, the
introduction of new diagnostic categories created what he calls a "looping effect": novel forms of experiences, new ways to relate to one's world,
and new ways of thinking and expression.[54] This is different from how
trauma is usually understood in popular culture and within some circles
in academia. Already in 1996, Allan Young identified an important split in
the historical inquiry into the origins of trauma. On one side are mostly,
but not exclusively, practitioners and advocates who think of PTSD as
a historically stable phenomenon. They project the category far into the
past, and find evidence of trauma and PTSD in Greek myths and Shake-
spearean plays.[55] This phenomenon was supposedly denied and white-
washed by an indifferent medical profession dominated by elite men who
saw trauma victims as shirkers, malingerers, and pretenders. Most victims
were common soldiers, women, workers, and other disadvantaged groups.

A number of insightful individuals fought bravely for these groups, but it was only after the 1960s that the disease was "discovered" and finally "understood." There is more than a grain of truth to this view. Thinking and research into the psychological suffering brought about by war and violence was often dominated by class, gender, and cultural norms. Most victims were disadvantaged, and faced discrimination. Figures like Kardiner, Lifton, Chaim Shatan, and others did fight admirably for recognition of their patients' suffering. But the picture was much more complex; more than just bias played a role here. The second group of scholars, mostly historians but also anthropologists and sociologists like Young, sees trauma as the product of a very particular and recent kind of modern experience, and believe that earlier generations simply did not experience suffering in the same way. This book largely concurs with the latter argument. Trauma was not denied; it was, arguably, not experienced as trauma until the historical and cultural conditions allowed for its development.

This was the exact problem that brought Lifton to Hiroshima. Lifton came to Japan in 1960 following his service in the Air Force, which had first brought him to Asia, and after his work on prisoners of war and other victims of Chinese "thought reform" in Hong Kong (a topic to which we will return). The Liftons were already making a name for themselves as researchers and committed activists. They had a strong interest in and passion for Asia in general, and Japan in particular. Lifton's first project in Japan was examining Japanese youth attitudes to historical change. Transcultural psychiatry, and the way survivors experienced nuclear trauma through a Japanese cultural sense, was of particular importance. When doing research in Japan, Lifton went through his notes with the psychologist Doi Takeo, whom Lifton had first met when he was stationed in Japan as an Air Force psychiatrist. Lifton regarded Doi as an "important influence and contributor" to his Hiroshima work, especially in regard to the way survivors experienced death and the loss of communal ties.[56] But this emphasis on the particularity of the Japanese experience was driven at the same time by "an important antiracist" impulse that saw Japanese as equal and worthy of research—not an uncontroversial attitude at the time.[57] Lifton was following the anthropologist Ruth Benedict, another important influence, and others in continuing a culturally sensitive yet universal tradition of research. He emphasized and practiced the shared human experience of victims, and aspired to practice scientifically based, yet politically informed research and advocacy.[58]

It was this impulse that inspired Lifton, as I have examined at length elsewhere, to connect the experience of Holocaust survivors and that of

INTRODUCTION   21

Hiroshima and Nagasaki survivors, and to formulate the "traits of the survivors," a study which eventually led to the establishment of PTSD as a category.[59] This was also Lifton's reason for meeting with Kubo, and this is why he stayed in Japan. Lifton drew on Kardiner, Freud, and various others, most importantly his mentor Erik Erikson, to articulate a theory of trauma that emphasized the joint psychological and cultural impact of mass death on the human psyche. Lifton was an heir of the long history and trajectory of research examined briefly above. But he was also reacting to the context of Hiroshima, antinuclear activism, nuclear weapon research, the history of bombing "psyches," and antiracist psychology. Kubo, as well, was heir to a particular history and confluence of influences. A former military doctor, like Lifton and almost all the researchers examined below, Kubo was influenced by German military psychiatry as well as British and American developments (he was in the Imperial Navy, which was, in medicine as in other fields, more open to British and American influences). For Kubo, the main reference point was military research and the experience of the World Wars. He also arguably inherited a certain suspicion of victims and an aspiration to practice his science "objectively," which further distanced him from the "stories and rhetorical flourishes" of his patients.[60] Lifton, as we shall see, was more open to victims' voices. However, Kubo and Lifton had much more in common than both realized. What brought them together, as well as what caused their roads to diverge, is the topic of this book.

Chapter Overview

The two main groups of researchers who examined the psychological reaction of the *hibakusha* and the victims of bombing in general were Japanese and American. Thus, although this author is, in general, opposed to the Japanese American focus that dominates so many works on Hiroshima and Nagasaki in particular, and Japanese studies in general, this book traverses mostly a transpacific research landscape. By way of balance, however, I have chosen to expand the focus of this work and triangulate the two foci of nuclear research with research on, and the history of the reactions of the professions and survivors to the horrors of, the Holocaust. Since I am relying on the fields and languages with which I am most familiar, most of the material is from Israel, Germany, and the Anglo-American world. As is, I hope, already clear to the reader, this is not a matter of simple comparison between two distinct fields. The history of psychiatry is an international and transnational history in which various research communities and trajectories have entangled with and exerted influence upon one another. This is especially so in the field of trauma, where there was a constant flow of ideas and people between Hiroshima, military psychiatry, and Holocaust discourses. Thus, as in most of my work so far, the main methodology this work seeks to employ is that of entangled histories, or *histoire croisée*. Jürgen Kocka succinctly summed up this kind of history as one that is "much less interested in similarities and differences [of different historical settings] . . . but rather in the processes of mutual influencing, in reciprocal or asymmetric perceptions, in entangled processes of constituting one another."[61] This is not to say that similarities and differences, as noted by more traditional comparative historians, are not a part of this work. But an entangled history is much better suited to the task of mapping the fluidity of categories and the way in which these develop through cross-influences and the global circulation of ideas. Thus, throughout this book, the historical lens narrows on Hiroshima and individual cases, and then widens to include other locales, weaving Hiroshima's story into the wider history of trauma.

This book is divided into two parts. The first part focuses mostly on American development up to roughly 1962 and Lifton's trip to Hiroshima, while the second part focuses on Japanese developments. The last chapter examines in greater detail what happened after the meeting, and how Lifton's time in Hiroshima impacted the history of trauma in Japan, the United States, and beyond. Throughout the book, and especially in its later parts, the history of nuclear trauma is connected to and compared with the history of Holocaust trauma. The book focuses on a number of important figures, as well as on the larger groups and networks around them. Those are, first and foremost, Robert Lifton and Kubo Yoshitoshi. The other main figures are the American psychiatrist Alexander Leighton and psychologist Irving Janis, the Canadian psychiatrist Brock Chisholm, the Japanese psychiatrist Konuma Masuho, and the Japanese American sociologist Yoshiharu Scott Matsumoto. These researchers and their trajectories serve as the focus of the chapters, with most of them standing at the center of individual chapters. One would immediately notice that this list is exclusively male. As already noted, this reflects the gendered history and division of labor between men, who did the research, and women who did the care work on the ground. Thus, chapter 8 looks jointly at the work of Lifton, and that of female social workers and community organizers in Hiroshima and Nagasaki who worked with *hibakusha*, developing

INTRODUCTION

23

practices and insights in dealing with the long-term human impact of the A-bomb.

Part 1 focuses on American developments and starts off with two chapters on the history of psychiatry and urban bombing. The focus of these two chapters is the work of the USSBS in 1945 and 1946. Chapter 1 sets up the theoretical and historical context of the survey, examining the transnational history of urban bombing and situating it in relation to the history of trauma, the concept of psychological morale, the rise of the figure of the "psychological expert," and USSBS work in Germany. Chapter 2 focuses on the work of the anthropologist and psychiatrist Alexander Leighton, the head of the Hiroshima team that interviewed hundreds of survivors in *hibakusha* in Hiroshima in 1945. The chapter follows him from his early work on Native Americans through his research in the internment camps (where he met and trained Scott Matsumoto), his work on psychological warfare, and finally his experiences in Hiroshima. The latter two chapters in part 1 examine the impact of USSBS research and the A-bomb in general on postwar American psychology and psychiatry. Chapter 3 focuses on the activism of psychiatrists and psychologists as they articulated a social and political critique of the nuclear age, relying on their experience and expertise. The focus is on USSBS veterans in the United States, and on the new emerging global networks in which they operated. Chapter 4 deals with American civil defense research in the 1950s, and especially the work of Irving Janis. Janis produced the most extensive research on nuclear trauma as part of his work at the RAND Corporation and various other government research bodies. The chapter focuses on the way USSBS research was integrated into an emerging body of knowledge on the impact of the A-bomb on American and Japanese minds.

Part 2 of the book takes us on the ground to Hiroshima and Nagasaki. Chapter 5 examines the psychological work done at the Atomic Bomb Casualty Commission (ABCC), which came out of the same intellectual "echo system" that produced the USSBS and civil defense research, and showed many continuities with them. Despite this, and although the central figure of this chapter, Scott Matsumoto, is an American, the location of his work in Hiroshima itself and the important impact the ABCC had on Japanese development situates this chapter as a sort of bridge between the two parts of this book. The chapter focuses on Matsumoto's work and that of the ABCC social workers he managed and trained. It examines how racial and gender politics and the ABCC's position in Hiroshima research impacted Matsumoto's work and the work of the social workers he supervised. Chapters 6 and 7 examine Japanese doctors, focusing respectively on the work of psychiatrist Konuma Masuho and psychologist Kubo Yoshitoshi. Chapter 6 examines Japanese military psychiatry and the longer history of trauma in Japan. It explores, through Konuma's research, the way military and civilian research intersected. It also examines research on survivors of the Holocaust in Israel and Germany, comparing and connecting their trajectories with the Japanese case. Chapter 7 focuses on Kubo's work and especially on how American research and methodologies impacted the move away from older German models. It examines Kubo's work with the American occupation, his research, his political activism, and his connection to the compensation movement. It also analyzes the case of Holocaust survivors and their struggles over compensation in relationship to the Hiroshima case. Chapter 8 takes us past 1962 into the 1980s and 1990s and the global rise of PTSD. Taking us beyond the Lifton-Kubo meeting, the chapter has a dual focus. First, it focuses on social workers' and sociologists' engagement with *hibakusha* in the stricken cities. It then focuses on the United States and the impact of Robert Jay Lifton's work and the road that led him to sit on the committee that established PTSD in *DSM III*. Both developments were very much connected to each other in the sense that reactions to Lifton's research and to Holocaust research were an important catalyst for Japanese research and the praxis of care (Hiroshima social workers even had a "Lifton study group").

This is a story, again, of the coming together of politics and psychiatry. It seems very fitting that as I write these lines in late 2020, psychiatrists once again use the tools of their trade to examine the polarized political atmosphere in the United States and elsewhere, and the fitness of political leaders. This unstable era in which we live sees not only the return of political psychiatry but also the return of public awareness to the involvement of psychiatrists and psychologists with military research—some of it, like CIA and Pentagon torture, ethically compromised. This book seeks to uncover the longer trajectories of this history and restore the place of Hiroshima and nuclear research not just in the historiography but also in the politics of psychiatry, society, and the multiple uses of trauma.

PART I
Bombing Minds

CHAPTER ONE

American Psychological Sciences and the Road to Hiroshima and Nagasaki

"In the coming war we shall fight not only on land, on the sea, and in the air. There will be a fourth theater of operations, the Inner Front. That front will decide the continued existence or the irrevocable death of the German nation." — Heinrich Himmler, September 1937[1]

A few weeks after the August 1945 bombing, the US Strategic Bombing Survey (USSBS) mission to Hiroshima set out in jeeps across the rubble to find eyewitnesses who could tell them about their experience of the atomic bomb. In bilingual forms, the young soldiers were instructed to ask the residents in Romanized Japanese, "*Genshibakudan ni tsuite do omowaremashitaka*?" or "What have you thought about the atomic bomb?"[2] This surreal scene, of dropping a weapon of mass destruction on a city and then going about with clipboards asking people politely how they felt about it (figure 1), encapsulates the zeitgeist of American social sciences' entanglement with bombing in general and the A-bomb in particular. The Hiroshima survey captured the hubris and pretense of scientific detachment, but counterintuitively, it was also an important break from wartime dehumanization, whether through abstraction or racism. It also showed how important psychology was in the employment and evaluation of wartime bombing. American psychological experts at the USSBS were the first researchers to interview and assess the mental state of *hibakusha*. Japanese researchers could not do such work under the American occupation, which left the field to the USSBS psychologists and psychiatrists. The USSBS researchers, however, were not there as medical personnel. and did not come to Hiroshima to heal its survivors. Their purpose was to assess the success of the A-bomb in shattering Japanese mental defenses, and to probe the links between individual mental damage and national morale.

HIROSHIMA, USSBS JEEP

KURE

FIGURE 1. USSBS teams in Hiroshima, and an image of bombed-out Kure from the USSBS official history. The juxtaposition of the two images further emphasizes the essential comparability of the two sites of bombing for the USSBS. Photo courtesy of the US National Archives.

AMERICAN PSYCHOLOGICAL SCIENCES

For the planners of bombing raids from Hamburg to Nagasaki and the survey researchers who evaluated their methods, individual civilians were ostensibly not the target. As David Fedman and Cary Karacas argued, "urbicide," or the intentional destruction of urban areas, had to be disguised "in order to justify the political violence inherent in the targeting of a city and its inhabitants."[3] The US Army Air Force (USAAF) thus had to conceptualize Hiroshima and other cities as military-worthy targets using terms like "industrial areas," "de-housing" of workers, and the like. President Harry S. Truman, for instance, told Americans on 9 August, "The world will note that the first atomic bomb was dropped on Hiroshima, a military base."[4] "Morale" was another abstraction that allowed for the indiscriminate killing of civilians. But unlike the other terms, it was intimately connected to the personal and psychological. American morale researchers, many of whom ended up working in psychological warfare and in the survey, saw nations as aggregates of their citizens' emotions. Morale was a back door through which the perspective of victims on the ground could enter the historical and military record. However, they were recorded in an extremely limited and circumventing manner. The development of morale studies paralleled the development of bombing theory and had important influence on war time campaigns.

USSBS research on the A-bomb's psychological impact was both a product of early ideas about the A-bomb's potential, and an important influence on shaping such understandings. In the mid-1940s, the A-bomb was seen as a war-winning psychological weapon which, in the words of a 1946 Report to the US military Joint Chiefs of Staff, was capable of "break[ing] the will of nations and of peoples."[5] This notion was the result of an unarticulated yet powerful theory of trauma that had a strong influence on the thinking about aerial bombing and its postwar evaluation. The theory was advanced by various thinkers on both the Axis and Allied sides, and was supposedly validated by USSBS researchers. Though by no means the only motive for bombing civilians, such ideas were crucial in connecting the severe emotional impact of bombing on individuals and the breaking of societal morale. The assumptions that underlined both the practice of bombing and its evaluation by the USSBS were developed throughout the first half of the twentieth century as military theorists, fantasy authors, and civil defense planners imagined the coming air war. This body of work structured the experience and practice of bombing for both the bombers and the people they bombed. Following the conclusions of morale theorists, the breaking of individual mental defenses was to lead to a similar impact on the national level. The anxiety, panic, and hysteria civilians were supposed to experience under the anticipated (and later very real) urbicide had become a problem of national defense. Even more important for our purposes, these ideas were influential in Cold War planning for nuclear war.

The USSBS set out to research scientifically whether such assumptions about bombing were correct. But even though they questioned thousands of individuals, the survey constantly moved away from the experience of the people whom they studied. The actual connections and mechanisms that led from high explosives, napalm, and atomic blasts to mental damage on the individual level, and how exactly these were connected to morale, were questions left largely unexplored. Although there already existed a body of research on the connection between "traumatic neurosis" and aerial warfare, even the very word "trauma" was rarely used. These developments had important consequences for subsequent research. As will be explored in more depth in later chapters, the long-term impact of mental breakdown was seen as negligible, and was not thoroughly researched by the surveys. USSBS researchers had a severely limited mandate from which they rarely strayed. And individual psychic trauma was not the USSBS's main concern. Furthermore, the individual experiences that were examined were obscured by a relentless drive for quantification and abstraction, with the horrors of war translated into graphs, charts, and indexes. The USSBS focus and methods were the results of a confluence of developments in the psychological sciences and the conduct of aerial bombing in Japan, Germany, the United States, and beyond. This chapter prepares the ground for later chapters by examining these developments, and charts the trajectory that led the USSBS to researching the A-bomb primarily through the lens of communal morale studies and, methodologically, through data collection. The chapter opens with a general overview of American psychological sciences' engagement with the war effort and the rise of morale studies, and then moves on to examine how aerial bombing was conceptualized and thought of as a psychological weapon. It ends with an examination of the USSBS experience in the European theater, the fragmentary way in which researchers conceptualized trauma, and the ways it connected with the practice of bombing civilians.

American Psychology Goes to War

As Sophia Dafinger has noted, the term "bombing research analyst" was often ambiguous.[6] Many such analysts were trained psychologists and psychiatrists. But the work they did was not confined to psychology, sociology, or any other discipline. When it came to the bombing surveys, the researchers who analyzed victims' minds employed a whole range of methods. Consequently, the definition of "psychological expert" that is used here is quite wide and includes anthropologists, psychiatrists, and others who used psychological categories. This eclectic definition was, to a large extent, a result of the wartime trajectory of these researchers. American psychological experts, many of whom were progressive and liberal—and quite a few of whom were influential émigrés from occupied Europe—were swept up in the enthusiasm for the great fight for democracy and against tyranny. American psychology and psychiatry benefited greatly from World War II. The profession rose in status and importance and expanded significantly.[7] The war gave American psychological sciences purpose and unity.[8] As Ellen Herman has argued, psychologists were well situated to deal with the world crisis, as they "possessed . . . a technology of behavior, a science of social relations, a theory of society, and a theology of emotional healing."[9] The government seized on psychological expertise and utilized it in various areas.

Drawing on the experience of World War I, noted psychologists set up the Emergency Committee on Psychology in 1939, to "prepare the profession for a great national crisis."[10] This committee was reorganized in 1940 as part of the National Research Council (NRC).[11] One particularly important branch of American psychology, social psychologists, organized itself under the "Society for the Psychological Study of Social Issues" (SPSSI), the most important organizational nucleus of wartime social psychology. Almost all psychologists who later joined the USSBS were also members of the SPSSI.[12] Another organization that was set up in 1940 was the Committee for National Morale (CNM), whose members included many of the psychologists, psychiatrists, and anthropologists we will meet in the following pages, including Gordon Allport (USSBS), Ruth Benedict (Office of War Information, or OWI), Erik Erikson (Robert Jay Lifton's mentor), Erich Fromm, Geoffrey Gorer (OWI), Kurt Lewin, Margaret Mead, Karl Menninger, Adolf Meyer (Alexander Leighton's mentor), and countless others.[13] Some psychologists were hesitant to make the move to the public and military spheres. Harvard's Gordon Allport, perhaps the most eminent social psychologist of his day, had little time for such doubts: "If the psychologist is tempted to say that he knows too little about the subject he may gain confidence by watching the inept way in which . . . men in public life fence with the problems of propaganda, public opinion, and morale. More often than not these men give the impression of playing a game with a red-hot poker."[14]

The study of morale was the main avenue through which psychologists studied victims of bombing. But it was far from being the only or even the primary pursuit of wartime psychology. The proliferation of organizations reflected the various roles the profession took upon itself. The two main fields of action can be roughly delineated to, first, the study of individual psyches, and second, research pertaining to societies and organizations. In the first realm, psychologists and psychiatrists advised the Army on its selection and training of men, and served as medical personnel both on the front lines and in military hospitals, tending to mentally wounded soldiers. The second set of professionals, who are the focus of this chapter, dealt not with individuals (though a significant number worked in both fields) but with populations. Morale was one of the main concepts that bridged the two realms. As Allport defined it, "Morale is a condition of physical and emotional well-being residing in the individual citizen . . . National problems . . . are nothing but personal problems shared by all citizens."[15] Herman, again, insightfully noted that the notion that the state of social morale was merely a reflection of individual morale multiplied (by a factor of millions!) was therefore a godsend for psychologists, as "it made systematic measurement and monitoring possible through an index comprising markers like suicide and crime rates, levels of industrial strife, and patterns of mental illness and disturbance."[16] The war meant that psychologists could leave their clinics, their labs, and the uncertainties of human psyche behind, and find comfort in numbers and "science." This move inevitably led from the personal and qualitative approach toward a quantitative one.

This development had its roots in New Deal use of public opinion surveys and psychological surveys done by the US Department of Agriculture. Rensis Likert, who would later work in the OWI and lead the USSBS Morale Division, pioneered the incorporation of interview techniques and public opinion surveys. The surveys were supposed to help the government assess the public impact of New Deal programs. These early efforts were incorporated into various attempts to measure the opinions and attitudes of US soldiers and, later, of occupied and bombed civilian populations.[17] One of the most important 1950s theorists of air war and emotional stress, Irving Janis, whom we will meet in chapter 4, worked with Likert on these surveys. The New Deal origins of wartime mobilization point to another salient feature of the group of psychologists in question: many came from progressive or even socialist and radical backgrounds. Allport, for instance, conducted seminal research into the psy-

AMERICAN PSYCHOLOGICAL SCIENCES

chological underpinnings of prejudice and discrimination. Edward and Rosamond Spicer, who worked in the internment camps, were socialist activists.[18] As we will see below, various aspects of the war, such as the internment of Japanese Americans and the bombing of civilians, made some social scientists uncomfortable. But most researchers did not protest the deportations, and even Spicer eventually took a job at the camps. The task at hand was just too important, not just for the country but for their profession. As Edward Strecker told the APA, "We are all engaged in the same task of defending the ramparts of democracy . . . our stake in the war is precious, for the discipline of psychiatry can only live and flower within the framework of democracy."[19] Thus, armed with scientific methodology and knowledge of the human psyche, psychological experts set out to defend democracy by aiding the prosecution of the war. Supporting the bombing of civilians was to become one of the main avenues through which they set out to do so.

Psychological Warfare via Napalm

The idea of bombing civilians from the air existed even before militaries even had the technological means to execute it. In his classic work on a worldwide conflict, *The War in the Air* (1907), H. G. Wells described a German and an "Asiatic Armada" destroying New York.[20] His description was prophetic: "As the airships sailed along, they smashed up the city as a child will shatter its cities of brick and card. Below, they left ruins and blazing conflagrations and heaped and scattered dead; men, women, and children mixed together as though they had been no more than Moors, or Zulus, or Chinese."[21] Beside its incredible foresight as to the nature of future wars, Wells's descriptions of the air war were notable for two reasons. First, Wells anticipated the emphasis future air strategists would put on causing social collapse. In one passage, his protagonists describe how, "once a red Asiatic flying-machine came fluttering after them . . . he followed them for a mile. Now they came to regions of panic, now to regions of destruction; here people were fighting for food."[22] A second important factor, in our context, in Wells' fictional account is the issue of race. For contemporary Americans and Europeans, the specter of New York being destroyed by a "confederation of East Asia," which proceeds to massacre Euro-Americans "as though they had been no more than Moors, or Zulus, or Chinese," was particularly troubling.[23] Bombing civilians was one way

34   CHAPTER ONE

in which modern technology, with its power of dehumanized and impersonal destruction, could turn Westerners into those whom they feared and loathed the most, the non-Western other.

Indeed, the argument can be made that the practice of bombing civilians was a particularly ironic case of colonial brutality coming home to roost. Western audiences paid no heed to the slaughter of non-Western civilians via modern technology from the machine gun to the bomber. Colonial powers widely applied the new theories of air power in non-Western settings. In the 1920s, the British bombed Iraqi and Somali villages, Spain and France bombed Morocco, and the Japanese bombed Taiwanese aboriginals, in some cases using gas bombs as well as regular munitions.[24] The issue of dehumanization and technology's ability to cause violence on a genocidal scale to enemy "others" would remain a constant issue up to and beyond the onset of the nuclear age. But this was only one part of the picture. Europeans were as capable of bombing and slaughtering each other's civilians as they were of doing the same to non-Europeans. The practice started during World War I, with the German bombing of London and subsequent Allied raids on Germany. Colonial bombing was an important factor in the development of bombing theories, but the actual practice of bombing cities started in Paris and London, not in Khartoum or Peking. The first theorists of the air war, first and foremost Italy's General Giulio Douhet, were planning for combat against other industrial powers in a total war. Douhet campaigned for a battle in which ferocious bombing of enemy cities with poison gas and incendiary and explosive munitions would bring about the swift capitulation of the enemy.[25] Ironically, he saw this as a more humanitarian way of fighting. Ending a war quickly was better, he argued, than the dragged-out stalemate of the Western Front. What Douhet and other theorists aimed at was a scenario like that in Germany in 1919, when the country collapsed from within after wide-scale societal upheaval.[26] German psychiatrists also made these connections. In their own version of the *Dolchstoßlegende* or "stab in the back" myth, some doctors viewed "shell shock" and its "sinister" social impact as the reason for Germany's defeat. Leading psychiatrists, many of whom became prominent Nazis, argued that "malingerers, cowards and left psychopaths" from the German army, instead of being shot, had been sent back to Germany for treatment, and there had poisoned the home front, infecting civilian morale with their degeneracy and defeatism."[27] After the war, "tens of thousands of psychopaths were cured as if by magic and became active and noisy revolutionaries."[28] Such ideas were an im-

AMERICAN PSYCHOLOGICAL SCIENCES

portant background to German ideas on civil defense and the practice of bombing civilians.

While scholars widely acknowledged the impact of Douhet and others on the bombing war in Europe, racial hatred, rather than the USAAF's professed goal of breaking the enemy's morale, takes central stage when examining Japan. In his work on the social scientists who worked in the War Department's Foreign Morale Analysis Division (FMAD), David Price, for instance, argued that the psychological warfare policies pushed for by FMAD were ultimately ignored. FMAD researchers, whose work we will return to in later chapters, argued that Japanese soldiers could be swayed to surrender through carefully crafted and culturally sensitive propaganda campaigns. Instead, Admiral Chester Nimitz and others "chose a strategy of massive destruction ... based on a shallow conception which took as a fact an imaginary situation actually created by Japanese propaganda itself: the delusion that the Japanese would never surrender."[29] While FMAD saw the Japanese as people, Nimitz and others saw them as subhuman. As John Dower has demonstrated, this attitude was indeed widespread, and had a significant impact on the prosecution of the war.[30] The fact that most Americans did not view Japanese as fully human certainly made it easier for the USAAF commanders to burn Japan's cities. As Conrad Crane has noted, if in Europe one sees "decreasing concern with civilian casualties, in the Pacific you see none at all."[31]

Thus, Price is not necessarily wrong in pointing out that race played a role in bombing. As Ronald Schaffer and others have pointed out, racism played a part in the decisions that led to the targeting of civilian Japanese population on a massive scale.[32] Faced with the brutality of the fire raids, these arguments seem quite compelling. One bombing raid, of Tokyo on 10 March 1945, exceeded even the destruction caused by the atomic bombings. The atomic bombings were not seen as completely separate from the fire-raid campaigns, and many argued that racism played a role in the decision to use nuclear weapons in Japan.[33] Race probably also played a role in firebombing, but it was not a primary motive in that campaign. The theory behind the bombing of Japan's cities, again, had been developed initially in Europe in the campaigns against Germany, and based on British and German practices. Furthermore, the A-bomb was deployed on the basis of the same basic doctrine that operated behind the burning to death of hundreds of thousands of Tokyoites and residents of other urban centers.

It should be noted that the actual deployment and the choice of targets for the A-bomb has a complex history of its own. The nuclear and the conventional bombings of Japan were not planned by the same people, and had somewhat different, if overlapping, goals.[34] While Japanese civilians' minds and bodies were the targets of conventional bombs, the nuclear attacks were aimed more at the minds of the leadership, and were intended to "'shock" the Japanese high command into a swift capitulation (or, as some have argued, to impress Stalin). This is why the USSBS had such difficulty in assessing the A-bomb. As we will see below, due largely to USAAF postwar goals, the USSBS made a concerted effort to "demystify" the A-bomb and present it as a conventional weapon, in direct opposition to the Manhattan Engineer District and others who sought to present it as something unique and different from the firebombing. However, both forms of bombing had much in common. First and foremost, for our purposes, was the emphasis on its morale-breaking role. Significantly, to return to Price, the goals of the USAAF and, even more important, the ways in which those goals were understood by postwar planners were in essence not very different from those of the FMAD's campaign. The main goal of the bombing campaign was not to blindly wreak destruction but to cause mental and societal collapse. It was psychological warfare via napalm.

As Sheldon Garon has demonstrated, the practice of bombing enemy cities was a transnational phenomenon that involved all World War II combatants.[35] Douhet's ideas were shared widely between allies and foes alike. Significantly, early air power simply could not deliver the kind of damage that air-war theorists and literary prophecies imagined. Airplanes and munitions were not capable of doing that until at least the late 1930s. Until then, bombing was ineffective and sporadic. But the randomness and novelty of the practice made it quite terrifying. British Brigadier General Cyril Newall, who headed the effort to bomb German factories behind the trenches, commented that the "material effect" of bombing vital industries "has not been very great ... but the morale effect has been considerable."[36] Air Chief Marshal Hugh Trenchard similarly believed that "the psychological 'yield' of his air attack on one Rhine town was twenty times larger than the actual physical damage."[37] This led Douhet and others to conclude that bombing cities with incendiary and gas bombs would produce effects on morale far greater than material damage.

This was still a forecast, however, rather than practical advice. Wells and other "prophets" of air war were important in this regard. The anticipatory anxiety that their works produced was as significant in the psychologization of the bombing war as was the work of military planners, if not

AMERICAN PSYCHOLOGICAL SCIENCES

more so. As Susan Grayzel has argued, the anxieties produced by the relatively few bombing raids on London profoundly impacted interwar thinking on the nature of future war on the "home front" (itself a completely new term).[38] Authors like Lewis Mumford, whose *The Culture of Cities* (1938) described a bombing as a "brief description of hell"; Olaf Stapledon, who in the 1930s predicted vast aerial gas attacks that would decimate Europe; Stanley Baldwin, who declared in 1932 that the "bomber will always get through"; and many others were significant in this regard. All these authors made Europe's cities an imagined battlefield years before bombing cities became a brutal reality. During World War I, bombing of civilian targets was rather sporadic and theorists had little to work with. The writings of Douhet, Trenchard, Billy Mitchell, and others were more a prediction of future war than a study based on actual warfare.[39]

The work of such authors, like bombing itself, was transnational. From the turn of the century onward, Japanese readers avidly consumed futuristic scenarios of new kinds of modern war in which Japanese cities were destroyed by mass bombing, death rays, and even atomic weapons.[40] Miyazaki Ichiu's 1922's *Nichibei miraisen* (The Future War between Japan and the United States) anticipated the use of kamikaze suicide bombers, massive airborne naval engagements, and cross-Pacific bombing raids.[41] Science fiction writers like Juza Unno produced countless novels that featured technologically advanced foes, and Japan itself, raining destruction from the sky. Some of the books, like the futuristic military fantasy *Chikyū yōsai* (Fortress Earth), were serialized and read avidly during the war itself, thus conflating lived experience, fantasy, and propaganda.[42] As Nakao Maika has argued, while World War I was the reference point for such cultural anxieties in the West, in Japan the 1923 Great Kanto Earthquake was the main impetus for such work.[43] This was true both in the realm of culture and in military planning. The breakdown of civil order and the onset of murderous riots in which thousands of Koreans and others were killed worried Japanese military planners. Following the 1923 quake, General Ugaki Kazushige, vice-minister of the army, recorded in his diary: "Chills run down my spine when I think that the next time Tokyo suffers a catastrophic fire and tragedy on this scale, it could come at the hands of an enemy air attack."[44] Officials fixated on the "'panic,' 'chaos' and 'moral collapse'" that would ensue among city people, especially the working classes, and could endanger the war effort.[45] Yamanashi Hanzō, who was the martial law commander of the Tokyo region after the quake, commented, "It is inevitable big cities will be targeted and bombed by air [in a future war]. . . . If this happens, public safety in the capital cannot be maintained without sending in large numbers of troops, as happened during the earthquake. I confess that I am extremely worried about the future of our national security. We must establish organizations and undertake training."[46] And indeed Japan, like Germany, the United Kingdom, and other combatants invested much energy in creating such organizations, often modeling their efforts on both German and British experience.

In this general atmosphere of anxiety, and especially after World War I, recent psychological notions like "shell shock" played a part in theorists' thinking. This was true both for the "bombed" and for the "bombers"—and all combatants, except Americans, were both. As Douhet wrote, "*Like intense artillery bombardments*, air raids would subject people in the target area to significant shock and stress" (my emphasis).[47] Reflecting such attitudes, when evaluating the bombing after the war, the USSBS, which frequently equated soldiers and civilian behavior, argued in its report on German morale that, though the air war did not achieve any significant slowdown of German war production, "the direct impact of air raids needs also to be considered, for obviously bombing presents all the traumatic conditions of front-line warfare, a warfare which strikes at the whole population."[48] The USSBS use of the term "trauma" was rare, but it emphasized the wide-ranging understanding that air war collapsed distinctions between the home front and the battle fronts. The psychological implications of this change were never fully theorized, but as bombing became a wartime reality, the premise that bombing could break the enemy's will to fight primarily through psychologically overwhelming city dwellers from the air became military common sense. The notion, formulated by morale studies, that societies and individuals operated along similar psychological lines contributed immensely to the shaping of bombing policies. Thus, British planners anticipated an "aerial holocaust, [which] it was assumed would not only kill civilians; it would also send them mad. There would be panic and hysteria, a danger of civil disorder; the planners 'accepted almost as a matter of course that widespread neurosis and panic would ensue.'"[49] In 1938, eighteen leading British psychiatrists warned "that in coming war three psychiatric casualties could be expected for every one physical. This would have meant . . . some 3–4 million cases of acute panic, hysteria and other neurotic conditions during the first six months of air attack."[50]

This was very similar to Japanese predictions and anxieties. Indeed, the psychologization of bombing was widely shared by both civil de-

AMERICAN PSYCHOLOGICAL SCIENCES

fense planners and airmen across the globe. This was regardless of the meager results achieved by actual bombing. The idea's hold on military and civilian minds alike was just too strong. The Japanese, drawing on French experience, enthusiastically embraced "political strategic bombing" (*senseiryaku bakugeki*). When bombing Chinese cities during the Second Sino-Japanese War in the mid- 1930s, air commanders' orders were to "break the enemy's will to continue the war." Pilots "need not directly hit the targets ... the primary objective is to sow terror in the enemy's morale."[51] The British experts who studied the campaign found that the Japanese bombing of Chinese civilians was counterproductive, as the "Japanese policy of indiscriminate airplane bombing aroused people in Shanghai and brought them against Japan.... Frightfulness united them as no peacetime propaganda could have," with the chief result being that the bombing of Canton "was to change the indifference of the south China masses to intense hatred of the Japanese."[52] Such evaluations did not change the course of action taken by either the Japanese or the Royal Air Force (RAF), which during the war, largely due to technological and material disadvantages, resorted also to the theory that massive destruction would break the German will to fight. By February 1942, the British Bomber Command concluded that the primary object of the bombing campaign was to break the morale of the enemy civilian population and, in particular, the industrial workers. This policy was called, in a famous memo, the "de-housing" of workers.[53]

The USAAF initially opted for precision bombing; but because of political and technological limitations, it adapted to British methods, first in Europe and then, from February 1945 onward, in Japan. The complex history behind its decision to move to bombing population centers, and the operational decisions that drove that campaign, are beyond the scope of this book. For our purposes it will be sufficient to note, first, that there was never one single theory, psychological or otherwise, that drove decisions. Our focus on psychological warfare does not mean that it was the only factor in the USAAF's turn toward terror bombing. A divided command structure; competition with the British, the Navy, and Army; the independence of people like General Curtis LeMay; and many other factors led the USAAF down the path to the torching of Tokyo and Hiroshima.[54] The bombing of civilian targets was the result of the many contradictory and entangled forces that drove total war. Racism, again, was also an important factor when the war moved to Japan. Another factor was what David Fedman and Cary Karakas have insightfully termed a "cartographic fade to black," as Japanese cities on US planning maps turned into "kill zones," "industrial areas," and other terms that turned cities into empty space and concealed the presence of the elderly, women, infants, and other civilians.[55] Thus, for instance, the Committee of Operations Analysts (COA), which was the highest planning organ at the USAAF, in a typical turn of phrase, estimated that "by destroying 70% of all housing in the above-mentioned cities (Tokyo, Osaka, Yokohama, Kawasaki, Nagoya, and Kobe)...Japan's industrial output would decrease by 15%."[56]

This drive to compute killing was part of an overall rationalization and quantification of bombing. Perhaps owning to this perceived chaos in decision making, there was a consistent effort to insert scientific thinking and planning into the process. Already in 1939 military reports concluded that "the most efficient way to defeat the enemy is to destroy, by means of bombardment from the air, its war making capacity; the means to this end is [to have] identified by *scientific analysis* those particular elements of his war potential the elimination of which will cripple either his war machine or *his will to continue to conflict*" (my emphasis).[57] Throughout the war, British and American commanders constantly tried to make bombing technologically efficient and scientifically advanced. Roland Schaffer saw this trend as leading to "technological amorality and fanaticism."[58] J. Enrique Zanetty, a Columbia University chemist who developed incendiary bombs, remarked, "Whether one is prepared to accept the long foreseen 'all-out' type of warfare, in which the destruction of civilian morale plays such an important part, or whether one condemns it as brutal, inhumane and uncivilized matters little. 'All-out' warfare is here and must be faced." Thus, Zanetti thought it was "elementary" to cause firestorms as the most efficient way to cause maximum damage to enemy morale.[59] Zanetti was not alone. The number of similar quotes is legion. Most discussion of fire raids of enemy cities was statistical. This led to some uneasiness among some decision makers. Even military men sometimes showed disquiet with the deliberations. At one targeting session, an officer pointed out that discussion was purely conducted "from a mathematical precision point of view," and wondered how the Japanese would react psychologically to the fire raids and whether "would bedlam be created."[60] This was the exact question that drove the turn to psychological experts. The USAAF move to rectify the gap between bombing praxis and theory led to the creation of USSBS and the conscription of "social scientists, [and] particularly psychologists," in order to "pursue the question of morale breaking more systematically."[61] American psychologists were more than happy to join the enterprise and lend their expertise to it. If until now the psychological dimensions of bombing had been stated only in broad terms and mostly by nonexperts, the USSBS was supposed to flush out and refine the concept, using the most advanced methods in the psychological arsenal for the scientific assessment of bombing.

The Strategic Bombing Survey in Germany

In 1944 the US War Department arranged to have Gordon Allport send a questionnaire to his colleagues on the CNM, and beyond that asked about the potential psychological impact of bombing on Japanese and German morale. Psychologists were divided on the issue. Some were sharply critical about the morality of the endeavor. Others, such as Ohio University's Horace B. English, had few qualms. English suggested "making Guinea pigs" of German civilian internees to see what methods would be effective in breaking their morale. English, who later served with the USSBS in Nagasaki, added that using internees was "done in Germany.... Let's find out now [as well], if we can."[62] Such references to Nazi practices were rare. But English's statement was a sort of Freudian textual slip that exposed how much was shared by psychologists and air theorists on both sides of the war. The practice of bombing, again, was a transnational process whereby combatants were learning from each other and adopting "best practices" for both breaking enemy morale and improving the defense of the home front.[63] Ideas about bombing psychology were part of this process. Himmler's 1937 quip about Germany's "inner front," quoted above, was not very different from the thinking of American commanders who were targeting Germans and Japanese minds.

The similarities between German and American ideas can be seen in the reports and activities of the USSBS in the European theater. The USSBS was created in late 1944 by the War Department to conduct "scientific investigation of all the evidence" of strategic bombing in the European theater, and to provide conclusions that would help to evaluate "the importance and potentialities of air power as an instrument of military strategy, for planning the future development of the U.S. Air Forces, and for determining future economic policies with respect to the national defense."[64] The emphasis on science and data was palpable in this and in many other statements and reports put out by the surveys. Furthermore, one finds in the drafts, correspondences, and reports of the German survey, for the first time, the contours of psychological theory that connected, however tenuously, the psychological shock the bombing caused to the morale of the German nation. This theory drew heavily on battlefield psychology but, again, was never quite pronounced. The surveys were mostly data-driven, leaving at times little room for nuance.

The USSBS reports were based on a number of sources. Researchers, many of whom were émigré Germans themselves, interviewed hundreds of German civilians and officials, checked German domestic intelligence reports on morale, and reviewed more than two thousand captured letters sent to the front by civilians.[65] These methods, not accidentally, were very similar to the ones used in the OWI. In terms of both personal and operational theory, the surveys were a continuation of the psychological warfare efforts of earlier war years. The morale survey final reports were somewhat ambivalent about the overall impact of the bombing and its contribution to the war effort. "Bombing," the report admitted, "was not the number one cause" but it "aided defeat" by "lowering morale." Decreased "civilian morale," the report continued, "expressed itself in somewhat diminished industrial productivity."[66] Thus, the very idea behind "dehousing" workers and the targeting of enemy civilians' minds was proved by the survey to have, if anything, only a "somewhat diminished" impact on the enemy's war economy. The authors of the report brushed aside this muted admission of defeat, however, and charged on to describe the various ways in which morale was impacted by the bombing. If bombing failed to impact war production, the impact on morale would be the "next best thing"—even if, as the authors admitted, it was not clear what exactly would be the contribution of such a vast loss of civilian lives to the Allies' victory.

Indeed, there are many inconsistencies in the survey's analyses of the term "morale" and the way in which the psychological impact of the bombing was connected to changes in "morale" and how they impacted the German effort. German émigrés who worked at the Office of Strategic Services (OSS), especially the noted scholars Franz Neumann and Herbert Marcuse, repeatedly and emphatically pointed out that the worsening "mood [*Stimmung*] of the Germans did not necessarily lead to erosion of support to the Nazi regime."[67] As Sophia Dafinger has demonstrated, different definitions of morale were used by different teams on the ground in Germany, and field teams differed in their application and parameters for morale from the final reports written by Likert and the analysts at headquarters.[68] In the final report, the survey found that the "main psychological effects" of bombings were "defeatism, fear, hopelessness, fatalism, and apathy."[69] The authors divided "psychological morale," defined as the "will to resist," from "behavioral morale," which was expressed in absenteeism and other more measurable factors.[70] This division was very similar to the way German home front organizations like the *Reichsluftschutzbund* (Reich Air Defense League, or RLB), and domestic intelligence viewed it. Echoing émigré experts, German reports often distinguished between *Stimmung* (mood), which was the way the people felt, and *Haltung* (attitude), which was the way civilians behaved.[71]

The psychological theory behind the surveys also contained many ambiguities and contradictions. The theory, again, was never fully spelled out, but it can be found in the way researchers tried to connect the two kinds of morale. Here the impact of both German psychological thinking and American battlefield psychiatry is notable. Significantly, the direct psychological impact of the bombing was seen as relatively short-lived. Like German psychiatrists, some American survey researchers saw permanent mental damage from bombing as a sign of earlier mental disease. In a section on suicide, USSBS consultant Halbert L. Dunn divided "healthy" responses into those of "extroverts," who "force such conflicting thoughts into separate compartments" of their minds, and those of "introverts," who might find peace in confessing to others or "to the listening ear of a benevolent God." What bombing victims needed was "adjustment! No other way is open. That is, except neurosis, which is nature's solution."[72] Putting the onus of "adjustment" to the reality of unceasing bombing campaigns on the victims was an extreme yet typical expression of a classic view of the role of psychologists in a capitalist society. From the mid-nineteenth century onward, psychologists saw their task as that of helping individuals adjust to the dislocations of the modern world. If a patient could not adjust, it was the fault not of society, or of any other environmental factor, but of the individual herself. German and particularly Nazi psychiatry took this logic to the extreme. The Nazis were obsessed with notions of health, and constantly used metaphors of illness, pollution, and disease in pushing their ideology. Nazi doctors saw mentally ill patients as a threat. They were not simply ill, but were themselves the disease that threatened the body politic, and which thus had to be eliminated. German psychiatrists played a key role in the Aktion T4 euthanasia program, in which the "mentally unfit" were murdered.[73]

American combat psychiatry was beginning to challenge such notions during the war. Front-line psychiatrists started to argue that individuals who had become psychologically unbalanced were responding quite normally to a troubling environment. Roy Grinker and John Spiegel, who worked with the US Army in Tunisia, argued, "The situations of war, for the civilized man, are completely abnormal and foreign to his background. It would seem to be a more rational question to ask why the soldier does not succumb to anxiety, rather than why he does."[74] Such notions were influential in shaping the way both strategists and researchers evaluated bombing. One can see the influence of both combat psychiatry and older bourgeois notions in the psychological theories outlined in the German reports. In several sections the survey argued that every person, no matter how "adjusted," would succumb to some sort of mental harm under the stress of bombing. After discussing the "traumatic conditions of front-line warfare," quoted above, the survey concluded that "soldiers learn to live in fox holes and some people manage to adapt to air raids. But the majority do not become adapted to bombing."[75] The survey found that "more than one-third of the people going through a big raid [suffered] relatively permanent psychological effects. That is, the terror transcends the immediate raid to such an extent that it is reinstated by the next alert."[76] In another section, the report spoke of the longer-term impact of the raids as being chiefly "apathy and fatigue," which the authors combined into one category. "As bombing increases," they concluded, "there is an increased apathetic reaction, and there is no diminution of this reaction in the cities undergoing the most severe attacks."[77] All of this would suggest a rather different view of the impact of bombing than the one presented above by Dunn. Bombing is seen as capable of causing permanent mental damage to healthy individuals, regardless of their capacity for adjustment.

In another section, however, in a discussion of "psychological morale," the report spoke of adverse reactions as "a reflection of deep-lying personality characteristics." Here the authors distinguished between "objective fear" and "sensitivity, or subjective fear."[78] "Objective fear" was seen as impacting most people, regardless of their mental health background, but "sensitivity relates to subjective processes, to apprehensions and expectations which differ markedly between individuals." Subjective fear led to "fright." The frightened were seen as more easily succumbing to anxieties.[79] Here again, the authors turned to battlefield examples, but they reached a different conclusion than in the "apathy" section: "The same phenomenon," of subjective and objective fear, "has been observed in battle, where men with good behavioral morale will experience fear under terrifying circumstances almost as much as men who run away. It is

AMERICAN PSYCHOLOGICAL SCIENCES

not so much whether people become frightened as what they do about it that affects the outcome."[80] Here the authors were likely referring to the work of the Yale psychiatrist John Dollard, who wrote a short influential pamphlet, *Fear in Battle*, and the even shorter *Twelve Rules on Meeting Battle Fear*. Both pamphlets were hugely popular and helped reform the way the US Army dealt with battlefield psychiatry.[81] Such ideas about "healthy fear" were advocated also by the future air theorist and psychologist Irving Janis, in his work on the American soldiers in battle, and were important in later thinking on nuclear civil defense.[82] Janis's contribution to *The American Soldier*, and the volume as a whole, would have significant impact in postwar discussions on nuclear defense.

It must be emphasized that it is only in retrospect and in reading against the grain of the report that one could ascertain the survey's definitions of trauma. The report, which spans a number of volumes and hundreds of pages, is not interested in trauma as a distinct phenomenon; the word "trauma" appears only once. In the interviews and other materials used to produce the report, one sees a much more consistent use of clinical terms and an interest in the precise psychiatric impact of bombing on the German people. The initial directive to field teams in the European theater asked them to seek "psychiatric evaluations [and seek] connections between bombing and acute neurosis," and to note the "diagnosis, number of raids experienced before the development of acute neuroses, general physical status, effect of less sleep in the etiology, location of casualty in relation to bomb hits and near misses," and the like.[83] The medical field teams noted in initial reports that there was an increase in "psychiatric cases" as well as "some increase in psychosomatic diseases in Germany."[84] In an interview with the Reich's health leader (*Reichsgesundheitsfuehrer*), Leonardo Conti, USSBS interviewers referred to the bombing campaign as a "war of vegetative neuroses." Conti noted that there was "a general increase in all vegetative diseases, although there was no pronounced increase in clear-cut psychiatric conditions." When prodded further about "the effect of the air war on the health of the civilian population of Germany," he answered that "we have covered that in the discussion of 'vegetative neuroses'; to me, this was the greatest effect of the air war on the people. The increase in all these neurogenic conditions is the greatest and most debilitating effect. It created [an] unseen enemy in our midst. An enemy that undermined every individual effort to the total war."[85]

Conti's reference to "vegetative neuroses" as an "unseen enemy in our midst" was, again, both an echo of Nazi attitudes to mental health and an affirmation of American bombing theory. However, very little of this language made it into the final report. Again, the authors of the report were interested not in the mental damage caused by the bombing to individuals, but in how bombing led to decreased morale in society at large. The authors repeatedly avoided illustrating the connections and mechanisms that led from individual fear, anxiety, and apathy to reduced support for the war effort. This is not to say that the survey did not acknowledge the existence of large-scale mental suffering. The authors provided a large number of examples that would prove the existence of what psychologists at the time were calling "traumatic neurosis" or "war neurosis."[86] Yet neither the authors of the report nor the German victims saw their experience through that lens. Instead, they used terms like "emotional shock," "wrecked nerves," a "shock to the soul," and the like. The survey did not distinguish between reactions, but bagged all of them under a number of general categories like "war weariness" and "apathy and fatigue," which it statistically connected to bomb tonnage and kinds of explosives on the one hand, and a quantified morale index on the other (see, for instance, the chart in figure 2). This was supposed to connect the sum of all these reactions to the impact of bombing on societal morale.[87] The survey connected numbers of bombs, weight and kind of ordnance, types of damage, and the like to changes in attitudes through a "morale index" and countless charts and statistics, which were supposed to show a connection between bombing praxis and the abstract notion of breaking an enemy's will. The mental health damage that supposedly led to these changes rarely made it into the charts.

Behind all of these numbers was real horror. One recoils when reading comments such as: "In the cross-sectional study in which people were asked directly about their experiences during raids, most of them talked freely about the psychological effect of the raids. More than one respondent, however, broke down and wept and could not go on with the interview when recalling the experiences under bombing."[88] Respondents were jumpy and easily spooked. Interviewees showed extreme anxiety when hearing airplanes overhead. In another instance the researcher reported that "twice during the interview some sort of explosive went off in the vicinity and the respondent jumped out of the chair both times with extreme fear in her expression."[89] In the many letters examined by the survey, one could also find many expressions of hurt and recognition by victims of the permanent mental damage done by the bombing. One woman wrote to her son at the front, "I saw people killed by falling bricks

FIGURE 2. "Variations in Morale Factors and Intensity of Bombing," from the USSBS German report. Photo courtesy of the US National Archives.

and heard the screams of others dying in the fire. I dragged my best friend from a burning building, and she died in my arms. I saw others who went stark mad. *The shock to my nerves and to the soul, one can never erase*" (my emphasis).[90] Another woman wrote from Dresden, "Believe me, we are trembling. The fright from the last time is still in our system." The survey would find very similar expressions of fear and shock in Japan.[91] But again, the authors of the reports were interested not in the symptoms and long-term impact of the bombing, but only in how it affected society at large and the German war effort. Regardless of all this suffering (and contradicting its own reports), urban bombing, the survey concluded, was a brilliant success: "It brought the economy which sustained the enemy's armed forces to virtual collapse. . . . [and] brought home to the German people the full impact of modern war with all its horror and suffering. Its impact on the German nation will be lasting."[92] Eventually, the survey analyzed the nation, not the individuals who composed it; and it brought the same attitudes and theories to the study of the A-bomb in Japan.

Conclusion: The Road to the Bomb

The survey's conclusions in its German reports were the product of developments in both the field of psychology and the development of bombing theory and praxis. The survey validated the psychological assumptions of military theorists and the air war prophets who had preceded them. The psychologization of bombing was, again, not the only reason why all combatants bombed civilian populations, but it was one of the major justifications for doing so. Enemy morale, an abstract and nebulous concept, became a valid military target—a decision that cost hundreds of thousands of civilian lives. This was a transnational development that one could see on both sides of the war, but it had its most drastic implications in the bombing campaign against Axis civilians. The rise of morale studies in the United States, and the active part psychological experts took in promoting such notions, had a direct bearing on this development. If a nation was an aggregate of individual citizens' emotions, one could break an enemy by damaging individuals psychologically. The psychological lessons of the trenches of World War I, the social upheaval that followed the war, and contemporary battlefield psychiatry were all important in formulating both the practice of bombing and, later on, the scientific evaluation of it. In a parallel development, the drive for quantifying bombing was

AMERICAN PSYCHOLOGICAL SCIENCES

also what drove the turn to bombing surveys. The survey's methods were a natural continuation of the ever-growing emphasis on technology and science in the conduct of bombing, on the one hand, and the evaluation of enemy psychology and morale, on the other. As a result, the language of bombing psychology, as in other fields that contributed to the targeting of civilians, from mapmaking to computing and math, remained largely abstract. The more technologically advanced and sophisticated bombing and its evaluation became, the more sterile were the concepts used, and the more it evaded the human price in the cities below. The A-bomb was the apex of such thinking. Perhaps nothing demonstrates this development more than photographs depicting the usual bird's-eye view of Hiroshima and Nagasaki, with miles upon miles of empty, blackened space. Humans are nowhere to be seen.

Therefore, as insensitive and surreal as it was to ask bombing victims in Hiroshima how they felt about the A-bomb and about their experience, it was in fact a radical break from what had come before it. Morale, in a way, was a back door through which the personal, psychological, and individual experience of the victims could be brought forward. It was also, importantly, a break from the racism that characterized so much of US wartime rhetoric and practice toward the Japanese. But the move toward humanization of bombing victims never materialized. First, morale studies were focused on communities and not individuals. Secondly, the psychological experts who filled the ranks of the surveys were as keen to quantify and compute suffering as were their scientist colleagues. They spent very little time on the actual experience of bombing victims. And more often than not, they rushed to translate it into charts and graphs. The experiences of victims were silenced and contextualized away, first, by being made into data, and second, by the connection to the larger question of morale and how best to break the will of communities. Still, by opening the door to individual experiences, and by including the human dimension of enemy civilians and treating them as fellow human beings, the USSBS was a first step toward a more expansive and humanistic assessment of the price of bombing.

CHAPTER TWO

Bombing "the Japanese Mind": Alexander Leighton's Hiroshima

"The urban area attacks continued ... until over 102 square miles of industrial urban areas of Tokyo, Yokohama, Nagoya, Osaka, and Kobe were destroyed. 'The target,' as one air commander put it, 'had become the Japanese mind.'" — USSBS report on Japanese morale, 1946[1]

When USSBS researchers interviewed the residents of Hiroshima and Nagasaki, they were instructed by their bilingual manual to open with the following statement: "We are interested in future good relations between the United States and Japan. As you know, good relations depend on good understanding. It is our task to learn as much as we can about living conditions and morale among the Japanese people, especially during the war" (figure 3).[2] Such an opening might seem odd for an interview that centered on the experience of bombing. How could bringing up and analyzing the painful experience of losing one's home and loved ones to American bombs contribute to "good relations" and "good understanding" between the US and Japan? Like asking *hibakusha* how they felt about the A-bomb, such an opening might look like sugarcoating and a thinly veiled ideological sleight of hand, intended to disguise the USSBS's true intentions. However, the survey was genuinely interested in how the bombing experience would affect the coming occupation and US-Japan relations. Counterintuitively, the psychological experts who studied bombed populations saw in their wartime experience a steppingstone for safeguarding the coming peace. Better understanding of the ravages of war and of their Japanese foe would help in both preventing the next war and in building a postwar Japanese democracy. Such feelings only went so far, of course, since in the same manual in which the researchers were instructed to profess their quest for understanding, they also were told to

INTERVIEWING, MORALE DIVISION

FIGURE 3. Morale Division interviews (location unknown), from the USSBS official history. USSBS interviews in Hiroshima and Nagasaki would have looked very much like these. Photo courtesy of the US National Archives.

keep survey results hidden from the Japanese.[3] The survey was still primarily a US military endeavor. It was concerned with US strategic needs, and was not primarily oriented toward US-Japan relations.

Such contradictions were the result of the complex trajectories that had led USSBS researchers to Hiroshima. The twin problems of race and trauma were at the heart of these histories. Many of the personnel who studied the way civilians reacted to bombing had come to the field from studying psychological warfare and management of interned populations. These inquiries were part of a struggle between a race-based understanding of Japanese behavior and more universalist, culture-oriented interpretations. Thus, although their work had developed within the context of what some termed a "race war" between the US and Japanese empires, the psychological experts who condoned bombing mostly professed a nonracist ethos.[4] USSBS research signified an important break in the way Western psychological researchers studied racial others. Psychology had a long history in justifying colonial racial hierarchies. Many wartime researchers had used psychological theories to explain Japanese aggression, and had viewed the Japanese as primitive, childish, and neurotic. The USSBS, however, dismissed race and racially motivated theories. The researchers were greatly affected by Boasian anthropology. They applied USSBS member Otto Klineberg's debunking of race, and followed the anthropologist Ruth Benedict's declaration that race was a useless concept for social scientists.[5] Ideas of science as an ideology-free and apolitical practice were an important part of this ethos. The approach allowed an erasure of racial difference, which in turn enabled the view of Japanese minds as being psychologically compatible with German and American minds, and the study of trauma in Japan side by side with other instances of bombing.

The career trajectory of the head of the Hiroshima mission, the psychiatrist Alexander Leighton, demonstrates the importance of these developments. Leighton's career had led him through many important posts along America's entanglement with Cold War Asia. He started studying "Japanese minds" at the Japanese internment camps. Afterward, he became chief of the Foreign Morale Analysis Division (FMAD) of the Office of War Information (OWI), where he sought ways to destabilize and demoralize Japanese soldiers. This, in turn, led him to Hiroshima after the bombing, where he researched *hibakusha*. After the war, Leighton worked in various roles within and outside the "military-educational complex," including work on atomic energy at the United Nations, and

BOMBING "THE JAPANESE MIND" 53

his work in Vietnam, where he was part of an effort to ascertain the effects of US chemical warfare. Leighton made this journey from the internment camps to Hiroshima and beyond together with a group of Japanese American social scientists, whom he had trained in the camps and who joined him in Japan.

Leighton's work, and that of most researchers examined here, moved on two axes. The first axis was between individual psychology and group psychology. The second was between a universalistic and humanist understanding of the Japanese "other," and a racialized notion of Japan. Leighton and others moved freely along both axes, and displayed many contradictory and ambivalent attitudes toward their research subjects. Most importantly, they rarely saw themselves as implicated in the very racially motivated policies that they both researched and condemned. But it was exactly these contradictions that came out of the study of bombed and policed "Japanese minds" that framed their knowledge and shaped their methods for pursuing the impact of nuclear weapons on the *hibakusha*. The USSBS's own history and methodological limitations, evident in its German work, had an important impact on Hiroshima research. Significantly, the survey sought to "demystify" the impact of the A-bomb and to normalize it as being not so different from the fire raids that had preceded it. This included a persistent belief in bombing's ultimate psychological role. Taken together, these trajectories led to a very narrow research focus, an emphasis on short-term damage to *hibakusha* psyches, and a denial of long-term damage. However, immediate postwar research, by virtue of its universalist ethos, enabled a possibility of later extension of ideas on psychic trauma. The deracialization of Japanese psychology and the larger experience of Hiroshima led, in turn, to the possibility of using such experiences in research on civil defense and possible American responses to the A-bomb, and also to the turn to peace activism by some psychological experts. Those subjects will be explored in later chapters of this book.

Interning Japanese American Minds

The study of internment was one of the first major undertakings of American psychological experts. Leighton was situated right at the heart of this enterprise. Having received his psychiatry degree from Johns Hopkins University, he was was also a trained anthropologist. The view of his mentor Adolf Meyer that psychopathology derived from multiple sources, including life experiences, was very influential in Leighton's later thinking. Following a short stint with Navy aviation, to which we will return shortly, Leighton worked as a team with his wife, Dorothea Cross, also a psychiatrist, on the Navajo of New Mexico and the Yupik people of Saint Lawrence Island, Alaska. While in New Mexico, the Leightons published a study of the impact of anxiety and depravation on Navajo men, titled *Gregorio, the Hand-Trembler: A Psychobiological Personality Study of a Navaho Indian.*[6] This study anticipated both scholars' lifelong study of environmental stress and psychological change. After his divorce from Cross, Leighton married another psychiatrist, Jane Murphy Leighton, with whom he also worked on his most influential and long-standing project, the Stirling County Study, which took the insights from his work on Navajo, Japanese, and Inuit, and applied them to white Canadians. Such husband-wife teams were not unusual at the time (Edward and Rosamond Spicer, who also worked in the camps, were also married). The fact that it was Alexander Leighton who got the prestigious positions at Columbia and Harvard while his wives' work remained less known was also not that unusual. Leighton's relationship with his Japanese American peers, who did most of the work for his internment research, followed a similar pattern. Another continuity was in Leighton's work on stress and anxiety in nonwhite ethnicities, and the way such knowledge was applied to Americans. As we saw, this trend was also in continuity with British military psychiatrists' involvement with non-Western communities during World War I. In the camps, Leighton developed a conception of trauma which was transmissible and could impact both victims and perpetrators of violence. His conception of trauma and ideas on race were important in the parallel development of the psychology of bombing and his later role at the USSBS.

The Leightons, the Spicers, and other psychological experts were sent to Poston, Arizona, in March 1942 by John Collier, the commissioner of Indian affairs, who was himself an anthropologist.[7] Poston had been chosen for his post because the War Relocation Authority (WRA) had a special arrangement with the Office of Indian Affairs (OIA), which managed the camp.[8] Poston was located on Navajo land, and as Leighton was at hand, he "was asked to carry out a study on the humane administration of people under stress in a Japanese Relocation Centre."[9] With Collier's encouragement, Leighton and his fellow social scientists established the Bureau of Sociological Research (BSR). Notably, Leighton recruited a large number of Japanese American graduates and trained them as community analysts in social research methods. He described the program as being "somewhat along the lines of a group carrying out clinical studies, but with the community rather than patients being the subject of study."[10] As in later USSBS research, the program was to extrapolate insights from individual cases and apply them widely to the whole community.

The goal of the BSR was, on the face of it, to help with the administration of the camp. But, as Brian Hayashi has demonstrated, the OIA believed that research in the camps could contribute to the war effort by "sharpening the US Navy's comprehension of Japanese psychology" and helping to prepare for the future US occupation of Japan.[11] In the context of our study, the BSR was important in two ways. First, it was an expression of the progressive and antiracist positions Leighton and his peers took toward Japanese psychology. This effort was in turn later connected to a larger Cold War effort to rebuild a postwar democratic Japan. Second, although with one significant exception, the connection with trauma was never fully theorized, a main strand of Leighton's research was the impact of extreme conditions and stress on the human mind. Leighton and his peers, including some of his Japanese American trainees, would continue from the BSR to serve in multiple posts and would have an important influence on subsequent social science research. The Japanese American researchers, like Tom Sasaki, Tamie Tsuchiyama, Iwao Ishino, and many others, continued with Leighton into the War Department, the USSBS, the American occupation, and beyond. Scott Matsumoto, the subject of chapter 5 in this book, continued on to the USSBS, SCAP, the ABCC, and the University of Hawaii.

In July 1942, shortly before starting his work in the camps, Leighton penned a short article for *Applied Anthropology* in which he called on social scientists of all disciplines to come together and join the war effort. But social science's war, according to Leighton, was not only against the Germans and Japanese but also against racism and unscientific thought in general. He wrote, "[For the] social sciences to develop fully all their potentialities as applied sciences, democratic thought and action may then incorporate the best of what science has to offer instead of political bias, hate reactions, and sentimental stabs in the dark. . . . One of the most important things that can be done here and now in preparation for postwar reconstruction is the training of social scientists with the demands of that period in view."[12] A number of important assumptions underlined this statement. First, Leighton saw in the war an opportunity for the expansion of social science's scope and influence. Using his experience with Native Americans, he argued that such enterprises "offer unparalleled opportunities to the social sciences which are yet mostly untapped."[13] Second, research on the camps was done with an eye to postwar occupation of Japan. Leighton was quite specific about this, writing, "Colonies of American Japanese have been formed and must be administered with sense, understanding, justice, and an eye for the future. Experience in such colonies can naturally lead to positions in reorganizing the Pacific areas when the war is over."[14] Such early emphasis on democratic governance was done for both practical and ideological considerations. The "liberal democratic way of management" was the preferred way for the Navy to administer territories. Admiral Ross McIntyre assigned Leighton to camps with instructions to find the best way for the Japanese to govern themselves, reasoning that "when it comes to administering retaken territory, the more efficient and self-regulating that administration makes the community[,] the fewer guards and soldiers will be needed[,] and therefore more men free for front line action."[15] On a deeper level, Leighton's ideas reflected belief in the connection between a psychologically healthy citizenry and democracy. Such ideas developed in the context of morale studies but were later applied widely in Europe and East Asia, as the United States tried to help building democratic (and anticommunist) citizens. As Jennifer Miller has shown, for US policy makers the ramparts of democracy were as much psychological as military.[16] Thus, it was important for Leighton to train and educate Nisei social scientists, and the community as a whole, in "democratic thought and action."[17]

Ironically, given the setting, such positions entailed the rejection of the racialized views of Japanese Americans that had led to their deportation in the first place. Leighton was not condemning the relocation of Japanese citizens per se. He was also not completely out of the colonial and racial woods. He had spent his career studying colonial "others," from Native Americans to Japanese Americans and, finally, Hmong communities during the Vietnam War. He strode around the Poston camp "resplendent in [naval] uniform" and, more than once, displayed condescending paternalistic attitudes toward his Japanese American trainees.[18] According to Arthur Hansen, who worked with him, Leighton "was very arrogant, almost like a British intellectual, [and] looked down his nose at you."[19] Many, both within and outside the administration, were hostile to Leighton's enterprise. After a visit to Poston, Stanford University's William Hopkins reported to Hansen on the frustration with Leighton: "'Who the hell is

Leighton?' They are wondering, and so am I, why a Navy lieutenant in full uniform should be wandering around a relocation center and why, if he's a medico, is he doing a social study?"[20]

Leighton was determined to examine Japanese Americans as people first. This was not easy or popular in wartime America. He had attitude issues, for sure, and was possibly also exploitative of others' work, but his studies were animated by a complete rejection of race. Leighton was quite hostile to camp administrators "as stereotype minded [individuals] who viewed internees as Japanese first and people second."[21] This came out of his deep convictions that, "due to the biological and psychological nature of man, one human community has fundamental similarities to all others."[22] This statement was made within the context of a tense racialized atmosphere, in regard to the Japanese internment. General John DeWitt, who oversaw the deportations, claimed that the operation was militarily necessary as "the Japanese race is an enemy race, whose racial strain remains undiluted."[23] As John Dower has demonstrated, this was not an exceptional view at the time. The war correspondent Ernie Pyle wrote from the Pacific that "in Europe we felt that our enemies, horrible and deadly as they were, were still people.... But out here I soon gathered that the Japanese were looked upon as something repulsive and subhuman; the way some people feel about cockroaches or mice."[24] Closer to home, the *Los Angeles Times* wrote in regards to the camps, "A viper is nonetheless a viper wherever the egg is hatched—so a Japanese-American, born of Japanese parents, grows up to be a Japanese not an American."[25] Seeing Japanese as being capable of "democratic thought and action," training Japanese American social scientists, and analyzing camp dwellers as autonomous individuals with complex life stories and psychologies was by no means a commonsense position at the time. A June 1945 *Times Magazine* review summed up Leighton's work at Poston: "Commander Leighton concluded that many an American simply fails to remember that U.S. Japanese are human beings."[26]

As Karen M. Inouye has demonstrated, the aspect that interested Leighton the most in studying Japanese Americans was the impact of continued stress on the internees. He called the experience "sociological earthquake."[27] And, like a real earthquake, the stress of camp life and forced deportations had a profound impact on internees' mental health. Breaking with Freudian orthodoxy with its focus on individual psyches, Leighton was interested in the connections between groups, environment, and individuals' mental developments. This is where his mentorship by

58 CHAPTER TWO

Adolf Meyer was important. Leighton, following Meyer, treated mental illness as a physiological susceptibility that could be activated by changes of circumstance.[28] He and the BSR researchers collected life histories, conducted intensive interviews and personality analysis, and gathered general sociological data by compiling employment and education records. This was done with an ultimate eye toward helping camp management. BSR staff wrote reports that predicted possible reactions to management decisions, and suggested possible psychological solutions. As Leighton wrote in one report, "The administrator who approaches turbulent people with reason is likely to get about as much result as if he were addressing a jungle."[29]

The violent metaphor of the jungle suggested the violence of camp life. This turned susceptible individuals but also, under enough stress, everyone into a potential neurotic. The concept of trauma did not dominate Leighton's and the BSR's work but, as Inouye has argued in retrospect, it was what the researchers were studying.[30] Leighton confronted the issue head-on in a 1943 lecture, where he connected combat psychiatry, camp life, and the issue of morale. Leighton drew on his work with pilots in Florida in a class led by John Embree, a noted Japan anthropologist, where, after detailing the many factors that led to "apathy" among internees, he spoke directly about "psychic trauma."

> There is something of a parallel to this thing in Flight Surgery. Before America went into the war, the British found out that the strain of too many flights made the aviators go "stale," as they called it. They would become listless and apathetic, and if something was not done, they would get into an empty depression in which they would sit around and do nothing. Some people called it "walking death." Then they began to look for ways to cure this. They discovered that if a man is kept under the strain of fighting on and on, he develops a mental state which incapacitates him.[31]

Leighton connected the mental state of "walking death" to overbearing mental stress that could overwhelm even the fittest pilots. This description was strikingly similar to the observations Lifton had made in Hiroshima two decades later on survivors' psychic numbing after their encounter with death. Furthermore, and again drawing on Inouye, Leighton connected the issue of trauma to the panic and aggression some guards displayed during a strike at Poston. This meant that the "adverse effects of stress—whether originating in combat flight or in internment—were

BOMBING "THE JAPANESE MIND" 59

transmittable, a disease both psychological and physiological."[32] This insight was at the very heart of the psychological warfare and bombing operations Leighton would take part in after Poston. However, in all three situations such insights were used not to heal minds, but to advise the military in how to better manage, propagandize, and eventually break enemy minds.

Propagandizing Japanese Minds

Following his work at the camps, Leighton was recruited by the OWI in 1943 to head the Foreign Morale Division. The OWI had been established in June 1942 to analyze foreign news and propaganda and generate domestic and foreign propaganda. George Taylor, the head of the OWI's Far East Division, brought Leighton on board, and together they collected a team of social scientists, chiefly psychologists and anthropologists, including many who had come with Leighton from the camps, such as John Embree, Leighton's wife Dorothea Cross Leighton, Morris Opler, and many Nisei researchers who had received their initial training at the BSR.[33] BSR staff assisted in the translation of enemy documents, including more than five thousand war diaries of Japanese soldiers that were recovered on Pacific islands.[34] FMAD analysts were supposed to analyze the Japanese enemy both in terms of "personality types" and as a nation, in what became known as national character studies. This was done in order to help prepare better and more effective propaganda, and to help policy makers in the conduct of the war. The memos and reports were heavily psychologized, reflecting the influence of psychologists and their ideas on wartime work. As Ellen Herman has argued, national character studies were typified by a blend of disciplines, "and at its heart lay the conviction that microscopic questions about individual personality and behavior and macroscopic questions about societal patterns and problems were nothing but two sides of the same coin."[35] Such studies contained many contradictions. Though many psychological experts rejected race as a category for the study of individuals, the very idea of assigning character traits and psychological attributes to a whole ethnic group was dangerously close to racism. On the other hand, experts were as ready to generalize about Westerners as they were about non-Westerners. Indeed, as with theories of bombing, such studies also started in Europe and were mostly related to the effort to explain the psychology of Nazism. Psychological insights into the emotional and irrational was especially important in this regard. As Leighton explained in his postwar account of his work, reflecting the consensus among students of morale examined above, "Societies move on the feelings of the individuals who compose them, and so do countries and nations. Very few internal policies and almost no international policies are predominantly the product of reason."[36]

The national character studies produced by the OWI were done in the context of the neo-Freudian movement and the revision of psychoanalytic orthodoxies. They were considered insufficiently attentive to the impact of social context on psychological development. The beginnings of the field can be traced to World War I, and to the work of Wilfred Trotter, a British surgeon connected with many early psychoanalysts, who wrote on the limits of reason and of individualism in his *Instincts of the Herd in Peace and War* (1916). In 1921, Sigmund Freud himself published *Group Psychology and the Analysis of the Ego*, which focused on how individual fears interacted with group dynamics. In the interwar years, together with the rise of fascism, many analysts found the concept of the superego, articulated by Freud in *Group Psychology* and in *The Ego and the Id* (1923), a useful concept in applying clinical knowledge to social and political problems.[37] Such thinking continued into the war years. Psychologists and the policy makers who sought their insights (but did not always heed their advice) operated on the assumption that psychology had an important role to play in understanding of the fascist powers. As Geoffrey Gorer, who worked in the camps and the OWI, explained, "Germany, and even more Japan, were acting irrationally and incomprehensibly by our standards; understanding them became an urgent military necessity, not only for psychological warfare—though that was important—but also for strategic and tactical reasons, to find out how to induce them to surrender, and having surrendered, to give information."[38] Leading analysts produced psychological profiles of Hitler and other Nazi leaders. Émigré psychologists were especially important in this regard. Bruno Bettelheim, who had been incarcerated in Dachau and Buchenwald before coming to the United States, saw the camp system as a disciplinary mechanism that pushed individuals into extreme behaviors. Notably, he generalized from the Jewish experience to the larger German one. In an explanation of the acceptance of authority in Nazi Germany, he wrote that "what happens in an extreme fashion to the prisoners who spend several years in the concentration camp happens in less exaggerated form to the inhabitants of the big concentration camp called greater Germany."[39]

Bettelheim was important in linking individual trauma and explanations for human aggression, as well as connecting and conflating victims and perpetrators. Pointing out that Jews and Germans, and even Americans, shared the same psychological vulnerabilities was not a popular stance at the time. Similarly, Leighton made such connections in his comments on stress at the Japanese internment camps. He and, to a lesser extent, Bettelheim insisted on the universalist potential of national character. They sought to treat all ethnic groups similarly without positioning nations on a developmental scale. Americans were not more "mature" than Japanese or Germans and, within cultural limits, were as open to aggression and fascism. But other experts used national studies as a foil for racist views of the Japanese. Leighton saw the liberal position not just as an ideological choice but as a more scientific and nuanced way to understand the Japanese. "Previous reports on Japanese military morale," he wrote, "took the view of a Shintoist fanatical enemy" who was radically different from Americans.[40] Leighton advocated for an "analysis of Japanese morale [based on] a number of basic assumptions regarding the nature of man derived from psychiatry and cultural anthropology."[41] He was particularly frustrated with "old Japan hands" who, he surmised, probably bought into the Japanese's own racialized propaganda.[42] He thought they had too much emotional attachment to Japan and not enough rigor. The "insecurity of the Japanese expert is an example of the ever-present insecurity of those with a reputation for intuitive judgment in the face of scientific method," he wrote.[43] Leighton brought in "men and women trained in cultural anthropology, sociology, and psychiatry rather than as experts on Japan."[44] There were some trained Japan experts, such as Embree, but for the most part Leighton and others relied on the Japanese Americans whom they trained: mostly much younger and less experienced researchers who were outranked by the white social scientists both militarily and academically.

Leighton's pragmatism dovetailed with his Boasian antiracism. Such stances were a break with the widespread use of psychology to justify and assist colonial rule over nonwhite people. As a profession that had risen in tandem with the spread of European imperialism in Africa and Asia, psychology was deeply implicated in colonial enterprises. Colonial people were often characterized as childlike and mentally immature.[45] As late as 1950, the French psychoanalyst Octave Mannoni justified continued French control of Madagascar by citing colonized peoples' "dependency complex," and branding anticolonial movements as "products of inchoate emotions."[46] Many psychologists and other social scientists clothed simple racism in psychological theories and language. Weston La Barre, a community analyst in the Topaz internment camp, was an anthropologist who applied psychiatric and psychoanalytic theories to ethnography. La Barre's hostility toward the internees permeated his writing. "The Japanese are probably the most compulsive people in the world's ethnological museum," he wrote.[47] La Barre even found proof of Japanese aggression in internees' politeness, seeing it, in classical orientalist fashion, as a cover for trickery. He was also quite supportive of the fire raids, writing, "[the] Japanese needed Pearl Harbor, and ultimately suicidal attack upon the powerful, disapproving authority, America. But like all compulsives, they have chosen the wrong object for aggression, they have not recognized the real internal enemy."[48]

Racism was rampant among OWI and FMAD psychological experts, but this was not a simple story of righteous antiracists versus racists. Leighton and Ruth Benedict, perhaps the most notable member of his team, were on one side of a spectrum while people like Geoffrey Gorer and Weston La Barre were on the other. Gorer, using a rather doctrinarian application of Freud, famously attributed Japanese aggression to strict toilet training, writing, "The motherly affection coupled with the severe toilet training, and culminating in the sudden loss of attention when the next child is born, creates an early sense of insecurity, which in turn produces an adult who is never absolutely sure of himself and who, through compensation, may become almost paranoiac."[49] This was racism clothed in psychological language. Gorer knew almost nothing about Japan, and like most other social scientists at the unit, he did not speak Japanese or have any training in the culture or history of that country. But his work was very influential; it formed part of the course material in the Far Eastern sections of the Army Specialized Training Program and the Civil Affairs Training Schools. At Yale University's civil affairs school, Gorer's arguments about the occupation of Japan were presented as the climax of the course, and in 1944 *Time* magazine did a full-length article on his work under the headline "Why Are Japs Japs?"[50]

Ruth Benedict, whose work *The Chrysanthemum and the Sword* was perhaps the most influential research that came out of the OWI, was quite hostile to notions such as Gorer's. Her work contained many psychological insights and methodologies, but was firmly cultural in emphasis. As Pauline Kent has demonstrated, Benedict rejected facile racist comparisons of Japanese to adolescents, and argued that the Japanese must be understood within their own cultural context.[51] The first task she chose to tackle in the OWI was a discussion of psychiatrists' problematic use of race-like categories, in an article titled "Problems in Japanese Morale Submitted for Study by Psychiatrists" (1944). She criticized such study as unduly Eurocentric, and argued that "Japanese behavior that would, in Western contexts, be considered atypical or even neurotic" made perfect sense within the Japanese cultural matrix.[52] After hearing about "neurotic" Japanese in a New York conference, John Embree also rejected such findings, arguing that "the same results would be achieved by substituting the word [Japanese] with 'American.'"[53] In the struggle for ideas between the likes of Gorer, on the one hand, and Benedict and Leighton on the other, the universalists emerged triumphant. In the USSBS and, later, in the American occupation of Japan, racially infused psychological language largely disappeared in favor of a universalist view that saw Japanese, Germans, and American psychology as largely comparable, and sought to study them side by side.

Surveying Japanese Minds

The USSBS teams that arrived in Japan in September 1945 were some of the first Americans to tour the country, some arriving as early as 4 September. The rest of the teams arrived throughout September, and fanned across Japan using four converted destroyers as floating regional headquarters. The survey set up its main headquarters right at the nerve center of the occupation: at the Meiji Seimei Kan building, which was adjunct to the Dai-Ichi Seimei Building used by General Douglas MacArthur, known as the Supreme Commander for the Allied Powers (SCAP), and his staff. The survey was divided into three groups: military, economic, and civilian studies. civilian studies were further divided into the Civil Defense Division, the Medical Division, and the Morale Division, which was the biggest of the three and one of the biggest in the whole survey.[54] Rensis Likert continued to head the division, which also saw many of the European personnel staying on for the Japan mission. Many former FMAD and internment camp personnel had also been recruited by the Japan mission. Besides Leighton, there were Conrad B. Arnsberg, who had worked with Leighton in Poston, Horace B. English, and the psychologist Egerton L. Ballachey, who also served with the OSS. The survey was augmented by a large number of Japanese speakers who formed a separate "language section." About one-third to one-half of language personnel were Nisei, many of whom had been recruited in the internment camps. The section also included, as the survey's official history put it, "twenty-one native helpers."[55]

This colonial-like reference to the defeated Japanese as "native" betrayed the ongoing and underlining problem of racial thinking in the survey's work in Japan. As noted above, the survey, for the most part, did not see the Japanese case as fundamentally different from the German one, or future American scenarios. The survey, however, was a creature of its time. The term "Jap" was constantly used, and casual racism was on display throughout the survey reports and memorandums.[56] There was one place, however, where race played an important role. Seeking to present the A-bomb as a legitimate weapon of war, the report engaged in what the historian Atsuko Shigesawa has insightfully called "the denial of awe" from the A-bomb.[57] In this context, the inability of the Japanese to deal with the A-bomb impact was attributed by some to their racial qualities. As one Civil Defense report noted, "The over-all picture of civilian defense in Japan is not a happy one.... Skillful national planning must provide for the unexpected and this the Japanese failed to do—just one more error of many committed by the little men who planned to rule the world."[58] The implication was, of course, that modern, rational American civil defense planning was superior to that of the "little men" of Japan, and would provide an answer to the threat of the A-bomb. As Sheldon Garon has noted, this was nothing more than hubris, as the Japanese were as sophisticated and as advanced in their thinking as any major combatants.[59]

This drive for demystification also meant that the A-bomb was studied side by side with conventional bombing. Radiation was mentioned only briefly in the Morale Division reports. Some of this lacuna can be attributed to the secrecy surrounding the A-bomb's radiological impact. But there was also an overall institutional drive for findings to enable the future use of the A-bomb by the Air Force.[60] In a briefing in late 1945, Major Curtis Enloe stated, "Our data on the atomic bomb is not yet complete, but from what I have seen in the papers, it is perfectly evident that the danger of atomic bomb is the danger of fire. The raid on Hiroshima and the raid on Nagasaki . . . were no worse—in fact, the Nagasaki raid was not nearly as bad as the area raid on the city of Hamburg."[61] Similarly, an initial urban area study of Hiroshima and Nagasaki claimed that "a calm appraisal of the atomic bombing does not change any of the results but comparison of the devastation with that found in Kobe, Osaka, and Tokyo raises the question of why there was so much emotion. The wasted areas in Hiroshima and Nagasaki do not differ materially, at least in outward appearances, from those in other Japanese cities which were ravaged by incendiary raids.... the ultimate result was identical—utter devastation."[62] Consequently, the A-bomb was studied side by side with Germany and the other urban fire raids on Japan. And as in other cases, the A-bomb's impact was seen largely in the context of short-term mental shock and anxiety, social panic, and the collapse of fighting spirit.

At the same time, institutional bias notwithstanding, it was very clear to the teams on the ground that the A-bomb was not just another weapon. As in Germany, there was much discrepancy between field reports and the eventual final reports composed in the United States. This reflected wide disagreement between researchers, administrative divisions, and field teams.[63] Even the survey's official history noted "sometimes bitter contention which arose in the drawing of conclusions and the making up of the reports."[64] Such disputes were occasionally laden with emotions. The A-bomb had truly shocked USSBS researchers. When Leighton and others entered Hiroshima, they immediately saw the A-bomb's possible impact on the United States and their own hometowns, and many were resolved to tell the world about the dangers inherent in the new atomic order. Ironically, both this newfound fear of an atomic war and the drive for demystification added to the already existing limitations on tackling psychological suffering seen in the German survey. Overall, researchers concentrated on social issues rather than individuals, and cared less about individual hurt and more about the larger challenges brought about by Hiroshima.

The work on Hiroshima was done at the same time as other fieldwork across Japan. The preliminary and later reports of the Morale Division, though differing on emphasis and some important conclusions (for example, on the relative weight of the atomic bomb on Japan's decision to surrender), saw the overall bombing campaign as a success. "Attack on 'total target' was successful ... [and] produced great social and psychological disruption," the report declared.[65] As in the German reports, mental damages were connected to declining morale, which the Japan team further defined as "a complex of factors which indicate the willingness and capacity of the Japanese to follow their leaders and to work and sacrifice to win the war."[66] The connection between individual hurt and social disruptions was not elaborated upon. The survey concluded, "The primary emotional response to the bombings was fright and terror."[67] According to the survey, this led to defeatism, absenteeism, and the like. Thus, "reactions to the explosions were indescribable terror and panic." But at the same time, the survey also admitted that as "physically devastating as the atomic bombs were in the cities of Hiroshima and Nagasaki, their effects on Japanese morale were limited."[68]

Methodological issues and institutional constraints pushed the survey in several directions. On one hand, it attempted to "demystify" the A-bomb's impact; but on the other, it wanted to show the overall bombing campaign as a success. This is why the survey, famously and controversially, concluded that the A-bomb did not lead to surrender and that nonnuclear conventional bombing would have caused Japan to surrender by November 1945 at the latest. Beyond the Morale Division, the UAD and the Civil Defense Division (CDD) emphasized the enormous destruction of the A-bomb while seeming to go out of their way in looking for positive conclusions that might be drawn from the bombing. Thus, the UAD emphasized that Hiroshima's economic and military potential was not severely impacted, and that the city—and Nagasaki even more so—could easily "bounce back" and return to normal. The CDD, for its part, manipulated data to show the effectiveness of shelters as a countermeasure for A-bomb damage.[69] The CDD's agenda was quite clear. As the report declared, "There is no reason for a 'nothing-can-be-done' attitude in this field. . . . It [is] reasonable to expect that something can be done to lessen the effects of atomic bombs on civilian populations."[70] But perhaps no division was as blatant in its embellishment of the situation in the bombed areas as was the Medical Division. Side by side with gut wrenching statistics about the impact of fire, radiation, and the horrendous post-bombing conditions on the civilian population, the division reported, "On the sanitation side the survey found that our incendiary bombs had cleaned out age-old areas of slums and filth, while affecting little the water supply or sewage facilities."[71]

When Alexander Leighton arrived in Hiroshima, he was told by a GI, "who had been through the city many times," that the city "don't look no different from any other bombed town. You soon get used to it. . . . They been exaggerating about that bomb."[72] Leighton, however, felt quite different. The destruction left a deep impression on him. He recalled that "the city seemed to have been stripped naked of everything but its cemeteries, which stood out in small granite clumps of orderly stones, gray and narrow . . . like teeth in a comb. . . . They appeared the hard remaining bones of the city after the flesh had dissolved."[73]

Leighton and the other field teams of Regional Group D arrived in Hiroshima in late September 1945 and spent several weeks in town. Initially, the teams operated from a converted destroyer, the "Sims," and later, on 8 October, a headquarters was established at the "damaged, but still passably habitable building of the Geibi [sic] Bank, which was centrally located for study purposes, being close to the zero point of the atomic bomb explosion."[74] Conditions on the ground were "undoubtably the worst in the survey."[75] In September a typhoon tore through Hiroshima, destroying much of what the A-bomb had spared and killing many survivors and rescuers. Everything and everyone had to be carried ashore by landing craft through heavily mined waters, then driven forty miles to the city over bombed-out and washed-out roads.

The teams "gathered in a small sample of the population from the ruins of the city." They then "sat all day [for] long interviews with these men and women—shopkeepers, factory workers, laborers, housewives, cooks, teachers, farmers, fishermen, and many more."[76] Other survey members sat down to interviews with local leaders: the chief of police, mayors of nearby towns, the governor of Hiroshima prefecture, and the like.[77] The fact that dozens of Americans could travel around the town so soon after the A-bomb was as incredible for researchers then as it seems to us today. Just a few weeks earlier, when the first Allied troops had entered Hiroshima, they had done so in full battle gear with drawn bayonets (the prefecture was occupied by British Commonwealth troops).[78] Hiroshima residents were suspicious. Some feared that Americans would rape and pillage their town. Women were told not to wear flashy clothes, men not to wear watches. Some people even escaped to the countryside.[79] As one interviewee told the survey, "I had heard that Americans were brutal because they took lunches to view lynching at which whites poured gasoline over Negroes who had attacked white women."[80] Yet neither the American surveyors nor any of the Japanese victims who were interviewed displayed much hostility. This transformation in attitudes, which I have explored in length elsewhere, was evident in the cooperation of many victims with the survey.[81] While some victims "were frightened and wordless," most interviewees were "talkative" and "willing [to cooperate]."[82] But the transcripts of these interviews make for harrowing reading. The field surveys and interviews are, in fact, the first testimonies produced by the *hibakusha*. Quite strikingly, most follow a format very similar to that of later testimonies, suggesting an important and quite unintended contribution of the survey and its format to later testimony culture in Hiroshima.[83] In another conspicuous parallel, the survey, like the later body of testimonies, "excluded Soldiers and Koreans" and focused exclusively on ethnic Japanese civilians,[84] thus already contributing to the later myth of an exclusively Japanese civilian victimization.

Researchers in Hiroshima followed the same bilingual manual (with Romanized Japanese translations) that was employed throughout Japan. The manual opened with the above-mentioned declaration of good will, which was followed by mostly general, freewheeling questions. Interviewers asked victims, "What did you think and feel about the atomic bomb?" "What bombing experiences have you personally had [*Jissai ni kushu ni awareta koto ga arimashitaka?*] . . . "Can you tell me more about your experiences? Tell me what happened, what you did, how you felt?" [*Sono koto wo motto kuawashiku hanashite kudasaimasenka? Donna guai deshitaka? Anata wa do saremashita? Donna kimochi deshita?*]"[85] Out of these interviews, surveyors were supposed to discern "the emotional status of the people . . . emotional changes [that] took place among the people during the war. . . . Were there changes toward aggression, panic or apathy and indifference?"[86] The surveyors were also asked to consult medical professionals, "to enquire as to hospitalization for psychosis and neuroses," and, "if possible . . . [to] get statistics" on suicide rates and other mental health phenomena.[87] As in Germany, these and other factors were calculated in endless charts and tables that added up to a "morale index." The index, developed first in Germany, was a "computation of the responses put into numbers," which sought to represent quantitatively the way that the mental and physical damage of bombing translated into an impact on morale.[88]

If one is to look beyond the numbers and charts into the raw "data" of the interviews at the field reports and those scattered through the official ones, a familiar pattern emerges. The emotional reactions recorded in Hiroshima were quite similar to results elsewhere in Japan and in Germany. A report on the victims of conventional bombing stated that "the people of the bombed areas are highly sensitive to all flashes of light and all types of sounds. Such a condition may be said to be a manifestation of the most primitive form of fear. To give instances: they are frightened by noises from radio, the whistle of trains, the roar of our own planes, the sparks from trolleys, etc."[89] A preliminary Hiroshima report stated that two-thirds of victims experienced "unqualified terror, strengthened by the sheer horror of the destruction and suffering witnessed and experienced by the survivors."[90] And, as in conventional bombing, such reactions persisted well after the bombing. "Whenever a plane was seen after that,

BOMBING "THE JAPANESE MIND"

people would rush into their shelters. They went in and out so much they did not have time to eat. They were so nervous they could not work."[91] A Japanese psychiatrist quoted by the survey described a situation similar to the German one: "The [people] lost their grip on reality and in many cases became quite apathetic. They were dazed and this feeling has persisted up to the present."[92] These speculations about longer impact were also the only place where radiation was mentioned in the report: "The sudden deaths produced by the bomb—days and even weeks after it was dropped—seem to have been particularly difficult to endure."[93] The word "radiation" itself was not used. A short section about "the long-term psychological effects of bombardment" consisted only of an anonymous psychiatrist's opinion and not much more. The authors concluded with their hope that their report might offer guidance "for the direction which future attitudinal developments may take, and some of the difficulties with which our occupation forces may in time have to contend."[94]

Leighton's findings supply us with further connections, beyond the German survey, to Poston and the OWI. Leighton's interviewees "were so nervous that any kind of spark would scare them, any kind of spark they saw. That was because of the A-bomb."[95] Such nervousness was coupled with apathy. Leighton observed that "the general manner [of interviewees] was one which might be interpreted as due either to apathy or absence of feeling consequent on schock [sic]."[96] Such observations were strikingly similar to findings in Germany and elsewhere. Even more importantly, Leighton employed the same jargon he used to describe reactions to stress in Poston in analyzing the reactions of Japanese survivors. Interestingly, after an interview with a Nisei woman, he described her as a "representative of [the] mannerism" of survivors. The mannerism "would appear when one spoke to her. She would look off in the distance and then, when it came her turn to reply, she would shut her eyes for a moment as if marshaling her forces to overcome something before she responded." Leighton then connected this "mannerism" to his own emotional responses and his "anger and pity" for the victims. He concluded, much as in his 1943 comments on "walking death," that this range of feelings in both researchers and survivors might be evidence of "semi-automatic devices of the mind for wading off its full poignancy."[97]

Little of what is described above found its way into the final reports. While the authors of the report admitted that "there are some experiences which cannot be described by cold figures," they surely did make a valiant effort to do just that. The vast amounts of data and interviews were taken back to the United States in May and June 1946. They were analyzed and coded at Swarthmore College—which, ironically, would later become a center of much antinuclear and peace activism. The psychologist David Krech and his students transformed the harrowing accounts of victims, hospitalization statistics, and studies of urban area damage into code and punch cards to be processed by IBM machines.[98] Thus, as in Germany, far from systematically studying the emotional suffering of survivors, the USSBS drowned it in data. Furthermore, even less than in the German case, little or no effort was made to connect the various dots or offer any theory of trauma that might explain psychological damage or even its connection to morale. As in the German report, the word "traumatic" appears only once in the field report, and even then in an offhanded manner.[99]

The A-bomb greatly affected researchers. However, this effect and the clear emotional angst the researchers themselves were experiencing served to further take away the focus from individual suffering and aid the shift toward loftier goals. Again, Leighton's unpublished and published work supplies us with the most direct evidence in this context. After his first tour of the city, he recalled, "I became aware of the emptiness that had been with me since I had entered Hiroshima, an emptiness that seemed to reflect the city." Leighton was first angry, then numb. "I felt like one in a dream trying to keep in a box hidden from sight a nameless something that struggled to come out. I put a box within a box and tied each down, but it was always there pushing against the last lid. . . . Amid this jumble of thought and feeling there came, like a huge round fish swimming out of green vagueness into sharp focus, the image of the white-face clock in the gloom below with its hands at 8:15."[100] Leighton was guilt-ridden and anxious throughout most of his time in Hiroshima. He reports an encounter with a survivor who made an especially vivid impression on him, and who admonished him, "If there is such a thing as ghosts, why don't they haunt the Americans?" Leighton added, "Perhaps they do."[101] Leighton felt that "the ghosts of Hiroshima can [still] have their reckoning." He saw in Hiroshima a "preview of the next war," which would be much closer to home. He looked at Hiroshima's ruins, and "could see other streets in days to come, looking just the same, but their names like 'Broadway,' 'Constitution Avenue,' 'Michigan Avenue' and 'Kearny Street.' And . . . under the rubble of those places, charred bodies that bore names with far more meaning than those of any street, and yet not one surviving except perhaps for a little while to endure pain and the realization of slow death."[102] Shaken, Leighton vowed to warn the people who had not seen Hiroshima what a nuclear weapon could do to a human city.

In Leighton's account of his wartime activities, he portrayed his Hiroshima experience as a steppingstone for a new role for psychiatry and psychology. This role, however, was not to heal the survivors. It was to prevent the next war. "Hiroshima with its clock at 8:10 [sic] brought realization that time has almost run out." For Leighton, no "problems of human relations" could be addressed outside the context of the nuclear age, and "no progress is of value unless it adds up to crossing soon the threshold between things as they are now and a world order in which there will be no war."[103] Leighton saw his wartime work, with its liberalism and especially its antiracist and integrationist vision, as a way forward for a world without the bomb. Ironically, he saw his active participation in locking up, bombing, and then researching and profiling Japanese Americans and the residents of Hiroshima as an experience he could draw on in bringing about this new world. He and other social scientists who had gone to war were now working for peace. But as for the actual victims of the A-bomb and the firebombing, they were left behind with their sorrows.

Conclusion: The A-Bomb, a Psychological Weapon?

As USSBS researchers were busy compiling their reports at Swarthmore, the United States was preparing to test further nuclear weapons over Bikini Atoll as part of Operation Crossroads. Crossroads was hugely controversial among the wider public, but the US military was determined to carry it through.[104] The military hoped that the test, like the USSBS, would help "demystify" the bomb's power. Rear Admiral William Parsons, who played an important part in the Manhattan Project and the Crossroads tests, told the press that the tests had "helped dispel 'atomic neuroses' about the bomb. . . . Operation Crossroads has gone a long way toward substituting a healthy fear of the known for an unhealthy fear of the unknown."[105] In their own reports, however, military men were less sanguine. Test results emphasized the deadly impact of radiation and displayed the military's inability to deal with its effect on Navy ships and personnel. Fear of radiation was seen as multiplying its deadly potential. As the report noted, "We can form no adequate mental picture of the multiple disasters which would befall a modern city, blasted by one or more bombs. . . . No survivor could be certain he was not among the doomed and so grasped by the very terror of the moment, thousands would be stricken with fear of death and the uncertainty of the time of its arrival."[106] Radiation, however, was seen not as a factor that should inhibit the use of such weapons, but as a "psychological bonus." The A-bomb was seen as the ultimate expression of the theory of strategic bombing that had burned German and Japanese cities. While the test failed to show the weapon's effectiveness against enemy fleets, the military insisted on its value as a psychological weapon, stating that "of primary military concern will be the bomb's potentiality to break the will of nations and of peoples by the stimulation of man's primordial fears, those of the unknown, the invisible, the mysterious." Combining again demystification and an emphasis on terror, the report continued, "The effective exploitation of the bomb's psychological implications will take precedence over the application of its destructive and lethal effects in deciding the issue of war."[107] Psychological considerations, the report concluded, "must constitute an element of paramount importance in the selection of atomic bomb targets."[108]

USSBS reports were already available to the writers of the report, but they were dismissed out of hand. The Crossroads researchers swatted aside one of the liberal pillars of the USSBS research, claiming that studying Japanese was just not relevant: "The mental makeup peculiar to the Japanese is probably at greater variance with that of Occidental peoples than the mental makeup of these peoples is, one from another. This would, of course, complicate evaluation."[109] This was not an isolated incident. In an April 1948 conference organized by the ABCC titled "Psychological Aspects of Radiation Hazards," the conference chairman, Austin Brues, dismissed psychological research on the A-bomb as "difficult to evaluate because of the differences between the Japanese pattern and our own."[110] That the premise of the universal application of psychological research, which drove so much of the work of Leighton and his peers was thus so easily dismissed points to the revolutionary and controversial nature of their work. One could condemn researchers' biases and contradictions, but their work allowed for serious examination of the impact of bombing on the Japanese as human beings. Racial and cultural difference would continue to be used as grounds for the denial of the validity or even desirability of research into the A-bomb's mental impact. But the trajectory that led Leighton from Poston to the OWI and then the USSBS allowed him and his peers to expose the wide-ranging damage done to the human psyche by exposure to the A-bomb's horrors.

This ethos did not necessarily lead to the development of a systematic theory of trauma. However, it was evident in fragmentary form. Researchers acknowledged and recorded the great suffering caused by conventional and atomic bombings, but concentrated on short-term im-

BOMBING "THE JAPANESE MIND"

pact and rarely went past the surface. The survey's institutional position and intellectual milieu led it in contradictory directions. On one hand, the USSBS sought to minimize the impact of the A-bomb and demystify it. Thus, the A-bomb was connected to research on firebombing. Such efforts, in turn, served to emphasize even more the similarity between German and Japanese reactions, while at the same time the focus on the connection between mental shocks and morale drew researchers away from the suffering of individuals to view them as part of communal and national entities. Researchers were also greatly affected by what they saw in Japan. They could see Japanese suffering as human suffering, and the destruction of Hiroshima as a preview for the destruction of American cities. Yet, here as well, the end result was ironically to draw the gaze of researchers away from individuals and toward communities, and from Hiroshima to the United States.

This was, after all, the whole point of the USSBS project: to learn what could be learned from Japan in order to protect Americans. Some saw this mandate quite narrowly and thought in terms of bomb shelters, dispersal of cities, and psychological inoculation and mobilization of Americans. Here the psychological implications of the report were paramount. As the Crossroads report noted, "Even a cursory examination of the characteristics of the American people . . . invites the conclusion that this nation is much more vulnerable to the psychological effects of the bomb than certain other nations. A study of the factors involved should not only assist us in determining the vulnerabilities of other nations, but, also, should lead to the development of measures to lessen the effects of these phenomena should we be attacked."[111] Others saw the role of future research in defending Americans in broader terms, namely in preventing war. USSBS veterans would play a central role in the scientists' peace movement. After investing so much time and money in creating the A-bomb, activists argued, now was the time to make sure it would never be used again. Ernest Hilgard captured the sentiment of many returning survey members when he wrote in 1945, "Millions of dollars invested in social science research in the immediate future would be a small price to pay if the costs of war could be avoided."[112] Thus, the legacy of USSBS research was not to lead to more research on the *hibakusha,* but to turn away from Hiroshima and aim the psychological sciences' gaze elsewhere.

CHAPTER THREE

Healing a Sick World: The Nuclear Age on the Analyst's Couch

"The bomb that fell on Hiroshima fell on America too. It fell on no city, no munitions plants, no public buildings, reduced no man to his atomic elements. But it fell, it fell. It burst. It shook the land." — Congressman Horace Jeremiah Voorhis, March 28, 1946[1]

"The physicists have an atom bomb; but psychiatry and social science have an atom bomb as well in the yet unknown discoveries of Sigmund Freud." — Weston La Barre, 1959[2]

In 1946 the Canadian psychiatrist Brock Chisholm, looking back at a half century of war, told the delegates of the preparatory committee of the World Health Organization (WHO), "The world was sick, and the ills from which it was suffering were mainly due to the perversion of man ... his inability to live at peace with himself."[3] Chisholm, a tough-spoken and controversial figure who had once blamed the idea of Santa Claus for undermining children's education and the cause of peace, certainly had a knack for provocative statements.[4] But as one of the founders of the World Federation for Mental Health (WFMH) and first director of the WHO, he also had an extraordinary feel for the state of his field, and his statement reflected the sense of mission and urgency shared by many psychiatrists and psychologists in North America at the end of the war. The world's sickness was far from being cured. With humanity threatened by the advent of the atomic bomb, its practitioners felt that the psychological sciences had to get out of the clinic and asylum in order to help guide North American society — and indeed the world — to a saner place. Chisholm and his peers stood at a crucial juncture in American psychological sciences. The postwar era saw a significant expansion in the professions and in the role of practitioners as social commentators, as well as significant anxiety about the implications of nuclear energy and warfare.

As Chisholm's friend and fellow Yale alumnus William Menninger, who led the drive to reform in the US, put it, the psychological sciences "can and will make an important contribution towards the solution . . . of our social problems."[5] And the most urgent problem, as Chisholm, Menninger, and others saw it, was the desperate need "to find ways and means of more satisfactorily sublimating man's aggressive instinct."[6] They feared that if psychiatrists and psychologists did not succeed, the world was doomed. As psychologist Abraham Maslow declared, "The world will be saved by psychologists—in the very broadest sense—or else it will not be saved at all."[7]

The psychological crusade for world peace was, as noted in the end of the previous chapter, one of the two main ways in which the professions reacted to Hiroshima and Nagasaki. At the same time that Maslow, Chisholm, and others were working to save the world, other psychological experts continued the wartime trajectory of the profession and used USSBS research in civil defense and strategic planning. This chapter focuses on the former development, while chapter 4 will take on the psychological experts who worked on defense issues. Although for the purpose of clarity the two fields of research are treated separately here, there was no actual separation between military and peace work. Most experts who drafted peace manifestos were veterans, and many were also employed by the defense and nuclear establishments, or were working with it closely. Furthermore, psychologists were more than accommodating to government positions on nuclear energy and the larger Cold War agenda.

Adjustment was a key word in the psychological sciences' drive for peace. Most early post-war psychiatrists and psychologists who tackled nuclear issues sought ways to help society deal with and adjust to the new nuclear reality, rather than resist it. Generally, they worked within state institutions rather than against them. Psychologists and psychiatrists also tended to focus on individuals' inability to adapt to society, and the threat this posed to the social order and world peace, rather than on the impact of violence on the individual human psyche. This development, as we will see in later chapters, had an adverse effect on research and care for survivors in Japan. A longer-term impact on Japan was the support given by psychological professions to the promotion of nuclear energy. Determined to see a silver lining in the advent of the nuclear age, psychological experts enthusiastically embraced nuclear energy. Significantly, they mostly sought ways to help society adjust to the march of progress and allay "irrational" fears and anxiety over radiation. After Chernobyl and

Fukushima, such attitudes may seem tragic and misguided to a twenty-first-century reader; yet at the time, psychological experts reflected the general scientific consensus.

The focus on social issues was, again, a move away from work on the actual victims of the A-bomb. Researchers were more concerned with society than with individuals, and that included the *hibakusha*. The first decade after the war saw a proliferation of writing by psychological experts on the impact of the A-bomb, but none of it involved studying the victims. However, the politicization of the professions was important in leading the way for a later critique of the new nuclear reality. The professions' reaction to Hiroshima was never monolithic. While the majority of experts worked with the establishment, many others were critical. And these critical voices were important for the developments that would lead to greater awareness of the plight of victims in the 1960s. This chapter examines these contradicting and complex reactions of American psychological experts to the A-bomb through an examination of the rise of psychiatry and psychology as social critique, and then moves to the role of USSBS veterans in this development, and the rise of left-wing critique. The chapter closes with a case study of the involvement of North American psychological experts in promoting nuclear energy at the United Nations, where again we meet Alexander Leighton and other USSBS researchers in their roles as advisors to the WHO committee on the mental health aspects of nuclear energy.

US Psychiatry and Psychology Enters the Nuclear Age

At the end of World War II, psychiatry and its allied professions received an extraordinary amount of attention in North America. As the historian Roy Porter has written, the decade after the war in the United States witnessed "the psychiatrization of everything."[8] Underpinning the popularity of the profession was a deep-seated notion that something was wrong with modern society. Not only individuals but modern culture as a whole was in need of psychiatric advice. As already noted, such notions had a long history. Already in 1936, Lawrence K. Frank, in a pivotal article, had called for putting society on the psychologist's couch: "There is a growing realization among thoughtful persons that our culture is sick, mentally disordered, and in need of treatment."[9] Much of this anxiety could be traced, on the one hand, to a growing sense of a "mental health crisis," a sense shared by both mental health professionals and society at large; and on the other, to the civilizational doubts and fears produced by the mushroom clouds over Japan. The sense of crisis was due to the exposure of large numbers of "mental defects" among the military during screening for conscription, as well as the large numbers of returning soldiers who suffered from anxiety.[10] As William Menninger disclosed during the first postwar gathering of the American Psychiatric Association (APA) in 1946, close to two million men were rejected for military service during the war as a result of "neuropsychiatric disorders," and an additional one million had become "neuropsychiatric admissions" to Army hospitals in the years from 1942 to 1945.[11] American psychiatrists, however, were more than willing to take on the challenge. This was part of a larger shift toward social medicine in the profession as a whole. For many leading physicians at the WHO and elsewhere, any improvement in public health would require social and economic measures in addition to strictly medical ones.[12] Affirming psychiatry's importance as part of the drive toward social medicine, Chisholm told the WHO, "The microbe was no longer the main enemy; science was sufficiently advanced to be able to cope admirably with it, if it were not [for] such barriers as superstition, ignorance, religious intolerance, misery and poverty. It was in man himself, therefore, that the cause of present evils should be sought; and these psychological evils must be understood in order that remedy might be prescribed."[13]

Chisholm was one of the main advocates for a more proactive profession, and was well situated within both the WHO and North American psychiatry to advance his agenda. In November 1945 he became the second recipient of the Lasker Award, given by the Academy of Medicine in New York City. The first Lasker prize had been awarded in 1944 to William Menninger. These awards were given on the recommendation of various American societies, including the National Committee against Mental Illness. Both Menninger and Chisholm had been senior officers during World War II, Menninger in charge of the US Army's Neuropsychiatry Division, and Chisholm in a similar role in the Canadian Army. Both men had also graduated from Yale University's Institute of Human Relations. Chisholm's prize indicated the high regard in which he was held in psychiatric circles in the United States. His friendship with Menninger tied him to a rising cohort of US psychiatrists who were redefining mental health and reforming the APA. William Menninger, together with his brother Karl, founded the Group for the Advancement of Psychiatry (GAP), which became the main vehicle for reform during the postwar.

GAP, which was to play a pivotal game in later debates, was described by Menninger as "a mobile strike force for American psychiatry, which would "invade" new fields and "lead the struggle for communal and individual health."[14] The martial language employed by Menninger reflected the impact of the military and war experience on postwar psychological sciences. Menninger and others saw the successful application of psychiatry on a large scale in the military as a steppingstone toward expansion in postwar society. In books like *Psychiatry in a Troubled World* (1948), Menninger drew on his experience of the war to offer solutions for the postwar world; chief among them was preserving the peace.[15]

After two world wars, and with the atomic bomb threatening the very survival of humanity, preserving peace was seen as an urgent task. "We have now reached a point where drastic readjustment for human personality and conduct appears necessary for survival," Chisholm wrote. "The reasons we found ourselves involved in war [are] all well-known and recognized neurotic symptoms. . . . All psychiatrists know where these symptoms come from. The burden of inferiority, guilt, and fear we have all carried lies at the root of this failure to mature successfully."[16] Maturing, for Chisholm, meant adequately dealing with the threatening new reality of the atomic age. The main argument was that it was not the atom (which frequently also stood for modern technology as a whole) that was dangerous, but the humans behind the atomic trigger. WFMH director Frank Fremont-Smith, a close colleague of Chisholm and of Lawrence K. Frank, wrote, "The real issue is not the peaceful use of atomic power but the peaceful use of human power . . . [and] for the management of human power we need experts in human relations."[17] This, of course, would entail increased budgets and investment in psychiatry and psychology. Pressing the urgency of the task, Fremont-Smith complained, "In the splendid program of the National Science Foundation, unfortunately, only a small fraction of its funds has been devoted . . . to social sciences." Quoting Margaret Mead, a cofounder of WFMH, he called for a new drive toward the establishment and expansion of what she called "human sciences."[18]

These scholars felt a visceral threat to human survival, and shared a progressive belief in the necessity of "a social leap that would save us from extinction."[19] This was done in the context of the early expansion of peace movements and anxiety over atomic war.[20] Research began as early as 1946, when the Social Science Research Council established a committee to study the social effects of the bomb. This was the first of many research projects that looked into the bomb's social effects, prompting some to call

HEALING A SICK WORLD

for "a second Manhattan project"—this time for the social sciences—to deal with the bomb's supposedly revolutionary impact on society, again echoing larger global trends about the supposed gap between technology and humanity's mental capabilities.[21] This move also reflected a blurring of boundaries between psychiatry and other social sciences—a continuation of wartime trends, and a conflation of social and mental problems that was common in Cold War social science.[22] This development was, in turn, closely connected to the expansion of psychiatry. When Menninger met with President Truman, the president, impressed by Menninger's arguments, declared, "*Never have we had a more pressing need for experts in human engineering.* The greatest prerequisite for peace, which is uppermost in the minds and hearts of all of us, must be sanity—sanity in its broadest sense, which permits clear thinking on the part of all citizens" (emphasis added).[23] To tackle these problems, psychiatrists argued for an increase in the number of psychiatrists and for elevating the role of psychiatry in government and society. Chisholm agreed. "We need in the USA some twenty thousand psychiatrists," he wrote. "We have only three thousand."[24]

The US president's call for recruiting "experts in human engineering" reflects both the important place that psychology and psychiatry played in the immediate postwar period and the authoritarian tendencies of some in the professions. As Michal Shapira has noted in the British context, "Psychoanalysis in this period played a crucial part in conceptualizing social reconstruction. It helped define both the optimism and the pessimism of social democracy and of the era in general."[25] Like Chisholm, psychologists and social workers urged the British government to devote more resources to fighting the scourge of asocial behavior, which they termed "the enemy within."[26] What psychoanalysis could do was help such people to "adjust" to social demands. Such tendencies were present on both sides of the Atlantic. As Daniel Pick has noted, developments in American psychology "built upon the idea that psychoanalysis should strengthen the patient's ego and help it to adapt to external reality. This might easily imply that health and conformity were one and the same thing."[27] Parents, especially mothers, were held mostly to blame for their children's failure to adapt. Chisholm, for instance, combined his Freudianism and environmentalism to hold parents responsible for "making a thousand neurotics for every one that psychiatrists can hope to help with."[28]

Notions of social "mental hygiene," the creation of a social environment that would foster a healthy development and maintain mental health, were important in this regard. In 1948 the psychiatrist Robert H. Felix, the first director of the National Institute of Mental Health (NIMH), summarized the postwar consensus of mainstream psychiatry when he proposed how "the impact of the social environment on the life history, and the relevance of the life history to mental illness are no longer in serious question as clinical and research findings."[29] Likewise, Bruno Bettelheim argued that "certain factors originating in society interfere with our work and create specific emotional difficulties."[30] Like Chisholm, Bettelheim was suspicious of parents' influence on the young. Bettelheim, who worked with emotionally disturbed youth, demanded that children at his school be kept as far removed from parents as possible, as he believed the parents' behavior "may actually impede mental health."[31] Such worries extended beyond children to returning GIs. Menninger, again, supplied us with perhaps the clearest illustration of this trend when he wrote in his book *You and Psychiatry*, "The pounding of German 88 guns and the diving Japanese Kamikazi [*sic*] planes are totally different stresses from living with a wife and three kids in the attic of an in-law's house or not being able to find a job. But the effect on the personality is very much the same."[32] Supplying GIs with a healthy environment and helping them to psychologically adjust to the pressures of peacetime society was not just a social debt owed to GIs for their service but, in the context of the time, an urgent need. Just as battle fatigue impacted morale in American units, so could the lack of adjustment to social pressure lead to disastrous consequences for American prospects. Psychological experts connected the perceived mental health crisis with the emerging Cold War and the need for social cohesiveness. The Yale psychologist Mark May, who wrote an important study on the psychological impact of various German weapons on American soldiers—including, incidentally, a paper on German 88 guns—advocated for the "need to build a healthy society for returning GIs and their many children in face of the threat of communism and nuclear attacks."[33]

The connection between mental stress and social health was directly related to wartime morale studies. If during the war, individual psychologies had been extended to encompass whole nations, now the whole of humanity, indeed the world, was on the metaphorical couch. In his 1947 address to the general conference of the American Medical Association's Women's Auxiliary in Chicago, Jules Masserman, the scientific director of the National Foundation of Psychiatric Research, warned of the psychological immaturity of modern man and advocated for studying the

HEALING A SICK WORLD

"biodynamics of world mental hygiene." The dangerous rise of mental health issues in the United States was due, he argued, to an inability to practice adjustment. "This principle, when applied to group psychology on a *terrestrial scale*, leads immediately to [this] simple but fundamental truth" (my emphasis).[34] But psychiatry was there to come to the rescue: "The psychiatrist, a lifelong student of human behavior, can also help analyze the social maladjustments of mankind and perhaps in this way to do his share in guiding those politicians who seem to prefer pretty famous or pompous pronouncements to precise and penetrating perceptions."[35] Such ideas went beyond psychiatry and psychology. In 1959 the anthropologist Weston La Barre, whom we have already met in the context of his wartime work wrote, "The fact is that psychoanalysis contains within itself not merely the therapy of individuals, but the revolutionary therapy of whole societies. . . . Thus it is not so much the failure of our social science in itself, as it is our failure to be scientific about our social selves."[36] As his above-mentioned quote on psychology's "atom bomb" demonstrated, some psychological experts truly saw themselves as almost messianic figures, as guardians of humanity against its darkest impulses, which now could lead to destruction. The A-bomb, then, supplied an opportunity for the psychological sciences not only to get out of the lab and clinic, but even to transition to a position of leadership among the sciences and in society at large, going beyond the individual, and even the community, to operate on a "terrestrial scale."

USSBS Veterans and Early Cold War Psychology

While psychiatry was transitioning out of the clinic, institutional psychology, which was historically more socially minded than psychiatry, was already well positioned for immediate intervention in public debates. Organizations like SPSSI and the many veterans of psychology's wartime mobilization played a central role in this effort. USSBS veterans like David Krech, Otto Klineberg, Rensis Likert, Horace English, and others who were closely affiliated with the survey, like Gordon Allport, took the lead in organizing a number of committees to examine "the psychological aspects of the present explosive situation which threatens the unity of mankind and of civilization itself."[37] This statement from the report of the APA Committee on the Implications of Atomic Energy captured the spirit of early efforts to tackle the problem of nuclear power. Like the efforts of the GAP and other psychiatry-centered groups, these committees operated out of a sense of extreme urgency. When the SPSSI created the Committee on International Peace in 1947, its first report stated bluntly, "Atomic Energy has become a psychological problem."[38] Significantly, the committee was chaired by David Krech, who was responsible for processing the Hiroshima data for the USSBS.

The APA and SPSSI efforts were a response to a request made by the Federation of American Scientists (FSA) in 1946 for psychologists to assist in understanding and controlling public attitudes regarding the atomic bomb crisis. The FSA was charging through an open door. Already in April 1945, SPSSI released a "psychologists' peace manifesto," which had grown out of a suggestion by Allport at a 1943 meeting. The statement, titled "Human Nature and Peace," was signed by more than two thousand members of the APA and summarized the lessons that socially oriented psychological experts had learned during the war, arguing that "an enduring peace can be attained if the human sciences are utilized by our statesmen and peacemakers."[39] USSBS and other psychological experts had come back from the war truly disturbed, and were resolved to use their wartime skills in the service of peace. As Alexander Leighton had written in 1949, "Social sciences have potentialities for development and use in human welfare that are comparable with what has been realized in other fields where the scientific method has been employed for several hundred years. . . . The need for better human relations both within nations and between nations is urgent. . . . It involves the twin problems of preventing war and utilizing present day knowledge and skills more effectively for the benefit of all mankind."[40] Leighton followed this sentiment by promoting what he called "behavioral weather stations" that were supposed to be established around the globe. The stations would use the methods of morale studies to constantly monitor levels of national and international aggression and hostility.[41]

Leighton and other psychological experts were influenced by the CNM and SPSSI member Kurt Lewin's idea of action-research. Lewin, a Jewish-German émigré and a leading member of the "Gestalt psychology" school, did work with minority groups in the late 1930s. He argued that researchers should not just observe the world, but should aspire to affect positive change through their research.[42] As we have already seen, with psychiatry's emergence from the clinic, such ideas were shared across the social sciences. Chisholm, Menninger, and others' work was not unrelated to the efforts of the SPSSI and others, as was evidenced by the participation

HEALING A SICK WORLD

of many psychologists in such efforts. Furthermore, practicing ideas of mental hygiene "on a terrestrial scale," and the use of terms such as "biodynamics" by psychiatrists like Jules Masserman, was further evidence of the ever-blurred line between the two professions that was straddled by psychological experts.

Those experts' organized efforts for peace were short-lived. The Krech committee, and similar ones (there were two others besides the two mentioned above) disbanded by the early 1950s, but were important in setting future trends. In the late 1950s, younger experts would pick up that particular torch and revolutionize medical activism. What perhaps caused the rapid decline in interest was the multiple and confused directions taken by researchers. Like the USSBS and morale studies, early postwar reactions to Hiroshima and Nagasaki displayed both liberal, even radical, trends and conservative ones. The researchers active in these organizations, who were all military veterans and were deeply involved with the emerging Cold War academic-defense nexus, could not bring themselves to identify the US government or any other clear political body as a target of criticism. If anything, their work played into the hands of those who wished to normalize nuclear weapons and energy. As Ellen Herman has noted, "Psychology's public face may have been turned optimistically toward peace, but wartime experts were working actively behind the scenes to ensure themselves a future in war as well."[43] Many of the same people who signed peace manifestos and wrote passionately about the need to control the atom would take part in Cold War research. Leighton's career path, as his later work in Vietnam demonstrated, supplies us with a rather typical career path of USSBS veterans. The above-mentioned emphasis on individual adjustment was another conservative trend.

The 1946 Krech report shows many of the contradictions of early postwar nuclear research. On one hand, the report started by stating its opposition to the "policy of military secrecy, military control, and the militarization of the Atom." Using the same language employed by Chisholm, Menninger, and others, the committee called American society, a "sick patient ridden by an ill-understood fear."[44] Society's sickness had to be understood and controlled, and again, psychological experts were the ones best situated to do so, as "no cannon, no airplane, no atomic bomb can declare war. Only men can do that. The atomic bomb has not plunged the world into an area of the dark and fearful unknown—Man's *psychology* is doing that. Just as atomic fission was accomplished by cooperative physical research, the fear which it created can and must be dispelled by cooperative social endeavor" (emphasis in original).[45] Again, the main problem was fear. "We will see threats to our safety everywhere," the report argued. "We will support the national policy of universal conscription, militarism, and political isolation. This panicky and distracted thinking is just the mental preparation which sets the stage for international conflict and violence."[46] The problem at hand was the suppression of fear. This was a familiar problem for veterans of morale studies. Fear, rumors, and irrationality, which were hindrances to victory during World War II, now could bring in a third world conflict. Controlling fear, however, could lead to an attack on Cold War fearmongering, and at the same time to a push for nuclear energy, along the lines the US government was promoting (the developments were not mutually exclusive). As we saw in Mark May's comment about the threat of communism, and will further see in defense intellectuals, anxiety over adjustment was connected to American Cold War readiness.

However, such anxieties were also connected—often by the same individuals—to worries about the rise of fascism at home. May, who worked with the American Council on Education as part of its advisory committee on motivational films for returning GIs, also produced films for reeducating Germans and Japanese during those countries' respective occupations.[47] May, who like Leighton also worked on psychological warfare and in Japan, was a strong believer in the psychological universality of all people. He saw the dangers of war and authoritarianism lurking both in the United States and in former Axis countries. Such concerns were connected to the wartime trajectory of morale studies and national character studies.

The Krech committee's attacks on "universal conscription, militarism, and political isolation" were the expression of a growing consensus among liberal psychologists that conservatism was a form of mental disease. As Michael Staub has argued, early postwar psychologists shared the idea that most Americans were likely to develop mental issues because of bad upbringing, and that many of them were at risk of being lured by right-wing extremists.[48] This was a direct result of concerns over both the large number of mentally unfit conscripts during wartime screening and efforts to understand the personality structures that had led to German and Japanese fascism. Such efforts peaked with Theodor Adorno, Else Frenkel-Brunswik, Daniel Levinson, and Nevitt Sanford's *The Authoritarian Personality*. As Jamie Cohen-Cole has noted, this demonstration of the cognitive deficits associated with racism and prejudice became a touchstone of Cold War social science.[49] In this line of thought, conservatism

HEALING A SICK WORLD

was a reflection of mental and developmental problems. The University of Pennsylvania psychiatrist Kenneth Appel insisted that conservatism was a psychiatric disorder. Arthur Schlesinger Jr. argued that many conservatives suffered from schizophrenia, while progressive thinkers like Nathan Glazer and Richard Hofstadter saw conservatism as an abnormal psychological phenomenon that came from failure to adjust to a complex modern world.[50] David Riesman, Lifton's friend and fellow antinuclear activist, in his *The Lonely Crowd* (1950), raised fears of an other-directed personality type that sought to conform to the values of "peer groups" and thus was vulnerable to demagogues.[51] Chisholm, as usual, supplies us with perhaps the most succinct statement of these trends: "Children must be immunized," he argued, "against the rubble rousers, demagogues, and neurotic power-demanding 'leaders' who will always appear in any country when enough unstable, frightened, guilty or inferiority-ridden people are available to provide a following."[52]

Such attacks on conservatism notwithstanding, most psychologists were not radical leftists. They were certainly not all antinuclear. As Jil Morawski and Sharon Goldstein remind us, "[psychological] research undertaken in the 15 years following World War II largely supported government policy in an attempt to socialize Americans to the benefits of atomic weaponry and energy."[53] The Krech report argued for just that, again using the language of rationality and reason: "The possible benefits of Atomic Energy must be emphasized and developed. The atmosphere of demoralizing fear which surrounds the phrase Atomic Energy can be reduced by presenting the facts. . . . Electricity was once feared because only its destructive manifestation, lighting, was familiar. [If] the boons to humanity which Atomic Energy promises must be exercised it must become familiar."[54] This call for familiarity and the normalization of atomic energy was a central effort of early postwar American administrations, and was used to distract the public from its more menacing aspects. And here as well, psychological experts were ready to oblige the government and jumped on its public relations wagon.

Atoms for Peace at the United Nations

The Krech committee's efforts to promote atomic energy were anticipating a campaign to portray it in a positive light at the United Nations, where psychological experts, including USSBS veterans, played a leading role. Here as elsewhere, the researchers avoided examining the impact of atomic energy on *hibakusha*. From 1953 onward, following President Dwight Eisenhower's "Atoms for Peace" UN address, the United States was engaged in a worldwide campaign to present the atom as a force for good. This effort intensified after the March 1954 *Lucky Dragon 5* incident, in which a Japanese fishing boat was blasted with radiation from the US hydrogen bomb tests in the Pacific Ocean. Following that incident and the radiation scares that came in its wake, the antinuclear movement received a tremendous boost, and the United States doubled down on its campaign to counter the rise in antinuclear feeling.[55] At the UN, the WHO, and other international bodies, many mental health professionals and social scientists cooperated with "Atoms for Peace" campaigns. As previously stated, the support by psychological experts and the United Nations for atomic power reflected an international consensus among social scientists, including those of socialist countries. Soviet representatives fully supported this agenda.[56] The Soviets had Atoms for Peace programs for their own satellite states, and, as Paul Josephson has demonstrated, they were as enamored by the promise of the atom as was the West.[57]

Chisholm and his team were at the center of this work at the WHO and at UNESCO.[58] Chisholm worked alongside leading social scientists, including luminaries like Margaret Mead and Claude Lévi-Strauss. American universities such as Columbia and Princeton also played a leading role in these efforts. Three of the four main psychiatrists working in WHO and UNESCO committees were North Americans who also had strong connections with the WFMH and the GAP. Chisholm and Mead at the WHO, and former WFMH president Otto Klineberg from Columbia University at UNESCO—a USSBS veteran—chaired their respective committees.[59] Alexander Leighton was the third prominent psychiatrist and second USSBS veteran on the roster. Another veteran of Hiroshima research was the biologist Austin Brues, who was one of the founders of the ABCC in Hiroshima. Hans Hoff, an Austrian psychiatrist from the University of Vienna who shared many of his North American peers' ideas, was also on the committee.[60] No Japanese or other non-Western scholars were present. The main thrust of these efforts was to argue that critics of atomic energy were emotional and suffered from what Hans Hoff called "irrational pathological fear."[61] A UNESCO report stated,

> It may be that the most important characteristic of [nuclear energy] is to be found not in the actual physical or economic implications of nuclear energy but

HEALING A SICK WORLD

in the psychological and social attitudes which it produces. . . . This particular topic was given careful consideration by the WHO expert committee which stressed the irrational fantasies which nuclear energy was capable of producing, and which might be related to those of early childhood.[62]

The WHO and UNESCO investigation into the mental health effects of nuclear energy reflected earlier debates in the WFMH.[63] These saw the atom as part of a larger development, including automation, to which humans had no choice but to adjust. As the UNESCO report stated, very much along the lines of the Krech report examined above:

> There are dangers in the peaceful uses of nuclear energy, but they should not be exaggerated, nor should it be forgotten that many other useful developments, in transportation, industrial production, medicine etc., have also their drawbacks. . . . [These fears] are rational. . . . A psychiatrist sees other, deeper fears and anxieties, not easily allayed by providing scientific information, because they are unconscious fantasies, and give rise to irrational reactions.[64]

Thus, psychiatry's role, as with other developments in modern capitalism, was to help those who could not adapt to the modern world

The WHO report showed a concern with the mental stability and preparedness of world leaders in dealing with nuclear issues. It complained that there were "even some in highly responsible positions, whose behavior is not entirely free from . . . unhealthy responses."[65] The main issue, the authors concluded, was that "the authorities like the general public do not always show the ability to make clear distinction between warlike and peaceful uses of atomic energy."[66] This the authors attributed to lack of information and proper understanding of the science involved: "Few if any [leaders], have [a] background which includes a thorough scientific training."[67] Leaders, the report argued, found themselves overwhelmed by the pace of technological change. This situation could cause them to "react at times with more or less irrational ideas and inconsistent acts." This, the authors continued, "sometimes takes the form of hostility to atomic energy as the cause of their dilemma and the rapidity of changes which have overwhelmed them."[68] The authors tried to remedy this situation through their research. They expressed their determination to treat these issues scientifically, in the hope that "people in positions of authority will accept its conclusion that the behavioral sciences can make a valuable and concrete contribution to the adaptation of mankind to the advent of atomic power, making it indeed as painless and as un-harmful as possible and allowing man to reap a rich harvest from the seed his inventive genius has sown."[69]

The WHO report on atomic energy defined its objective as examining atomic energy's "effects on mental health [which] can come, either directly from influence of radiation on the nervous system or strong psychological [i.e., nonsomatic] reactions . . . that will have to be considered more or less pathological," or caused by "man's encounter . . . [with the] shattering possibilities of atomic power."[70] Despite Leighton's and Klineberg's presence, the Hiroshima and Nagasaki survivors' mental experiences—which of course were shattering in ways other than the metaphysical—were hardly mentioned in these deliberations. After examining in some detail the actual physical damage done by radiation, citing American and Japanese research on *hibakusha* brain damage, and ascertaining the nature of physical health risks, the WHO committee turned away from the *hibakusha* to examine the "thoughts and fantasies about the danger of the nuclear bomb" among the general population.[71] Following widespread assumptions in American and other professional literature, the WHO also launched "an enquiry into what was thought might turn out to be a hidden reservoir of anxiety in the population." However, this research, which included surveys of psychiatrists in eight countries on both sides of the Iron Curtain, "gave surprisingly blank results," with no mention of nuclear energy in the "expressed content of psychiatric patients, whether psychotic or psychoneurotic."[72] The lack of empirical evidence, however, did not discourage the WHO, which went on to recommend the incorporation and expansion of the mental health profession to help leaders and populations as well as the fledging International Atomic Energy Agency (IAEA). Echoing Chisholm and others, the authors called for more mental health experts within the IAEA and other nuclear energy-related bodies and activities.[73] Echoing Leighton's suggestion for a "behavioral weather station," they recommended creating a network of psychiatrists who would advise governments "in order to plan a rational local mental health program" that would help countries deal with the rapid expansion of atomic power, especially in the event of "accidents and unexpected hazards."[74]

Both UNESCO and WFMH/WHO actions came after an October 1957 nuclear accident at the Windscale plant in Cumberland (now Sellafield, Cumbria), England. Rather than alarming scientists about the dangers of nuclear energy, the accident spurred the United Nations to further combat what they saw as the prejudices exhibited by local populations. WFMH director Frank Fremont-Smith pointed out that the accident "produced something approaching panic among the local population."[75] This "panic" had wide impacts on local resistance to nuclear plants. The WHO report decried the fact that "although [they] have been presented with evidence that atomic energy has no health risk to population around the plant," local communities "irrationally oppose atomic plants." According to the report, the resistance of the population was "an expression of fear which is displaced and irrational."[76] Anxieties about atomic energy were connected to "thoughts and fantasies about the danger of the nuclear bomb." These fantasies included "irrational fears" following nuclear tests which were in "conflict with many official pronouncements put out about risks and safety measures" by authorities.[77] To tackle the irrational fears and anxieties supposedly plaguing the public, the study group recommended an expanded mental hygiene program, and greater rationalization and expansion of mental health in the community.

The WHO, UNESCO, and other bodies made a very strong connection between mental health, as advocated by early postwar American psychiatrists, and the accepted integration of atomic energy in global society. The study group recommended that governments work toward "1) an upbringing free from anxiety and hate 2) creation of good human relations in the family . . . 3) education of those in responsible positions in public life . . . in mental health requirements, [and] 4) relief of the healthy from the burden of the mentally ill."[78] This move, in turn, was tied to the implied unpreparedness of non-Western societies to deal with the fruits of science. UNESCO, in a separate report, emphasized its efforts in educating populations and incorporating science into local cultures "Otherwise, forced acceleration of the uses of atomic energy might have dangerous repercussions upon local cultures which have lagged behind in the past."[79] In this effort, past traditions of scientific education and rationalization of society and current anxieties over new technologies and the impact of modernity came together in a campaign to push atomic energy (and science as a whole) as the cure to the very conditions brought about by rapid technological change. Indeed, UNESCO aptly called this effort the "domestication" of atomic energy.[80] Thus, the cure for anxiety over that most emblematic of modern science's advances, the atom, was a greater acceptance of psychiatric science. The emphasis in the UN report—as in postwar psychiatry as a whole—was on science's capacity to solve problems, rather than on the destruction it caused. As David Serlin put it in a different context, psychiatrists sought to normalize the terms under which "modern science could absorb its capacity for recklessness and turn trauma into opportunity."[81] This approach allowed them to repackage the bomb and nuclear energy not as political problems but as psychological ones, thereby further deflecting the hard questions brought about by modernity's worst war.

Conclusion

The twin quotes by La Barre and California's Congressman Horace Voorhis of a poem by Hermann Hagedorn, with which this chapter opens, captured much of the zeitgeist of the early Cold War encounter with the A-bomb. The bomb had an unprecedented impact on the minds of Americans. The United States was not harmed physically by it, or by any type of bombing of major cities for that matter, but the psychological impact of the event was perceived to be considerable. The psychologists and psychiatrists who made such observations, as well as the many commentators who echoed similar messages, saw the A-bomb as a deadly symptom of a wider disease from which modern man was suffering. The bomb proved to the psychological sciences that the disease of war and aggression could lead to the death of humanity. Such worries were not new. Freud himself, in a 1931 letter to Albert Einstein, worried about "man's inherent drive for destruction," and emphasized the psychological reasons for the outbreak of wars.[82] The A-bomb, however, added much urgency to the problem, and the psychological sciences were poised, as Weston La Barre summed it up, to diffuse the atomic bombs that lie in the depth of the human psyche.

Thus, psychologists and psychiatrists—encouraged by the significant roles they had had during the war, armed with new insights into human nature, and greatly worried by the mental health crisis their mobilization had uncovered—set up to reform postwar society. The A-bomb presented an opportunity and a challenge which the professions were happy to take on. Thus, the experts wrote books, formed committees, and joined governmental bodies to advise, warn, and plot humanity's first steps in dealing with the nuclear age. USSBS researchers played an important role in these efforts. David Krech and others in the APA, Otto Klineberg and Leighton at the UN, and many more individuals have left their mark on early Cold War research. The impact of Hiroshima was very real for people like Leighton, and they were determined to prevent the use of nuclear weapons in future wars. But if survey personnel played a role,

USSBS research and the people whom researchers interviewed did not. Psychologists' mobilization left the actual victims of Hiroshima and Nagasaki behind. The problem was with American minds (and, by extension, the minds of citizens of Russia and other nuclear powers), not with Japanese ones. The experts did not tackle individual minds, but worked on a national and even global scale. It was indeed only fitting that figures like Chisholm and Leighton moved away from research on individual soldiers to work on communities and nations, and finally to work in the United Nations on the anxieties that plagued the whole world. Hiroshima itself was seen more as a symbol and a warning than an actual place with actual people and actual suffering.

Early Cold War research, however, was not without its importance for Hiroshima and its victims. While in the short run an emphasis on peace problems discouraged work on the more concrete psychological problems of individuals, in the long run the politicization of the professions and the emergence of "action-research" had profound implications for the stricken cities. Early Cold War research had multiple, often contradictory, trajectories. While the majority of experts, including USSBS veterans and leading psychiatrists like Menninger and Chisholm, emphasized the individual need to adjust to nuclear reality, they were also worried about the meaning of nuclear anxieties for the potential rise of fascism. Thus, Leighton and Chisholm could condemn resistance to nuclear energy and the emerging nuclear order as irrational, and as a manifestation of dark phobias. But at the same time, they worried about leaders' mental health and the susceptibility of the common man to the temptations of authoritarianism. Surveying organized psychology forays into nuclear research and popular attitudes to the A-bomb, Goldstein and Morawsky pointed out that some psychologists, who were worried about public inaction in face of the nuclear threat, "without any explicit sense of irony . . . concluded that people had relinquished responsibility to expert authorities."[83] Psychologists' worry about the authorities' mental capacities rarely expanded to any sense of self-doubt. Another decade would pass before before action-research would expand to include a questioning of the profession's involvement with the nuclear order and its neglect of nuclear victims. However, in the first decade, and for some (like Leighton) well beyond it, the psychological experts worked well within the consensus and the established organizations that sustained it. The A-bomb may have shown us that the world was sick, but the doctors were working for the government that had dropped it.

CHAPTER FOUR

Nuclear Trauma and Panic in the United States

"The bombed populations of Europe and Asia stood up to bombing far better than had been anticipated. . . . The dire predictions made by many self-styled 'experts' on mass behavior failed to take account of the psychological stamina of the average civilian."—Irving Janis, 1949[1]

On 15 May 1952 the Federal Civil Defense Administration's "Alert America" convoy rolled into Los Angeles. The traveling exhibit was part of the FCDA's campaign to promote awareness for efforts to prepare Americans for the possibility of a nuclear strike on the US mainland. The exhibit presented a mixture of grim propaganda regarding the dangers of modern warfare, including Soviet psychological warfare and sabotage, and an upbeat and optimistic view of the American population's ability to withstand nuclear attack. In Los Angeles, the latter cheerful view was on clear display. When the convoy arrived, the lead truck driver, Corporal Samuel Leible, was greeted by "Miss Alert America," Jeanne Lambros, and two "hostesses," one of whom bestowed a Hawaiian lei around his neck, while visitors were greeted by sales of "atomic cheesecake."[2] With proper preparations and planning, the exhibit's argument went, US cities, not unlike British, German, and Japanese cities, could withstand urban bombing even by nuclear weapons, and keep up the fight. As the word "alert" in the convoy's title suggested, one of the main goals of the campaign was to turn terror of nuclear attack into a healthy awareness and vigilance. Given such emphasis, the presence of a group of Japanese American survivors of Hiroshima on the premises might seem contrary to the exhibit's goals. The *Los Angeles Times* informed its readers that the survivors, who had immigrated or repatriated to the United States after the war, "were there when the first Atom bomb was dropped on Hiroshima and ... [will] tell their experiences during that historic holocaust at the Alert America show."[3] The use of the word "holocaust," even if at the time it carried different meanings than in its current usage, added to the peculiarity of the *hibakusha*'s presence at the event.

Significantly, the testimonies of what the newspaper called the "Hiroshima blast witnesses" were presented not as a story of torment, but as one of nuclear preparedness. As Naoko Wake has demonstrated, Japanese American *hibakusha*, conforming to FCDA and larger mainstream expectations, mostly presented themselves as rescuers rather than as sufferers.[4] One of the survivors who in the show, Jack Dairiki, a Nisei born in Sacramento in 1930, was later interviewed for a California Civil Defense radio show, which used his story to assure state residents that "[even if] an atomic bomb [were] dropped over the city ... many will survive if they simply observe the fundamental rules of survival."[5] The way *hibakusha* testimonies were construed, both by civil defense authorities and, more importantly, by the *hibakusha* themselves, attests to the strength of ideological constraints that shaped the perception of Hiroshima survivors' experience. Such constraints also had a powerful impact on the way psychological experts viewed the reactions to and long-term damage from an atomic explosion. Research on mental damage to *hibakusha* in the first decade after Hiroshima was primarily done in the context of US preparations for future nuclear confrontation with the Soviets. The focus on civil defense, this chapter argues, precluded any attention to long-term mental damage. Short-term emotional shock was seen as temporary and treatable. Like the bigger civil defense project, mental health damage was seen as manageable, and, significantly, not very different from the experience of World War II combat troops and of conventional bombing.

As mentioned at the end of chapter 2, civil defense research was the second main avenue through which American psychological experts reacted to the dropping of the atomic bombs. The resources devoted to such research and the sheer volume of it far outweighed any research done in Japan by either Japanese or American researchers. In direct continuation of the work done by the USSBS, psychological researchers tackled the emotional impact of bombing, the efficacy of shelters, and the possible impact of nuclear weapons on society and morale. Indeed, one salient feature of this body of research is the extent which it relied on USSBS work in Japan. Although, as we have just seen, there were *hibakusha* present in the United States and a significant American medical research establishment in the stricken Japanese cities, all the work done in the US was based on the work of the USSBS and a small number of translated testimonies. Researchers frequently complained about the paucity of data, but no researcher ever traveled to Japan or gathered Japanese materials. With only one minor exception, most researchers also did not contact Japanese or American professionals in Japan or try to do any follow-up research on USSBS work. The reliance on USSBS work, most of which was done in the first couple of weeks after the bombings, had a further detrimental effect on civil defense research. The impact of radiation and related anxieties, as well as other long-term mental health damage, was never researched by the USSBS. This dependency on short-term research made it easier for later researchers, who were in any case focused on short-term damage, to ignore the long-term psychological impact of the A-bomb.

Most civil defense researchers were World War II veterans. Thus, unsurprisingly, military psychiatry and wartime research featured prominently in atomic psychological research. The military approaches to trauma made their way seamlessly into research on civilians. This was part of a larger trend within civil defense that noted the increased militarization of American civilian life during the Cold War. As a result, as was done in the military and due to civil defense priorities, the problem of trauma was dealt with in relation to the larger issue of group behavior and morale. Still, work on psychological trauma on civilians was an important aspect of civil defense research. This body of work was recognized neither by researchers of civil defense nor by historians of trauma. Historians of civil defense focused much of their attention on the way concerns over panic and morale contributed to the militarization of American society and psychiatry's concern with anxiety. This focus, of course, is not wrong per se, but it does obscure the work done on individual trauma. Likewise, trauma studies tend to concentrate on military psychiatry, and overlook work on civilians and strategic bombing. However, examining trauma work in the context of civilian bombing and nuclear history shows important precursors to later work on PTSD. Researchers also drew on a whole range of work on "extreme situations," from concentration camps to mine explosions, and sought to expand their work beyond the confines of military psychiatry. These inquiries had a direct impact on the later development of clinical categories. They were also part of a transnational effort to understand the impact of bombing on civilians. Unfortunately for the victims, however, this transnational consensus, and bombing research as a whole, tended to be conservative in its assumptions and tended to reinforce the dismissal of long-term mental damage.

This chapter examines the work on individual psychological trauma within the context of the larger work done on panic and other mass reactions to bombing. It begins with a survey of such work and its relations to military psychiatry, Cold War strategy, the importance of culture (or lack thereof), and the emergence of the military-academic complex. It then focuses in depth on the work of Irving Janis, a Yale psychologist whose work extensively built and elaborated on USSBS research. Janis was one of the architects of what Guy Oakes has insightfully called the system of "emotional management" of the American population in the early Cold War.[6] However, Janis was a critic of the notion of panic, and saw mass psychological trauma as the real threat facing the United States. The chapter concludes with a short discussion of the Desert Rock maneuvers, in which thousands of American soldiers who participated in live nuclear tests were examined by psychologists, and the larger significance of Cold War and civil defense psychological research on contemporary culture, as well as post-Fifties research on *hibakusha* mental health.

The Problem of Panic

Civil defense research on possible American psychological reactions to nuclear attacks was a direct continuation of wartime research. As Mathew Farish aptly described it, during the war, "German and Japanese spaces were turned into sites for collection of evidence and testing of previously vague theories, a place where the principles and methods of cutting-edge social science could be applied to a definite geography later carried over to American environs."[7] The same techniques and assumptions that underlined bombing research were employed now on the US mainland. Strategic considerations were paramount in this move. As the civil defense planner Joseph McLean put it, "America's 'glass jaw'" in the conflict with the Soviets was the lack of preparedness and the doubtful ability of Americans to handle the effects of bombing. A 1951 report by the GAP titled "Psychiatric Aspects of Civil Defense" defined this thinking, quoting S. L. A. Marshall, as "a curious transposition whereby the civil mass becomes the shield covering the body of the military, and whereat the prospect for final military success lies in the chance that the shield will be able to sustain the shock, and the will and productiveness of the civil population can be maintained until the military body can make decisive use of its weapons."[8] Civil defense psychological experts were intensely worried about the civilian shield's ability to "sustain the shock" of nuclear warfare. "Can a free people organize and discipline themselves," McLean asked, "on both an individual and collective basis, to avoid paralysis by fear, defeat through despair, and fatal inaction and indecision induced by apathy?"[9] He and others were not so sure. Thus, they embarked on a campaign to determine what could be the possible behaviors of Americans under future attacks, and, not less importantly, to transform American attitudes toward such scenarios.

From the mid-1940s onward, a growing body of research in the United States sought to determine how civilians and soldiers would respond to a nuclear attack. The USSBS findings consisted of much of the data on which these researchers relied. Speaking no Japanese, and working for the most part from their US labs, the researchers did not conduct their own field research but relied on USSBS data, research on US combat reactions, and research into other civilian disasters. Most work on the A-bomb's psychological impact was related to this kind of nuclear and civil defense research. Psychological experts sought to use Hiroshima and Nagasaki research to demonstrate the ability of civil defense medical personnel to deal adequately with psychological trauma and keep morale high. They mostly minimized the A-bomb's impact and presented it as manageable and containable, soothing the populace's fear of nuclear attack and enabling the home front to support a future war with the USSR. They were not intentionally blind to the long-term impacts of the bomb, but their politics and basic assumptions about trauma steered them away from recognizing the implications of their research.

As Gerald Grob has noted, World War II had a paradoxical influence on psychiatry. On one hand, the huge increase in mental disorders exposed by wartime screening caused much anxiety in the profession.[10] On the other, psychiatrists were confident of their ability, based on their wartime experience, to help individuals and, indeed, society as a whole to adjust to the needs of peacetime.[11] This sense of confidence was displayed both in psychiatrists' newfound appetite for social action and, within psychiatry, in their perceived ability to treat and contain the impact of war trauma on veterans. Notably, however, the long-term impact of wartime trauma was not thoroughly examined by postwar American psychiatry. It was felt that psychiatry was capable of helping veterans completely overcome battle-related mental issues. The vast majority of men, psychiatrists reported, were responding remarkably well to treatment and new therapies. As the war correspondent John Hersey, who became famous for his Hiroshima story in the *New Yorker*, observed in a long piece in *Life* magazine about a veteran hospital, the modern therapies received by returning soldiers meant that most of them were "no worse off, in fact sometimes better off, than millions of their fellow citizens with minor neuropsychiatric disorders who have not had the benefit of a psychiatric service like that of the U.S. Army."[12] Thus, science was seen as being capable of overcoming and healing the suffering caused by war.

US research broke with a long tradition in psychiatry that viewed trauma victims suspiciously. After 1945, for the first time, war trauma victims were getting recognition from a wide range of fields. Before the 1970s, however, veterans' long-term trauma was not acknowledged as a permanent condition or as deserving of financial compensation by many psychiatrists or by the US Veterans Administration. The emphasis in the postwar era was on psychiatry's ability to cure combat-related mental damage. Those who were not cured were suspect. The culprits, however, were not just the veterans themselves, but their mothers and wives who had failed to care for their husbands or raise their sons properly—a theory that came to be known as "momism."[13] Brock Chisholm blamed the high percentage of breakdowns in the Canadian military on mental defects caused by bad upbringing.[14] Trauma, for Chisholm and many other establishment psychiatrists and psychologists, was a result not of the dehumanizing experience of war, but of childhood experiences or somatic issues that "predisposed" people to trauma.[15] These notions were challenged during the war by the likes of Roy Grinker and John Spiegel, who argued that even under the best circumstances and with the healthiest of minds, anybody who is exposed for prolonged periods to the brutal realities of war could be broken, as "traumatic stimuli" could combine "to produce a potential war neurosis in every soldier."[16] This had important implications for scholars like Erik Erikson, Robert Lifton's mentor, who in the 1950s challenged the primacy of childhood in psychiatry and psychology and opened the way to more open engagement with the ability of adult trauma ability to alter personality structures.[17]

Where such attitudes to trauma intersected most clearly with nuclear issues was in the field of civil defense. The basic assumptions about trauma, and optimism regarding psychiatrists' ability to deal adequately and rationally with the long-term implications of nuclear warfare, resonated across civil defense studies. These trends, in turn, intersected with a similar optimism about humanity's ability to use the atom for good, and US military planners' confidence in their ability to fight and win a nuclear war. As previously examined, for many psychiatrists within the defense establishment, the crisis of veterans' mental health represented a crucial weakness of the United States in its global struggle with the Soviet Union. With the Cold War intensifying in the late Forties and early Fifties, a new group of postwar psychiatrists, many of whom were veterans of military psychiatry, started to think seriously about how to help the United States win a nuclear war when it inevitably came, by preventing panic and helping Americans adjust to the new nuclear reality. As Paul Boyer has noted, for psychological experts, "disruptive or immobilizing emotional reactions [were] increasingly defined as the central hazards confronting civilian population."[18] Nuclear anxiety in these studies was medicalized and dealt with scientifically by the growing number of psychiatrists within the defense establishment. This expansion of the role of psychiatry in the realm of defense was closely connected to the growing role of psychiatry in society as a whole. As Andrea Tone has pointed out, campaigns to market tranquilizers to stressed housewives and businessmen were happening at the same time as the FCDA was urging Americans to stay calm under nuclear attack.[19] As the *New Yorker* declared in the mid-Fifties, when the Milltown pill was introduced to the American market, "an age in which nations threaten each other with guided missiles and hydrogen bombs is one that can use any calm it can get, and calm is what the American pharmaceutical industry now abundantly offers."[20] Indeed, the FCDA itself was urging Americans to stock their fallout shelters with tranquilizers. "A bottle of a hundred should be adequate for a family of four," the government declared.[21]

Psychiatrists' work on defense issues was part of the US government's drive to enlist expert academic advice in preparing the American public for the prospect of nuclear war. The central enterprise for these efforts was Project East River.[22] The reports resulting from this project became a blueprint for civil defense "emotional management" in the early Cold War.[23] As with massive aerial bombing during World War II, US planners in the early 1950s saw the primary value of the bomb in its "psychological implications" and its ability to "shatter enemy civilians' morale."[24] US planners continued to use the wartime "morale shattering" arguments in their strategic planning for an attack on the Soviet Union. At the same time, FCDA planners were using USSBS research to claim that nuclear bombs were not so different from regular bombing, and thus that the psychological damage they produced was manageable. This was another arena for the expansion of psychiatry, and a catalyst for much research on the impact of aerial bombing on the human psyche. The psychiatrist Dale

Cameron, who wrote the East River report on the problem of panic and was the assistant director of the National Institute of Mental Health from 1945 to 1950, defined the profession's mission in 1949 when he asked, "What can psychiatry and its allied professions, psychology and sociology, contribute to the prevention of untoward mass reactions and to the prevention of individual personality disorders?"[25] Psychiatry, argued Cameron, drawing on William Menninger's work, should include "professional concern with environmental, interpersonal, and intrapersonal problems which may contribute to personality disorders."[26] The interplay of mental damage, group behavior, and environment had important implications for civil defense, as "fear, with its attendant panic, might preclude the resumption of organized, constructive activity."[27] But fear and panic were not inevitable. This "defeatist picture," Cameron argued, could be countered with organized research.[28]

Cameron praised the work of the RAND Corporation and Irving Janis in taking the first steps in this direction, in order to "counteract possible unrealistic attitudes of fear and futility ... [providing] positive information concerning the effect and particularly the limitations of new weapons."[29] Cameron himself drew on Janis and the USSBS in his 1952 report for the East River project. Panic and fear were the main focus of the report. Cameron did not doubt that Americans *would* panic. "The possibility of panic must be taken as a working assumption" for future research, he argued.[30] He defined panic as "a highly excited individual or group behavior characterized by aimless, unorganized, unreasoning, non-constructive activity ... resulting ordinarily from sudden, extreme and often groundless fear."[31] The same conditions, according to the report, might lead to "apathy" and "demoralization." Drawing on military research, Cameron cautioned his readers that fear is a normal reaction to dangerous situations. The way to counter fear and prevent spread of untoward reactions from individual to the group was through training and information: "The likelihood of panic or other disorganized behavior increases to the extent that ... the individual is not trained in organized response [and] no external guidance to organize responses is furnished."[32] Cameron advocated military-style training for the general public, so that people could "recognize the main sources of danger in foreseeable emergencies. ... As in combat training, every approach toward realism into training situations will be gained as much as it guarantees greater transfers of the learned responses to the situation of real danger."[33]

Cameron's work had multiple continuities with the work of Alexander Leighton and other USSBS researchers. As with the USSBS, Cameron did not elaborate on the mechanism that connected individual mental damage to group behavior. Like Leighton, Cameron accepted that such reactions were transmittable and were directly linked to mental health, panic, and aggression. In a further continuity, he saw racial tensions as a significant barrier to effective prevention and understanding of future panic. In a section on the dangers of mob behavior, he warned, "What is the likelihood during a raid upon our cities that mob aggression would seek and find scapegoats to destroy instead of the real enemy? The fact of lynching, race riots, and other well-known attacks on scapegoats in our society is not reassuring."[34] Cameron's antiracism was not exceptional among his peers, but he also directly linked "mob behavior" with McCarthyism and the wartime internment of Japanese Americans. He condemned "public opinion which readily supported the indiscriminate seizure of Japanese Americans in World War II, [and] the present atmosphere, to the extent that it condones aggression toward merely unorthodox persons as symbols of communism."[35] The presence of such condemnation of Cold War fear mongering and racial policies in one of the most quintessential works of the Cold War academic-military complex seems paradoxical. But, as we saw with Leighton and others, most psychological experts saw themselves as progressive, and possessed a strong belief in rationality and scientific objectivity. For such experts, Cold War work meant continuing their wartime commitment to defend those values in the face of totalitarianism. Preventing panic at the home front, therefore, was part of a wider struggle for freedom, which Cameron and his peers did not see as inherently conservative or militarist. If anything, the defensive nature of such work made panic prevention much more acceptable than bombing work.

The Imagination of Disaster

The same liberal and progressive bodies that issued peace manifestos and warned against the danger of nuclear war also worked with the defense establishment on plans to prepare the public for nuclear war. GAP issued a report in mid-1951 that sought to help military and civilian bodies to prepare for a nuclear attack. The report displayed liberal paradoxes similar to those of to the East River one. Using the aforementioned quote from S. L. A. Marshall, the authors bemoaned the way modern warfare made citizens targets. GAP, even more directly than Cameron, condemned racism as a "mental illness." Racial tensions, which like Cameron they connected to panic and mob violence, were dangerous, as "both those who are prejudiced and those who were the victims of prejudice can easily displace their unresolved resentments upon their leaders when threatened by overwhelming disaster."[36] GAP advocated a mental hygiene program and democratic education as preventive measures. Racial fears underlined much of the discussion about panic. More conservative pundits, like the FCDA consultant and popular author Philip Wylie, were more inclined to use racial tensions as a scare tactic to get the American public to mobilize against the Soviet enemy. In his 1954 article "Panic, Psychology, and the Bomb," Wylie warned of the danger of urban masses pillaging the countryside and suburbs after a nuclear attack. Using a series of not very subtle references to minorities, Wylie wrote, "Six percent of the population of every big city is criminal. Half the hospital beds are occupied by the mentally ill. In every city, thousands cannot read English. The bomb would turn them all loose."[37]

Compared to Wylie, the GAP report was measured and calm. It dealt with both group and individual responses. As in most work examined here, its authors began by decrying the paucity of research and sources. Like the WHO and GAP accounts, the report warned of the existence of "diffused anxieties rooted in the unconscious which can be stirred by the awareness that a truly cataclysmic disaster has occurred or may be imminent."[38] Drawing on behavioralism, the authors argued, "One of the strongest and most lasting emotional supports for positive motivation in stress situations is an individual's identification with a specific group in the sense that he feels the group is responsible for him and he is responsible for it."[39] As Edward Geist pointed out, behavioralism wielded significant influence in American defense policy circles during the opening years of the Cold War.[40] Behavioral theory argued that "fundamental social factors, such as membership in primary groups and social networks," determined human behavior.[41] Behavioralism also always aspired to generalization. The theory was particularly suited to the practice of psychological experts that developed during the war, as it "sought to break down disciplinary barriers in an attempt to create a generalized theory of human behavior."[42] Geist traced the rise of behavioralism to the 1949 book *The American Soldier*, which used this framework to explain the wartime behavior of GIs (Irving Janis also contributed a chapter). The theory "found favor in think tanks such as RAND ... as well as among philanthropic foundations such as the Ford Foundation."[43]

Behavioral theory, with its focus on group cohesion on one hand, and behavioralists' penchant for overgeneralization on the other, made drawing on military psychiatric theory easier. The GAP report emphasized leadership, motivation, and information as the best measures for creating individual and group mental resilience. Individual reactions depended on group cohesion, and vice versa. The GAP report advised the public that "unusual emotional reactions" were to be expected.[44] Just as military psychiatrists had advised soldiers, it said that fear reactions should be seen as normal. But it cautioned that a small minority of people would experience "disabling anxiety manifested by physical symptoms, irritability and aggressiveness, flight, fury apathy, varying degrees of depression, loss of motivation and initiative, departure from the group, minor misdemeanors, immature reactions (with regression to infantile behavior), passivity and even denial of the situation to a psychotic degree."[45] Most people affected would quickly experience "a period of recoil" with "a gradual return of self-consciousness and awareness for the majority."[46] The emphasis on the temporary nature of traumatic experience was not unusual. The GAP report, however, stood out in talking about the "actions of the post-traumatic period," which were "closer to those clinical pictures which psychiatrists are usually familiar with—'the post-traumatic reactions.'" Such reactions included "persistent anxiety states, fatigue stays, recurrent traumatic dreams, depressive reactions, rage, etc. The post-traumatic syndromes or neurosis become apparent during this period."[47]

The 1951 report was one of only two reports that discussed "posttrauma" at any length, and it was remarkably close in its clinical definition to what would later be called PTSD. Significantly, posttraumatic impact was also not limited to those already suffering from mental illness. The GAP report drew on the work of James Tyhurst, who formulated the theory in some length in his 1951 article "Individual Reactions to Community Disaster."[48] Tyhurst relied on the work of Abram Kardiner and on British psychiatrists who worked on the impact of the Blitz. The latter included the British psychiatrist E. Stengel's work on "air-raid phobia," as well as the work of other British researchers. Likewise, Donald Michael's 1955 work, discussed below, refers to British work as a counterpoint to the work of Irving Janis and others, who argued that "prolonged, incapacitating symptoms [were] likely to occur only in markedly predisposed personalities."[49] On the other hand, Michael concluded, similarly relying on British work, that "neurosis is likely to follow severe air raid experiences which at the time upset the individual emotionally or produced a serious upset in the pattern of his living. . . . Both previously stable and previously unstable personalities showed neurotic symptoms."[50] British researchers, however, found that the "effects were generally more persistent among those with personality defects."[51]

But the GAP and Michael reports were more the exceptions than the rule in the 1950s. Postwar work overwhelmingly emphasized the temporary nature of traumatic reactions to bombing and combat—that is, if it looked at individual reactions at all. Generally speaking, psychological research was much more concerned with group behavior and the problem of panic. Panic was what most scholarly attention and resources were focused on. The first interdisciplinary conference on "morale and the prevention of panic" was held in February 1951 in New York City under the sponsorship of the New York Academy of Medicine and the Joshua Macy Jr. Foundation. More than fifty participants from across the social sciences attended. The conference featured a large array of opinions both in support of and opposition to the government position on panic.[52] The organizers were skeptical of the "fear technique" that the government had so far employed, and they encouraged "teams of social scientists and other leaders who have knowledge of human behavior" to participate in promoting research that would be "morale-building rather than panic-building."[53] A follow-up conference was held in 1954. In between, three mini-conferences on "morale problems" were held in Chicago, Boston, and Washington. The "morale problem" conferences were among two hundred conferences organized by the foundation in its mission to promote research into problems of health that fell "between the sciences," in what organizers called "a new psychosocial" field.[54] Alexander Leighton, as well as many others whose work is examined here, such as Dwight Chapman, Frank Fremont-Smith, Albert Glass, and Roy Grineker, were in attendance. Also in attendance were Robert Jay Lifton and Jerome D. Frank. Frank, like Lifton, would later become a leading dissenter on nuclear issues.[55] Despite their opposition, both men continued to engage with establishment psychiatry and, as will be examined later, civil defense forums. In the early Fifties the Macy, Rockefeller, and other foundations, as well as many of the psychiatrists and social scientists who participated in these conferences, were part of an expanding world of "human sciences" that at least partially fed into the emerging "military-academic complex," in which nuclear issues played a key role. This had an important influence on the research trajectory of Lifton and other dissidents. Those researchers, though they were writing in opposition to the military-academic complex, came out of it and were influenced by it.

Despite the presence of Grinker, Glass, Leighton, Lifton, and others, the proceedings of the "Morale and the Prevention of Panic" conference contained only one report, by Joost Meerloo, on possible individual reactions to nuclear bombing. The majority of the discussion revolved around issues of morale. Meerloo, a Dutch American psychiatrist better known for his work on brainwashing techniques during the Korean War, served with the Dutch Army in exile during World War II. The connection between trauma research and "brainwashing" was not coincidental. Two other principal figures in our study, Janis and Lifton, wrote on mind manipulation techniques. As the title of Meerloo's book *The Rape of the Mind* demonstrates, brainwashing was seen as the deliberate destruction of the prisoner's mental defenses.[56] This was exactly what terror bombing was supposed to achieve, and what researchers sought to evaluate and defend against. Meerloo's view of victims as reverting to "a more primitive and infantile" state was a direct link to his work on brainwashing and the power of suggestion to guide the traumatic mind to reveal its secrets. The connection between suggestion and trauma had a long history, going back to the work of Jean Martin Charcot, Pierre Janet, and W. H. R. Rivers, who connected suggestion to his work with "primitives."[57]

Significantly, for Meerloo trauma was not a phenomenon limited to those predisposed to psychiatric illness: "Special catastrophes such as an earthquake, a railway wreck, or a direct bomb hit may throw everybody into such a temporary infantile state."[58] But such states were temporary, he argued, and could be treated by following a few "simple rules." "If a population is well prepared and morale is good nearly everyone will have the jitters, but only for a short time," he wrote.[59] Meerloo's somewhat dismissive tone toward mental symptoms (or jitters) and even more toward the victims whose symptoms persisted, is indicative of his training in the German tradition. Though he was critical of past dismissal of shell shock, his attitude was quite paternalistic. The "crying child' in the victim asks for paternal understanding," he opined. "Every hostile attitude toward a panicky person increases his panic. During the First World War there existed a rather hostile attitude towards the so-called malingerers which was expressed in the use of electrotherapy. We could not cure them with that. These victims are sick and need help."[60] For Meerloo, the majority of those experiencing shock should be able to recover quickly. He recognized that some bombing victims would not return to normal behavior. He did not elaborate on the reasons for this, or on the role, if any, of "personality defects" in the persistence of symptoms. He suggested the use of hypnosis and suggestion as well as, in more extreme cases, "hypnocatharsis and narcoanalysis," which would "bring the patient . . . to reexperience in his mind the frightening impact so that he will gradually be able to halt his pathological behavior."[61] Meerloo here was reiterating the acceptable World War II–era methods developed by the American and British armies.

Meerloo's positions were perhaps expressed in a tone most American doctors would not have employed. But his methods and conclusions on the treatment of trauma were accepted practice in the United States. Meerloo also shared with his colleagues a dislike of racism (a Dutch Jew, he had lost his family in the Holocaust), fearmongering, and the "mass hysteria over Communism" in the US.[62] Race and ethnicity, however, continued to be used by Meerloo and others in explaining varying responses to bombing. This was especially the case in Hiroshima research. Japanese cultural stereotypes often played a role in the thinking of researchers such as Dwight Chapman, another veteran of military psychiatry who cooperated with Janis and the aforementioned John Spiegel (who had worked on combat trauma in Tunisia during World War II) on research for the FCDA.[63] Chapman, like Janis, was skeptical of the emphasis on panic in civil defense research. Drawing on the USSBS research, he assured his readers that "there was no panic in Hiroshima."[64] He attributed this to "Japanese stoicism" and implied, in the same manner the USSBS Morale Division was sometimes prone to, that the American people could learn a thing or two from the Japanese on the matter of having a fighting spirit.[65] Likewise, Donald Michael argued that, though Europeans and Japanese were better prepared psychologically for bombing, "the Japanese . . . have a way of life and philosophy which inured them to hardships and thereby, perhaps, permitted them a more rapid and extensive recovery from the initial shock than could be expected of Americans."[66] The use of Japanese examples came in the context of profound distress among experts about Americans, who, some complained, were "corrupted by mass consumption . . . addicted to pleasure and . . . had become morally decadent."[67] Americans needed to be educated, informed, and managed. The alternative was panic and mayhem. As Chapman argued, "The outright psychiatric effects of air attack observed during the last war are not alarming. On the other hand, however, some rather small disasters in American communities have produced some psychosomatic complaints among survivors and put extra strain on doctors and hospitals."[68]

Michael, who relied heavily on work of the USSBS and John Hersey, was quite somber in his assessment of the lessons of Hiroshima. He was also one of the only researchers to pay any attention to radiation, which, he argued, would make psychological damage worse in the United States. Michael was already writing after the 1954 Bikini tests and fallout scares. The Japanese did not know of or expect radiation sickness, but Americans were already "familiar with the threat of radiation sickness. Therefore," Michael argued, "it may well be that post-attack emotional disturbances will be expressed in a new form: pseudo-radiation sickness, presenting a serious morale and medical problem which, by the very nature of the situation, will be unprecedented."[69] Michael here was employing the same logic of psychological warfare via radiation which the authors of the Crossroads Reports had speculated on, and was applying it to the American home front with terrifying implications. He and other dissenters exposed the inherent contradictions of civil defense research, which sought to present the coming nuclear bombing scenarios as manageable, but relied on USSBS and other materials that emphasized the success of strategic bombing in destroying the very mental defenses that psychological experts insisted could hold in America. Michael and Chapman reversed the logic of the USSBS "little men" argument in regard to the inadequacy of Japanese civil defense, and insisted that the Japanese, rather than the Americans, were the ones who could withstand bombing.

Even more devastating, Michael and a few other psychiatrists doubted the very basic premise of psychological defense studies. The very idea of studying Hiroshima and Nagasaki and other bombing scenarios in order to learn about American behavior was suspect, "as . . . the environment preceding the atomic bombings of Hiroshima and Nagasaki was so different from what we might expect as to be worthless from our standpoint."[70] Both the situation after nuclear attacks and the US social landscape were just too radically different from Japanese wartime realities. "Therefore," Michael argued, "disturbing as it is, we should recognize that our data are almost useless as a basis for predicting with any assurance whether, in the period immediately preceding the attack, Americans will panic wildly, be reduced to terrified paralysis, or carry out a disciplined evacuation."[71] Roy Grinker went even further. At a 1954 debate he told his colleagues, "Today, we see in psychiatric practice an extension of psychiatric concepts from individuals to groups." But, he continued, when a psychiatrist is asked to make statements about

> groups, group action, group morale, he is pretty well frustrated because he cannot apply, legitimately, what he knows about an individual to group structure and function. Yet, he very frequently utilizes his special brand of knowledge

authoritatively, to interpret what happened post hoc to the group, but often he is incorrect. Unfortunately, he is the one in the community who is asked to make very frequent pronouncements to lay people through lectures and what not.[72]

This was a devastating critique. Yet it remained unanswered. Grinker, Michael, and other dissenters were lone voices. Most psychological experts could not look beyond the limitations of their enterprise, and were eager to jump on the defense research bandwagon.

Irving Janis and the Work of Emotional Inoculation

The work of Irving Janis represented the most sustained and thorough engagement with Hiroshima and Nagasaki research in the United States prior to the work of Robert Jay Lifton. Janis, a Columbia University PhD, was an advisee of USSBS veteran Otto Klineberg. He followed Klineberg to the War Department, where he worked closely with Samuel Stouffer and Carl Hovland in designing surveys and field experiments on determinants of military morale. These studies were eventually published in the aforementioned work *The American Soldier*. After the war, Janis returned to Columbia University, where he completed a dissertation on the cognitive and emotional effects of electroconvulsive treatments of psychotics. In 1947 he was recruited by Yale University in 1947, where he worked mostly on the issue of psychological stress. Parallel to this work, he continued his engagement with military research through consulting with the RAND Corporation and, from 1951 onward, through serving on the National Research Council (NRC) Disaster Research Committee. Janis is mostly known for his antiwar stance and his work on what he termed "groupthink," which examined bias and conformity pressures in the process of decision making in government.[73] His work on bombing and trauma is less known. Nevertheless, among scholars who examined civil defense research, Janis is acknowledged as "one of the chief theoreticians of the system of emotion management developed by the civil defense establishment," and the "author of one of the earliest and most influential psychological studies of strategic bombardment."[74]

Janis's importance to and impact on defense planning is demonstrated by a series of memos written by Carlton Savage, a member of the policy planning staff at the US Department of State, to Paul H. Nitze, then director of planning and the principal author of NSC 68, the foundational 1950 policy paper that outlined US Cold War strategy.[75] Savage called Janis's report "well written," and supplied Nitze with an extremely detailed survey of Janis's 1950 report "Air War and Emotional Stress."[76] He detailed to Nitze the implications of Janis's research to Cold War Strategy, arguing—very much along the lines of the East River and other reports, that "the psychological impact of an atomic bomb upon the American people might prove as shattering as the physical devastation." The main dangers to the home front, according to Savage's reading of Janis's work, was "emotional shock and disorganized behavior." The danger of the A-bomb lay not with radiation but with its greater psychological impact, as "one of the striking differences between conventional bombing and atomic bombing is that the intense heat generated by the explosion of an atomic bomb leaves the victims with a horribly altered physical appearance. This [would] make it difficult for relief workers to do their jobs unless they have had 'emotional inoculation.'"[77]

The idea of emotional inoculation was Janis's main contribution to civil defense and the treatment and prevention of trauma. Just like with physical disease, Janis argued, a low exposure to traumatic sights would numb people enough to be able to withstand trauma. Emotional inoculation, together with proper leadership and education, was for Janis the only means to prevent mass breakdowns. For Savage, such preparatory work was critical, as "in an atomic war, these reactions on a mass scale might become a crucial deterrent to national recovery." To prevent such responses, the US had to be prepared for the coming onslaught on the American psyche. "The impact of this book underlines . . . that unless we remedy our civil defense deficiency of vulnerability to attack, it will deter us from using our atomic weapons except for retaliation if the USSR initiates atomic war," Savage argued.[78] Thus, repeating the "glass jaw" argument, preventing mass psychological reactions through "emotional management" was seen as crucial as other military preparations for US nuclear deterrence.

Janis was located at the heart of discussions on civil defense both at the RAND Corporation and at the NRC. In the early 1950s the NRC set out to institutionalize preparations under the umbrella of the Committee on Disaster Studies. The committee was funded by the Ford Foundation and recruited, besides Janis, many psychological experts. Glen Finch, head of the NRC division of anthropology and psychology, outlined in a letter to the Ford Foundation the major interests of the committee in "the patterns of social interaction and communication before, during, and after the [nuclear] disaster, from the dysfunction of panic to the functional development of 'therapeutic community' through citizen solidarity."[79] Finch's statement demonstrated the importance of behavioral theory with its emphasis on groups and group dynamics for individual mental health, as well as the main issue the committee was interested in: panic. The impact of behavioral theory can be seen in the large number of analogous cases the committee sought to draw on for the purpose of supplementing USSBS research. What Sharon Ghamari-Tabrizi called the "grand analogy" involved "nonchalantly transpos[ing] incommensurable fields and historical experiences into the world of atomic war."[80] The first study released by the Committee on Disaster Studies was "Human Behavior in Extreme Situations." The study examined existing literature on a whole range of issues ranging from atomic and conventional bombardment to combat stress in the Battle of Guadalcanal and the Battle of the Bulge, massacres and pogroms, concentration camps, and prisoner-of-war internment camps, and labor strikes.[81]

Janis, especially in his work on shelters and long-term confinement, was likewise a proponent of the grand analogy. Especially important for our purposes is the early use by Janis and others of Holocaust research in disaster studies. One researcher bluntly summarized the issue at hand: "How could one design a shelter so that people would not kill, cannibalize, violate one another, or commit suicide?"[82] Janis was confident in the defense establishment's ability to rationally and efficiently prepare the population for nuclear war and shelter life. Just as with the issue of emotional shock, Janis proposed that emotional inoculation would be developed as a result of individuals' rehearsal of shelter situations. Training would lead an individual to "vividly to imagine himself as a survivor in the future danger situation."[83] Janis proposed mass experiments in long-term confinement, which, together with the studies of confinement in other contexts from the Holocaust to North Pole research stations, would produce a system of emotional inoculation. He told his colleagues, "I feel it is quite feasible to duplicate most of the essential psychological features of a wartime shelter confinement situation in an experimental [setting]."[84] Dwight Chapman, who attended the shelter meeting, thought the very premises of Janis's system were improbable. Echoing Michael and Grinker, he argued that Americans were incapable of imagining themselves involved in nuclear war or as survivors of war.[85] Robert Jay Lifton and others would go even further and argue that the very exercise of using conventional analogies for understanding unconventional warfare was a contradiction in terms. Yet at the time, the majority of disaster researchers enthusiastically supported such positions.

Janis was also a dissenter of sorts. He was almost alone in the field of disaster studies in arguing against the emphasis on panic. His position on panic was stated most clearly in a lecture he gave to Army cadets in 1954, in which he dismissed the assumption of Wylie, whom he mentioned by name and called "extreme," and others that panic would be the dominant reaction to the A-bomb. After surveying his work at the NRC, Janis declared, "We [at the NRC] soon found that the evidence [of panic theorists] fell far short of minimal scientific standards—to put it mildly. The instances of authenticated mass panic known to have occurred in the last 50 years have been very few in number and have been very restricted in their effect."[86] What concerned Janis was not panic but what he called, betraying the influence of military morale studies, "excessive absenteeism." His "excessive absenteeism" amalgamated a number of phenomena: "1. Traumatic neurosis. 2. Emotional shock. 3. Apathy and hopelessness. 4. Docility and constriction. 5. Apprehensive, self-protective attitudes toward self and family."[87] Like the psychological experts before him, Janis was concerned not with the health impact of bombing, but with the impact of psychological damage on individual contribution to the war effort. He argued, "All five of these [maladies] have this in common: they are psychological reactions which result in a marked reduction in job efficiency and in job output. Each of them can produce actual physical absenteeism— that is, the person is physically capable of doing a job but simply does not show up."[88]

Notably, however, following the conventional understating of trauma in military psychiatry, Janis was excessively optimistic about psychiatrists' ability to handle the psychological problems he outlined. For instance, he defined "traumatic neurosis" as a "set of severe symptoms such as persistent anxiety attacks, sleeplessness, and extreme irritability" which could persist for weeks or even months.[89] But proper treatment—or even better, immediate "psychiatric first aid," he argued—could "speed up" recovery considerably, or even prevent the onset of neurosis altogether.[90] Janis's belief in the ability of psychiatric science to adequately manage and even prevent psychological damage cannot be overestimated. Like Cameron, who called such attitudes defeatist, Janis saw excessive fear of the A-bomb as dangerous and unscientific. He firmly believed that psychological reactions to nuclear weapons would be temporary in nature, and similar to reactions to conventional weapons. He told his listeners, "The acute emotional symptoms among the A-bombed survivors do not differ from those observed among the British, Germans, and Japanese subjected to exceptionally severe air attacks with conventional bombs."[91]

These acute symptoms, in turn, were not chronic. As early as 1949, Janis wrote, taking aim at the twin issues of panic and chronic neurosis, and echoing Edward Glover's arguments from 1940:

> Prior to World War Two government circles in Britain believed that if their cities were ever subjected to heavy air raids a high percentage of the bombed civilian population would breakdown mentally and become chronically psychotic or neurotic. This belief based on predictions made by various specialists proved to be a myth. Already there are some indications that a similar kind of myth is beginning to develop with respect to future A-bomb attacks: the belief that the news of the first A-bomb attacks in this country will produce panic in the residents of un-bombed Metropolitan centers and industrial areas"[92]

Janis argued that traumatic neuroses and related phenomena were a real problem for civilian morale, but that they rarely lasted. There appeared to be a "low frequency" of "psychoses, traumatic neuroses, prolonged depressive states, and other persistent disorders" following bombing. Janis argued, based on the work of British researchers, that "the incidence of bomb neuroses was 'astonishingly small'" following the Blitz.[93] He did not mention Tyhurst or Stengel's work on air phobia and post-trauma. Instead, he turned to German psychiatry, where, he pointed out, based on USSBS work, there was universal agreement that "neither organic neurologic diseases nor psychiatric disorders can be attributed to, nor are they conditioned by, the air attacks."[94] This dismayed American researchers. Janis quoted an anonymous USSBS researcher who commented that "in view of the tremendous exogenous stimuli which offered a fertile ground for the development of psychosomatic complaints, the relative infrequency of the development of these disorders among the population is striking."[95] As we have already seen, other USSBS officers had different views. One explanation for this discrepancy, offered by Ben Shepard, was that civilians were mostly dealt with in hospitals that were "run by tough-minded veterans of the First World War, determined not in any way to encourage neurosis." This was in stark opposition to the much more open-minded approach of military psychiatrists, many of whom "were younger, quasi-Freudian analysts from the Tavistock" and similar progressive clinics.[96]

The difference between American expectations of widespread mental issues and what European medical establishments claimed was the absence of them on the ground was a topic of some discussion in US military psychiatry circles.[97] The émigré psychiatrist Lothar Kalinowsky, who served with the US Army, toured Germany before the Nuremberg trials in connection with the trials of German psychiatrists who had taken part in the T4 euthanasia program.[98] Kalinowsky was interested in the discrepancy between the exceptionally high number of mental casualties in the US Army and the very low number of such casualties in Europe, where "shell shock cases were rare among soldiers . . . [and] even the heaviest air raids seem to affect the mental health the civilian population in a very negligible way."[99] This was also a very different picture from World War I, in which shell shock cases had been common. Kalinowsky concluded that this resulted from a number of factors but, first and foremost, from a different attitude to the management of trauma. As examined in detail in chapter 6, the main cause for posttraumatic reactions, according to continental psychiatry, was not to be found in the experience of war. As Kalinowsky succinctly put it, "After many scientific discussions during and after the First World War, German psychiatry accepted the view that war and other traumatic neuroses are not caused by the war experiences as such but by secondary psychological mechanisms, [like] the negative wish to escape from danger and, eventually, to receive financial compensation."[100] In the case of civilian populations, Kalinowsky speculated that the strength of the herd instinct among people from the same locality gathered together in communal shelters, and the fact that breakdown did not provide an escape from danger or a claim for compensation, must have prevented mass neurosis.[101]

Like Janis and his German colleagues, Kalinowsky argued that the war showed that humans were extremely resilient to mental damage. Based on extensive correspondence with his colleagues, he claimed that "psychiatrists in many countries who studied this question reported the astounding fact that there seems to be hardly any limit to men's ability to stand terrifying experiences."[102] Kalinowsky, alone among all the psychological experts examined in this chapter, reached out to a Japanese colleague, Hosokoshi Masaichi, who verified to him that in "Japan, where Neurotic reactions among soldiers were also rare, psychiatric manifestation had even less importance among civilians in the atomic bomb raids on Hiroshima and Nagasaki."[103] Hosokoshi, a military psychiatrist who had written his dissertation on "war hysteria" (*sensō hisuterī*), was notoriously hostile to the notion of trauma, and described military psychiatry wards as "hotbeds of hysteria."[104] His attitude was typical, and it reflected the Japanese connection to German psychiatry and its wartime hostility to psychiatric casualties in the Imperial Army. Thus, Janis drew on this consensus among British, German, and Japanese psychiatrists in regard to the rarity of long-term trauma, to argue for the civilian population's capacity to adjust to war conditions and prevent the onset of severe psychological reactions.

Janis did not deny the existence of long-term damage. But given the international consensus in the field and the way such conclusions fitted with his greater argument, it is not surprising that he also attributed the persistence of psychological damage to preexisting conditions. Surveying the available research, he concluded that "emotional shocks . . . tend to subside spontaneously," and that "chronic traumatic reactions to air raids tend to occur predominantly among persons with pre-existing psychoneurotic tendencies."[105] Thus, "the difference between a predisposed personality and a normal one lies solely in the failure of recuperation."[106] This was true for both nuclear and nonnuclear scenarios. Although the "exceptionally intense stress of an atomic disaster" was likely to produce "insidious, delayed effects" and "unusually persistent anxiety reactions, prolonged apathy, or other sustained symptoms," Janis again found that "none of the effects appears to differ from those which have been noted among the English, German, and Japanese people who were exposed to 'conventional' air attacks."[107] Thus, even though he broke with earlier research on the issue of panic, Janis, like the USSBS and other military planners, saw the A-bomb as just a bigger bomb. The A-bomb could produce more damage, but it was not fundamentally a new phenomenon. Janis did speculate that radiation could be a factor in prolonging damage, as it "may have played some role in reviving and strengthening disturbing memories of the disaster"; but he did not dwell on the topic.[108]

One obvious problem in Janis's conclusions, as in practically all US work at the time, is the very limited source base he used. Janis relied solely on the USSBS material, with occasional references to the testimonies brought by John Hersey in his Hiroshima book, and Takashi Nagai's 1949 work *The Bells of Nagasaki*. Janis did not read Japanese reports (or German reports, for that matter). He did not interview a single *hibakusha*, nor did he reach out to colleagues in Japan or at the ABCC. Furthermore, he displayed at times a rather dismissive attitude to Nagai and other Japanese sources. In a section on survivor guilt, Janis quotes Nagai, who wrote, "We carry deep in our hearts, every one of us, stubborn, unhealing wounds. When we are alone, we brood upon them, and when we see our neighbors, we are again reminded of them; theirs as well as ours." Yet Janis attributed this notion to Nagai's particular predicament. Nagai suffered from radiation sickness and was confined to his home. Janis argued that Nagai's observations therefore were quite limited, and that "survivor guilt" was not "an inevitable consequence of atomic bombing." He argued that Nagai's experience could not be generalized, as "although there are independent observations which indicate that some survivors experienced temporary guilt reactions following the A-bombings, there is no satisfactory evidence to support the claim that such reactions persisted in large numbers of survivors."[109] He based his conclusion on the USSBS research, where "in the entire sample.... of morale interviews there were found only a few cases who made comments suggesting that they had experienced feelings of guilt, sadness, hopelessness, or apathy during the postdisaster period."[110] The USSBS had interviewed only a couple of hundred survivors, almost all before the end of 1945. Thus, it is hard to see how Janis could use their research to dispute Nagai's observations.

The lack of long-term impact and large-scale panic, however, did not mean that the bomb produce no impact at all. Quite the contrary, Janis argued for the existence of extensive short- and medium-term psychological damage in Hiroshima and Nagasaki. Trauma, rather than panic, was for him the main threat of nuclear attack. Mental damage was produced by the "double emotional shock" of being hit by the bomb and seeing "large numbers of burned, cut, and maimed bodies, [which] was a major source of emotional trauma."[111] Janis spent some time examining the experience of "near-miss" reactions among "people who undergo direct exposure to actual danger. This may involve a narrow escape from death, being wounded, witnessing the destruction of persons close by, or suffering the loss of a loved one."[112] Here, the "traumatizing experience of violent physical concussion" and "violent kinesthetic and disequilibrium sensations ... probably played a primary role" in touching off "a complex pattern of unusual and intense stimuli."[113] Like German researchers, Janis emphasized the likely physical causes of emotional trauma; but he placed them in a relationship with emotional stimuli. He relied heavily on combat psychiatry in reaching this conclusion. He cited Abraham Kardiner, who already in 1940 had argued for trauma having both biological and mental origins, and other military psychiatrists, if somewhat selectively. Janis used combat psychiatry research to argue that the situation in Hiroshima was not unusual in producing a "sizable incidence of acute reactions with transient symptoms that could be characterized as a 'temporary traumatic neurosis.'"[114] Continuing his line of argument from his work in the *American Soldier*, he argued that this was normal behavior that could "be regarded as an extreme form of emotional reaction to objective conditions of danger."[115]

Janis shared with combat psychiatrists, though not with Kardiner, a basic optimism in regard to the ability of training and preparation to minimize fear reactions and mental damage, as "to the extent that the public is informed about ways and means of coping with the dangers and trained to participate in civil defense, disruptive fear reactions will be minimized."[116] He spent much time on adaptation mechanisms and other factors that could produce emotional inoculation to bombing damage. He examined group loyalty, leadership, and similar factors, but also superstitions, magical beliefs, and rituals, all of which proved helpful in reducing fear reactions in combat troops. But training and infrastructure were the most crucial elements in preventing future damage. Janis wanted civil defense workers to watch "realistic sound films (preferably in color) showing actual disaster scenes." Another method of "emotional inoculation" that would "enable trainees to become emotionally adapted to the sight of the dead and injured are tours of the local morgue, courses in human anatomy, and disaster exhibits using a World's Fair type of presentation, e.g., blown-up photographs of damage, full-scale models of destroyed communities, and lifelike plaster dummies to demonstrate each type of casualty."[117] In addition, Janis wanted more psychiatrists employed in civil defense. He bemoaned the lack of trained psychological experts to operate the rest camps and first aid stations he wanted to see installed, and thus "proposed . . . to offer special inducements to attract more women into psychiatry."[118] Unlike Cameron and others, Janis, following the bombing survey's lead, did not see Japanese culture as a factor. He treated Japanese accounts mostly the same as he did British and German ones.

In this and many other aspects, Janis continued much of the work done at the USSBS. He argued for the demystification and conventionalization of A-bomb damage. He overlooked or minimized radiation responses and dismissed long-term damage, while at the same time arguing for the existence of widespread short-term damage and traumatic reactions induced by the bombing of civilians. His emphasis was on the temporary nature of the symptoms, which could be relieved with proper and immediate psychiatric attention; a sort of psychiatric triage that would be set up close to stricken cities.[119] Of course, while the USSBS and air-war theorists developed their thinking in the context of deploying strategic bombing against enemy civilians, Janis approached the problem from a different angle: how to protect American civilians from such damage. Hence his emphasis on "emotional inoculation" and induced numbness that would enable Americans to deal with the coming nuclear attacks. Janis broke with the

USSBS and much of the disaster studies field on the subject of panic. He saw mass psychological casualties as being much more of a danger than widespread panic. He did not think nuclear weapons could "break nations," but focused on individuals. As we saw with Savage's memos, however, the defense establishment mostly ignored such nuances, and used Janis to support large-scale civil defense research, deploying his meticulous suggestions for inculcating first responders in the emotional management of the American people as a whole. Most importantly in our context, Janis's work, and the work of other disaster researchers, with its wide-raging analogies and its attention to individual trauma, prepared the ground for later research, which would be done, this time, not within the academic-defense establishment but consciously in opposition to it.

Conclusion: The Desert Rock Exercises and the Praxis of Nuclear Trauma

Research on Hiroshima and Nagasaki survivors' psychological reactions was almost exclusively done in the US as a part of defense-related work. This research was an overlooked yet important part of the history of trauma and the history of civil defense. It was part of a transnational, if limited, effort to examine the impact of bombing on civilians, which connected with work on combat veterans and military psychiatry, and reflected consensus among German, American, and Japanese psychiatrists as to the absence of long-term, clinical, and significant damage as a result of urban bombing. Ironically, researchers tended to minimize the effects of the bomb while at the same time insisting on the need for more psychiatrists to deal with these same effects. In a further irony, much of this defense research was often done by the same people who sought to deploy psychological science in order to prevent war. As Robert Jacobs noted, "paradoxically and typically," that Janis's work advocating for more planning and preparation for nuclear war, as well as much of the work cited above, "was reprinted in the *Bulletin of Atomic Scientists*—the primary vehicle of scientists working against any planning for nuclear war."[120] It is hard to overestimate the significance of early Cold War psychological work. Millions of children went through the unnerving experience of practicing "duck and cover" exercises and being exposed to endless talk of nuclear war. As Joseph Masco has shown, the civil defense project amounted to a new social contract between citizen and state based on defense from nuclear disaster, where the primary obligation of the citizens was to be ever-prepared for their own annihilation, and where "it has become a civic obligation to collectively imagine, and at times theatrically enact through 'civil defense,' the physical destruction of the nation-state."[121] This had wide-ranging consequences that are still felt today in our relationship to the threat of terrorism, the culture of prepping for disaster, and the militarization of American society. (One can, for instance, draw a direct link between "duck and cover" and "active shooter" exercises in schools.)

More immediately, drawing on the work of Janis and others, the US military intentionally exposed tens of thousands of soldiers to radiation in nuclear tests that were, among other aims, supposed to "mentally condition" soldiers for nuclear war.[122] In a 1948 speech, Colonel James P. Coney, chief of the radiological branch division of military application at the AEC, complained, "I have observed the reactions of the military [personnel], who were not acquainted with the technical details on two missions, Bikini and Eniwetok, and the few reactions of the uninitiated is [sic] appalling. . . . It could well interfere with an important military mission in time of war."[123] Coney argued that "psychological training for the military level of acceptable radiation hazard is possible and should be prosecuted."[124] The Joint Panel on Medical Aspects of Atomic Warfare followed through on these recommendations, and advised the military to "continue studies in psychology of panic; seek technics [sic] for reducing apprehension and for producing psychologic resistance to fear and panic, especially in presence of radiation hazard (emotional vaccination) . . . and prepare to make psychologic observations at and after bomb tests."[125] Thus, Janis's "emotional inoculation"—or, to use the Department of Defense language, "emotional vaccination"—contributed to the largest human subject experiments in history.

In what became known as the "Desert Rock" exercises, the US Army and Marines sent thousands of ground troops to atomic test sites in Nevada, where they were examined by psychological and medical teams. Psychologists from George Washington University in Washington, DC, established the Human Resources Research Office (HumRRO), which focused on gauging the effectiveness of the education and indoctrination programs presented to troops who took part in atomic tests. Human-behavior specialists from the Johns Hopkins University Operations Research Office (ORO) set out to measure troops' levels of fear and anxiety during the actual weapons tests.[126] Though fascinating, as they did not engage with Hiroshima, such reports lay outside the scope of this book. For our purposes it is sufficient to note that, as in the work on bombing, military thinkers saw no difference between nuclear and other battlefields. "The same over-all mission of the rifle squad on the atomic battlefield remains much the same as in the past," wrote Colonel George W. Dickerson, "with few modifications to keep step with the faster tempo imposed by swifter means of transportation and greater destructive force."[127] Army psychiatrists like Albert Glass relied heavily on Janis in arguing for the basic similarity of nuclear and conventional combat. Glass went further than Janis in arguing that "psychoses and neuroses are not caused by an external trauma, as shown by the lack of any appreciable number of cases attributable to massive aerial bombardment, intense combat, civil disaster, or to the atomic destruction of Hiroshima and Nagasaki."[128] Glass's work is evident in training films for management of atomic psychological casualties, which minimized radiation (soldiers were told some of their peers could "believe they have radiation or heart disease," and that it was just an expression of anxiety) and sought to show future psychological damage as manageable and treatable.[129] The result of such attitudes in Nevada was the exposure of thousands of American soldiers to radiation, and lifelong struggles with the medical and psychological impact of those experiences.[130]

Glass, Janis, and others relied heavily on USSBS research. This body of evidence was extremely small. None of the researchers quoted above had been in Hiroshima, spoke Japanese, or even met a survivor. Yet beyond the United States, their research had a profound effect on the fate of research done in Hiroshima. The denial of long-term effects and the tendency to minimize the A-bomb's damage disincentivized further investigations and concentrated what little research there was only on the short-term impact of the A-bomb. American researchers, unlike some German ones, were not outright hostile to bombing victims; the victims just did not enter into their calculations. The "grand analogies" that Janis and other researchers used were projected into a possible postnuclear future, and had only limited use for the present and very real suffering of *hibakusha*. The impact of the A-bomb on the difficulties experienced by survivors, many of whom lived in the US and even worked with civil defense, was ignored. Yet in important ways—as in the politicization of the professions examined earlier—civil defense research, especially its emphasis on connecting and learning from extreme situations such as the Holocaust and combat reactions, prepared the ground for the next generation of researchers.

PART 2

Researching Minds, Healing Minds

CHAPTER FIVE

Y. Scott Matsumoto, the ABCC, and A-Bomb Social Work

"I am willing to believe that Dr. Shimizu's erroneous inferences stem from his justified hatred of the Bomb that took his son, and from sentimentality toward the survivors. But . . . he is obviously *unable to tolerate our objectivity* and will make a career out of being sentimentalist about the survivors." — Gilbert W. Beebe, 1959[1]

In 1953, In the midst of the Desert Rock nuclear tests, US Army Resources Research Office (HumRRO) psychologists distributed a list of questions to the soldiers preparing to experience a live nuclear explosion. The questionnaire sought to gauge the GIs' knowledge of the effect of the A-bomb, and their levels of premaneuver anxiety. The soldiers were asked whether it was true or false that "children born in Japan now are deformed because of the 1945 A-bombs," if "sexual potency is reduced by a bomb explosion four miles away," whether "it is safe to walk through Ground Zero immediately after an A- bomb air burst"; if "man became permanently sterile" by exposure to radiation, and if "radiation . . . from an A-bomb explosion can make men unable to have intercourse."[2] According to the answer sheet, based on research done in Japan, the correct answer to all the questions was "false."[3] The sexual nature of many of these questions spoke volumes on the psychological attitudes and assumptions of the HumRRO researchers as much as on those of the soldiers. Psychological experts saw fear of the bomb as an atavistic force which connected to the libido and other irrational forces in the depth of the human mind. Information and research from Japan played an important role in demystifying nuclear weapons and their psychological effects, and helping Americans adjust to the new "nuclear normal." This effort had already started with the USSBS and continued well beyond the 1940s.

The drive for rational management of the atomic threat and its psychological implications, this chapter argues, underlined much of the American research of A-bomb survivors in Japan and was the most significant factor in the American denial of long-term mental damage in the stricken cities. As will become clear in the following chapters, the ABCC's inability and unwillingness to tackle mental damage had, in turn, a significant impact on Japanese research.

The ABCC was established in 1946 to research the long-term medical and biological impact of the bombing of Hiroshima and Nagasaki, and played an outsized role in those efforts. Situated in the bombed cities as a permanent research facility, its goals were more than purely scientific. The ABCC played an important diplomatic, ideological, and arguably psychological role in the United States and Japan, soothing and explaining away fears of radiation, sterility, and deformed babies. Americans hailed it as a beacon of international cooperation, a place of science and objectivity, a unique place with world-historical significance, and even a sign of American benevolence toward the Japanese. The uniqueness and status of the *hibakusha* played an important role in this world view. This did not necessitate any special care on the part of the ABCC in their relationship with the survivors. Quite the contrary; this special status led American doctors in Hiroshima to see researching the *hibakusha* as their right and duty. As Susan Lindee has argued, the survivors' "unique historical place as the first victims of atomic weaponry" was what drove the ABCC's infamous no-treatment policy, under which it conducted research but supplied no medical treatment to survivors.[4] American scientists' sense of entitlement also led to the abuse and violation of survivors' bodies, as this chapter demonstrates. The ABCC's sense of mission also underlined a single-minded drive toward what ABCC scientists saw as objective and rational research. The ABCC was born in the mid- to late 1940s out of the same intellectual community and zeitgeist that had seen USSBS send researchers into the rubble of Hiroshima asking survivors about their feelings, and the US Army to order thousands of GIs to march into mushroom clouds. The bomb, the argument went, could be managed. It could be explained, and its impact conquered, through reason and science. This particular brand of mid-century technocratic rationalism saw criticism of its goals and methods as emotional and irrational. Science — cool, rational, and deliberative — would guide civil defense at home, and research in Hiroshima.

It was within this context that research into the mental impact of atomic weapons, or rather the lack of such research, should be thought of. This chapter, indeed, deals with the lack of research and what was *not done* at the ABCC as much as what was done to tackle the mental anguish caused by the A-bomb. I argue that denial of suffering, and the various strategies deployed by the ABCC that resulted in such denial, did not mean a simple cover-up. The reasons for dismissal and lack of attention to long-term mental damage were multiple. The drive toward rational management of the bomb's effects was paramount, but other factors included the ABCC's diplomatic and psychological role vis-à-vis both the Japanese and American publics, as well as the ABCC focus on somatic issues—a result of Washington's priorities and the fact that most of the leadership came from biology and medicine. Personal circumstances and intellectual backgrounds also played an important role in the turn away from psychological research. The ABCC leadership was aware of the need to tackle the psychological and social impact of the A-bomb. The leaders contemplated hiring a psychiatrist, and even created a department, Medical Sociology, where such research was undertaken, if in a limited and sporadic way. But research on psychology was secondary to the department's main task, which was to maintain ties with the survivor community and facilitate cooperation with the ABCC.

The medical sociologist Y. Scott Matsumoto, who created the department and is the main figure in this chapter, played an important if contradictory role at the heart of the ABCC's struggles with the psychological fallout from the bomb. Anxiety, hostility, and other psychological issues impacted *hibakusha* cooperation, which Matsumoto was made responsible for. Like the problem of morale, survivors' attitudes and willingness to cooperate were ambiguous goals; they were hard to quantify and gauge, but that nonetheless guided psychological research. Significantly, the work was entrusted mostly to Japanese women, who took on the thankless task of dealing with the day-to-day consequences of lives and minds shattered by the bomb and its aftereffects. A second goal of the department, public relations, also shaped attitudes toward survivors. Furthermore, Matsumoto's unique status as one of the few Japanese American professionals at the ABCC with a leadership role, as well as his personal journey and history, also impacted his research. Matsumoto's life and intellectual pursuits brought him into contact with all the main figures and fields examined in this book. He had been a student of Alexander Leighton in the camps, and had gone with him to Washington, and then with the USSBS to Tokyo and Hiroshima. He met Lifton a number of times, both in Hiroshima and in later civil defense meetings. He was a friend of Konuma Masuho, and worked with Kubo Yoshitoshi in Hiroshima and Tokyo. Indeed, Matsumoto stood at the heart of the Japanese and American effort to tackle the long-term mental impact of the A-bomb.

The chapter starts with a survey of the ABCC's early forays into the psychological impact of the A-bomb, its propaganda role, and its early dismissal of psychiatry. It then takes on Matsumoto's personal history at the internment camps, in the rubble of Hiroshima, and through his journey and life in Hiroshima. We conclude by looking at the department's social work and the work of medical social worker (MSW) Kodama Aki and other women who went into the community in the service of the ABCC to help *hibakusha*, but also to facilitate the ABCC's goals and public image.

ABCC and A-Bomb Psychology

The ABCC was established as a permanent research facility in Japan following a directive by President Truman in December 1946. The directive was the result of a letter by Shields Warren, a Harvard-trained pathologist and radiation expert. Using what was one of the main tropes of debate around the ABCC, Warren told Truman that the *hibakusha* offered a "unique opportunity for the study of the medical and biological effects of radiation which is of utmost importance to the United States."[5] As Susan Lindee has argued, the AEC set up the ABCC initially because it wanted to establish safety standards for exposure for workers in nuclear plants, and allay public fears of radiation.[6] Supporters of the commission specifically mentioned the importance of the research for "future wars" and civil defense planning.[7] Thus, from the start the ABCC was concerned not with the survivors themselves, but with instrumentalizing and learning from their damaged bodies. The research had a rocky start. Funding was not assured for a time, and the relationship with the AEC and other agencies was stormy at times. In Hiroshima, the committee had trouble acquiring a suitable location, settling eventually for a location on top of a hill overlooking the city called Hijiyama, which was the site of a Japanese military cemetery. The removal of the cemetery for the purpose of building the ABCC's research facility was controversial, and it added to the local residents' general suspicion of the Americans' motives. The researchers' expectations for cooperation from the Japanese, both survivors and scientists, were high. But as early as 1946, some on the committee were worried that "recovered persons will probably prefer to forget their tragic experience rather than submit themselves for examination."[8] Such worries continued to haunt the committee's work.

The 1946 Truman letter was the culmination of almost a year of work by teams in both Japan and the United States. Following the USSBS's initial investigations, three separate military teams surveyed the bombed cities. Efforts to centralize and manage information from Japan culminated in November 1946 when Austin M. Brues and Paul S. Henshaw visited the country to prepare for the setting up of the committee. They were joined in Japan by representatives of the different military teams. In its report, which was republished in the *Bulletin of the Atomic Scientists* in 1947, the team surveyed the state of research and conditions in Japan.[9] Their comments, both public and private, were telling. In many ways these early reports and activities, with their focus on public relations and diplomacy, established much of the organization's "DNA." The reports displayed a mixture of misunderstandings, exoticism, hubris, and condescending attitudes toward the Japanese that characterized much of the occupation era, but they also contained much praise for Japanese efforts. Brues and Henshaw found that the Japanese had already set up a significant research apparatus, with 119 papers already written on the topic, and noted that "practically all the approaches considered by the commission had also been visualized by the Japanese."[10] They found the Japanese work "somewhat lacking in critical analysis according to the best scientific methods, [but] they nevertheless represent work carried out under the most difficult circumstances and covering a set of conditions which cannot be reproduced."[11] They believed critical thinking was lacking because "most of the Japanese scientists, through their contacts with Teutonic science of a few decades ago, have been less exposed to the attitude of free criticism and more inclined to academic authoritarianism than Americans."[12] But the problem went well beyond German influence. The report went into much detail into the problem of authoritarianism, which permeated Japanese culture. It digressed from discussion of nuclear medicine and went into great sociological and anthropological detail on Japanese conditions. Echoing the anthropological discussions in the camps, the report declared "the Japanese" to be "stolid people." It surveyed family systems and values, emphasizing that "every Japanese must have a master," and even went into child rearing, commenting that "Japanese babies never cry."[13]

Science in general and the ABCC in particular played an important role in the effort to "democratize the enemy."[14] Brues and Henshaw correctly predicted a shift from German to American influence and models in Japan. Japanese scientists were eager to work with the Americans, and "everywhere there is a sincere hope and effort to learn our manner of thinking."[15] Henshaw saw this development as a "remarkable opportunity for cultivating international relations of the highest type."[16] The ABCC would be a place of cooperation, "a place where the war could be forgotten, and science existed as a language and culture all on its own."[17] This was important, the report argued, as "Japan at this moment is extremely plastic and has great respect for the occupation. If we continue to handle Japan intelligently during the next few years while the new policios [sic] are being established, she will be our friend and ally for many years to come; if we handle her unwisely, she will drift to other ideologies. The ABCC or its successor may be able to play a role in this."[18] It was up to scientists to take up the mantle of leadership in shaping Japan, as "American science must of necessity accept a large measure of the responsibility for this development."[19] This sense of mission and American responsibility (and superiority) continued to shape the public message of the committee. A 1952 summary of the ABCC's activities during the occupation closed by emphasizing that "a tribute of American sympathy for human suffering that one of the earliest activities of the occupation forces in Japan was the careful study of the survivors of the Hiroshima & Nagasaki bombing and the instruction by American physicians of their Japanese colleagues in all the advances in medicine. . . . Thus, many of the injured that survived would otherwise have died."[20]

The ABCC was supposed to impress not only Japanese but, first and foremost, Americans. One of the committee's roles in the United States was public relations. The first (and arguably last) major effort in tackling the psychological impact of the A-bomb was a part of this effort: the conference titled "Psychological Aspects of Radiation Hazards," convened in Washington on 22 January 1948. The conference dealt very little with the problem of emotional shock and the A-bomb's impact on *hibakusha*; its primary purpose was public relations. And the psychological hazards it was concerned with were not those of the *hibakusha*, but the American public's willingness to support an atomic energy and weapons program, and to help civil defense planning.

The conference had its origins in discussions held at the NRC following the 1946 Bikini tests. Fredrick R. Hanson, the military psychiatrist who coined the term "combat fatigue," was the one who initiated these discussions.[21] Hanson wrote to Edward A. Strecker, a neuropsychiatrist with the NRC's medical division, asking that the NRC committee on neuropsychiatry take on "the problem of the Psychological Aspects of Atomic and other newer forms of warfare." Hanson was concerned about the lack of psychiatrists in the NRC's nascent efforts, then led by Vannevar Bush, to evaluate the medical impact of the A-bomb, and he argued that "it would be a mistake to let this problem be dealt with primarily by the psychologists."[22] Hanson's letter led to a flurry of correspondence within the NRC. In September, John C. Rensmeir, a Medical Division executive, wrote to Strecker saying that the matter should be taken up by the "Council's new Committee on Atomic Casualties, which ... had discussed it in preliminary fashion at an early meeting and recognizes the seriousness of the problem, as well as the need for constructive action."[23] Momentum was building toward entrusting the ABCC with the problem. Throughout these conversations, however, Hansen's initial concerns with individual psychic trauma were transformed, like so many contemporary debates, into discussions on possible "widespread panic reaction which might have both disruptive and paralyzing effect upon the national resistance in event of atomic attack."[24]

Significantly, the USSBS veteran Rensis Likert became involved in the effort. Likert, who was then at the University of Michigan, was invited to participate by Charles Dollard, vice president of the Carnegie Foundation. In a letter to Lewis Weed, chairman of the Medical Division, Dollard presented Likert as someone who "had large share in the work of the recent study of Public Reactions to the Bikini experiment financed by the corporation and the Rockefeller Foundation."[25] Stafford Warren, another Crossroads and Manhattan Project veteran, also got on board and was supposed to chair the conference. Thomas Rivers, chairman of the Committee on Atomic Casualties (the NRC-NAS body that supervised the ABCC's work), was weary of Warren's "tendency to panic the public rather than bring calm to it." He told Weed, "If there is one thing we don't want, it is panic."[26] Again, panic and its implications for civil defense were what was at stake. In a letter to Carroll L. Wilson, the general manager of the AEC, Weed warned, "There is danger that . . . civil defense planning would be seriously handicapped by the present state of public knowledge. The fear stimulus in atomic energy stems . . . from the radiological effects and panic is almost an inevitable reaction to be expected from a condition of public misunderstanding and absence of factual information."[27]

When the conference was convened in January 1948, it was attended by high-level military and civilian doctors and officials. Its goal was to plan for a "program worldwide in scope that [is] aimed at increasing factual information of the public in order to provide a basis for reasonable, logical thought in this matter."[28] Much of the worry about radiation anxiety came from the military's experience at Crossroads. Rear Admiral William S. Parsons. another Manhattan Project veteran, reported on the problem of radiation anxiety at Bikini. "In dealing with atomic bombs, [the military] had to avoid psychological difficulties in personnel," Parsons reported. "To this end they developed a 'nuts and bolts' attitude. . . . [An] educational program was aimed at developing in the men a 'healthy familiarity.' To accomplish this, it was necessary to develop a combination of phlegmatism, alertness, and intelligence as opposed to tension."[29] Parsons's "healthy familiarity" was, of course, what had led to Desert Rock and similar experiences that had left subject populations, GIs, and downwinders with poisoned bodies and minds.

The World War II experience and the USSBS were prominently mentioned at the gathering. Likert, for instance, after talking about Bikini, referred to the work of the USSBS as a "useful source of information pertaining to the problem at hand," as well as reports he had prepared for the SSRC and similar bodies on Crossroads. Another USSBS veteran, Gordon Allport, spoke on the "problem of morale," which, "if an atomic war should come . . . would be overwhelming." Other participants referred to World War II bombing experience and the need to build a system based on the civil defense model of the British. What was almost completely absent from the conference was any discussion of Hiroshima and Nagasaki. The only sustained comments on Japan were in a survey from Brues, who summarized the bomb's impact based on his above-mentioned 1946 trip to Japan. When it came to mental issues, Brues told the committee, referring dismissively, to rumors about radiation sickness in the stricken cities, that "the population appeared to unduly believe anything they heard."[30] As for more immediate psychiatric issues as noted above, Brues concluded, "This is difficult to evaluate because of the differences between the Japanese pattern and our own."[31] Such dismissal, and use of cultural justifications, were the first of what would be repeated attempts by the ABCC leadership to avoid the problem.

The conference results were widely disseminated, and they attracted much interest from other agencies, the State Department, and the military. Though no follow-up research was suggested, and though the ABCC did not take on psychological research, the conference created a blueprint for the use of the ABCC and radiation research in public relations. These attitudes reflected the role of psychological sciences in early Cold War

America. However, there was another, more pressing reason for the move to public relations. The committee was under constant threat of being shut down by Washington. Thus, it had to make itself useful for the AEC and its agenda of promoting the atom. At one point in 1951, at the height of the Korea War, the AEC did not allocate any budget to the ABCC, and thus essentially terminated it. Some felt that the money on long-term research should go elsewhere. As one detractor argued, "With the likelihood that atomic bombing of the United States may occur in the near future, thought may be given to the abandonment of the present project and the preparation of plans for study of populations elsewhere."[32] The AEC's decision, however, caused an outcry. Wadsworth Likely, the reporter who broke the story, wrote that the AEC was "killing the only research program able to tell Americans what the long-range effects of an A-bomb attack would be on physical and mental health."[33]

The ABCC was saved in 1951. Long-term effects on mental health, however, were not on its research agenda. Despite the early efforts, the committee continued to neglect the issue. This led to much criticism, which ABCC leadership met with deflection. In a 1952 report to Washington, Grant Taylor, then head of the ABCC, told his superiors, "With regard to the need for [a] psychiatrist for a short period with the ABCC, we have been repeatedly criticized for our limited approach to the problem of survivors of the atomic bomb. We have examined the body and neglected the mind. This criticism has come from numerous consultants who have come to the theater and from sociologists, cultural anthropologists, etc." Taylor mentioned University of Michigan anthropologist Robert Hall, who had set up a center in Okayama, as possible consultant who might be able to survey the issue. Another person that he considered was Roy M. Docus, whom he knew from university, and who, he emphasized, was "able to get along as a psychologist with M.D.s even in Los Angeles."[34] Aside from his humorous, if important, mention of hostility to psychologists, Taylor did acknowledge the need to address the problem. Nevertheless, he was not interested in genuinely researching it. "It is the view of many, which I share, that the *problem of psychic trauma* should be surveyed by a competent authority and a statement written," he wrote. "I am confident such a survey would *absolve the ABCC of this responsibility and nullify the critics*" (my emphasis).[35] Taylor saw the issue through a political rather than a research lens, showing yet again how politics intruded into medicine in trauma research. Even more important was his mentioning of the "problem of psychic trauma" specifically as a medical issue that the ABCC was aware of. This did not mean that he or others understood it in the same way as we do today. But, unlike most survivors and Japanese researchers, who have not used the term till decades later, the term was available as an interpretative category for Taylor and his peers.

Robert Livingstone, in his reply, further minimized the issue, suggesting that getting a biophysicist was more important than a psychiatrist, and that "Dr. Folley or you could write a statement which would cover the responsibility of the ABCC for an investigation in the field of psychiatry. It is clear that whatever problems existed in 1945, it could not very well now be isolated from many other important events of that era."[36] Livingstone's reference to the difficulties of causation to dismiss psychic trauma and his reference to the messiness of evidence would be important tools in the arsenal of denialists. As will be examined below, both in nuclear and Holocaust trauma history, those who denied recognition, such as German doctors, saw themselves as objective and scientific, while they perceived their opponents as too emotional and subjective. In a later communication with James Neel, Taylor retreated from his earlier suggestion and wrote that although he "emphasize[d] the need for a psychiatrist to make a statement of the responsibility for making a psychiatric survey, this need should be balanced against our need for a biophysicist—the latter is acute, and the former might well be met by a U.S. Army psychiatric consultant." Taylor also pointed out that Hall would, in any case, not be a suitable candidate: "It would be ill advised to approach Dr. Hall. He has been very critical of our program for the very reason we would be asking his advice." Taylor concluded, again recognizing the problem, and clarifying the political nature of his inquiry: "It is well known that problem does exist, as it does in the wake of any catastrophe. Our request actually stemmed from a desire to relieve the Council and the ABCC of the responsibility of conducting such a survey."[37] Thus, though the ABCC and leading individuals within the NRC were aware of the problem of psychic damage from at least 1946 and the Hanson memo, they did not see it as a central problem they should tackle.

Taylor did emphasize that "it is our feeling that such a statement should come from someone qualified in the psycho-sociologic world."[38] But took no steps to achieve that goal; neither he nor Jarrett Folley ever issued a statement. The ABCC saw the psychological hazards of the A-bomb primarily as social and diplomatic in nature, and the problem was sidelined in the first decade after the war. When the ABCC eventually did take it on, it focused on issues of panic and civil defense, thereby following the lead of the larger intellectual American ecosystem. Cultural biases, scientific hubris, and the politics of medicine and "objectivity" further led to exclusion of the issue. By the mid-1950s, however, with the occupation over and survivors' cooperation in decline, the ABCC faced a need to tackle the social and psychological aspects of the A-bomb. They turned to a young Japanese American sociologist, Scott Matsumoto, to take it on.

Scott Matsumoto, Medical Sociology, and the Nisei Dilemma

In 1949 the ABCC hired Scott Matsumoto, a Nisei sociologist from Fresno, California, and an USSBS and BSR veteran, to tackle the problem of *hibakusha* cooperation. Reflecting its faith in Matsumoto's abilities, and the growing significance of the problem, the committee entrusted him with patient contacting, which was elevated to a fully-fledged Medical Sociology Department in the late 1950s. This was not an obvious choice. Although many Nisei were employed as linguists and in other low-level jobs, only a handful became part of the ABCC leadership.[39] In many ways, Matsumoto shared much of the ABCC's world view, though his was a much more nuanced and even tortured path toward such a view. Like that of his early mentor, Alexander Leighton, Matsumoto's research was shaped by the confluence of problems of race, science, and war. The sociology he had learned from Leighton greatly impacted his views. As Henry Yu noted, "the sociological perspective" that Matsumoto and his peers had first encountered in the BSR, and in Chicago together with other Asian American intellectuals, "gave them the freedom to distance themselves from the pain, anger, and emotion wrought by discrimination against Orientals."[40] However, it was this exact detachment that made Matsumoto suspicious of trauma. Furthermore, like so many Asian American intellectuals, he was operating on "a stage already set" by white American scientists, and he faced multiple "constraints that limited the possibilities for Asian-American intellectuals in the twentieth century."[41] As Eiichiro Azuma has argued for other Nisei in occupied Japan, the unique position and relative freedom Matsumoto and other Nisei enjoyed "came with white supervision," which was a further impetus for Matsumoto to steer away from controversy and toe the ABCC "party line" on psychological trauma.[42]

Matsumoto had become acutely aware of the problem of race during his internment at Poston. Expulsion to the camps badly shook Matsumoto's world. Writing in 1943, he emphasized his feeling of powerlessness when his family entered the camps: "I recalled the procedure [and the] feeling we were regimented and pushed about like a bunch of hogs."[43] The experience drove Matsumoto and many of his peers to look for answers in wartime sociological and psychological theories and their attendant antiracist progressivism. Many BSR Nisei veterans saw rationality, science, and a New Deal–like belief in American progressive values as means to counter racism. Social science was more than just a scholarly pursuit for Matsumoto. Scholarship was his ticket out of the camps, and out of marginalization. It also gave him the position and language to understand and deal with the experience of being a Nisei intellectual. In late 1943 Tamie Tsuchiyama, a fellow BSR trainee, wrote to Dorothy Thomas, who headed a project similar to Leighton's, that "according to [Edward] Spicer, Scotty Matsumoto, the best of the evacuee staff, was going to spend several months in Chicago going over the notes and writing up [the] sociological study of Poston."[44] Chicago deeply impacted Matsumoto. Chicago sociologists had developed methods of sociological research, such as life history surveys, and theories that gave Asian Americans "a whole new way to think of themselves."[45] Matsumoto and his peers endorsed this language, which, very much like the Boasian anthropology that had impacted Leighton, rejected racial categories in favor of social science. Chicago also taught Matsumoto to endorse his position in between cultures. He made full use of the experience in forwarding his career and getting further away from the camps. Matsumoto followed Leighton to the War Office, where he worked on psychological warfare, and then went to Japan with the USSBS.

Matsumoto's encounter with Japan, which he had never before visited, was as empowering as it was shocking. He was first sent to Akita with team 7 of the USSBS Morale Division.[46] Akita had suffered a particularly heavy bombing on the very eve of surrender, on 14 August 1945, when 134 B-29 airplanes dropped thousands of tons of explosives and napalm on the city and surrounding areas. Matsumoto, who interviewed town residents, encountered in Akita the same stories of horror and shock as are detailed in earlier chapters of this book. After Akita, in November 1945, Matsumoto and Tom T. Sasaki, another BSR veteran, were sent for thirty days to Hiroshima, Hagi, and Tsuno-gun, as "civilian consultants.[47] Matsumoto never mentioned this early visit in later writings. But again, to judge by the report he and others filed, he experienced and heard much that left an impression on him while interviewing survivors and just walking around the rubble of Hiroshima only a few weeks after the A-bomb. He worked throughout December, with Leighton and individually, interviewing officials, journalists, and regular townspeople.[48] Matsumoto stayed in Japan after his contract with the USSBS ended in February 1946 and worked for a time in Tokyo, probably as a linguist for military intelligence, from an office in the Wako Jewelry store in Ginza.[49]

Matsumoto was hired by SCAP as a researcher in the Public Opinion and Sociological Research Unit of the Civil Information and Education Section of GHQ. There he worked alongside Kubo Yoshitoshi, who partnered with the unit—an episode to which we will return in later chapters. In September 1949 he was hired by the ABCC. In his curriculum vitae, he described his position as "chief. Dept. of patient contacting" for the ABCC, with an annual salary of "$5,768 per annum." The position and salary were significant material and professional advancements for Matsumoto. He described the department role as "the important duty of representing the Commission to the great majority of his Japanese Contacts in the research programs," which meant contacting and arranging for survivors to come and get tested. The department also handled "reception of care before and after the clinical examination," which "was likewise in the hands of this Department." This was done not only to help the subjects but to "determine the reaction of the patient and to obtain all related information which might be of significance to the public relation aspect of the organization."[50] This candid description of patient contacting as primarily subject procurement and public relations operation betrayed the naked interests that governed the ABCC and the *hibakusha* relationship. The department had grown from just two people to a staff of sixty-four when Matsumoto completed his appointment in September 1953 to begin study toward a PhD at American University in Washington.

Initially the ABCC had little need for PR or persuasion. During the early phases of the occupation the ABCC, as part of the occupation forces, could simply force survivors to cooperate. Multiple testimonies by survivors tell of being rounded up and taken off the street by armed soldiers. Hashizume Bun, who was fourteen in 1947, recalled being taken by American soldiers in a jeep to the ABCC. In a scene reminiscent of the concentration camps, Bun and other survivors were then "put into a room with a group of people, men, women, old people.... American soldiers who stood around [the room] ordered us to undress. We did not understand English. I was scared." When she tried to keep her undergarments on, Bun was told by the soldiers to undress completely, and was handed a sheet with a hole in the middle. "I was completely naked, completely bare," she recalled, and "the soldier was looking me over." The whole experience made her feel inhuman, "like a commodity [*shina mono*]."[51] There were no interpreters or "contact persons" involved. Likewise, other survivors recalled being taken by force to the ABCC. Schools were a particularly frequent target. A Japanese Canadian named Joe Ōhori, who was a student at the time, remembered that ABCC "trucks began to come to 'round up' student survivors and demanded blood samples etc." Not wishing to go, whenever the "ABCC truck showed up, [Ōhori] hid in his school's bathroom."[52] Another survivor remembered a pistol-wielding MP taking him from class and forcing him (*muriyari tsurete ikareru*) into a jeep with other students.[53] Similar stories abounded. Much of the resistance was due to reports, to which we will return below, of young female survivors being forced to undress and be photographed. In a 1952 meeting, one Japanese ABCC contractor said that "many of the students dislike pick-up at schools as the other students tease them by saying 'he (or she) is going to ABCC for a "strip" like the strip-tease dancer.' "[54]

As this last quote demonstrates, the ABCC was aware of the problematic nature of its methods. Matsumoto's initiative for exit interviews was part of a program, supported by the ABCC leadership, to ameliorate the problems in its relationship with survivors (figure 4). The interviews were supposed to evaluate patient experience and facilitate greater cooperation. In an unpublished June 1950 report, which served as the first draft for the exit interview program, Matsumoto registered a note of protest regarding earlier attitudes, commenting that with the approaching peace treaty there was a need to improve patient relations. "The ABCC is still regarded by most Japanese as a portion of the Occupation forces," he wrote. "Many patients come in unwillingly, because ABCC is tied up with the Allied occupation in their minds. Time is short in which to develop a much more vigorous program of understanding . . . to insure [*sic*] future cooperation from the Hiroshima population."[55] Matsumoto pushed for implanting a program that would be run by "people sensitive to human relations." He saw the increasing need to reach out to the medical and local community, and to solve the treatment issue: "The problem of treatment needs solutions as soon as possible." Matsumoto hoped that his meetings with the Hiroshima medical association might offer a route for doing so.[56] The ABCC's refusal to provide treatment had been a constant and growing problem for the committee. As Susan Lindee has pointed out, the ABCC's reason for not providing treatment was political.[57] It did not

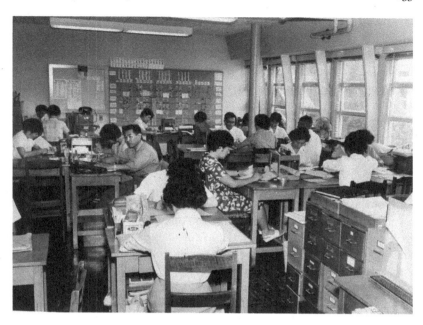

FIGURE 4. ABCC Medical Sociology interview room, Hiroshima. Photo courtesy of the McGovern Historical Center, Texas Medical Center Library.

want treatment to be seen as acknowledging responsibility for the victims' suffering. In a published report on exit interviews, Matsumoto admitted as much, candidly writing, "No monetary or other reimbursements are offered.... No treatment is given; the examinations are suggested purely for diagnostic purposes. Furthermore, no air of atonement is suggested in any way by the commission."[58]

Matsumoto finished his first stint with the committee in 1953, and went back to the States with his wife, Nobue, a Kure native who worked at the ABCC, to complete his doctoral degree in sociology. His adviser, Irene N. Taeuber, with whom he'd had a long professional relationship since their meeting in Hiroshima in 1952, was quite enthusiastic about his potential. Taeuber worked relentlessly to ensure him funding and publication venues. Matsumoto named one of his daughters after her, and they maintained a correspondence long after his graduation. Still, Taeuber as well saw him through a racial and cultural lens. In a letter, she characterized Matsumoto as "an exemplary individual in that he is completely American in loyalty but basically bi-cultural." Further building on these wartime tropes, she continued, "He has the industrial character and the loyalties that we associate with the Japanese, the Intellectual habits and skepticism that we associate with American scholarship."[59] Thus, Matsumoto was again presented as a model Japanese American. This was very much along the trajectory of transformation presented for Japan in the 1946 Brues and Henshaw report. It was also a view that Matsumoto, at least outwardly, fully embraced. In the same application he wrote, "It is the writer's desire to seek an opportunity to services [sic] a link, however small, between two hemispheres and two traditions. It is his sincere hope that pursuit of academic knowledge and skills will provide him with tools with which will better prepare him to participate in future study of vital meaningful problems of East and West."[60] As Naoko Wake has noted, the postwar idea of a "model minority," held by both Asian Americans and their supporters, included a denial of race, which we have already examined with Leighton, and was both a reaction to wartime racism and an affirmation of Asian Americans' ability to overcome it.[61]

Matsumoto completed his doctoral degree in 1957, writing his thesis on the "individual and group" in contemporary Japan. He did not train as a medical sociologist, and his passion seems to have been elsewhere. But he struggled with publication of the dissertation as a manuscript, and could not secure an academic appointment. There was probably an element of discrimination in these rejections. In one recommendation letter Taeuber emphasized, again, that Matsumoto was a "young American" with promising abilities. One can assume that this emphasis would not have been necessary for a white graduate. In May 1957, with two young children, and with his wife increasingly unhappy with life in the United States, Matsumoto was offered a job by Felix Moore in Boston that would involve a return to Japan, and he immediately took it. The family left San Francisco for Tokyo on Japan Airlines on 7 September 1957.[62] Matsumoto kept working with Taeuber and sending her materials. He also secured her an appointment as a consultant for a new research project with the committee.

The two met in Tokyo in December 1957, shortly after his return there. Matsumoto was tasked with identifying the main factors that led to persistent anxiety and social problems of the *hibakusha*. This was considered to have an impact on cooperation with the ABCC. Matsumoto described his conversation with Taeuber in a report to ABCC director George Darling, noting that "the basic importance of asking whether a difference is brought about by exposure to the A-bomb or by some socio-economic factor was consistently stressed." Taeuber and Matsumoto wondered whether the increased social problems, chronic health issues, and anxiety suffered by *hibakusha* were "known effect[s] distinctive to irradiation." They argued, "The need is great to guard against selective factors. . . . In the concern to weigh the factor exposure versus non-exposure there may be real danger of becoming myopic to the influences and consequences of socio-environmental dynamics." Matsumoto further elaborated that the A-bombs in both Hiroshima and Nagasaki were dropped on areas "likely inhabited by low-income groups." Focusing, like Janis and the USSBS, on the problem of absenteeism, Taeuber suggested "the study of the short leaves of absence (3 days or less) as a source of evaluating the extent of 'hypochondriasis' or 'suggestibility' towards illness caused by psychosomatic influences among the exposed people." She argued that it was not the A-bomb that was the cause of these problems: "The predisposition to 'suggestibility' has social and psychological as well as somatic aspects. . . . With the greater sensitivity to a-bomb exposure built up through press and propaganda, has there been an increase in absenteeism by exposed persons in recent years?" What Taeuber and Matsumoto proposed was that other factors, namely "press and propaganda," were responsible for the social and psychological problems of *hibakusha*. Long-term impacts and the persistence of radiation, or "somatic aspect," were not denied. But the emphasis was on the environment, especially the media and the peace movement, building a greater sensitivity among *hibakusha*, and the possible predisposition of survivors to mental illness.[63]

This conclusion was very much a reflection of contemporary thinking on the long-term impact of war neurosis and related conditions. It was the survivors' environment, rather than their wartime experience, that was the cause for persistent mental and related issues. This tendency was reinforced by the skepticism and the detached empiricism Matsumoto had brought from Chicago. Matsumoto and Taeuber agreed that there was a need "to evaluate the socio-psychological consequences of exposure to the A-bomb." But "even more than in medical and biological research, there will be need for caution in determining whether an effect has been brought about by irradiation or by socio-environmental components."[64] Emphasizing "caution," and acknowledging that it was "difficult to propose a measurement technique suitable" for the task, Matsumoto proposed studying the impact of media on the survivors through a "content analysis within a socio-psychological framework," as well as a study of the "power structure" of the survivor community.[65]

In a letter to Taeuber, Matsumoto reported, "Dr. Darling seems to love the memo and agreed with all its points except the study of the 'power structure,' which he correctly surmises may be misunderstood by Japanese as a sort of 'intelligence.'"[66] Darling's concern was genuine. The ABCC did whatever it could to distance itself from military and intelligence research. Anti-American feelings were running high in the mid- to late 1950s, with the position of the ABCC in Hiroshima greatly imperiled by the rise of the antibomb movement following the *Lucky Dragon 5* incident of 1954, in which Japanese fishermen were exposed and fell ill following the Bravo H-bomb test on Bikini. Darling and the ABCC went on a PR blitz in Hiroshima, which included persuading the city of Hiroshima to include Atoms for Peace materials in its Peace Museum.[67] It was in the context of increasing worry by ABCC leadership about the committee's deteriorating standing, and in relation to his work with Taeuber, that Matsumoto was tasked with reforming patient contacting. In September 1958, Matsumoto submitted his report on the current operation of patient contacting. His report was critical. Contractors (as the investigators and others were called—they were external employees) had low morale: "The tendency [in Hiroshima patient contacting] appears to be towards apathy and withdrawal." Matsumoto attributed some of these issues to lack of cooperation and frustration with medical doctors' attitude. He implored his colleagues, "The ABCC medical program requires an additional skill focused specifically on the patient as an individual. . . . The patient is not just a series of laboratory tests or just a Master File number with a series of punched holes on an IBM Hollerith card." But significantly, Matsumoto couched his criticism within the bigger mission of the ABCC: "The voluntary and satisfactory relationship of Japanese patients with ABCC, upon which the entire medical program rests, can only be gained and maintained through constant interest in the feelings, attitudes, emotions and welfare of each individual patient." In order to achieve this, he wanted to establish an "elite crop of contractors to work as ambassadors of ABCC and who will carry out their role with dignity and a spirit of service."[68]

The ABCC leadership was completely on board with Matsumoto's initiative. In a letter to Darling, the epidemiologist and statistician Gilbert W. Beebe "concur[red] heartily in Dr. Matsumoto's recommendations of 19 September 1958." Beebe went further than Matsumoto, and "urged that any such department be given a research function. . . . There are research areas of genuine interest to ABCC that are not likely to be entered by biologically trained scientists." Displaying a typical lack of self-awareness, Beebe asked, "We are confronted with a degree cf apathy and/ or hostility ... and need to know the sources of these attitudes." Echoing Matsumoto's earlier conversations with Taeuber, he continued, "Is the anxiety level abnormal? If so, how it is generally manifested? What are the major sources of attitudes toward health and illness? What is the economic significance of illness? The social significance?" Beebe forcefully argued that "the ABCC needs more sociological and social-psychological emphasis in its work.... [The] new proposed Department should include individuals with training in those fields and if they are selected in part for research competence investigating work in those areas should proceed." He cautioned, however, that it would be hard for the ABCC to work directly in the community, specifically because of the hostility and suspicion toward the commission, which he wanted Matsumoto to research. Thus, the ABCC should "encourage research on the part of groups outside the ABCC enjoying a more neutral status in the community. Its strength would lie in providing stimulation technical aid in design funds and perhaps assistance in machine processing of data." This new emphasis played an important role in the work of Japanese researchers, which will be examined below. Significantly, Beebe referred to USSES veterans as an inspiraticn: "Professor Likert's recent visit to Hiroshima University is one small measure of the level of interest here in social surveys, and it would be my hope that such interest could be encouraged by the new proposed department."[69]

Matsumoto's new department, the Department of Medical Sociology, was established in January 1959. Its "primary responsibility ... [was in] constantly gauging and improving the relation of the ABCC with each patient ... and with the community at large." For this purpose, the department was instructed to "carry out projects and research programs designed to improve relationship with patient and community." This included researching "social attitudes ... and [conducting] demographic analyses and investigation of social and psychological aspects of medical studies in cooperation with the department of epidemiology, department of statistics, and department of medicine." This initial task was later extended to that of providing social services to survivors. This was done not out of concern for the well-being of the survivors, but in order to facilitate cooperation with the ABCC research program. As the directive establishing the department reminded its prospective head, an "important function of the department would be the broad surveillance of the community's sentiments and attitudes towards the Commission."[70] The department's broad mandate, however, did not result in much psychological and sociological research. As Beebe predicted, it was hard for Matsumoto to conduct independent research, and he spent more time in searching for external collaborators and surveying outside efforts than in doing any research. In any case, his heart was probably not in it. In a 1961 letter to Darling, he complained that it was impossible "getting actual research [done] under my own specialty. Correspondence from my professional colleagues in the United States constantly remind me not to neglect this. . . . From a career point of view, the longer my stay with the ABCC is without research of my own, the worse it will be for me later."[71] Darling's response is not recorded.

The department did complete one significant piece of research on the "social impact on bomb survivors."[72] The report argued, very much along the lines of the Taeuber research, that survivors did not suffer disproportionally, as "statistics on health, life span, marriage, divorce, migration, and other social factors . . . [do] not support or tend to negate some commonly proffered conceptions regarding suicide and marriage patterns among the survivors."[73] Furthermore, Matsumoto argued that even though the ABCC maintained social caseworkers for patients, "there is no overwhelming social welfare work being performed from the closely exposed as compared with the non-exposed."[74] This was the farthest Medical Sociology went in denying long-term social and psychological damage. Yet the context for this report is crucial. The intended audience was the American defense establishment and Matsumoto's peers. The immediate impetus for the work was an invitation received by Matsumoto and a number of other ABCC officials and veterans, including the geneticist William J. Schull, Stafford Warren, and Austin Brues, from WFMH director Frank Fremont-Smith to attend a conference on the "long range biomedical and psychosocial effects of nuclear war" at the New York Academy of Science in January 1967. Fremont-Smith's invitation was part of an ongoing series of conferences and meetings on civil defense and nuclear weapons with which he was involved from the mid-Fifties onward. Like the panic conferences, these conferences involved leading social scientists as well as scientists in an effort to find interdisciplinary solutions for civil defense issues.

The conference was directly sponsored by the Pentagon's Defense Atomic Support Agency (DASA). Like the previous conferences, it involved leading "dissidents," including Robert Jay Lifton and Jerome Frank. Matsumoto and Lifton shared a panel, chaired by Brues, on the psychological and social aspects of the bombing. We will briefly return to that topic in the

MATSUMOTO, THE ABCC, AND SOCIAL WORK 141

last chapter of this book. For our purposes here, it will suffice to note that, with the Vietnam War raging, the mood at the conference was much more skeptical and the resistance to the military establishment's ideas about nuclear weapons much more vocal than in the mid-Fifties. Lifton and Frank pushed quite relentlessly against the idea of a "winnable" or "manageable" nuclear war, with Lifton deploying his Hiroshima research to great effect. Matsumoto, however, was not joining Lifton and Frank on the antiwar barricades. His skepticism was deployed not vis-à-vis the Pentagon, but toward assertions by Lifton and others of long-term psychological damage to survivors. In a discussion about the prevalence of trauma, for instance, Matsumoto wondered if there really was significant psychological damage in Hiroshima: "At Hiroshima University a professor of neuropsychiatry (Konuma Masuho) has tried to obtain figures, but as far as he can surmise, he feels that there has been no increase of psychosis because of the A-bomb experience. For what few cases they have, it seems very difficult whether to relate the psychosis to atomic bomb experience, per se, or to some other personal experience."[75] Matsumoto's strategy here was in line with earlier denials of a causal connection between the A-bomb experience and long-term damage. Significantly, as will be examined below, these were the exact arguments deployed by German doctors to deny compensation to Holocaust survivors.

This was not Lifton and Matsumoto's first meeting. They had already met, along with other ABCC members, in Hiroshima in 1962. That meeting had been far from a success. Lifton was under the impression that Darling, a fellow Yale professor, "had an unmistakable tone of minimizing the effects of the bomb. He stressed how much these effects had been exaggerated by people who wish to embarrass America and how . . . any illness in Hiroshima [is attributed] to the effects of the bomb." Lifton also mentioned Matsumoto, if not by name, as "a full time Nisei sociologist who evaluate[s] their work."[76] He had very little positive to say about the encounter. The feeling was mutual. The ABCC kept a file on Lifton, and seems to have regarded his whole body of work with suspicion. In his own account, George Darling complained that Lifton "did not wish his 'objectivity' to be tarnished in Hiroshima by any association with ABCC." According to Darling, Lifton had accepted Japanese accounts of the ABCC and was motivated by an animosity toward the commission. He wrote, "If you have read his book as I have (without reward) you will have seen that this preoccupation together with the need to expand a very short series of case studies into a 600-page book still obtains." Darling recalled a lunch with Lifton, Matsumoto, and others at which he protested that the ABCC had been "giving considerable attention to this area and even had the benefit of psychiatric consultation." Darling was referring to Ralph Gerard from the Michigan Mental Health Institute, a member of the NAS-NRC committee who had visited in March 1961. In 1962, Matsumoto's cultural expertise was enlisted by Darling to counter Lifton's findings. Lifton spoke little Japanese; Darling spoke none. Thus, implying his inadequacy for the task, Darling recalled that "Dr. Matsumoto stressed the necessity for a binational team approach using psychiatrists or psychologists each well acquainted not only with the other's language but with the other's cultural frame of reference." Darling, Matsumoto, and others further "thought there was a great danger in assuming that the Neo-Freudian interpretations following the psychoanalytic pattern would be misleading in the extreme if used as an explanation of Japanese behavior which presumably responded in a different way to totally different set of values." This was a familiar line of attack. Darling, however, took this further. He wrote, "Dr. Lifton seemed to feel that as a psychiatrist he was dealing with the varieties of human behavior as true in Hiroshima as in German extermination camps and stressed what he believed were the similarities between the responsibilities of those responsible—a point of view to which I cannot agree."[77] Thus, Darling rejected the whole basis of what would eventually become PTSD—namely, the universal nature of human experience. Matsumoto's "native" authority was deployed by the ABCC in the service of this goal.

This attitude seems to have also much to do with Darling's views of psychiatry. Darling admitted, "It is true that the psychological aspects of the bombing of Hiroshima and Nagasaki are very important. I am sorry that the skills of the psychologists and psychiatrists have apparently not yet developed far enough today to permit the undertaking of a really objective analysis." He ended on a high note, which said as much about him, and about the ABCC's view of itself, as about Lifton:

Unfortunately, Dr. Lifton refuses to grant . . . the courage and even grandeur with which most of the survivors met their catastrophic experiences. . . . He denigrates the one great role that should help sustain the [survivors]. Their unwilling sacrifice, necessary or not, did save untold lives American as well as Japanese. It seems especially degrading to these people to painstakingly paw over their mental associations in an effort to explain through some psychoanalytic nit-picking why they were stunned or afraid. As though some weakness,

physical or mental[,] was needed to explain why they broke down or had night-
mares, or regretted they had not behaved like heroes. To me this is the unkind-
est act of all. The leftist will remember that he was American, that he treated 70
Japanese as Guinea pigs.[78]

One cannot help but think that Darling, by supposedly taking the side of
the *hibakusha* and calling Lifton's interviewees "guinea pigs," was projecting criticism of the ABCC onto Lifton. In both upholding the saintly role
of the *hibakusha* and taking offense at Lifton's "tarring" of the survivors
with the stigma of mental disease, he was also advocating the exact arguments that led the *hibakusha* movement to largely reject Lifton's work.
The ABCC and Darling did not quite deny psychic trauma, yet they did
what they could to minimize and dismiss it. Matsumoto's reasons for joining this particular crusade against "neo-Freudian" ideas like trauma are
complex. But being who he was, he had to be even more "detached" and
"objective," and more "on message," than his white colleagues. Yet, with
ABCC work generating more and controversy in Hiroshima, even he had
reached his breaking point.

A-Bomb Social Work and Social Research

George A. Hardie, a consultant to the Atomic Energy Commission who
visited Hiroshima in the mid-1950s, described patient contacting as the
ABCC's "wastebasket," a department that took over "things that other
departments don't want to handle."[79] Medical Sociology's main function
turned out to be not research, but something more along the lines of Hardie's description. These operations fell mostly under community relations
and social work. MSWs often dealt with "problematic" patients and situations that might reflect badly on the ABCC. One of Matsumoto's main
innovations was introducing social workers to handle cases in which external factors impacted patient cooperation and diagnosis. This was done
mainly to facilitate return visits, which were crucial for the ABCC. As
Matsumoto wrote already in 1954, "We must be able to gauge what the
patient will say to his family, his neighbors, and his friends about ABCC
upon his return home. His comments in his own community may decide
whether others will cooperate with ABCC or not."[80] The MSWs also were
supposed to have a research function. Looking back in 1969, Matsumoto
wrote, "By casual conversations and by skillful observations a great deal

FIGURE 5. ABCC Medical Sociology group photo (1950). Dr. Matsumoto is at the center of the front row. Note the large number of women. Photo courtesy of the McGovern Historical Center, Texas Medical Center Library.

of social information could be documented leading to analysis and research papers.... In the past, I have incorporated the field of social casework into the contacting operation to give it a firm technical and professional basis."[81] The ABCC's MSWs were indeed guided by a sense of professionalism and a scientific ethos. But their job often entailed hard choices and not a little politics. They also fulfilled a great need in the community. The MSWs were the ones who eventually dealt not only with what other departments did not want to handle, but with what Hiroshima society and the medical establishment at large chose to ignore. Such issues often touched on sensitive political and social issues. This meant that they did not, indeed could not, always live up to the ideals of professionalism professed by Matsumoto.

In a sense, these very ideals, of scientific detachment and rationalism, undermined much of what the MSWs were trying to achieve. Like the rest of the ABCC, the MSWs could not recognize their own biases. They saw themselves as professionals: objective, technical, rational, and modern, but also compassionate and understanding—seeing, as Matsumoto wanted, the patient as a whole person. Significantly, the great majority of MSWs were women. The ABCC had a policy of employing only women for patient contacting. Continuing this gendered practice, the department hired mostly married women as MSWs (figure 5). As Matsumoto wrote, "The prerequisites for being a good contractor, obviously, were the same as for a good wife."[82] Much of this preference was rooted in a classic patriarchal understanding of womanly virtues. But this was not all about feminine intuition, warmth, and care. Social work was one of the new post-occupation professions in which woman could practice modern, science-based work. Like the home economics experts examined by Mire Koikari in Okinawa, women MSWs were engaging in a Cold War civilizing and modernizing mission that had complex roots in prewar ideas of modern womanhood and domesticity, namely the legacies of *ryōsai kenbo* ("good wife, wise mother") and wartime mobilization, as well as in the activism of New Deal American and American-educated women, who promoted a sort of "manifest domesticity."[83] Like home economics, medical social work gave Japanese women a sphere of action in which they could participate in the rebuilding of Japan along modern scientific lines.

Kodama Aki, who headed the MSW section in Hiroshima, embodied many of these qualities. A survivor herself, she was the public face of the MSW section, appearing on television and radio, writing reports, and handling the most difficult cases at the committee. Significantly, Kodama credited the introduction of MSW to the work of occupation reformers, who "sought to solve problems of poverty, [and] crime . . . that are detrimental to the welfare of the nation, not as charity work but as social welfare work with the introduction of scientific techniques."[84] One such reformer who promoted modern "scientific techniques" was Dorothy Dessau, who had come to Hiroshima as a social worker with the occupation, and eventually taught at Doshisha University in Kyoto in 1951. Dessau was responsible for many social initiatives in Hiroshima, including introducing modern, American-style clinical social work.[85] The twin pillars of social work for her were "Christianity and democracy," and, "just as it was the work of Christian missionaries to preach the gospel of Christ, so Dessau 'preached' the American clinical social work."[86] Dessau and her peers, such as the American-educated sociologist Fusa Asaka, who worked with the Ministry of Health and Welfare and was Dessau's colleague, were the ones responsible for shaping postwar medical sociology. Fusa was in touch with Matsumoto, and introduced her students to him to work as MSWs in Hiroshima.[87]

146   CHAPTER FIVE

It is unclear whether Kodama worked with Dessau or Fusa. But they shared much in terms of conviction and methods. Kodama started her career not at the ABCC but with Hiroshima hospitals, and was recruited by Matsumoto in 1960. Matsumoto first met her in 1959 as part of a "seminar group on problems of anxiety among A-bomb survivors," organized by survivor organizations. Even before joining the ABCC, Kodama had shared much with Matsumoto's cautious approach toward survivor problems, including a dislike of the media and a suspicion of the new psychological and all-encompassing definition of A-bomb disease and neurosis. She also showed a no-nonsense "tough love" approach toward survivors. Such attitudes were in full display at the seminar. When a woman representative of a *hibakusha* organization argued that "because of exposure to irradiation many women feel somehow being less than human," Kodama replied, "A great deal of this is irresponsibility of mass communication."[88] In another exchange she said, "The term A-bomb sickness is for political use. No illness is diagnosed as such. . . . at the A-bomb hospital. Doctors called leukemia, leukemia." Matsumoto added that the ABCC also refrained from using the term "A-bomb sickness." Kodama continued, "An important factor, it seems to me, is *how* the particular A-bomb survivor has accepted the fact of exposure; *how* does he live with his experience and himself? How the individual reacts to all kinds of problems seems to stem from this adjustment" (emphasis in original). Kodama echoed American psychologists' positions and emphasized the survivor's own responsibility to accept her condition and adjust to postwar society.[89]

In another exchange regarding the inability of female *hibakusha* to maintain steady jobs, Kodama argued, "Isn't there a need for the exposed to have stronger determination to work and live and not to give up so easily?" (Ironically, it turned out that the woman in question had quit to become a social worker.) In a heated exchange with the survivor and activist Kikkawa Kiyoshi, she told the seminar, "Many . . . feel psychologically that they are 'special.' Some seek special privileges and attempt to take advantages of all and any assistance they feel due them. They seek special attention. Although there are other laws to take care of their particular needs, some survivors feel that the A-Bomb Hospital *must* do as they wish" (emphasis in original). Kikkawa protested. And, probably feeling she had gone too far, Kodama added, "Please don't misunderstand what [I] have said. I too am exposed and lost my only child. I am not being critical of the exposed people. But we need to realize that many problems which are brought to physicians have no relations to them." This was a

MATSUMOTO, THE ABCC, AND SOCIAL WORK

rare glimpse of the emotional toll and sense of mission guiding Kodama. She may have been harsh, but she was determined to help survivors help themselves. Furthermore, she was also overworked and overwhelmed by the huge need for social welfare in the survivor community. She told the seminar, "In August [alone], during 25 work days at the A-bomb hospital, 402 cases concerning survivors were handled."[90] Until the mid-Fifties, survivors received no financial aid toward their medical needs, and their social needs were only starting to be addressed by the mid-Sixties. MSWs at hospitals and the ABCC could address only a fraction of the problems facing survivors. The result was ongoing anxiety and escalating mental problems, alcoholism, and family problems.

The attitude of the ABCC and contemporary MSWs toward these problems was, again, an emphasis on self-help and adjustment. In a 1968 summary of her first years at the ABCC, Kodama succinctly reviewed her own position.

> Since the survivors have psychological problems attributed both to apprehension of radiation disturbances and to social problems resulting from the sudden loss of many family members and the breaking up of their homes, and are affected also by the interaction of those problems, the need for casework has been great. The subjects suffer because they have encountered those difficulties not singularly, but in multiplicity. They fall into agony [kunō], a state of ambivalence [hantai kanjō ryōritsu. or conflicting emotions], and loss of self, and in many cases this leads to misfortune. Therefore, the social worker, on the basis of mutual rapport with the subject, has to help them stabilize their emotions and work toward their self-recovery and re-adaptation to medical treatment and to society.[91]

This passage is noteworthy in a number of ways. Kodama insightfully assessed the multilayered and intricate problems facing *hibakusha* as well as the dynamic nature of the problem. Secondly, Kodama was completely aware of the psychological price that radiation and fear of radiation extracted from the survivors' psyches. There was, however, beyond talk of the "sudden loss of family members," no mention of the actual shock of the A-bomb. Kodama and the MSWs generally did not talk with survivors about their A-bomb experience. Their focus was on long-range psychological and social problems. Finally, there is no talk of specialized psychological help; the emphasis is on "stabilizing emotions" through "self-recovery" and "re-adaptation."

In a summary of casework written by Kodama, these features of the ABCC's MSWs are quite evident. One particularly noteworthy feature of the summary is, again, an almost complete absence of the A-bomb or the A-bomb experience. Survivor status is mentioned mostly in passing, often through a sentence indicating distance from the epicenter of an explosion. Also, there is a repeated emphasis on survivors' problems of self-confidence and emotional instability, which is implicitly contrasted with the MSWs' technical competence and professional calm. The MSWs' job was, again, helping survivors help themselves. As Nishimura Kiyoto, a student of Fusa who was recruited in 1964 by Matsumoto, recalled, "My job was to help survivors with such problems or difficulties to adapt themselves to these processes, so they could resolve or lessen their psychological and social problems *on their own*" (my emphasis).[92] These cases and recollections are, of course, selective. Yet, especially because these are the ones the ABCC chose to publish, one can see more clearly here the value system that MSWs professed to uphold. Thus, Kodama brought a case "of an exposed survivor who thought that his various physical troubles were due to the effects of exposure to the atomic bomb. This is to report how he was rehabilitated, relieved of his anxiety by examination at ABCC."[93] The survivor complained that "life since the A-bomb until now has been lonely and difficult. . . . I have no confidence in my health . . . [and] I feel increasingly impatient and disturbed."[94] Since an examination showed no immediate signs of radiation, the MSWs did not see a reason for such feelings to persist. Kodama wrote, "Although A-bomb survivors are prone to feel uneasy and dread the effects of radiation, the problem is largely of an *unscientific nature, a matter of emotion*, that is, apprehension of the unknown and fear aroused by indefinite information" (my emphasis). Kodama by no means ignored the psychological issues facing the survivor; she wrote in his case file that "the emotional instability of a survivor resulting from sickness is especially marked."[95] Yet, for her the only way forward was for the survivor to accept the "unscientific" and irrational nature of his emotional issues, and to rationally and calmly reorder his life: "The most important thing was to help him determine whether radiation effects were present or not so that he might recover emotional stability and return to suitable life."[96]

Women survivors were seen as especially prone to emotional instability in the case files. Kodama said of a survivor who was upset about her divorce (there is no mention of exposure) that "the patient's emotional instability and antagonistic attitude toward physicians and nurses greatly interfered with treatment."[97] After dealing with legal issues and helping the survivor get into a hospital, "the caseworker helped her to gain emotional release and regain reason."[98] One phrase that is repeatedly brought up is "inferiority complex" (*rettō-kan*). Thus, one case spoke of a "housewife who because of an inferiority complex hesitated to undergo operation for chronic sclerosing osteomyelitis [*kōkasei mansei kotsuzuien*]." It is, again, unclear whether the woman's medical issues were due to exposure. The MSW wrote that, "as a physically delicate woman having spent years in hospital ... she suffers a great sense of humility toward her husband and his relatives who are strong and healthy." Kodama's diagnosis was that "the patient needs support in her loneliness, psychosocial help to relieve her of her inferiority complex, and coverage of her medical expenses. The case worker ... helped her to attain spiritual growth and to gain full coverage of medical expenses through application of the Law Concerning Medical Treatment of A-Bomb Survivors."[99] Much of the MSWs' work was just that: identifying resources and benefits, including the ABCC's own Social Welfare Funding, and helping the patient gain access to them. But it is clear that Kodama and others saw their work as also involving what she called here a "spiritual" or moral dimension of uplifting survivors.

Significantly, although Kodama dismissed psychological problems as "unscientific" and "emotional"—she never used any psychological categories—she repeatedly saw the survivor's problems as chiefly psychological, and located the solution within the survivor's own psyche. MSWs had to "create an opportunity" for survivors, such as a female *hibakusha* whose marital issues were compounded by poor health, "to make judgements objectively [*kakkanteki ni kangaeru yō ni enjo shite*] together with the caseworker in regard to the doctor's diagnosis and her present symptoms. She will be helped to examine herself as to her self-centered critical attitude [*jikochūshinteki hihan taido*] and distrust of doctors and public health nurses, attributable to disappointment in her hope of recovery."[100] After a number of sessions, the patient did make progress: "Asked about the contradiction of the two conflicting feelings of confidence and anxiety [*jishin to fuan*], the patient criticized herself objectively [*kakkanteki ni jiko naisei*], stating that she probably had to act strong, though actually she was sick and weak, because her future with no hope of marriage or employment was pitiful and she did not wish to cause her parents worry."[101] This was a rather extreme case, but the general tendency in all case files was toward patient self-reflection and "objective" understanding of their situation. Again, the A-bomb was rarely mentioned, and the problems of the *hibakusha* were mostly presented as being of their own making. All patients in the published case files recovered and were thankful, and were able to return to normal life. They also were all eventually able to resume regular visits to the ABCC. This was, of course, the main reason behind supplying the service. It was also good public relations. It should be noted that all ABCC social work and funds were reimbursed by the Japanese government. Thus, the ABCC was not unduly generous in this regard.[102] Nonetheless, it did provide a valuable service to survivors.

Unpublished case files and Medical Sociology, however, paint a rather different picture. The MSWs' main function at the ABCC was as a sort of fire brigade, dispatched to investigate and handle problems with patients and the community at large. One such notable case was criticism of the ABCC's handling of cases of children who had been exposed to radiation in utero and had developed mental retardation and microcephaly. Parents of such children formed an organization, *Kinoko no kai* (the Mushroom Cloud Organization), which demanded recognition from the ABCC, to no avail. The father of one of these children, Hatanaka Yuriko, took the unprecedented step of writing to the commander of the US base in Iwakuni, demanding US and Japanese government help and accountability. The letter caused somewhat of a minor diplomatic incident. Then, "a few days later, Kodama Aki, a medical caseworker at ABCC, arrived at our house in a jeep. She said, 'If you plan to put Yuriko in a facility, I'll take care of her.' " After offering help, "Mrs. Kodama said, 'Microcephaly is not caused only by the atomic bomb. . . . It can also be caused by normal circumstances, so we cannot say that Yuriko suffered from microcephaly because of the atomic bombing."[103] We do not have Kodama's account of that particular exchange, but other evidence points out to a cover-up of the issue by the ABCC. When the journalist Ōmuta Minoru asked the ABCC for a response to Hatanaka and other parents' accusations, "we were told that microcephalic cases were something that had already happened, and not something just discovered or to be discovered in the future, so that there was no justification for imposing an unnecessary psychological strain on other victims."[104]

This was not a denial per se, but as in other cases, it was very much in line with the ABCC stance on anxiety and related issues: Discussing ongoing medical issues was what supposedly caused mental strain, not the actual conditions of the survivors. Ōmuta's piece and the Iwakuni incident caused a small crisis within the ABCC. Efforts were made to find who had said what to Ōmuta and the families, and when. In a letter to Darling,

FIGURE 6. Dr. Darling (right) and Dr. Maki (left) present Dr. Matsumoto (center) with a certificate. Photo courtesy of the McGovern Historical Center, Texas Medical Center Library.

Gilbert Beebe advised dispatching MSWs to investigate, significantly adding, "It is possible that, had all of Dr. Matsumoto's social work effort and funds been poured into these cases, ABCC could still have been accused of covering up, but one would think that here were some medical welfare problems of first order."[105] In his typically candid manner, Beebe here basically showed the rationale for ABCC social work to be one of buying survivors' silence. After some back-and-forth, and with the issues refusing to die down, Matsumoto was contacted by Darling, who said, "I know that you and Mrs. Kodama worked hard with some of the cases reported in this article. Please give me what you can on contacts and efforts for and with those people" (figure 6).[106] Matsumoto submitted a detailed report on the issue, which categorized families as "difficult" or "cooperative." On the Hatanaka family, Matsumoto noted, "Mrs. Kodama undertook to do social case work and made numerous visits to the family's home in Iwakuni."[107]

Another investigation undertaken by Matsumoto concerned the treatment of young female survivors at the ABCC. Here, aspects of gender and power imbalance between Japanese female patients and American male doctors, as well as a medical culture that was, more often than not, flippant about patient rights, combined in abuse and violation of survivors' bodies. In his report, Matsumoto noted, "From approximately 1953 to 1957, the general rumor that women and adolescent girls were stripped naked, photographed in the nude, and forcibly subjected to gynecological examination at ABCC circulated widely within the Hiroshima community."[108] Matsumoto sent out female MSWs and other staff to collect evidence, and was able to verify and bring multiple cases of abuse of women. "We are unable to quantitate the various attitudes; however, *all* of the 17 contractors engaged in the current ME-200 program have experienced difficult cases due to past vaginal examinations" (emphasis in original). The evidence included women and girls, some as young as fourteen and fifteen, who had experienced being stripped naked and forced to wait for long periods of time in cold rooms, being photographed in the nude without consent, having vaginal bleeding due to rough examinations, and even experiencing what seems to have been borderline sexual assault.

One patient stated "that at the time of the gynecological examination, the interpreter told her that she must have the examination for possible cancer. Although she desperately tried to make the interpreter communicate her refusal to the doctor, she was forcibly placed on the examination table. A chattering foreign doctor inserted his fingers turning it around and round and said that the purpose was to obtain vaginal discharge. It was despicable." Matsumoto recounts over twenty cases. Significantly, he termed the testimonies of younger patients the "traumatic experiences of adolescent girls," thus showing an understanding of trauma very similar to our own. One could only imagine the sense of helplessness, humiliation, and vulnerability these women felt. They were surrounded by foreign men, with no understanding of the language and what was happening around them, and were forced to undergo invasive procedures. Seventy years after it was written, Matsumoto's anger and frustration with his colleagues is clearly evident. He insisted that his medical colleagues respect female patients' right to consent. "The Japanese, especially the female," he wrote, "seems often unable to state verbally a definite *no*. Such hesitation should not be interpreted immediately as consent. Pelvic examination should not be considered part of a routine procedure" (emphasis in original). Matsumoto demanded that such examinations be done by a "mature female doctor," preferably Japanese, and that "procedures should be firmly established so that any patient requesting consultation because of discomforts following pelvic examination is adequately and courteously handled."[109]

But, even here, Matsumoto was still being a team player. He insisted on the need of "persuading the patient that the modern vaginal examination is ethically acceptable and clinically desirable," and explained that "the desire to cooperate and the feeling of compassion of female patients are mingled with those of discomfort and avoidance." Matsumoto wrote that he was convinced "that with the proper kind of personnel, with the proper kind of approach there are probably few Hiroshima citizens who will not wholeheartedly participate in the ABCC medical program." As with the MSW program and his bigger approach to problems of anxiety and care, Matsumoto insisted on the rational nature of the survivors. All they needed was for the ABCC to properly reason with them, as "as genuine understanding of the meaning and benefit of the pelvic examination must dissipate anxieties. A distressing experience is sure to result if the female patient feels that she surrenders herself to the wishes of others (hence "forced") and submits passively to what she considers an assault upon her person."[110] Matsumoto denounced such "assaults." But unlike some of his white colleagues, such as Earl Reynolds, who quit the ABCC over similar concerns, he did not have the privilege to rebel fully. We should remember that Matsumoto was in a precarious position academically, professionally, and, for lack of other words, racially. He tried to use his academic and cultural knowledge and authority as a Japanese American to right this particular wrong. But this could only go so far. He, Kodama, and others were operating on a very uneven playing field. They were caught in between the Hiroshima community, their ABCC colleagues, and their sense of professional responsibility and ethos. The odds were very much against them. Yet eventually, Matsumoto made his stand.

Conclusion: The Problem of Denial

Following yet another public relations crisis, caused by sociologist Shimizu Kiyoshi's survey of ABCC handling of survivors' emotional and social issues, Beebe, yet again acting as the ABCC's unofficial id to Darling's super-ego, penned the quote that appears at the top of this chapter, about Shimizu's inability "to tolerate our objectivity" and his sentimentality toward survivors. Beebe was upset about the supposed added psychological suffering that journalistic pieces like Shimizu's were causing survivors. Significantly, he quoted Lifton approvingly, and showed an understanding of the connections between trauma and radiation which was rarely shown by anyone at the ABCC: "The loss of parents and spouses, and of property, was common to all these cities [that were bombed]. What are unique here are the psychic trauma associated with the sudden, overwhelming, massive, and unprecedented character of the experience that produces the psychic trauma Lifton writes about, and the radiation that we are studying."[111] Yet Beebe attributed the ongoing suffering not to what we would now call post-traumatic disorders, nor to the ongoing impact of radiation, but to the media and the peace movement's "exploitation" of survivor suffering. What concerned Beebe was "the realization of the full extent to which the A-bomb survivor is being victimized and neglected, and were I not at ABCC, and thus certain to be disbelieved, I would write a piece for public consumption in Japan, perhaps with the title A-bomb victims— twice martyred." Beebe believed "it is to the interest of those who exploit the [survivors] to exaggerate their ills, to blame too much on radiation, and to keep alive the anxiety of the survivors." Circling back to the strategy of demystifying the bomb and equating it with strategic bombing, he concluded, "This seems to result in a kind of conspiracy to keep from them any balanced view of the research findings. . . . Even Dr. Shimizu, who must know the facts as to the devastation and loss of life in Tokyo, Osaka, etc. can say in his article that the bombs had not only psychological and biological effects, but economic and social effects, and imply that these are somehow unique in Hiroshima."[112]

Beebe's letter succinctly demonstrates the various mechanisms and factors that led to denial of suffering. Beebe was aware of psychic trauma and its ongoing toll, as were Matsumoto, Darling, and others who specifically mentioned it. He even approved of Lifton's work. But he and others repeatedly attributed the continued suffering to other causes that muddled the diagnostic waters. The blame lay with the Japanese: either with the community, or, as in the MSW approach, with the survivors themselves. Trauma—a word rarely used—was something survivors could and should overcome. Through retrospection and "objective" assessment, survivors could regain emotional stability. But the Hiroshima environment, with its constant emphasis on the A-bomb, supposedly made it impossible for them to do so, unlike the inhabitants of other bombed cities. The problem was one of public relations as well as psychology. If the ABCC and Beebe could engage in rational discussion on the matter, then the "true" situation of the *hibakusha* would be known. Yet this was impossible, due to the ABCC's position. Beebe was not wrong about that last point; he was unable to truly help the survivors. But that was not because, as he claimed, no one would believe him. It was because his training, ideology, and position made him unable to see the interplay of initial psychological damage, social discrimination, and radiation anxiety that perpetuated and maintained long-term mental problems among survivors. This background was only reinforced through the ABCC's public relations, diplomatic, and psychological role that led researchers, almost reflexively, to minimize and contextualize damage.

Matsumoto's case proved this last point to the fullest. He and his department were in the best position to evaluate and research psychic trauma in Hiroshima. Yet, like Beebe, and even more so as a Japanese American, he found that his whole career and life trajectory made him recoil from the subject. If he did raise the alarm publicly, and not just in internal memos, he would in all probability be accused, like Shimizu, as being unobjective, emotional, unscientific, and too sympathetic toward survivors. Matsumoto could not escape the racial straitjacket imposed on even the most successful Japanese American intellectuals by their white environment. It was people like Beebe and Darling who were rational and objective. Nonwhites were sentimental, unable to act objectively. The same could be said of women care workers. The gendered division of labor, in which men did research while women provided care, was quite obvious at the ABCC, where patient contact and social work was done almost exclusively by women.

But for both female MSWs and Japanese Americans, marginal status did not lead to a different understanding of trauma. Quite the contrary. Kodama and Matsumoto were, in a way, even more prone than their white male colleagues to employ skeptical, detached, and "objective" methods when examining and caring for mentally damaged survivors. Kodama was a survivor herself, which seems to have had little impact on her attitude toward fellow survivors. Matsumoto and Kodama's background, of course, was not the only factor here. Denial was not a simple cover-up. It was an inability and sometimes a refusal to see the problem. It was shared throughout the ABCC and the bigger medico-legal world that defined and dealt with survivors' issues. This inability to tackle trauma at the ABCC was significant, and had far-reaching implications for Japanese research. The ABCC was the bridgehead for American medical and sociological understanding of psychic trauma in Hiroshima. It represented the most modern and scientific methods, and had enormous prestige. The ABCC supplied data, funding, and, perhaps more importantly, scientific prestige and opportunity, which many Japanese researchers sought to utilize. As Iida Kaori has noted, the ABCC was as much a part of a "Japanese landscape" as the American one, as it "provided [Japanese] access to new information, techniques, materials, and scholarly networks."[112] Much of Japanese medical research on survivors was done with or in response to ABCC support. This was true to all medical research, including psychological research. Kubo Yoshitoshi and Konuma Masuho, the two most prolific researchers on survivors' psyches before the mid-1960s, both worked either with or in response to the ABCC, and it is to their work we must now turn.

CHAPTER SIX

Konuma Masuho and the Psychiatry of the A-Bomb

"'The best of us did not return.' I used to feel a twinge when I read those words that Viktor Frankl used at the opening of *Man's Search for Meaning*. I can perhaps restate them in this way: 'The best of myself did not return either.'"—Ishihara Yoshirō[1]

In a 1958 letter to Irene Taeuber, Scott Matsumoto told her of his developing friendship with "Professor M. Konuma who is the head of the neuropsychiatry department of Hiroshima University School of Medicine" (figure 7). Matsumoto explained that Konuma "has a wide range of interest in social and cultural component in illness, quite unlike the typical Japanese psychiatrist who is deeply embedded in the German tradition with almost complete focus on neurology and biological medicine. It has been refreshing to meet someone who can talk the 'same language' on the sociological influences on personality formation and psychiatric disorders." Matsumoto hoped "that Dr. Konuma and I may combine skills in some sort of collaborative research in psychosomatic medicine." In their conversation, they were exploring a "wide variety of subject matters related to mental illness and social environment." The topic of most immediate concern to both, one would assume (and as this author certainly hoped when first reading this letter), would have been the impact of the atomic bomb on the human mind. But what Matsumoto and Konuma spoke about instead was an "area of mutual interest ... the study of the social and cultural reasons for a great number of consanguineous marriages in this area."[2] Matsumoto and Konuma's mutual interest in incest was less puzzling than it seems on first sight. Sexuality, and especially its "darker" side, has the habit of showing up in rather unexpected places with Konuma Masuho. It is also, as we saw with the Desert Rock

FIGURE 7. Konuma Masuho. Photo courtesy of the Department of Psychiatry and Neurosciences, Hiroshima University.

maneuvers, not completely unrelated to nuclear psychology. Konuma's interest in psychoanalysis, a relative rarity among his peers at the time, was driven by his fascination with errant sexuality. This training in psychology was one of the important factors that impacted his research, which was the most thorough psychiatric examination of *hibakusha* before the 1960s. Konuma also had a strong connection with military medicine, and researched the psychological cost of Japan's long war. His association with Matsumoto was also not a coincidence. Konuma's research was initiated in response to the ABCC's continuous failure to tackle the issue, and he and his peers were in constant conversation and contact with the ABCC. This conversation was always in the background as researchers constantly measured themselves against what was done, or not done, at Hijiyama.

Focusing on the work of Konuma and related research, this chapter seeks to uncover the myriad ways in which Japanese psychiatry understood the psychic damage done by the atomic bomb. Psychological trauma was not an important category in this effort. Most of the current literature on Hiroshima and Nagasaki survivors' mental suffering frames earlier research, and indeed the whole issue, through the prism of PTSD. As Richard McNally has argued, such "retrospective historical diagnoses of PTSD constitute a psychiatric version of the 'Whig interpretation of history,'" wherein a few brave prophets foreshadowed the future advance of PTSD.[3] The actual historical records are far more confusing, and point in multiple directions. Neither survivors nor researchers understood what had happened in terms of trauma. This was true in Japan as well as in the West, in its dealing with the aftermath of the Holocaust. Eva Hoffmann, who grew up with survivor parents and writes extensively on the Holocaust, recalled that her parents did not see themselves as being "traumatized." They suffered, yes, but so did everyone else around them. "To me, they were not survivors," she wrote; "they were only people who had undergone extremity and were now living another stage of their lives. Their very human condition did not appear to me as a condition, nor did it seem susceptible to being parsed into diagnostic categories."[4] This particular experience was even more prevalent in Japan, where the term was rare even in medical circles, let alone ouside them. This is not to say that research into war experience was not influential. Quite the contrary; the development of and relationship between civil and military research into the mental price of war and disasters had a crucial impact on the history examined below. The trajectory of Japanese military and general psychiatry's effort to deal with "traumatic neurosis" (*kizusei shinkeishō*; usually relating to physical wounds), "war neurosis" (*sensō shinkeishō*), "disaster neurosis" (*saigai shinkeishō*), and the numerous other terms used from the nineteenth century onward is important in showing the many ways in which psychiatrists tried to deal with the mental price of war, most of which pointed away from the usual trajectory that led to PTSD. These categories were not aberrations. They were the rule.

Konuma's unorthodox figure made him a fitting man to tackle A-bomb psychiatry. As someone who cultivated an image of an eccentric, he no doubt would have been pleased by Matsumoto's description of him as a quixotic figure taking on the establishment. Konuma, however, was a man of his time. At the end of the day, he did not stray too far from the mainstream, opting for biological over psychogenic explanations and urging caution in evaluating both soldiers' and survivors' mental hurt. Despite his efforts, which were considerable, his research did not lead to a breakthrough in the research of A-bomb mental damage. In more ways than he would have liked to admit, Konuma reflected the general trajectory of transwar social scientists in Japan. Like Kubo Yoshitoshi, the subject of our next chapter, Konuma was part of a generation who were all "men of one age ... [who] read the same books, talk[ed] together, and wrote for each other's journals."[5] Like other psychological experts examined here, including his peers in the USSBS and the German and Israeli experts treated below, he was a former military man, an elitist, and a firm believer in the republic of science and its universal language of objectivity and the scientific method. Such preference for the "universal" was made even more acute considering the Japanese need to appear as scientific and objective as ABCC researchers. Though he talked of sociological and anthropological influences, "the cultural component in illness" was perhaps a subject of his conversation over drinks, but it never entered much into his research. Neither did the victims' voices, politics, culture, or any other experiences that went beyond the measurable and scientifically verifiable. Konuma shared with Matsumoto the unspoken disadvantage of being a nonwhite scientist in a world dominated by Western scientists who took their objectivity for granted. This, together with a general suspicion of traumatic neurosis in Japanese psychiatry, the lack of resources, the need to appear scientific vis-à-vis the ABCC, and the very complex links between radiation damage and psychiatric effects combined to make research difficult, and eventually led him away from the field of enquiry.

Framing Konuma's research both within the longer history of research into traumatic neurosis in Japan, especially in the military, and the wider global trajectories, this chapter starts with a survey of Konuma's army work within the context of Japanese military psychiatry's World War II experience. It then examines Konuma and the half dozen or so other psychiatrists who worked with survivors before the 1960s in Hiroshima and Nagasaki. The chapter concludes with a comparative look at the Israeli and German psychiatry histories with both soldiers and civilian survivors. Examining the history beyond Japan shows that Konuma was well within the bounds of international consensus. Furthermore, as in Japan, the connection between military and civilian victims were myriad and multiple, and had a dialectic impact on each other as well as on research in other places. It was these connections, between civilians and soldiers as well as between locales, that would put American and then global psychiatry on the path to accepting the concept of PTSD in the 1970s. But in the 1950s, the results of such connections were very different indeed.

Konuma Masuho and Japanese Psychiatry's Attitudes to Trauma

Konuma Masuho graduated from Keio University's faculty of medicine in 1931. He stayed on in Keio's Department of Neurology until he entered government service, becoming involved with Japan's war effort in 1935 at the Japan Institute of Labor Sciences research at first, and then, more directly, when he was mobilized and assigned to the Tokyo Third Army Hospital in 1938, becoming a lieutenant.[6] He focused on neurology, and mostly worked with soldiers suffering from head wounds. This was usual for a man of his training and stature. But, reflecting on his career in 1964, Konuma claimed the mantle of rebel against his field. "Because I had set my sights on an unorthodox research project," he told his students, "my life in the medical office was also full of troubles. Therefore, I had to throw myself into [work] with the field army [hospital]. . . . I was [indeed] a battle-hardened warrior who differed from most of the other professors in my career."[7] Konuma's "unorthodoxy" was, according to his memoir, a mixture of old-school humanism, which he attributed to the spirit of Keio's founder and liberal thinker Fukuzawa Yukichi, and an American-inspired attachment to dynamic psychiatry, which he had gotten through his professor Uematsu Shichikuro, who had been trained in the United States. Konuma emphasized that he had been "baptized in the American way of doing things at a time when German medicine was universal . . . [and when] psychoanalytical research was a taboo subject at many universities," and that it was only thanks to Uematsu that he managed to present his work.[8] This account is probably an exaggeration. Konuma, again, was mostly operating within the bounds of his class and profession. But his first academic enterprise was, indeed, a 1933 translation of Freud's work on "hysterical psychogenesis" (*hisuterī no shinri naruse*), which was unusual for neurologically trained psychiatrists.[9] This was also Konuma's first venture into the field of trauma research and sexuality, two topics he would continue researching throughout his career.

Konuma's involvement with the translation of Freud's work on hysteria, as well as his later work in the labor institute, in the army, and on sexuality, connected him to ongoing debates in Japanese psychiatry about the nature of hysteria, neurasthenia, and traumatic neurosis. As in Western debates, these terms were used at various times to designate various reactions to mental shock. As Akihito Suzuki has argued, debates in Japanese psychiatry closely followed Euro-American debate. New technologies and therapies, such as insulin treatment or the use of electric shock, were "all introduced into Japan almost immediately."[10] Already in 1890, Tsuboi Hayamai had reported on George Beard's work on neurasthenia as a "morbid emblem of the age of openness" that was caused by fatigue, which is the "product of the struggle for wealth and power."[11] Following this early intervention, the work of Oppenheim, Charcot, Janet, and Freud was translated and debated upon in Japan through the 1890s and early 1900s. As in the West, industrialization, the introduction of railroads and modern mining (with its attendant accidents), and the onset of modern warfare were important catalysts for debate.[12] And also as in the West, increasing recognition of "traumatic neurosis" met with pushback. In 1926, the same year in which the German war pensions administration reached a similar conclusion, the Japanese government's "investigative committee on traumatic neurosis" (*Gaishōsei shinkeishō chōsa iinkai*) concluded that traumatic neurosis was "not caused by direct [physical] trauma," and thus did not merit compensation.[13] Medical consensus was that what caused symptoms was not accidents, but workers' desire for compensation. After this decision, cases plummeted.

When in 1939 a munitions factory doctor asked on the pages of *Nihon igyō shinpō* (Japan Medical Journal) for opinions concerning the condition, most respondents claimed, "They rarely see any cases anymore and 'had to look for them.'"[14] The 1939 debate was telling on many levels. While some doctors directly referred to the 1926 committee decisions as the reason for the situation, Nagoya Imperial University's Sugita Naoki tied the disappearance of the disease to the revival of Japanese values since the Manchurian incident. Before modernization, Sugita claimed, the Japanese showed resignation and a Buddhist-like understanding of the suffering of life. All this changed with the modernization and Westernization of the Meiji era, which brought with it the weaknesses and degeneration that caused traumatic neurosis. "This syndrome is one of the diseases of [Western] civilization and should be called a manifestation of the non-Japanese spirit," he continued. "It seems to have appeared in British and French soldiers [during World War I], but there are no such ill-intentioned people in our Imperial Army."[15]

Sugita's position reflected a growing trend in Japanese psychiatry. In 1937, for instance, the military psychiatrist Kamata Shirabe told doctors, "Unlike the Western militaries during the First World War, there has been no neurotic illness called war neurosis in the Japanese military since the present war [the Asia-Pacific War] broke out. I'm proud as a member of the military of the emperor that the fact shows people of the Japanese Empire have especially high morale."[16] Significantly, only a few years earlier, these very same anxieties over race and values had led psychiatrists like Habuto Eiji to pin the blame not on the West, but on Japanese traditional mores. Habuto saw homosexuality and masturbation in the ranks of the Japanese military as a "threat to the physical and moral fiber of the race."[17] Excessive masturbation was seen as leading to exhaustion and neurasthenia (*shinkei suijaku*). The homosocial setting of the military was seen as "a breeding ground for the affliction," which doctors traced to "vices of bushido" (male-to-male sex being quite common before Meiji).[18]

This arbitrary use of "spirit" in the 1930s and 1940s as an explanation for the supposed lack of mental injuries in the Imperial Army, coupled with Japanese psychiatry's adherence to the German tradition, led to wide-scale dismissal of mental injuries during the war. There was only one military psychiatric hospital, the Kōnodai hospital in Chiba, which throughout the war admitted a mere ten thousand cases from the ranks of an army that numbered in the millions. Military psychiatry's status was not very high, and doctors rarely acknowledged psychological injuries.[19] Significantly, they used the exact same language as German doctors to dismiss traumatized soldiers' claims for compensation. Soldiers who claimed to be mentally hurt during their service suffered from a "compensation neurosis" (*hoshō shinkeishō*), which corresponded to the German *Rentenneurose*.[20] In the ranks, especially as the army started to experience defeats, the situation was much worse. Some Japanese prisoners of war told their US interrogators that "[all] of the soldiers who went mad in the mountains were shot to death because they might be found by enemies."[21]

By and large, Japanese military psychiatry's wartime record was, even by contemporary standards, not the most humane. However, wartime research and treatment were far from being one-dimensional. In late 1945, US Navy teams met with Japanese military psychiatrists and produced a detailed report about the state of Japanese military psychiatry during the war. The US Navy reports are unique if flawed documents; produced in haste and through translators, they reflected much of the biases of the American researchers. They displayed considerable bias (calling Japanese research "primitive") but also, like the USSBS reports, a progressive and universalist attitude.[22] The report stated that "the indoctrinated, disciplined, and repressed individual typified by the average Japanese might have been expected to react to combat situations with the brutality and excesses that he sometimes showed. At the same time, *mankind being basically the same*, psychologically, the world over [and] having taken the 'conditioning' of the Japanese into consideration, it was to be expected that he would be affected by the same emotional, nervous, and fatigue factors as the occidental" (my emphasis).[23] The US Navy teams met with a number of psychiatrists, most notably with academic psychiatrists like Uchimura Yūshi and Sugita Naoki, as well as military doctors Sakurai Tsunao, Kasamtsu Akira, Suwa Keishiro, and others.

Of particular importance to us is a section in the report detailing attitudes to the "manifestation and development of war neuroses." One of the main figures whose research was highlighted in the report is Sakurai Tsunao. Sakurai saw traumatic reactions as the result of "the interaction of the patient's bad disposition due to his character and circumstantial and external factors." War neurosis, for Sakurai, was "a type of psychogenetic reaction." The disease was "'provoked' by the circumstances of the war," and the "appearance of a utilitarian sense," by which Sakurai meant a flight into illness and a desire for monetary or other gains.[24] Sakurai argued "that individuals with these latent conditions did not even have to experience combat and could go into profound shock merely by receiving a draft notice."[25] The doctor's role, according to Sakurai, was "to smash feelings of wishes or expectations accompanying them and rectify patient's psychical attitude."[26] Sakurai's attitude should be understood within the broader framework of military compensation and pensions. As Nakamura Eri has demonstrated, psychiatrists saw their role in protecting the state from undue demands by malingering soldiers.[27] Here the contribution of Nagino Iwao was crucial. Nagino proposed translating the German word *Kriegsneurose* (war neurosis) not into *sensō-shinkeishō* (war neurosis), but "*senji-shinkeishō*" (neurosis in wartime), thus showing the disease to be something that happened *not because of the war* but something that happened to individuals who could develop neurosis independent of it *during* wartime.[28] This definition enabled the army to dismiss pension claims and the harmful impact of war on soldiers' minds, implying that those who broke were weak individuals.

Kasamatsu Akira, while relying on Sakai, had a more nuanced view of psychic damage. Kasamatsu saw war trauma as a "continuum from fright reaction on the front to hysteria close to malingering." Like Sakurai, he saw the disease as primarily a "psychogenetic reaction," but he also argued for a whole spectrum of reactions that depended on the interplay of environment and constitution. Those who broke were not necessarily weaklings.

Kasamatsu argued that "some soldiers—even dedicated soldiers—can have short term breakdown as 'defense mechanism.'" This developed "out of a 'sense of duty' which they could not fulfill," a reaction typical of "Japanese characteristics."[29] Kasamatsu separated hysterical reactions, fright, and depression, but also a "wish of death."[30] Such a death wish was not always negative. As Janice Matsumura and Diana Wright have noted, Japanese military psychiatrists, such as Ōnishi Yoshie, developed a theory of "bad" and "good" suicides. For Ōnishi, "war with China restored the traditional, earnest, pure-hearted and serious suicide," and reduced "frivolous, rebellious, playful, and vain cases of suicide," which he equated with love-related suicides and other self-centered (and Westernized) acts.[31] Kasamtsu's research was also driven by "the question of how the elements, war and race, are pathoplastically shown on the aspects of disease." Implicitly condemning the soldiers who broke down for the "wrong" reasons, he concluded, "After all, war offers opportunities to examine the strong and weak points of races."[32]

Kasamatsu's racially driven reasoning was used differently by others in the military. For instance, in the Navy, doctors often used disciplinary rather than medical actions in tackling traumatic responses, "self-discipline being a supposedly already acquired characteristic of the 'true Japanese.'"[33] As one interviewee stated, "As a general rule, nervousness and fear in combat seemed to have been treated more by a severe reprimand from the line officers than by sympathetic therapy from their medical officer . . . [and] in the hospitals all 'nervous' patients were carefully examined for evidence of malingering."[34] Indeed, Sakurai and others often treated patients with disdain. Sakurai characterized "the personality of these patients as 'having a strong tendency to be degenerate,' 'selfish, immoral, filled with self-interest,' and 'very insidious and egoistic.'"[35] Nakamura and other scholars also show, however, that dealing with psychiatric casualties in the military was a complex and fraught process. Doctors negotiated with soldiers who did not want to be seen as "defeatists" and "deserters," and who were frightened of the consequences for themselves and their families if they were released or sent back to the front. Soldiers, however, had little autonomy or control. Former patients "recalled in tears the incomprehension of doctors," and denounced doctors for considering them "dim [morō] and ill-witted."[36]

The situation in the air force was much better for victims. This is demonstrated by Uchimura's work as a civilian consultant with pilots in Reboul. Uchimura also advised the army on conscription issues, and "with our bombing of TOKYO his advice was sought on behald [*sic*] of civilians."[37] In his memoirs, Uchimura recalled the Reboul episode in some detail. Uchimura and Katsunuma Seizō were sent to Reboul by Tanaka Tarō, who was the director general of the navy's medical bureau. The navy "wanted to somehow raise the morale of these air crews," and the psychiatrists "were tasked with the problem of finding a limited number of measures to do so."[38] Uchimura claimed he saw "only a small number of airmen below the rank of petty officer who complained of nervous breakdown. I did not see a single case of what could be called a clear psychogenic reaction, let alone florid hysterical symptoms." Uchimura concluded that "this is not surprising, since they have all been trained in the military spirit for many years and are still living under strict military discipline." Uchimura conceded, however, that a more thorough examination by experts might find out that "many of them had latent neurosis [while] on the front lines."[39] Uchimura and Katsunuma recommended a better rotation-and-rest policy. After the war, Uchimura told his interrogators that he "was dubious there was any application of his recommendations."[40]

Uchimura was much less compassionate toward his civilian counterparts. He stayed in Tokyo through the firebombing. Uchimura, who followed reports from Europe, "heard that refugees from bombed-out London had suffered from emotional paralysis and depersonalization." He also discusses at some length his own disturbed mental state, which, he claimed, quickly improved after the war.[41] But he also argued that the air raids improved civilians' mental state. He wrote in his diary, "It's amazing how great is people's power to adapt [*tekiōryoku*]; it seems that people have gotten used to the situation and no longer feel so anxious."[42] Uchimura brought a few examples from his own experience, as well as that of a Taiwanese doctor, of how the danger of the air raids cured dementia and other conditions. He concluded that wartime experience "makes us realize that emergencies themselves do not necessarily have only negative effects on human spiritual life, and . . . spiritual health." Like Sugita, he blamed the modern Westernized lifestyle for mental issues. But during war, "overprotection and easy living are not allowed, and each person must take responsibility, . . . endure the inconveniences of life, and actively defend himself without depending on others. It goes without saying that such a situation is better for one's mental health than one in which one can act as one pleases."[43]

Uchimura did speculate, based on his own experience and "psychological condition" as "the houses in my neighborhood were burned down

KONUMA AND THE PSYCHIATRY OF THE BOMB

one after another and . . . people lost their lives and relatives," that one might want to factor "psychological anxieties" into future psychiatric research.[44] But when, after the war, he had a chance to research the experience of *hibakusha*, he completely refrained from any use of psychological methods and relied entirely on neurological and physiological inquiries. His contradictory attitude was reflective of the greater state of Japanese psychiatry during the war. Not all doctors adhered to harsh positivism. Nakamura Tsuyoshi, for instance, who worked in the Kokura Army hospital, argued that "Dr. Sakurai attributes the increase in war neurosis to the progress of the compensation system for war wounds, but I believe that the increase in the power of modern warfare, the increase in the use of firearms, and the increased terror and ferocity of the dangers of warfare are also significant factors."[45] Korumaru Masashiro, who worked in Kure, also opted for a more compassionate approach. Korumaru refused to use electric shock and other punitive methods. He found that psychiatric patients' complaints were not recognized. They were mostly in the general wards, where they "were being slapped by their superiors for being lazy and sluggish."[46] Kuromaru moved the patients to his ward, and often issued them medical certificates that exempted them from military service.

As far as one can judge from the limited information available, Konuma, who worked mostly with the physically wounded at the army hospital, encountered most of his psychiatric patients at the Shimofusa Sanatorium. In an early postwar article, he recalled focusing "mostly on occupational therapy and vocational guidance."[47] He did not mention any punitive methods, nor did he doubt his patients' sincerity. War neurosis was not mentioned, but he diagnosed patients with schizophrenia, depression, and the like. We must remember, however, that he wrote the article in 1948, in a radically different social environment and under an American censorship regime. For instance, he emphasized that "in general, we agree with the opinions of American and European experts who have noted occupational therapy's [benefits], as well as [those] with advanced opinions of our country" who promoted such ideas.[48] But Konuma's recollections were mostly verified by his colleagues Katō Fusajirō and Katō Masaaki. Katō Fusajirō, who incidentally was one of the only psychiatrists to write on Japanese war crimes, and Katō Masaaki, whose experience in Burma led him to social psychiatry and to work on the cultural basis of psychiatry, are fascinating characters.[49] For our purposes, it will suffice to note that Katō Masaaki, who worked in the Kōnodai hospital before Shimofusa, showed a positive attitude toward psychoanalysis and toward creating a "family-like" relationship with his patients. He noted that such attitudes became very much en vogue after the war, but were not possible in the Imperial Army.[50]

Konuma, then, was working in a different environment than Kōnodai. But variation in attitude between him and the likes of Sakurai had its limits. Konuma also came from an intellectual tradition that greatly curtailed unorthodox attitudes to war-related injuries, emphasized the physical over the psychological, and was deeply suspicious of patients' motives. Kuromaru, Kato, and others were exceptions to the rule. By and large, military psychiatrists were not receptive to either innovation or compassion. This was not just caution and academic aloofness. As Okada Yasuo and others demonstrated, psychiatrists were deeply involved in some of the military's worst excesses. Uchimura, in particular, is singled out by Okada for conducting human experiments "not unlike the Nazis," infecting patients with dengue fever, and doing work that "provided theoretical support for the National Eugenics Law."[51] These were not the kind of men who would conduct a campaign on behalf of their patients. These trajectories had important impact on A-bomb psychiatry, all of which was conducted by military veterans using mostly a transwar methodology. Thus, it is no surprise that they produced only meager results.

Early Psychiatric Research in Hiroshima and Nagasaki

When Kuromaru Shoshiro was asked by an interviewer in 1982 about his experience in Hiroshima, to which he was dispatched from the Kure Naval Hospital on 6 August, Kuromaru told him that the state of "medical treatment [in Hiroshima] was extremely miserable," but refused to elaborate. He told the interviewer, "I am not going to tell anyone about this, no matter who asks me."[52] Psychiatric issues were, understandably, not a top priority for Hiroshima doctors in the early postwar period. Immediately after the bombing, the Japanese military sent to the two cities a medical and scientific delegation that included two psychiatrists sent by Uchimura, who was tasked with helping the survey. Reflecting the preference for somatic research, however, the two young researchers, Okada Kei and Shimizano Yasuo, were sent not to question survivors, but to perform autopsies and collect samples of brains for the purpose of ascertaining radiation damage. Furthermore, Uchimura's research notes were confiscated by the Americans, and not much seems to have come out of this initial foray

KONUMA AND THE PSYCHIATRY OF THE BOMB

into Hiroshima.[53] It is safe to assume that even if doctors were interested in conducting research, American censorship and the harsh conditions of the early occupation would have made such projects difficult to execute.

It took a full four years for Japanese research to begin in earnest. The first survey was done in 1949 at Kyushu University by Okumura Nikichi and Hitsuda Heizaburō.[54] Okumura's team surveyed fifty patients treated at Nagasaki's Omura Hospital, and studied them for three months. The team found that all patients experienced "emotional turmoil" (*jōchobanmei*) and "emotional overload" (*kanjō mitsurujutsu*), which led many of them to a state of "*Affektstupor*, a condition in which the patient has lost the ability to feel" (the German word appears in the original). However, while most patients recovered normal functions, the patients who were "predisposed" were in danger of developing symptoms.[55] Okumura's team recognized the initial impact of psychological shock, but for an explanation for any long-term damage, they argued for a combination of environmental, hereditary, and radiation impacts. They concluded that in "later stages, the deterioration of the environment and [the impact of] personal characteristics (i.e.. predisposition) caused by the bombing led to the development of osteoporosis and psychosis."[56]

Another early research effort by Tsuiki Shiro and others, also in Nagasaki, reached conclusions similar to Okumura's. Tsuiki, significantly, was in touch with Konuma in Hiroshima and worked with the ABCC. Like Konuma, he bemoaned the ABCC's lack of attention to psychiatric issues, but also worked closely with the commission. Tsuiki examined eighty-three patients who had developed "anxiety neurosis, hysteria, and nervous breakdowns." His team asked the ABCC "to examine them in detail for a wide variety of organic disorders," and the ABCC found no abnormalities.[57] Tsuiki found a correlation between the severity of "regular" diseases and neuropsychiatric symptoms like "fatigue, introversion, memory loss and the like," but concluded that there was a need for further research to better understand the relation between the A-bomb and psychiatric symptoms.[58] He continued this effort with Nishikawa Taneo at Nagasaki University. The Nishikawa team's efforts coincided with the campaign to pass the *hibakusha* relief bill, and the establishment of *Hidankyō* (the *hibakusha* relief organization). The Nishikawa team was part of a bigger effort by Nagasaki University, which examined 7,297 survivors, the biggest number to date. They identified 469 neurotic cases. Again, working closely with the ABCC to rule out neurological and other cases, they sent out questioners and further examined about half of the original cases.[59] They eventually identified a 7.3 percent neurosis rate ten years after the event. They concluded, however, staying well within medical orthodoxy, that "although some of the subjects showed symptoms that could be considered psychogenic neurosis," because most severe cases also suffered from radiation-related diseases, "it seems logical to think that the disease is a kind of encephalocele or somatose based on organic or functional damage."[60] Such inconclusive results and tendency toward organic explanations were a persistent feature of early research. As I have examined elsewhere, this was a typical conclusion in the dozen or so research schemes that were initiated in the 1950s and early 1960s.[61]

In 1954, the Hiroshima doctor Oho Gensaku told a reporter, who attended a monthly counseling session at a *hibakusha* relief organization, that many of his patients got "tired easily, [complained of] lack of patience, muscle pain in various parts of the body, get sick easily, and [in general] lack of desire for life." Oho noted that "survivors are always anxious. Of course, some patients have heart disease, leukemia, and other medical conditions, but most patients" suffered from no more than "a moderate level of poverty and neuroses. I'm calling it the 'Hiroshima disease,' if you will." Oho further complained that neither the ABCC nor the Hiroshima medical establishment provided any explanation. Significantly, he stated that the new condition was "different from war neurosis [*sensō shinkeibyō*] and external traumatic neurosis [*gaishōjū shinkeibyō*]," and claimed that the condition was unique to *hibakusha*. Oho's effort to distinguish war neurosis from "Hiroshima disease" demonstrates the stigma attached to these conditions and the fear of *hibakusha* of being labeled as idle or lazy. In a meeting of Hiroshima doctors in 1990, Oho recalled the negative meanings attached to what doctors began calling "idling disease" (*bura bura byō* in the Japanese text, more commonly translated as fatigue).[62] The attitude of other doctors in that meeting was telling. Nakayama Hiromi, following Oho, speculated, as did many at the time, that there was a "food shortage nationwide . . . [and] the living environment was inferior. Everything was attributed to that, wasn't it?" Complaints were again attributed to environmental concerns. Furthermore, patients' motives were suspect. Nakayama argued that "there were neurotic people who attributed any sickness to A-bomb disease."[63] Harada Tomin, perhaps the most notable of the Hiroshima doctor activists, agreed, and added, with some condescension, "Probably due to an obsessive idea, anything is attributed to the A-bombing. This is the case with most of the A-bomb survivors residing in the United States."[64]

KONUMA AND THE PSYCHIATRY OF THE BOMB

Terms like *bura bura byō*, "A-bomb neurosis," and "Hiroshima disease" carried multiple and ambiguous meanings. Some, like Kodama Aki and Scott Matsumoto, saw these terms as political. Others saw them as forms of stigmata that ennobled their survivors' suffering. The conversation was about much more than medicine. But almost all actors tried to distance themselves from the psychological. Activist doctors, in particular, tried to show *hibakusha* complaints as legitimate, and "war neurosis" and related terms carried a negative label. What Konuma and others were trying to do was give psychiatric concerns a scientific basis, which meant a somatic explanation. Purely psychological explanations were suspect, and it is not surprising that psychiatric research on survivors' mental injuries was sporadic and not part of a consistent research effort. Mental damage was just not a priority. This resulted in little research being done. This was acknowledged at the time by Konuma, who wrote in 1963, "Both in terms of intellectual [pursuit] and [pushing for] financial [compensation], only a few [researchers] have adequately grappled with the psychiatric aftereffects of the atomic bomb so far."[65]

Konuma's Research into A-Bomb Psychiatry

Konuma arrived at Hiroshima in 1949, but he did not publish on *hibakusha* psychiatry until the mid-1950s. He spent the first few postwar years focusing on military veterans and following his interest in the Oedipus complex, researching errant sexuality in Tanizaki Jun'ichirō's *Makioka Sisters*.[66] Konuma was exceptional among military doctors in conducting follow-up research on veterans. After the war, only a handful of dedicated long-term studies were conducted on military veterans. Besides the above-mentioned Katō Masaaki's 1955 work, another notable exception was Meguro Katsumi, who worked in Kōnodai, which was made into a national hospital in the early 1960s, and still found wartime patients there. Meguro's work, due to its late date, is beyond the scope of this chapter, but it is important to note that he found that at least 25 percent of Japanese veterans suffered from persistent war neurosis.[67] Konuma researched veterans from 1949 to 1953 to determine the causes for long-term neuropsychiatric and psychiatric "functional disturbances [which] stand stationary in spite of ample surgical viz. orthopaedical treatment, thereby including some veteran cases of Chino-Japanese (1894–95) and Russo-Japanese (1904–05) wars."[68] The research could not have been possibly conducted on veterans of these turn-of-the-century wars. Konuma mentions "a case of a 26 year old with a bullet wound," and it almost certain that this was later research (indeed, the original 1949 Japanese-language article does not mention it, and later articles refer to soldiers who were shot in 1938).[69] This reference to earlier wars is significant; it shows the very serious limitations faced by Konuma and his colleagues, as in all probability Konuma inserted this sentence to evade censorship. In 1948–49 military-related research, like *hibakusha* research, was heavily curtailed. The political atmosphere and the general reluctance to deal with the military and veterans in general was a contributing factor to the paucity of research. As the Ishihara Yoshirō quote at the beginning of this chapter attests, soldiers, like Holocaust survivors, felt rejected and misunderstood. And society, as well as medicine, preferred to look the other way.[70]

Furthermore, Konuma, following German precedent and contemporary practice, insisted on somatic explanations to his patients' neuroses and related psychiatric issues. As in German research, which we examine below, Konuma looked for brain lesions, which he claimed were hard to diagnose; he cautioned that "they are very often looked upon as simply psychogenesis or neurotic; especially when there is [*sic*] no foci symptoms with skull fractures."[71] Konuma insisted that "head trauma often has a *neurotic coating* but it is not just neurosis" (my emphasis).[72] Notably, Konuma was not satisfied with "simply psychogenetic" explanations, and argued for damage to the central nervous system as the cause of latent and persisting psychiatric issues. This damage was caused by "heavy brain concussion, which must in turn cause injuries in the midbrain-hypophyseal system."[73] This was a classic "shell shock" assessment that looked for concussions, damage from shelling, and other physical factors as explanations for persistent psychiatric issues. German psychiatrists persisted with such diagnoses well into the 1960s. Konuma reached a similar conclusion in all research he produced on head injuries, and was relying on German psychiatric literature as corroboration.

Like Nishikawa, Oho, and others, Konuma traced the beginning of his research to frustration with the ABCC inaction on psychiatry. He claimed that right after moving to Hiroshima he had planned to approach the ABCC, but that "to this day, they do not involve themselves with such issues or give any consideration [to psychiatry]."[74] Konuma did work with the ABCC occasionally. At one point, probably referring to Matsumoto, he acknowledged that the "ABCC has lacked a research staff on this topic since the beginning, but we do receive occasional research [requests] and contacts from sociological experts in the committee."[75] But, most of the time, when mentioning the ABCC, Konuma did it in the context of its neglect of psychiatry. Starting in 1953, he started his survey, examining hundreds of *hibakusha* in Otake, just outside Hiroshima. Significantly, he took on the problem of A-bomb fatigue and, unlike Oho, made connections between military and *hibakusha* research. In Otake he found "autonomic ataxia (lack of muscle coordination), dizziness, headaches, sleep disorders . . . insomnia, vertigo, emotional intolerance, amnesia and difficulties in mental work, intolerance to mental shocks, and so on." The long list of complaints "appeared after the atomic bomb diseases and remained stationary till now."[76] Notably, just as in his research on veterans, Konuma noted that these symptoms were usually the result of brain injury, and, "there was not supposed, that their complaints and symptoms are merely neurotic ones."[77] In his first articles in connection with this research, he maintained ambiguity over the causes of these symptoms. Like his other colleagues in Hiroshima and Nagasaki, he concluded, "It is supposed or recognizable that there lie diencephalic, namely central regulation disturbances of autonomic nervous functions as the after-effects of A.B. [Atomic Bomb] casualties. . . . But it is not yet concluded that the facts have direct relation to A.B. casualties. As the exact cause of the disorders being not clarified."[78]

Such inconclusiveness continued in later research. In a 1960 article, part of a symposium on the "psychiatric effects of [the] A-bomb," Konuma noted, "As we [continue] to deepen our understating of 'the symptoms of and distress [caused] by head trauma' [and] neuroses . . . we still cannot [positively] recognize that [these symptoms] are the 'after effects of A-bomb disease.'"[79] Konuma surveyed his research, also using his work on military casualties, as well as other psychiatrists' work on the topic so far, and he strongly gestured to (but still refrained from positively linking) a connection between the A-bomb and the varied symptoms suffered by *hibakusha*. He still insisted on physical damage as the main cause of mental disease, but he also added environmental and social concerns as contributing factor. "The atomic bomb is *Noxe*; it has a [harmful] impact, socially and personally, on both body and mind. Even if *Noxe* disappears, the mental effect is of [these combined factors]" (German word appears in original).[80] For Konuma, however, acknowledging the social and economic impact of the A-bomb just further muddied the diagnostic waters. In a 1963 report, getting back to his original Otake research, Konuma noted that that living conditions of *hibakusha* were generally poor, "and

174 CHAPTER SIX

he could also see arteriosclerosis, beriberi, stomach disorder, parasites, and intellectual insufficiency [in patients] ... [and thus] it is difficult to judge whether the cause of the symptoms is due to the living conditions or the impact of the atomic bomb."[81]

Konuma, however, did gradually come to see a clearer connection between the A-bomb and *hibakusha* mental health issues, and even attributed some of them to nonsomatic factors. At the same aforementioned 1963 symposium, he argued for the existence of outside factors—"namely the startle response (to the A-bomb) and radiation," as major contributors to the onset of neurosis.[82] A later, 1965 report, listed "psychogenic psychosis," as one of the "A-bomb aftereffects," as well as "anxiety disease at the time of atomic bomb exposure."[83] Konuma then added, "Those exposed within two kilometers [of ground zero] suffer from psychogenic psychosis, which often leads to suicide attempts. Such psychological symptoms, which [existed] at the time of the bombing, as well as the chronic symptoms [from which *hibakusha* still suffer] should be understood as psychogenic reactions."[84] Konuma speculated that what was understood as "A-bomb disease" (*genbaku byō*) was actually schizophrenia.[85] He was conforming to contemporary trends in which shell shock and other similar conditions were often being diagnosed as schizophrenia or other personality disorders.[86] This was still a departure of sorts from the organic, but the apparent turn away from somatic explanations was not followed through. Most of the paper stuck to examination of brain waves, blood circulation, and possible central nervous system damage, but Konuma did speculate that there was interaction between psychogenic and organic factors that produced the "interbrain syndromes" his patients suffered from. Thus, Konuma, almost alone among his peers, did finally reach beyond somatic explanations for *hibakusha* mental suffering. Yet he as well did not reach out to psychologists or try to coordinate a coherent care program. Konuma published no new research on *hibakusha* after the abovementioned article, and moved on to work on alcoholism, masturbation, and other issues.

Konuma's and other researchers work was not insignificant, but it remained far removed from the day-to-day life of *hibakusha*. The profession's isolation from the community is demonstrated by an exchange that took place at the 1959 seminar recorded by Matsumoto. Asada Shigeyo, who worked with Konuma in Otake, told the seminar that since 1949, "we have had no specific psychiatric case called to our attention at the medical school whose symptoms can be said clearly to be related to the atomic bomb." In a typical manner, Asada added, "Neurosis of a mild nature may be prevalent among the survivors, but this must await the results of future research." Continuing with his inconclusive stance while also making connections to military psychiatry, he answered a question about amnesia: "I participated in studying head casualties of war survivors where damage to the nervous system has affected memory. [But] it is hard to determine whether it is entirely physical or mental." Asada told the participants that the "term 'atomic bomb neurosis' was coined by the Nagasaki Medical School in 1951. We have had no actual experiences in our clinic ourselves." He conceded, "In the Otake study we found a higher proportion of exposed persons who reacted intensely to a loud crash or sound."[87] Despite this, he insisted when pressed by Kikkawa Kiyoshi, that "the reactions following disaster experience are usually temporary." Finally, when Kodama Aki asked for his help with a survivor, Asada seemed to have gone out of his way not to see the patient: "I would be very happy to help in any way, but it must be emphasized that these things probably are not related in any way to atomic bomb exposure. This would be very difficult if not impossible to evaluate."[88] This attitude was, again, telling. Still, we must remember that Konuma's team, Asada included, came closer than others to conducting a sustainable research campaign, and was able to reach conclusions that, however tentative, could have served as a basis for treatment and advocacy for his patients. But he, as well, stopped short. The forces that guided Konuma and the profession—his elite status, his German education, and his wartime experience—constrained his research and made recognition of long-term psychological damage in the 1950s impossible.

Veterans and Civilian Victims in Germany and Israel

Writing in a Greek medical journal, Nakazawa Masao, looking back in 1985 on forty years of research following Konuma's early research into A-bomb fatigue, *bura bura byō*, and related psychiatric concerns, harshly criticized his profession. "There was no research carried on to supplement these two pioneers' works, and atomic bura-bura disease was often regarded as 'hypochondria' or 'laziness.'" This, he bemoaned, caused "double suffering for the hibakusha," as "psychiatry did not pay sufficient anthropological attention to what psychological effects were inflicted on hibakusha by their experiences of being bombed and surviving, and by their torturous lives afterwards. Hiroshima did not have its Frankl to handle those problems."[89] As a longtime advocate for *hibakusha* welfare, Nakazawa's frustration with his peers is understandable. The situation in the mid-1980s regarding research and care for Holocaust survivors was far better than that of the *hibakusha*. Japanese psychiatry, indeed, did not have public figures such as Leo Eitinger and others who worked across disciplinary boundaries and actively campaigned for recognition for victims (Frankl's own record was mixed). But until the mid-1960s, the attitudes of Japanese psychiatrists were very much in line with mainstream global psychiatry. Survivor psychiatrists in the West were fighting an uphill battle against establishment psychiatry. And recognition for Holocaust victims did not come easily, or instantly.

When comparing the German and Israeli records with that of Japanese psychiatry, one finds that the latter was not exceptional in its attitude to either soldiers or survivors. In both Israel and West Germany, psychiatrists had to work in similar environments very similar to those of their Japanese peers. They examined soldiers, survivors of concentration camps, and of prisoner-of-war (POW) camps, using the very same terms and methodologies as in *hibakusha* research, and they reached similar conclusions. This is less surprising than it might seem given the widely varied histories and circumstances. In all three situations, the psychiatric establishment was dominated by a cadre of German educated-professionals. Most of the researchers were military men (female professionals being rare in all three countries), and the impact of wartime psychiatry, especially from World War I, was strong. Israeli and German doctors showed an aversion to using the language of trauma that was similar to Japan's. As Svenja Goltermann has argued regarding the German record, the "concept of trauma offers a misleading answer to [the] causes and consequences" of psychological damage suffered by veterans, as psychological issues were not seen as an inevitable reaction to stress, and what the historical record shows is a "polyphony of responses."[90]

Despite its appalling wartime record, the German psychiatric profession emerged relatively unscathed from World War II, as "denazification was particularly skimpy in the medical profession."[91] Even doctors who had worked in the concentration camps continued to publish and work mostly undisturbed, going so far as publishing work on human psychiatry in "extreme conditions" based on their camp work. Psychiatrists like Ernest Gunther Schneck, who was tried for conducting starvation experiments in Mauthausen (he was acquitted for "lack of evidence"), and Heinrich

Berning, who had done similar experiments with Soviet POWs, managed to reinvent themselves as experts on German POWs and their psychiatric complaints. The profession, still rife with anti-Semitism and a general hostility to war victims, was unsympathetic to Jewish and other survivors of German camps. But the doctors were just as harsh to German veterans. Following their World War I and interwar trajectory, German psychiatrists mostly dismissed psychological damage. Damage was seen as temporary, and if it persisted it was often connected to either lack of adequate nutrition and general bad health, or to a desire for pensions. In a development rife with historical irony, German soldiers only gained recognition for wartime mental injuries after the recognition of Jewish suffering. This history, which led directly to the making of PTSD, was entangled with the Hiroshima case and impacted it.

The German record in the war itself was also comparable to the Japanese record. The German profession was better organized, and had a much more robust presence in the field, but suspicions abut war neuroses were widespread (albeit for different reasons than in Japan). Even more than in the Japanese case, being psychiatrically ill was a mortal danger for the German soldier. Determined to prevent another epidemic of war shakers, "German doctors outdid each other in demanding that dangerous elements should be kept away from the home front, either by being shot or being sent to concentration camps."[92] Such concerns were rooted in ideas about morale, examined in earlier chapters of this book, which tied the German collapse in 1918 to the rise of shell shock. This, however, did not mean that there were no psychiatric hospitals cr treatment. As in Japan's Imperial Army, there was variation between services, fronts, and locations. The surgeon general (*Heeressanitätsinspektion*, or Inspectorate for the Army Medical Services) and the air force favored psychotherapy, while the army opted for "active treatment."[93] The latter usually meant punitive treatment, such as electric shocks, that were supposed to cure soldiers from their desire for gain (*Begehrungsvorstellungen*), which was seen as the primary cause of neurosis.[94] In a sign of the struggle between the hard-liners, like Friedrich Passen, and their detractors, in 1944 the high command prohibited the use of the term "neurosis" and ordered it to be replaced by abnormal mental reaction (*abnorme seelische Reaktion*). Labels such as "war neurotic," "war trembler," and "war hysteric" were explicitly prohibited. This was done to fight the stigma attached to these terms, but also to avoid "any causal relationship between war and psychological disorder."[95]

After the war, Wehrmacht veterans were routinely denied pensions in West Germany, as doctors insisted on finding physical causes for psychiatric ills. As the psychiatrist Kurt Schneider wrote in 1947, in case of pension evaluation, "under no circumstances do physical impairments that are expressions of emotions, for example, a psychogenic gait impairment following fright, qualify as a pathological physical change [for pension]." German POWs who came back from the Soviet Union and suffered from a range of psychiatric issues were, according to psychiatrists, "being ill without a disease."[96] Most German doctors saw nothing in their World War II experience that fundamentally altered what they had seen as a proven and tested body of knowledge that went back to World War I. Many doctors echoed Karl Bonhoeffer's comment that the experience of the war had further demonstrated the "extraordinary capacity of the healthy brain for resistance and adjustment."[97] Thus, doctors saw any prolonged suffering as abnormal. Neurosis in returning soldiers derived primarily from "endogenous factors . . . [it] manifested itself in an insufficient capacity toward all the demands of the new life."[98] This was very similar to what Kodama Aki, Uchimura, and others saw in ill-adjusted victims. The patients were the problem, and their symptoms stemmed from either hereditary issues or psychological immaturity.

A further diagnosis was "dystrophy," which attributed erratic behavior to prolonged malnutrition. Dystrophy, as Frank Biess has argued, "offered a seemingly objective, scientific justification for ascribing a victim status to returning POWs."[99] The diagnosis was based on World War I studies on Russian and other POWs, and on the concentration camp research. As in the anxieties over poverty and food insecurity in Hiroshima, however, it was also a way to draw the gaze of the medical profession away from the war and to the material concerns of the present. The situation was temporary and was supposed to disappear with improving conditions. But, as Svenja Goltermann has argued, the diagnosis was important, as it was a "bridge to exogenous explanations."[100] Dystrophy opened the door to further recognition of environmental factors while at the same time shielding veterans from the stigma of mental illness. The Association of Returnees (VdH) argued that the "aftereffects of dystrophy affected not only individuals with a 'deficient brain' [*Hirnschwäche*] or 'weaklings,' but also highly educated people."[101]

The recognition of suffering, however, only came in the late 1950s. In the first decade after the war and for some time afterward, doctors rarely acknowledged the long-term psychological suffering of soldiers or of bombing victims and camp survivors. As in Japan, civilian victims of bombing received very little attention from German doctors. The conclusions reached by German doctors about the impact of the bombing are in complete contrast to what their peers were telling the USSBS immediately after the war. While USSBS interviews with medical authorities and victims resulted in reports on widespread psychic damage, postwar psychiatrists saw remarkably little of that. Following an inquiry from occupation authorities, a Berlin psychiatrist reported in 1946 that "there are no abnormalities in civilian behavior, [and] despite justified fears there is no illness" among bombed populations. What he did see was mostly a sense of "dullness and surrendering to fate."[102] For Wilhelm Gerstaecker, like for Bonhoeffer and Uchimura, the bombing demonstrated that the "human organism had an astonishing capacity for equilibrium under extreme mental stress."[103] And for Hans-Werner Janz, the supposed lack of illness in civilians corroborated what he saw in soldiers. Despite "the worst possible horrors of war," and despite all the hardship and misery civilians suffered, the "classical clinical pictures of hysterical mechanism" had completely disappeared.[104]

The lack of recognition of suffering and the rejection of pensions led to a political struggle against the German state by war victims. Wehrmacht and SS veterans were, again, quite ironically finding themselves in the same situation as their Jewish and other victims in this struggle for recognition against Federal Republic of Germany bureaucrats. We will return to this history in the next chapter. For our purposes here, it is sufficient to show the stark difference between Japanese and German veteran organizations. The VdH and other German organizations created their own medical boards which provided second opinions to veterans and protested government doctors' insensitivity. In a letter to the Ministry of Labor, the veteran association skillfully and without shame used the memory of Nazi victims to advance its own cause, wondering, "Are the gentlemen blind and deaf that they did not notice long ago the misery they have inflicted through such nonsense and injustice? Do they . . . [know] how many disabled veterans threw away their lives because they were unable to bear the injustice of having their pensions revoked on such ridiculous grounds? During the Third Reich people were gassed and shot, today the bureaucracy cruelly drives people to throw away their own lives . . . or can you explain why we are treated as second-class citizens vis-à-vis those who were persecuted by the Nazis?"[105] Such appeals to German victimhood (vis-à-vis the state and the Jews) were quite effective, as we will shortly see, in turning the tide of political and medical opinion.

Japanese veteran organizations, for their part, while not engaging in any such cynically competitive victimhood, displayed a very unsympathetic attitude toward their comrades. Many former mental patients ended up as "white gown soldiers" (*hakui no yūshi*).[106] These often disabled former soldiers were ubiquitous in early postwar Japan, begging for alms in shrines and on street corners, clothed in white gowns. The Japanese Disabled Veterans Association (JDVA, or *Nippon shōigunjin kai*) saw the white gown soldiers as negative role models who symbolized the despondence and despair of veterans. The JDVA wanted veterans to be "honorable role models in accordance with the JDVA charter."[107] The US occupation forbade any kind of military pensions, including for disabled veterans, and many of those veterans ended on the street. Many suffered from severe, undiagnosed psychological problems.[108] Echoing ABCC social workers, the JDVA was resolved to help veterans help themselves. They called on beggars to get off the street, and conducted a large-scale moral persuasion campaign. A 1954 leaflet, for instance, berated the veterans: "Anyone who has a will should rehabilitate himself." Another told ex-soldiers, "You cannot be allowed to solicit donations publicly since it causes considerable discomfort to the general public. If you make the most of your abilities, you can survive one way or another. Our comrades have already demonstrated this in the whole country."[109] So, instead of shaming the public as the Germans did, the JDVA shamed the soldiers themselves. Again, they were blaming the victims of war for their own misery.

In Israel as well, despite the presence of a very large survivor population, veterans and survivors felt bound by social norms to integrate and make a quick recovery. It should be noted that, as Rakefet Zalashik has argued, such similarities were not a simple case of German influence. American models of mental hygiene, with their emphasis on communal mental health, also facilitated this push for integration.[110] Israeli society was not welcoming to immigrants with mental illness. They were seen as a potential burden on the fledging state, and unsuitable "human material" for nation building.[111] The situation was symbolically captured by a rumor, circulating in 1951, of a ship carrying a thousand mental patients from Germany to Israel. The rumor had no basis whatsoever, but it demonstrated the level of anxiety many felt regarding mentally wounded Holocaust survivors.[112] Unlike *hibakusha*, Holocaust survivors did gain recognition for their psychological suffering. But for them as well, recognition also took much time, at least until the late 1960s, and a concentrated effort by physicians and survivor-activists, to which we will return in the next chapter.[113] As late as 1956, the German-Jewish psychiatrist H. H. Fleischhacker wrote on Jewish refugees, "Personality disorders and neuroses were very rare among Jews" (in displaced persons—DP—camps); and in 1961, Viktor Frankl, who, as we have seen, was an early influence on Japan, wrote, "Neuroses in the narrower sense . . . were not observable in the concentration camps; neurotics healed there."[114] But it was not just doctors' attitudes that hindered recognition. As the psychiatric researcher Judith Stern has argued, there was "an unspoken agreement between the therapist and the survivor [which] held that the best way to cope was to leave the hellish period behind and deal only with current problems."[115]

Survivors of the Holocaust and mental patients were seen at the time as a potential burden and a threat to a newly emerging, still fragile society within the fledgling state of Israel.[116] There was a notable emphasis among psychiatrists in the postwar period on working with youth and on transforming survivors into healthy Israelis. Psychiatrists saw their mission as showing that survivors could return to "normalcy" in the "healthy" environment of Israel.[117] Doctors were aware of research in Europe, mostly done outside Germany but also done by sympathetic Germans like Ulrich Venzlaff and Helmut Paul; but they dismissed it: "We don't find too many similar cases among victims in Israel, due to the transcendental strength of Israel which is exercised upon the Jew."[118] Thus, if survivors could not adjust to Israel, it was somehow their fault. Doctors were aware of the horrors of the Holocaust, and some, like Fishel Shneerson and Leo Srole, who worked in the DP camps, were quite sympathetic. Like Konuma, Srole was exceptional in suggesting that the survivors' symptoms were similar to those of soldiers who had previously been diagnosed with "shell shock." He recommended similar treatment for the DPs, but was ignored; and it took more than twenty years for the psychiatric profession to appreciate his work properly. Shneerson was much more typical in advocating an optimistic theory, which emphasized survivors' ability to overcome their suffering. Shneerson saw some survivors' behaviors—their eagerness to learn and return to life—as a sign of "immunization from trauma."[119] Like Frankl, Uchimura, and others, Shneerson saw their suffering as leading to resilience and strength.

When doctors spoke with survivors, they often attributed their suffering either to preexisting conditions or to their lack of ability to integrate. Doctors, like ABCC social workers, often mentioned the war and camps in just a few lines. Details like losing (and often witnessing the killing) of one's whole family, spending years in hiding, and so on, were glossed over. For example, one psychiatric file simply mentioned that a female patient had been "in a few concentration camps," before discussing her suffering from postpartum psychosis.[120] The war experiences of another survivor, who was diagnosed as having "borderline intelligence, low social understanding, an infantile personality, and an *inferiority complex*" (my emphasis), received only five lines in a three-page patient background analysis. The report stated, "In 1941, at the time of the World War, the patient was taken to work camps and since was separated from his family. At the camps he did not suffer any illness. After liberation from the concentration camps, he returned to Romania and found out his family was exterminated." Despite this, the doctors connected his diagnosis to childhood trauma.[121] Israeli doctors who examined survivors wishing to receive compensation from Germany were sometimes as hostile as German doctors. We will examine this issue in greater depth later, but for our purposes here it is sufficient to note that many victims were seen as unwilling or unable to integrate due to hereditary mental health issues. This preference for organic explanations was displayed also by more sympathetic doctors like Leo Eitinger. A Holocaust survivor himself, Eitinger examined close to thirteen thousand Danish former political prisoners from 1947 to 1952. He found "restlessness, fatigue, increased smoking, irritability, complaints of defective memory, and vegetative nervous systems." He termed the condition "repatriation neurosis."[122] but like Konuma and other "A-bomb neurosis" researchers, as well as contemporary German research, Eitinger also found that the condition "seems to be the result of organic changes in the brain caused by mechanical and toxic injuries as well as by starvation and exhaustion."[123]

Political prisoners in Europe were treated much better by their respective societies than were other survivors. Resistance fighters especially were held in high regard, as they supposedly had upheld national honor while the official state capitulated to the Nazis. It was research on political prisoners that initiated changes in attitudes. Given Israel's emphasis on national rebirth and military strength, which was contrasted with the shame of survivors who had not resisted, one would have expected much less hostility to soldiers than to survivors in Israel. But in the first decade after the war, outside the United States and to a lesser extent the United Kingdom, the suffering of soldiers was also not recognized. In fact, it will be hard to separate the histories of survivors and soldiers in 1940s and 1950s Israel, as so many soldiers were also survivors. The ideological imperatives were even stronger in military psychiatry, and there as well, many doctors were German émigrés, including veterans of World War I.

But, here again, a plurality of attitudes and reactions can be perceived among doctors and patients. Because Israeli medicine was dominated by immigrants, British and American Army veteran doctors played an important role in early military psychiatry and implemented many of the methods learned in North Africa and Europe. Overall, however, the overwhelming emphasis was on short-term treatment if there was any, and soldiers' experiences varied greatly according to location and doctors.

In her work on "war trauma" in Israel, Irit Keynan roundly condemns the Israeli military establishment's attitude toward mentally wounded soldiers. She and others argue that "battle shock" (*helem krav*)—or battle reaction (*tguvat krav*), as the syndrome was called by the Israeli Defense Forces (IDF)—was not recognized in Israel before the 1973 Yom Kippur and 1982 Lebanon wars, "even though it is obvious that many of the fighters in all previous wars experienced battle reaction."[124] Putting aside the ahistorical and sloppy retroactive use of contemporary medical categories to diagnose victims of past wars, the historical evidence points to a much more complex situation. As Rakefet Zalashik has argued, the history of "mental injuries" (as they were then called) is one of the cycles of learning and forgetting. Health professionals were aware of the mental price of war, and made plans to address these injuries, though they often attributed them to the soldiers' background rather than to war itself.[125]

It is here, with the emphasis on patients' "background," that the history of victims and soldiers was most entangled. Survivors were not seen as reliable soldiers, and were perceived to lack the ideological fervor of native-born Israelis. The 1948 war was a particularly brutal ethnic conflict that saw significant atrocities committed by both sides. The ethos that guided the socialist founders of Israel in that war was the Soviet resistance to Germany. This ethos bore much more resemblance to German and Japanese myths of soldierly resilience than to Anglo-American ones. Thus, Benjamin Wolman, in a typical fashion, saw numerous cases of neurasthenia among officers and hysteria among privates. He saw the latter as a result of "conflict between the urge for self-defense and the national roles and ideals."[126] Thus, when no such conflict existed, the number of mental injuries declined. Wolman argued that "in Russia at the time of the Nazi invasion, the percentage of neurological diseases was much lower.... There is no doubt that the wonderful mental health of the Soviet soldier must be attributed to his intense love for his homeland." Wolman likewise argued that "there is no doubt that the Hebrew soldier has a very high moral and ideological level. Hebrew youth are imbued with patriotic love,

184   CHAPTER SIX

and its desire is to faithfully serve its people and country.... The moral order of the nation and the natural instinct of self-defense are not contrary to the Hebrew soldier."[127] Wolman attributed the supposed lack of mental health issues to this ideological fervor.

This was not the case with Holocaust survivors. Letz Halpern, at the Jerusalem front, likewise saw few mental problems with the native soldiers there, as "the hearts of our soldiers pulsed with a steady and brave spirit." However, Halpern mentioned "A whole different psychopathological issue are the cases among the newcomers. ... Many manifest the shocks of the past in various ways of mental and spiritual disturbances. Well-known are the adjustment difficulties of this group in days of peace and more so in times of war."[128] Halpern noted that many survivors "are still not free from the mental bruises [*khabalot nafhsiot*], both evident and hidden, of their tragic pasts at the extermination camps of their countries of origin, and are unable to withstand the further shocks of war."[129] Another doctor, Ernst Kalmus, at a Tel Aviv hospital, was a World War I veteran of the German military medicine. Kalmus brought with him German methods and ways of thinking. He boasted an experience of treating more than three thousand cases during World War I. Some of the cases were the result of "degeneration and hereditary issues," while others were completely "psychogenic" and could be cured by hypnosis or "suggestive electricity." The latter, Kalmus wrote with no small pride, was "an easy method which was used by the Jewish doctor Kaufman of Mannheim, who discovered in 1916 the surprising discovery that one can cure in that way war neurosis [*nivroza milkhamtit*]."[130] Following mainstream German examples, Kalmus saw psychogenic cases of war neurosis "as in all traumatic neurotics [*nivrotim travmataiim*], in the conscious desire to avoid military service (and often desiring compensation) by the operation of the hysterical mechanism [*mekhanismus histeri*]."[131]

Kalmus clearly never left the German fold (he often used Hebraicized German terms). But it should be noted that he and other doctors, whom Irit Keynan and others point out as examples of the cold-heartedness of the medical establishment, served side by side with others who showed completely different attitudes toward mental injuries. In fact, the fledging military psychiatry section of the IDF was dominated by British and American army veterans who drew on their recent experience, and saw mental injuries not as ideological weakness or desire for gain, but as a normal response that could be treated by applying the correct methods. A historical project commissioned by the IDF in the 1990s found widespread neglect and hostility toward mental injuries (in people who were often called "degim," short for *degenratim*, or degenerates), but also an organized response by volunteer doctors such as the British Army veteran Norman Cohen, who ran a military psychiatry in Sarafand (Tzrifin), and the South African Louise Miller, who had served in Italy, and ran the PI psychiatric facility in Jaffa. The Anglo-American contingent based its treatment on the work of Grinker and Spiegel, and emphasized drug treatment and psychotherapy.[132] Gerald Cohen in Haifa even sent psychiatric nurses and others to units to lecture on battle shock, and asked commanders to send him wounded soldiers.[133] Holocaust survivors were only mentioned as one group among other immigrant groups who lacked support networks and family, and who thus were more prone to long-term damage.[134] The mental health system built by the Anglo-American doctors, however, was dismantled after the war. They were, as one doctor recalled, "low priority" for the army, "like *Khevra kadisah* (burial society)."[135]

Subsequent wars saw similar cycles of learning and forgetting at the IDF. That fascinating history, however, is beyond the purview of this chapter. We should note that the fact that such knowledge was forgotten shows the low status and attention given to this issue in all countries under consideration. Mental injuries were a low priority for both armies and bureaucrats. Patients were either suspect or did not receive adequate care, and their fate very much depended on which doctor saw them and in which hospital they ended up. There was much variation. But the overall picture in Israel was not very different from the treatment of soldiers and survivors in Japan. Much of this was due to the transnational nature of mid-century psychiatry. There were close connections between different countries, and methods and ideas traveled back and forth. In all three of the countries just discussed here, the beginning of change in attitudes was due to the interplay of influences between sites of research and between military and civilian medicine. Change within German medicine, rising American influence, and the rise of more progressive forces within US psychiatry, were all part of this change. The crux of these developments was the struggle about compensation and pensions in both the West and Japan. We will pick up this thread in the next chapter.

Conclusion: The Curse of Objectivity I

In a draft of an unpublished 1955 paper, Konuma Masuho departed from his usual dry and scientific manner of writing and conveyed the words of his research subjects. He quoted complaints like "It's so bad that I can't even talk about it," "I forget what I just said," "My children say that my mother must have become stupid," "I sometimes forget what I'm holding in my hand," "I forget things immediately after I put them down," and the like. These were followed by complaints on excessive fatigue, and of easily "losing patience." In the draft, however, this section is crossed out, and the article instead opts for detailing percentages of amnesia, mental intolerance, and the like.[136] This incorporation and eventual erasure of victims' voices is symbolic of Konuma's overall research. Konuma, more than any other psychiatrist, came close to incorporating the nonsomatic and psychological complaints of *hibakusha*. Significantly, he did integrate psychoanalysis into his research. His exposure to and interest in psychoanalysis and atypical military experience at the military sanatorium allowed him to go beyond the narrow confines of previous research. But he eventually stayed in lane, opting for the "scientific" over the subjective. In a letter to Nakazawa Masao, "Konuma admitted that as a researcher, he maintained a firm positivist stance [*jisshō shugi no tachiba*] and did not base his argument on phenomenological theories [*genshō-ron*], especially those based on mere complaints and interviews."[137] This absence of victims' voices was typical of the profession as a whole.

The result of this stance was a persistent inability to connect the "phenomena" of memory loss, fatigue, and the like to the organic and "objective" changes Konuma was after. He and other researchers recognized the damage done by the bomb, but did not use "traumatic neurosis" and related terms. And even in the military, where such terms were used, they were mostly related to flight into illness, desire for compensation, and so on. It would be easy to condemn Konuma's and others' excessive caution. Indeed, as we saw with Asada's attitude in 1959 and survivors' responses, psychiatrists could be easily perceived as callous and disconnected. But we must remember that the situation in which doctors were operating was not conducive to research. This was the result of several factors. First, severe censorship by SCAP in the early years after the war curtailed any research related to the bomb. Second, cultural and social taboos prevented many survivors from seeking help or even openly talking about their suffering. Third, as we saw with military research, Japanese psychiatry was traditionally hostile to psychological trauma. Fourth, the peculiar nature of radiation and its unknown character made it hard to distinguish between physical and mental effects. Fifth, and because of the above, no reparation schemes were set for mental injuries, so there was no institutional incentive to evaluate survivors. Finally, as we saw in the Israeli and

KONUMA AND THE PSYCHIATRY OF THE BOMB

German cases, Japanese psychiatry was operating well within the medical consensus outside the United States.

Except for the US Navy reports and Matsumoto's brief encounter with Konuma, American medicine indeed was curiously absent from A-bomb psychiatric research. This is not to say that US researchers had no impact. American methods were important in Israeli battlefield psychiatry, and German émigrés serving with the United States, like Kalinowsky, were important conduits of knowledge. (Uchimura, as well, mentions his connection with an émigré US military psychiatrist with whom he studied.)[138] American influence was on the rise. But in Israel, Japan, and, of course West Germany, this was still very much a German world In Hiroshima and Nagasaki, American medicine was more important in what it did not do (i.e., tackle psychiatry) than in what it did. Konuma, Nishikawa, Oho, and almost all psychiatrists who worked on A-bomb research invoked ABCC inaction as an important motivation. On the other hand, all researchers, Konuma included, also worked at times directly with the ABCC and were in contact with researchers there. Relations with the ABCC were a primary mover of Japanese research in other fields as well. As Iida Kaori shows, this combination of resistance and co-option was typical of the Japanese medical profession's relationship to the ABCC, and that of science as a whole.[139]

The institution was a colossus in the stricken cities, and its influence impacted research in many unpredicted ways. Konuma and other Japanese scientists had a very good reason to stick to the objective and scientific. Japanese doctors had to "out-objectify" the ABCC and be more scientific and cautious than any American doctors. As we saw in the previous chapter, with the accusations hurled at Shimizu Kiyoshi and others, Japanese researchers were often suspected of being sentimental and unobjective. Therefore, not unlike in USSBS research, there are almost no victims' voices in psychiatric research, but only numbers and charts. There is also no culture or politics. The complete lack of any attention to cultural factors is very much in contrast to both wartime military psychiatry's emphasis on Japanese spirit, and Matsumoto's use of culture in his encounter with Lifton. This can be explained by the discrediting of racialist thinking, as well as the power relations between the ABCC and Japanese researchers. The language of science and objectivity was the only way through which Japanese scientists could hope to reintegrate into an American-dominated world.

This was not a new experience for Japanese researchers. Konuma's predecessors had to prove to a similarly skeptical nineteenth-century medical world that Japanese could be as objective and scientific as Europeans. This constant suspicion of researchers' motives and their outsider status had an outsized impact on both *hibakusha* and Holocaust research. While in the 1950s medical consensus made it difficult to prove connections between the experience of mass death and long-term damage, this was beginning to change as a result of a struggle by sympathetic doctors who fought for the rights of survivors and veterans. These German, American, and Israeli researchers brought morality and politics into their research in ways that were unthinkable in 1950s Japanese research. Japanese researchers as well, from the mid-1950s onward, started to connect their research with politics in a similar struggle for rights. But, as we will see in the next chapter, the consequences of such struggle and the entry of politics into science was quite different for Hiroshima and Holocaust research.

CHAPTER SEVEN

Kubo Yoshitoshi and the Psychology of Peace

"Isn't it the duty of the A-bombed nation to produce a white paper on the A-bomb, based on advanced scientific research as cold and detached [*reigen na kagakuteki sōgō kenkyū*] as that which was conducted on the manufacture of the A-bomb, and present it to the world so that Hiroshima will never be repeated?" — Kanai Tashirō, 1958[1]

In late 1945 the US Army produced a training film for US troops heading to Japan. The film, *Our Job in Japan* — written by Theodor S. Geisel, better known by his pen name, Dr. Seuss, and directed by Frank Capra — was a sharp departure from earlier training materials that had told soldiers to expect "a knife in your back" from the vengeful Japanese.[2] *Our Job in Japan* saw the US mission as a benevolent one, and the role of the Army not as fighting and subjecting the Japanese, but educating them. While showing pictures of regular Japanese going about their business, the film asked, "What does a conquering army do with seventy million people? . . . What do we do with the Japanese people when the military leaders they followed are gone? They can still make trouble, or they can make sense. We have decided to make sure they make sense." Then, focusing on what appears to be a Japanese scientist in a lab coat, the film went on: "Our job starts here. Our problems are in the brain inside of the Japanese head." Over an uncanny background image of brains floating in space, the narrator continued, "There are seventy million of these in Japan, physically no different than any other brains in the world, actually all made of exactly the same stuff as ours. These brains, like our brains, can do good things or bad things, all depending on the kind of ideas that are put inside" (figure 8).[3]

The focus on the figure of the scientist was not accidental. As we have seen in the 1946 ABCC mission, scientists were given a special role in

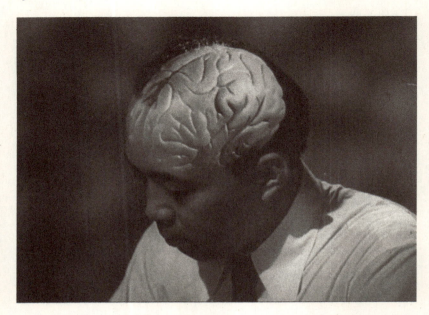

FIGURE 8. "The Japanese brain." From the US Army training film *Our Job in Japan* (Washington: National Audio-Visual Center, 2015).

the occupation's project of transforming Japan. Progressive ideas gained much traction after that country's defeat, as the United States tried to incorporate Japan and other Asian countries into its Cold War camp. And postwar reconstruction was promoted by many in psychological terms. As Jennifer Miller has argued, American policy makers came to believe that for democracy to "endure [it] required a psychologically strong citizenry that was capable of remaining vigilant about protecting democratic values while distinguishing between healthy and harmful ideas."[4] Indeed, there is a straight line leading from the firebombings of Tokyo to the seminars in psychology given by American scholars to their peers in the late 1940s. Both were intended to teach the Japanese "to make sense," and to put the "right kind of ideas inside" their heads. Both bombs and sociological theories were aimed at the "Japanese mind." Though such campaigns professed equality between Japanese and Americans, there was no doubt about the hierarchies involved in the enterprise. The "common sense" and science that Japanese were taught was American. But Japanese scientists, like the society around them, embraced American ideas and sought to use them in building a democratic and peaceful country. Japanese scientists also wanted to use American resources and networks to promote their own status and agendas, not all of which coincided with American goals.

Focusing on Kubo Yoshitoshi (figure 9), this chapter examines the way A-bomb psychology was entangled with the postwar transformation of Japan. The chapter, in many ways, takes us back to the ideas and struggles examined in the earlier chapters. The campaign by Alexander Leighton and his peers to teach Japanese Americans "democratic thought and action" was adopted wholeheartedly by SCAP. The contradictions inherent in this project were carried over to Japan as well. The legacy of occupation and war and the ever-growing impact of the United States were perpetually present in Kubo's life and work. Kubo had a long personal relationship with the United States. He had spent his early childhood in Worcester, Massachusetts, where his father, Kubo Yoshihide, obtained a PhD in

FIGURE 9. Kubo Yoshitoshi. Photo courtesy of the *Chugoku Shinbun* company.

psychology from Clark University. Kubo was in direct contact with many American organizations and academics. He had worked with the American occupation, and later with the ABCC. His concern with political action, his connection of the experience of the A-bomb with peace activism, and his belief in the role of scholars in promoting such goals paralleled and was connected to the activities of American psychological experts. In many ways, Kubo, with his focus on opinion polls and the gauging of survivor attitudes, continued the work of the USSBS. Like his American peers, he was interested in panic and the short-term impact of the A-bomb, on one hand, and the larger impact of the bomb and the war on society, on the other. And for his as for others, trauma (a word he never used) was not an important category.

Kubo and his peers had their own agenda. As his involvement with antinuclear work deepened, his research was framed more and more in opposition to the ABCC and American research. The move from working with the Americans to a more oppositional stance paralleled a move in his work from working for peace and reconciliation to promoting nuclear disarmament and *hibakusha* relief. Kubo saw the insertion of *hibakusha* voices and opinions into public debates on nuclear disarmament as the ultimate goal of his research. But he did it in his own "scientific" way. With his commission to survey *hibakusha* psychological and sociological difficulties, he was also drawn more and more into the contentious politics of the time, which did not sit well with his ideas of "objective" science. He kept working with the ABCC and, even more importantly, within the contours of American ideas of Cold War science. Kubo and his peers aspired to the scientific and objective, and kept their distance from emotion, even while calling for a more empathetic view of victims' suffering. This was a picture very different from that of Holocaust victims and veterans, where activist researchers moved away from "cold" and objective science and toward a more empathetic science—a position in complete opposition to the ideas of Hiroshima scientists.

This chapter begins by exploring the meeting of American and Japanese social sciences under the occupation, and the implications of the project of creating a "democratic mind." It then examines Kubo's participation in "peace psychology," his subsequent research into *hibakusha* experiences, and his involvement with peace circles, the ABCC, and the compensation movement. The chapter ends with a comparative look at developments in Japan and the West as psychological experts in both settings struggled for recognition of their patients' rights as part of the larger struggles of the

1950s and early 1960s. The chapter carries us all the way to 1962 and the meeting between Kubo and Lifton, which demonstrated the many ways both men were at the same time of the same mind, yet quite apart.

The Democratic Mind

In December 1945, echoing the arguments of *Our Job in Japan*, President Truman's adviser James Byrnes said, "So now we have come to the second phase of our war against Japan—what might be called the spiritual disarmament of the people of that nation—to make them want peace instead of wanting war. This is in some respects a more difficult task than that of effecting physical disarmament. Attitudes of minds cannot be changed at the points of bayonets or merely by issuance of edicts."[5] Byrnes's emphasis of the continuities between wartime "disarmament" and postwar "spiritual disarmament" was telling. In many ways, democratizing Japanese minds was a continuation of wartime campaigns; and psychological experts, yet again, played a leading role. Bruno Bettelheim, for instance, argued for "designing a blueprint for psychological reconstruction on a mass scale that would bring the national characters of Germany and Japan back into the normal range, away from perverse dependence and toward a healthy self-reliance."[6] This was an ethos that, developed as it was in the context of the Japanese American camps and in OWI, was quite flawed; but it had enormous influence on the way Americans and Japanese dealt not only with reconstruction but with the legacy of the bombing raids that devastated the very minds and bodies of the enemy subjects whom researchers aimed to reform.

The principal organ of educating the Japanese was SCAP's Civil Information and Education (CIE) unit. CIE was, as Miriam Kingsberg Kadia has argued, "the primary institutional mechanism through which U.S. human scientists transmitted putatively American values to Japan."[7] At the CIE, its Public Opinion and Sociological Research Division (PO&SR) functioned very similarly to the BSR. The similarities were not accidental. In terms of both personnel and ideology, PO&SR was continuing the BSR's work. The unit was run by Herbert Passin, who worked in the camps. Clyde Kluckhohn, also an internment camps and OWI veteran, was another influential member.[8] Kluckhohn, who would later work at RAND with Irving Janis, was also involved in introducing Matsumoto to the ABCC.[9] Matsumoto was one of several Nisei social scientists, and a University of Chicago alumnus (Passin was also a Chicago graduate) employed by PO&SR. Chicago and BSR sociology were thus important influences on the unit. Like the BSR, PO&SR was tasked with surveying Japanese attitudes toward the occupation reforms and the administration of the country. And, as in the camps, PO&SR was a training ground for "native" social scientists who served as both local "informants" and "models" for the transformation of their fellow citizens. Transitioning from "authoritarian" German to American models was an important trope in this enterprise. Kluckhohn, for instance, argued "that Germanic logic, philosophy, and ideas of law and the state had molded prewar Japanese research into a means of promoting autocracy within and aggression without . . . not something based on free inquiry resulting in universal good."[10]

Japanese social scientists had much to gain from this enterprise. Many Americans accepted their Japanese peers as equal. The occupation saw a jettisoning of psychological racism of the kind that was practiced by the likes of Geoffrey Gorer. Ruth Benedict's work was particularly important in the development of such ideas, as it argued for the Japanese ability to change and accept democracy. Working with the Americans offered not just steady employment at a time when academic positions were scarce and many were struggling to make ends meet, but also an opportunity to reconnect with international research networks. As Miriam Kingsberg Kadia has argued, participating in social science networks was beneficial for both Japanese and Americans, as "recognition of Japan's ability to formulate objective knowledge allowed the nation to enter the Euro-American intellectual community, transforming it from a Western into a truly transnational network."[11] On a less sanguine note, this move also allowed Japanese (and German) social scientists who worked with the Americans to elide complicated questions of their own war responsibility and engage in "soul searching" in the name of science, calling on Japanese to be more progressive, scientific, and rational.

Kubo Yoshitoshi fitted right in with this move. During the war he was with the Imperial Navy Technological Research Institute, where he engaged in tests on human/machine interaction and the improvement of fleet watchers' ability to recognize enemy planes.[12] Kubo's work with naval aviation was a continuation of a tradition of sorts within Japanese psychology. The Aviation Research Institute at Tokyo Imperial University was founded in 1918 by Matsumoto Matatarō, one of the first to introduce applied psychology to Japan, and Obonai Torao. The profession was also long connected with the navy.[13] As Brian McVeigh has demonstrated, Japanese psychology—like its American and German counterparts, though on a much smaller scale—was wholly mobilized at the service of the imperial state. Besides working with the navy and army, psychologists also worked in moral suasion campaigns and mobilization as part of the education ministry.[14] The Naval Research Institute, where Kubo worked, was one of the main organs of wartime psychological research, employing more than a hundred psychologists.[15] The relatively small scale of the enterprise, however, reflected the small size of the profession and its relative lack of influence as compared to psychiatry and other disciplines. Arguably until the 1920s, psychology was not seen as important by the state. No students were sent abroad to study it, and it was imported into Japan mostly through individual initiatives. Thus, unlike psychiatry, where specialized journals and societies existed from the 1880s, psychology only became a specialized course in Tokyo Imperial University, under Motora Yūjirō, in 1903.[16] Like psychiatry, however, the discipline was heavily influenced by German psychology. Also, like psychiatry, the discipline was relatively indifferent to Freud and his associates. Significantly, one of the few in Japan who had written on Freud was Kubo's father, Kubo Yoshihide, who had been exposed to Freud's work in the United States.[17]

As Osaka Eiko has demonstrated, the occupation heralded a shift in Japanese psychology toward American methodologies.[18] This shift continued after the occupation ended in 1952, as Japanese researchers tried to integrate themselves into the American-dominated Cold War world of postwar research.[19] Kubo was at the heart of this shift. PO&SR and other CIE initiatives played an important role in this development. During the occupation, GHQ set up the Institute for Educational Leadership (IFEL) under CIE, whose mission "was to create new educational leader groups in the principles of the new democratic education."[20] The institute had an important role in disseminating postwar psychology. Other CIE initiatives also brought in psychologists from the United States, such as Clarence Henry Graham of Columbia University, who gave lectures to about thirty Japanese psychologists in Kyoto.[21] This was part of a larger initiative by the CIE of conducting American studies seminars, based on work done in Europe.[22] Policy makers had been planning this campaign from the early days of the occupation. According to Kawashima Takefumi, Colonel Kermit R. Dyke, the first chief of CIE and a former executive of the NBC broadcasting network in the United States, had already told him in late 1945 that he needed his help to recruit "sociologists and psychologists . . . in order to overcome the backwardness of Japanese opinion polling" methods.[23] Kubo and his Navy peers were important in this recruitment drive. Psychologists in the army were suspect, but psychologists with the Naval Technology Research Institute were neither subject to expulsion nor barred from the public office and therefore could fulfill the new roles CIE had envisioned for them.[24]

The transformation of the social sciences was by no means solely an American imposition. Japanese social scientists were very much the driving force in the movement to democratize Japanese minds. Dyke's campaign resulted in the establishment not only of PO&SR, but also of related organs outside SCAP, such as the cabinet information bureau's Public Opinion Research Division (*Nihon yoron kenkyūjo*); the Japan Public Opinion Research Association (*Nihon yoron chōsa kenkyūkai*), founded in 1948 with American help; and the Association for the Scientific Study of Public Opinion (*Yoron kagaku kyōkai*). The members of the Navy's Technical Research Institute group were also the founding members of the Scientific Association. Kubo served as executive director while the president was the sociologist Toda Teizō, who worked with PO&SR. Other psychologists were Kaneko Hiroshi (also a PO&SR consultant), Hatano Kanji, and Togawa Yuiko.[25] The institute sought to reform Japan's public opinion surveys on the basis of American models. Members introduced methods like random sampling, aiming at representing "mass opinion" scientifically and increasing the importance of public opinion in the new democratic politics, which members contrasted with the elitism of prewar methods.[26] Yet the institute's budgetary allocations, networks, and affiliation with the Agriculture, Forestry, and Fisheries Ministry was very much a carryover from the wartime surveillance state. The ministry, very much like the New Deal surveys conducted by Rensis Likert in the United States, had a network of rural informants, which the occupation sought to use for its own ends. SCAP abolished the old structure, which it saw as being too close to the Special Higher Police network, but it retained the budget. The ministry, which "wanted to use this budget to capture the trend of rural public opinion from an impartial standpoint," then turned to Kubo and Kaneko.[27]

The institute initially operated independently of SCAP, but, as Kaneko recalled, "one day a Nisei officer in army uniform came to the offices of the association . . . and said they [association officers] were needed at G1 [the Civil Information and Education Section, or CIE] at [occupation] headquarters. It was not a good feeling. It was like being summoned to the magistrate during the oppression of the Edo period."[28] Association leadership met with Passin, "who was very appreciative of their methods," and "started to work very closely with CIE."[29] PO&SR's Seki Keigo recalled, "The room [where we worked] was filled with [the Institute's] public opinion people and others who were trying to use new methods of surveying."[30] The ideas that radiated from PO&SR outward were in the same language of science and objectivity that was used by Leighton and Matsumoto (a civilian employee of PO&SR) at the USSBS and later at the ABCC. There was much overlap between the surveys conducted on bombed populations and those done during the later occupation by Kubo and others to gauge the impact of land reform on rural populations. While in the United States researchers progressed from rural civilian surveys to the BSR work in the camps, and then to militarized public opinion or morale studies, in Japan the research started with morale and then moved to civilian surveys to gauge the progress of democratization.

When he turned to *hibakusha* research in the late 1940s, Kubo carried with him these very methods and convictions. As Osaka Eiko has noted, Kubo's was the only article on the A-bomb by a psychologist to be published during the occupation. The article adopted American-style sampling and other survey methods, reflecting Kubo's experience at the association.[31] Kubo approached the problem from the angle of *hibakusha* experience and its impact on public opinion, and like his peers at the association, he sought to include common survivor voices in public conversations on peace, democracy, and the A-bomb. Knowingly or not, he was continuing the wartime work of the USSBS and the BSR, once again surveying bombed populations—not for the purpose of healing, but to connect his research on survivors to the pursuit of "higher" political goals through "objective" and scientific methods.

Kubo Yoshitoshi and the Psychology of War and Peace

Kubo left the Association for the Scientific Study of Public Opinion in 1949, for a position at Hiroshima University. His father, Kubo Yoshihide, who had founded the university's psychology department in 1929, had died in 1942, but the family had stayed in Hiroshima. It is not clear how much his father's position had influenced the university's decision to hire Kubo, or whether he had been slated to fill the job while he was away with the Navy. But the family was in Hiroshima on 6 August 1945, and Kubo's mother, wife, and eldest daughter were exposed to the A-bomb at their home in the Sendamachi neighborhood, about three kilometers from the epicenter. Kubo could not get in touch with his family almost until October, when he went to visit them. He recalled, "I was so shocked by the destruction, I could not even shed a tear."[32] Kubo connected his turn to psychological research on the bombing survivors directly to his personal and family experience. As he would recall in 1977, he was convinced of the importance of the survivor experience to the goal of peace: "My research led me to believe that the feelings and attitudes of A-bomb survivors toward the atomic bombing and the war should be pursued by all fields of science, not to mention psychology and sociology, and that there was much potential for change [in general attitudes] as the period of the bombing and defeat in the war passed."[33] This statement was no doubt colored by his later experiences, but one could see similar rationales in Kubo's writing as early as 1950.

Kubo first published his research on survivors in April 1950, in a handwritten circular within Hiroshima University. A slightly altered version was published in 1952. Unusually for an academic work, the research garnered media attention. Explaining his work in an interview in June 1950, Kubo noted the disproportionate attention given to the American opinions about the A-bomb, which, he emphasized, were researched with funds from Carnegie, Rockefeller, and other institutions at Gallup and other surveys. But Kubo protested, "What about the issue of [our] people's attitudes and opinions toward the atomic bomb and nuclear power? Although a few articles by [Japanese] experts have been published in newspapers and magazines, there has been no comprehensive study of the attitudes and opinions of the general public, especially those who experienced the atomic bombing." Kubo, together with other social scientists and activists, was tasked by the city of Hiroshima with collecting testimonies of survivors, and he was moved by them. He was convinced of the importance of disseminating them and bringing *hibakusha* voices to the public, telling a reporter, "Only those who have been exposed to the atomic bomb once [can] know whether it is right or wrong to use it on ordinary people."[34]

Kubo was not interested in victims' personal stories per se, but, following the usual trajectory of psychological experts at the time, he wanted to research how the experience connected to the bigger agenda of peace and reconciliation, namely the survivors' commitment to peace. Presenting the connection as self-evident, he wrote, "The unprecedented experience of the atomic bombing *naturally* had an enormous impact on the attitudes and opinions of the *hibakusha*, so researching nuclear [science] from the perspective of the social sciences must *naturally* include a comprehensive survey of the attitudes and opinions of the *hibakusha* in this regard" (my emphasis). Furthermore, Kubo was not going to present the testimonies unmediated and unfiltered, as the research would "not be served by listing individual stories or by skillful reportage and rhetorical alterations." Kubo was aiming at scientific accuracy. He did not trust survivors' subjective testimony. He explained: "Since the atomic bombing was an unprecedented experience, many stories have been told by *hibakusha* to each other and to people who were not exposed to the bomb, and I imagine that there are many cases in which people unwittingly confuse their own experiences with those of others, or consciously or unconsciously exaggerate their own experiences."[35] Thus, while elevating *hibakusha* voices, he was at the same time suspicious of the *hibakusha* testimony, and argued for the need to mediate their voices through his own scientific expertise. As in the greater project of democracy in occupied Japan, the people's voices were important in principle, but they required the intervention of experts in the public sphere.

Kubo's distrust of *hibakusha* voices was very much connected to the "unprecedented experience" of being A-bombed. Later thinkers in trauma studies, such as the psychologist Dori Laub and the literary scholar Cathy Caruth, accorded the witness to mass violence a special "truth" value, which not only complemented but even at times was considered superior to historical or juridical knowledge. Such debates are particularly passionate in regard to the Holocaust, as most "factual" and documentary evidence in that case was produced by the Nazis.[36] Kubo's episteme could not have been more different. Measuring himself against the American ideas of science, he aspired to the objective. Thus, given what he saw as the rhetorical embellishments in testimonies, he defined the "target of the survey" as "find[ing] out whether the reported experiences were true or not." This impacted both the kind of testimonies he examined and his methodology. Reflecting his elitism, almost all fifty-four of his interviewees were academics, as "it was necessary to select survey targets who have a high degree of accuracy in the reported course of action."[37] In the revised version of his article published in 1952, Kubo was even more pointed, writing that he had limited the survey to Hiroshima academics in order to "select people who could reliably report their behavioral experiences," and who were "well educated and aware of the value of social research."[38] The need for accuracy was magnified by the nature of the experience. The major reaction Kubo identified, following the trajectory of American civil defense researchers, was panic. However, "in general, behavior in paniclike situations is fragmentary . . . and is expressed in fragmentary language and speech. Therefore, in analyzing panic behavior, we must take the position opposite to reportage; that is, instead of compiling fragments, we must further fragment the fragmented nature expressed in the spoken language." Kubo was after general patterns. So he deconstructed the various testimonies, and on the basis of social "scientific method," he searched for commonalities to ensure that the "analysis is as objective as possible."[39] For Kubo, it was the very fragmentary nature of what we now call traumatic memory that made it problematic, and victims' testimony unreliable and unscientific. The victims' own words, as in Konuma and most of the American surveys, were almost nowhere to be found.

In direct contrast with earlier USSBS research, however, Kubo sought to find the exact mechanism that led from violent psychological shock (intense stimuli) to the change of political attitudes. His main theoretical references were SSRC reports into American opinions, and, significantly, Hadley Cantril's 1940 *Invasion from Mars* and the idea of "frames of references." Cantril defined the term as the psychological makeup that structured an individual response to panic-induced events. But Kubo seemed to imply that this could also mean the survivors' larger psychological makeup and political attitudes and outlook (he did not follow on this in the 1950 research). It is quite telling that Cantril's work on a fictional alien invasion would serve as a primary reference for Kubo's tackling of the very real experience of A-bomb victims. Cantril's American credentials, the importance of his work on panic, and the general importance given to work on panic in American psychology enabled Kubo's use of Cantril's work; but it also demonstrated the extent to which myth and fantasy were intermixed with scientific work on the impact of the A-bomb.

The main use of Cantril's work by Kubo was in showing how the A-bomb destroyed older ways of thinking and frames of reference, and led to new ones. Kubo argued, "The goal is to establish a behavioral framework for the unprecedented panic of the AB bombing, and to clarify the special attitudinal formation process of AB survivors."[40] Kubo divided survivors' reactions into four stages: "instinctive action," "panic," "quasi-panic," and a "blank" (stupefied) stage. None of these stages, however, lasted beyond a week or two after the bomb.[41] Kubo, like Janis, divided the various shocks into groups, noting that the shock of the bomb event was compounded by the sight of dead and wounded, which was particularly gruesome in Hiroshima. Survivors constantly looked for familiar patterns to understand the situation, as "the 'frame of reference' [English in original] that had been the standard of behavior was now completely destroyed.... When we are in such a 'critical situation' [English in original]—that is, when we are looking for a standard or frame to interpret again—we receive stimuli such as injured people, voices calling for help, and smell of fire."[42] This led to panic and chaos; but as Japan was still at war, many reverted to a wartime mode of behavior. Kubo noted that, "while some people escaped and others were apathetic, many were angered by the bomb and sought to fight the United States "as a suicide squad."[43]

Kubo added the surrender as the final group of stimuli. The defeat led to a final change, as "frustration disappeared completely, leaving only emptiness and escape." But how does this emptiness lead to current attitudes toward war? Kubo left this question unanswered. His research ends with the defeat. "We can hardly estimate the next stage," he concluded, "but perhaps some time afterward, every respondent succeeded in slowly adjusting to their circumstances."[44] Kubo acknowledged the limitations of his survey: "Since this survey was based on behavior immediately after the bombing, the effect on attitudes or frame of reference is not known, but about half of the 54 respondents reported this aspect of their behavior." *Hibakusha* noted that they felt different, "that it was very unpleasant for others to see the keloids caused by the bombing, that they should wear badges to identify them as *hibakusha* (like the wounded soldier insignia) ... [and] that it was inconceivable that those who died in the bombing would be in heaven."[45] Yet Kubo did not follow up in his research beyond the immediate experience, and just assumed that the shock of the bomb led to a change that lasted until the 1950s. The experience of discrimination, he conceded, showed that "the influence [of the experience] is very strong, and [the difference in] the frame of reference between the experienced and the inexperienced is nonexistent."[46] But Kubo stopped short of examining conditions and long-term damage, and did not detail the long-term mechanism that connected the initial shock with issues like anxiety, numbness and the like, which were already known at the time.

Kubo's insistence on scientific patterns and distrust of victims' stories should be understood in the context of both the nature of the testimonies he heard, and the political and scholarly world in which he was operating. Transcripts of Kubo's interviews were circulating among Hiroshima activists, and a number of them made it into private correspondence between Ogura Kaoru (a Seattle-born city official and translator) and the author

Robert Jungk, a German-Jewish émigré who wrote extensively on the A-bomb. Ogura passed to Jungk, in installments, the "compiled report of 42 reports of University professors of their experience both in action and in mind on the particular August 6 and the following 7th," the content of which was quite graphic.[47] A typical testimony Ogura translated, written by a "Professor of Eastern History," spoke of how "corpses are seen only along the roads. . . . [many are] facing towards heaven, some are sitting dead with intestines exposed. And some are dead in the air-raid shelter. . . . Hiroshima City is an entirely scorched and a devastated plain. This is terrible. [I] thought we are annihilated. [I] felt completely defeated."[48] Similar descriptions abound in Kubo's testimonies. This was not an easy material to generalize or write a scientific treatise about. With a few exceptions, such accounts were heavily censored in Japan. Not until 1952, with the publication of accounts such as the *Asahi gurafu* exposé, were they more openly discussed.

Furthermore, such descriptions of horror did not fit with the optimistic outlook and spirit of reconciliation that Kubo was actively promoting at the time, both within Hiroshima and through the institutions of Japanese psychology. On 3 April 1950, the same month his first draft of the Hiroshima research was circulating, Japanese psychologists met at the fourteenth annual conference of the Japanese Psychological Association (JPA). Kubo was one of "seven leading psychologists [who] issued a 'peace appeal to American psychologists.' "[49] This was the start of an organizational drive under the banner "Japanese Psychologists for Peace" (JPP). The peace appeal made a point of the Japanese psychologists' unique situation as citizens of "the country [which] experienced the terrors of the atomic bombs in Hiroshima and Nagasaki."[50] The fact of American responsibility for this "experience" was not mentioned. Emphasizing their cooperation with the US reformist agenda, the psychologists stated that "after the war, we, Japanese psychologists, have made every effort to democratize our country and to establish the [*sic*] academic freedom. We can never forget the great contribution of peace-loving scientists in the United States to the establishment of academic freedom in Japan." The declaration vaguely referred to Japan's recent imperialist past, and demonstrated its ignorance of or disagreement with Freud, when it stated: "We know that 'aggression' is not human instinct and that development of this kind of behaviors mostly depends upon some historical and social circumstances." But the statement did not develop the point any further. The declaration ended on a very optimistic note, with a call for world peace.[51]

This was no place for recollecting the horrible suffering that had been meted on Hiroshima by the USAAF.

Notably, the statement was building on the above-mentioned 1944 appeal, initiated by Gordon Allport in "Human Nature and Peace," and the 1948 "Statement by Scientists in Japan on the Problem of Peace," both which appeared in a volume edited by Hadley Cantril.[52] The latter statement was part of a campaign to promote "peace thought" by both Japanese and American social scientists, through groups such as JPP and "the Peace Study Group" in Japan, and SPSSI in the United States.[53] Cantril was connected with SPSSI and other groups in which USSBS veterans like David Krech operated. Allport, who had worked with Cantril in the 1930s, and others were active in the movement.[54] Cantril's peace activism helps further to explain Kubo's choice of his work. This was another important link between the work done by American psychologists and Japanese psychologists, who shared a very similar agenda. Besides the shared belief in the duty of behavioral scientists to help promote peace in both countries, the concern of psychologists was not with the impact of the A-bomb on individual mental health, but with greater social issues, first and foremost the problems of aggression and war.

After the 1950 meeting, JPP established a number of "study objects." These included "'experience of the atomic bombs,' 'Nazi concentration camps,' 'war psychology,' and 'peace consciousness of the adolescents.'"[55] This early juxtaposition with Holocaust work was important. But, again, this was not done out of concern for damage to individuals. Rather, work on the A-bomb was subsumed under a general framework that connected to problems of totalitarianism and war, and the general experience of Japanese under fascism. It indicated the impact of American thinking, where the experience of the camps was also mostly thought of in the context of the problem of totalitarianism, and the relative ease with which Japanese social scientists identified with the experience of victimization. Two essays on the work of Bruno Bettelheim by the psychologists Shimizu Ikutarō and Kido Kōtarō clearly illustrated these points.

Shimizu connected his reading of Bettelheim to the outbreak of the Korean War, as "once the war broke out, the situation Bettelheim had described was far more difficult to deal with."[56] Shimizu was referring to the fear among intellectuals regarding the return of totalitarianism with the outbreak of war. As Jennifer Miller has noted, "The Korean War altered the landscape of anxieties" in Japan.[57] Shimizu reflected this as he wrote that reading Bettelheim reminded him of Bronisław Malinowski's

204   CHAPTER SEVEN

Freedom and Civilization, in which "Malinowski passionately teaches that even democracies must inevitably become totalitarian as soon as they begin to prepare for war. . . . We live in a world where [Bettelheim's] work is still not out of date."[58] Shimizu summarized Bettelheim's 1943 work "Individual and Mass Behavior in Extreme Situations," focusing on the "initial shock and collapse of self" that occurred as prisoners arrived in the camp, and the "prisoners' regression into infantile phase where man became what the Nazis wanted him to be."[59] Shimizu's main interest was in the collapse of mental defenses, which led to loss of individuality and humanity. Such understanding of the camp experience was parallel to the contemporary understanding of those experiencing traumatic neurosis, "brainwashing," "battle shock" and so on, which were seen in various locales, as "regression to the infantile." But Shimizu was not interested in trauma. He was after an explanation of why prisoners obeyed, why they "mimicked the Gestapo," and how group solidarity was broken.[60] Shimizu was not misreading Bettelheim. These things were very much what Bettelheim himself was interested in, comparing the prisoners' obedience to the camp guards to Germans' obedience to Hitler. Bettelheim, who had spent time in Dachau and Buchenwald after Kristallnacht but had managed to flee Germany, did not see the camps as primarily an anti-Jewish institution. As he wrote in his review of Hannah Arendt's *Eichmann in Jerusalem*, the camps were "merely one part of the master plan to create the thousand-year totalitarian Reich." And, for him, Arendt, and many others, the Holocaust "was not the last chapter in anti-Semitism but rather one of the first chapters in modern totalitarianism."[61]

Most Japanese intellectuals thought of the experience of the camps through the lens of totalitarianism. Kido Kōtarō made this connection explicit in his 1955 essay *Tamashī no setusujin ichi ichi kyōseishūyōsho to ningen* (The Killing of Every Soul: Humans and the Concentration Camps). Kido, unlike Shimizu, did mention Bethlehem's Jewishness, if only in passing, but he was much more interested in his status as an academic who "used himself as a guinea pig . . . [and] analyzed the psychological mechanism of 'soul murder,' but saved his own soul." Kido argued that Bettelheim had done so by "splitting his ego into 'observing ego' and 'real ego.'"[62] Kido's summary of Bettelheim did not differ much from Shimizu's. Kido likewise focused on the loss of humanity and "the process of disintegration of the personality in the camps . . . where human dignity is shredded like a piece of paper, and torture labor turns people into slaves more obedient than bass [fish]."[63] The connection between suffering, dehuman-

KUBO AND THE PSYCHOLOGY OF PEACE

ization, and the power of objective observation was important for later researchers like Ishida Tadashi. Ishida, who was also influenced by Holocaust psychology, would use these insights to formulate a psychological theory of A-bomb suffering and healing through observation and struggle.

Herein lies the importance of the Japanese psychologists' mid-Fifties engagement with Bettelheim. Unlike Ishida and Lifton, Kido and his contemporaries connected the Holocaust not to A-bomb psychology but to the question of authoritarianism. Kido, for instance, emphasized regression, as prisoners "regressed to the childish belief that the Gestapo is righteous and kind, which they have received as an image of the Almighty Father."[64] He emphasized the coercive power of the group on the individual prisoner and the ingenuity of the Gestapo, in that by "throwing the individual into ... the group, they have, by both external and internal pressure, regressed the individual into a childlike mode of behavior and blind obedience to the will of the leader."[65] Kido made this coded reference to Japanese fascism explicit when he wrote that Bettelheim's work "reminds us of the Japanese military." Wartime Japan was a "concentration camp [organized] by the ruling class to deprive the people of their critical spirit and instill a spirit of obedience." Referring to the concept of a "vacuum zone" of nonthought, developed by the writer Noma Hiroshi, Kido argued that "the vicious cycle of adaptation and regression was extended to the entire nation, turning the whole of Japan into a 'vacuum zone' and a concentration camp."[66]

The psychologist Shimoyama Tokuji was an exception to this general trend. Shimoyama translated Viktor Frankl's *Man's Search for Meaning* into Japanese with the peculiar title *Yoru to kiri*, "Night and Fog," which is also the title of a film by Alain Resnais that came out the same year and had no relation to Frankl. In their comments on Frankl, Shimoyama and his unnamed publisher compared the experience of Auschwitz not to the oppression of Japanese by the militarists, but to the "Nanking Incident of 1937, in which Japanese troops, after occupying Nanking, shot, burned, tortured, raped, and murdered an estimated two hundred thousand innocent civilians." Auschwitz and Nanking, they wrote, "make us ashamed to be human. These events occurred in relation to the war, not in the war itself, but rather in [connection to] the internal politics of the nation and its people."[67] This was a departure from the conflation of war and fascism by Kido and Shimizu, which blurred the boundaries between victims and victimizers. Shimoyama here invited his readers to reflect on their role in the tragedy; but at the same time, his call for reflection was only implicit:

he was ashamed to be human, not to be Japanese. He was much more concerned with the issues of modernity and mechanized mass killing, writing, "This was not the result of primitive impulses or temporary excitement, but rather the organization, efficiency, and circumscription based on calm and careful planning . . . where 'modern mass-production industries were mobilized to reduce man from a vertical walking animal to a kilogram of ash.' "[68] This move was capped by a reference to Hiroshima and Nagasaki, which served as a grim warning for "the unfolding possibility of a new tragedy" and an example of the "correlation between technology and politics in the new machine age."[69] Thus, here as well, Hiroshima was eventually seen as the more appropriate equivalent to Auschwitz and the horrors of the new age, while Nanking was conjured to be the more "primitive" impulse—and, by implication, a thing of the past that the new Japan left behind). This does not mean that Shimoyama gave himself and his countrymen a free pass. Reflecting the general trends in mid-century psychology, he saw the real enemy as being within. Referring to these same "raw" impulses and the danger of the "cross-section of modern history and the pathology of politics and war," he asked, "Who is to say this story will not end in a different form? If we do not fight the snake?"[70]

Such debates, as fascinating as they are, were not about the victims but about the larger political and historical questions. The snake within was a metaphor, not a psychological category, and one concerned with perpetrators as such. Trauma, again, was just not a category that interested psychologists at the time. Even psychologists who worked on both Hiroshima and the camps, like Miyagi Otoya, did not make the connection. Miyagi, whose work "Psychology of Obedience to Authority" examined emperor worship in a manner similar to that of Shimizu and Kido, was part of a group that investigated the *hibakusha* in the early 1950s.[71] In 1952, as a result by efforts of JPP, the JPA decided to start an "investigation on the effects of the A-Bomb of Hiroshima," which they did in 1952, with Miyagi and two other directors (all of whom were also signatories on the 1950 peace declaration) heading the project. Kubo's work was the "flagship" of this research effort.[72] The only other work that came out of the project, however, was a round-table discussion convened by Miyagi at Hiroshima and published in 1952.

The round-table was notable in that, it had two military men as interviewees, and also in its constant use of supernatural metaphors and images by the *hibakusha*, a feature completely absent in Kubo's work, or any other work examined here. Miyagi interviewed Lieutenant General

KUBO AND THE PSYCHOLOGY OF PEACE

Matsumura Shūitsu, the former chief of staff of the Chūgoku Military District, and Major General Abe Masaya, who had served under him in the 59th Army. Matsumura and Abe were both seriously injured, and Matsumura had also been purged by the occupation for his wartime activities. The inclusion of the soldiers in the round-table was rather exceptional, as most Hiroshima testimonies circulating at the time were those of civilians. For practical reasons (most soldiers having left Hiroshima) and ideological ones (the emphasis on Hiroshima's victimization), the main image of survivors was one of noncombatants. Both Matsumura and Abe, as well as the civilians in the group, spoke of the horror of the Hiroshima bombing, retelling the story, familiar by now, of where they had been when the A-bomb hit, the flash, and then the dreadful sights around them. However, Matsumura and Abe were exceptional in emphasizing, not unlike American survivors of the time, their role as rescuers. Both also showed particular resentment at having been examined by Americans at the Iwakuni air base and at a Hiroshima hospital, where Abe ran away and hid from visiting American researchers.[73]

Both ex-soldiers and civilians spoke of ghosts (*yūrei*) and of the wounded being ghostlike (*yūrei no yō ni*), and also emphasized the long-term physical and mental price of the A-bomb. For instance, Matsumura, who was buried alive by the initial blast, recalled: "Ever since then, even when I was inside the house, when I was sleeping I felt afraid of the beams, which I didn't feel before, but I began to feel that I was in danger if they fell on me." Mori Michiko, a company employee, mentioned symptoms similar to A-bomb fatigue, and the failure of the ABCC to diagnose her.[74] Much as in Kubo's contemporary research, Miyagi's only diagnostic comment was to relate these difficulties to the shock of the A-bomb, or the "startle response" that hit "the surface of your consciousness. If the [shock] is severe enough, the patient may lose consciousness and become unable to recognize things" around him. This, he told the survivors, "causes memory problems. Not only in the case of the atomic bombing, but in other cases as well."[75] This was as far as any psychological expert went in connecting the A-bomb to other war experiences. It was also the only recognition of any long-term damage. But again, Miyagi did not develop this further, or publish further on the topic.

Kubo was operating not just within JPP, but in Hiroshima's own scholarly environment. In August 1950, the new president of Hiroshima University, the economist and former minister of education Morito Tatsuo, proposed establishing a social science research center that would focus on the problem of peace. Morito, a center socialist who had served time in jail before the war for his opinions, was well respected in Hiroshima. He was also one of the main promoters of what Nemoto Masaya insightfully called the "Hiroshima Paradox," where Hiroshima intellectuals claimed that the experience of being bombed (*hibaku taiken*) endowed them with a unique victim status, but also repudiated any notion of a particular victimizer (i.e., the United States).[76] Thus, Morito condemned "outsiders" who tried to spoil Hiroshima's faith in "the constructive power of the human spirit" and its quest for peace. In a particular twist in the USSBS quest to demystify the bomb, Morito added: "There is a deplorable tendency among the promoters of the peace movement. That is, their overemphasis on the destructivity of atom bombs, just to stir up antagonistic national sentiment."[77] Building on such sentiment, both Kubo and Morito joined the World Brotherhood (WB) organization. Kubo became the the executive director of the Hiroshima branch. The organization, launched in 1950 at UNESCO in Paris, as an offshoot of the National Conference of Christians and Jews in the United States, had been established on the basis of "a belie[f] in a spiritual interpretation of the universe to promoting justice, understanding, and cooperation among people varying as to religion, race, or nation."[78] WB had a whole number of luminaries on its board, including German Chancellor Konrad Adenauer, William Benton (US senator, assistant secretary of state, VP University of Chicago), Arthur H. Compton, and others. Notably, the list also included as "notable supporters ... John Foster Dulles, Allen W. Dulles (CIA director), [and] Henry R. Luce (owner of Life and Time magazine)."[79] Besides Allen Dulles, many WB figures were heavily involved in CIA psychological warfare and propaganda across Asia. As Audra Wolfe has argued, the CIA "had its fingers in many similar pies," often either setting up such organizations or covertly funding them when they suited its needs.[80]

This is not to say that Kubo and Morito were actual agents, or that the WB was a false organization, but it does explain Kubo and Morito's reluctance to come out against the ABCC, and their general pro-American stance. Kubo tried to get WB involvement and funding for Morito's initiative, and he corresponded with Everett R. Clinchy, an American sociologist and one of the founders of WB, about "establishing a Human Relations Center at Hiroshima."[81] Kubo complained about the lack of funds, but according to the press, Morito had already received pledges for about six and half million yen from the treasury, a considerable sum at the time. The institute was conceived as complementing American efforts, as "while

KUBO AND THE PSYCHOLOGY OF PEACE

the ABCC . . . is steadily completing a comprehensive study of the effects of the atomic bombing on the natural sciences in Hiroshima, there seems to be a strong desire to focus on research on the social scientific effects of the bombing, which is easier for the Japanese to do."[82] Another newspaper report emphasized that "the project would focus on the social effects of the atomic bombing from the standpoint of social science, which are difficult for outsiders to access . . . and will help to scientifically clarify not only the direct effects of the atomic bombing on the human body, but also the horror of the social effects." If Kubo and his peers were to succeed, one commentator noted, "they would surely receive the Nobel Prize for their efforts."[83]

As the report noted, the initiative was a direct response to the ABCC pressuring the government to include questions about *hibakusha* status in the 1950 census. The goal was to create a nationwide database of people who were exposed to the A-bomb, which was not available at the time. While the ABCC got its census question, Morito's institute did not materialize. The efforts of Kubo and others continued, however, and in 1953 Kubo joined fifty other professors in the Heiwa to gakumon o mamoru daigakujin no kai (University Scholars Society for the Preservation of Peace and Scholarship), which aimed "to defend peace and protect freedom of conscience and learning."[84] Other noted members were the sociologist Nakano Seiichi and the philosopher-activist Moritaki Ichirō. In the same year, Kubo also received an education ministry grant of 320,000 yen for his project on the "Socio-Psychological Effect of Atomic Energy and the Atomic Bomb." Kubo told the press that he wanted to expand the study beyond *hibakusha* and "study . . . feelings toward the US, the difference [of *hibakusha* in Hiroshima] from *hibakusha* in Nagasaki . . . and the difference [of *hibakusha*] from war sufferers in general. [And finally,] I would like to conduct an opinion poll about atomic energy."[85]

Kubo's focus, again, shows many continuities with the priorities of American social scientists, with whom he was in contact and whose agenda he shared. Like his American peers, he was promoting an ideal of social science that sought to help society in general. Part of this project, for Kubo and for others in the scholars' society, was support for nuclear power. Kubo's 1954 project again emphasized the need to listen to survivors, but also imposed his own interpretation and "objective" analysis on his subjects. Echoing and building on his earlier article, Kubo's "Attitudes toward the Atom and Hydrogen Bombs [*Gensuibaku e no taido*]" defined attitudes as "intrinsic tendencies that are prepared in advance in human beings about how to respond to a given stimulus."[86] For Kubo, beliefs were the result of attitudes, and were a result of the way one responded to one's surroundings. Drawing again on Cantril, he argued, "When we acquire judgmental standards at a young age and frameworks (general views such as progressive and conservative, etc.) at a slightly older age, we form a worldview and a view of life that can only be changed by strong stimuli."[87] The A-bomb was such a stimulus; "but if it did not lead to death or psychosis, after a temporary catastrophe, the process of reintegration will be solidified."[88]

Such processes, Kubo argued, resulted in "the extremely strong feelings of fear, dread, and unease [that] were the basis in all people [*subete no hito*] of homogenous and stable beliefs and attitudes, as well as their ideas about the atom and hydrogen bombs, and . . . [which also] form the context for their beliefs, attitudes, and ideas regarding the United States."[89] Kubo admitted that this imposed homogeneity was based on "guesses based mainly on indirect sources" (*Kansetsu shiryō o omo to shita suisatsu*).[90] Such methodological "shortcuts" could be explained by the political urgency of the work. Kubo's main goal was, again, not to examine survivors' psychology, but to use their experience to sway American public opinion, which was once again "headed into the vicious cycle of war," and to mobilize "social scientists in the United States [and Japan] to cooperate with the UN commissioners" and work for peace.[91] Kubo was by no means trying to silence *hibakusha* or prevent them from receiving treatment. His priorities simply lay elsewhere. They could be explained by his own trajectory from the end of the war to the 1960s. Kubo was a product of a transwar generation of social scientists who were pro-American, liberal, and rational. As Miriam Kingsberg Kadia has argued, these men believed that "by furnishing 'objective' evidence of Japan's progress toward democracy, capitalism, and peace, [they] established their place within the new transnational network of knowledge production undergirding American hegemony."[92] For Kubo, it seems, the main struggles were at the United Nations and for "world peace," not at the A-bomb slum and the day-to-day struggles of the *hibakusha*.

Compensation Struggles after Hiroshima and Auschwitz

Kubo's 1954 survey was published at the University Scholars Society side by side with Nakano Seiichi's "Sociological Study of the Effects of the Atomic Bombing," which examined the long-term psychological and social damage to *hibakusha* life. Focusing on "family disintegration and [*hibakusha*] abnormal human relations," Nakano and other sociologists were tackling issues that had been sidelined in the work of Kubo, Konuma, and other psychological experts.[93] Hiroshima-based sociologists like Nakano and Yamate Shigeru, also a Scholars Society member, and the social worker Watanabe Shōji, were hugely influential in initiating the struggle for recognition of *hibakusha* suffering, and for adequate compensation from the Japanese government. The focus of the movement was on sociological impact, and psychology was a secondary issue. Kubo was initially a part of this movement, yet his impact was limited. This had much to do with the growing emphasis on political action and survivors' care. Masaharu Hamatani, who took part in the second phase of the movement, recalled that right after the occupation, sociologists and social workers "started the steady work of caretakers, going door to door to the homes of the *hibakusha*, talking with them, encouraging them to join the [survivors] organization, and resolving the various complaints and demands they raised, starting with what they could do." Scholars, "at the same time, conducted a campaign to write [survivor] testimonies in order to appeal to the whole world, and [show] through the words of the *hibakusha* themselves the horrors of the atomic bombing and the need for peace."[94]

This dual movement of supplying care and mobilizing *hibakusha* experience for the cause of peace was a feature of the compensation movement that was tied to the bigger antinuclear movement from its inception. Hamatani, writing in the 1970s, probably exaggerated the role of *hibakusha* care in the early 1950s. With the Korean War raging, intellectuals at the time were much more concerned with high politics and the general problems of democracy and peace than with *hibakusha* care. But the movement did pick up in the mid-1950s and, following the 1954 *Lucky Dragon 5* incident and the nuclear scare that followed, *hibakusha* care came increasingly to the fore. Much of this was due to the rising visibility of *hibakusha* themselves. As I have argued extensively elsewhere, the mid-Fifties saw the rise of the figure of the *hibakusha* in their role as witnesses to nuclear holocaust.[95] With their rising importance, they demanded greater awareness of their day-to-day struggle against discrimination, poverty, and the multiple lingering impacts of the A-bomb.

One of the immediate results of this struggle was the establishment of the Hiroshima City Atomic Bomb Casualty Treatment Council (Hiroshim-shi genbaku shōgaisha chiryō taisaku kyōgikai: Gentaikyō) in 1953, which was followed by similar efforts at the national level. The first big victory of *gentaikyō* and *Hidankyō* was the 1956 law that recognized the *hibakusha* needs for special medical care. The law, however, did not provide compensation for anything but bodily injury. Government surveys did not see significant differences between *hibakusha* and others in health and living conditions, and saw no need for further action.[96] This lacuna incensed activists who accused the government of having "abandoned *hibakusha*.... [It] never conducted a comprehensive damage survey, and closed its door to save *hibakusha* who suffered from illness and poverty by declining to attribute their illness to the effects of atomic bombings."[97] Thus, activists resolved to conduct surveys themselves. In 1956, the *gensuikyō*s' newly formed Atomic Bomb Victims Relief Committee asked the University Scholars Society to conduct a survey of five to six thousand survivors. The survey was headed by Kubo Yoshitoshi and Yamate Shigeru. It was envisioned as encompassing a "mental, medical, and economic survey" and, it was reported, would be done in cooperation with the prefectural and city government and the ABCC.[98] Kubo and Yamate recruited about fifty female students (women, again, doing most of the legwork), who throughout July 1956, surveyed one thousand survivors. The survivors were chosen randomly from a list of 35,000 names on the *gentaikyō* rolls. They were asked "about forty questions relating to hibakusha health, residence, employment and job search, marriage and family issues eleven years after the bomb." The ultimate goal was to produce a "white paper on the victims on 6 August ... to better understand *hibakusha* needs," and get a better picture of their suffering.[99]

The survey was presented to *gensuikyō* at Nagasaki in August 1956. By that time the ABCC, which was never seriously involved, was not mentioned as a sponsor. Kubo and Yamate emphasized the *hibakusha* role in the peace movement as they "overcame their physical and mental suffering and went east and west to make the devastation of the atomic bombing known, inspired by the desire that no human being should ever have to suffer this agony again." This was not a simple offhand remark. Although the idea was in its infancy in the mid-Fifties, later sociologists would develop the concept of "overcoming suffering" (*kutsū o norikoeru*) through activism into a defining feature of their theory of survivors' mental suffering. Another important feature was the insistence on the special nature of *hibakusha* suffering, and the bomb's "unique and profound impact on the economic and spiritual aspects of life due to the [survivors'] exceptional circumstances and the permanent and semipermanent nature of its physical effects." The insistence on the A-bomb's distinctive impact also emerged later as a major trope, separating *hibakusha* from other war victims. Here as well, Kubo and Yamate insisted on the special role of social science in dealing with the bomb. The two researchers stated, "In terms of scientific research on the damage caused by the atomic bombings, there have been significant achievements in medicine, but these alone cannot provide a complete picture of the damage caused by the atomic bombings. The damage caused by the atomic bombings is not only physical, but also deep and wide, covering all aspects of people's lives. Therefore, it must be studied by sociology and human science as well." Finally, the authors emphasized the objective and scientific nature of their appeal: "To date, the damage caused by the atomic bombings has been reported mainly in the form of literature, films, and other art forms, which have deeply touched a wide range of people. However, these mainly *appeal to the emotions*, and cannot be said to be sufficient on their own" (my emphasis).[100]

Thus, the report was framed as an uniquely objective contribution, based on science and not mere emotions. The report subjects, the *hibakusha*, just as with the ABCC—one may recall Darling's retort to Lifton—were seen as unique and noble "victim-heroes" whose suffering was fundamentally different from that of other war victims. Thus, Kubo and Yamate, like the compensation movement as a whole, tried to undo the early move by the USSBS that treated the bomb as no different from the firebombing. However, reflecting their long-standing entanglement with American social science, Kubo and Yamate produced a report that looked very much like those produced by the USSBS, the ABCC, Janis, and others. It was full of charts and figures that tried to quantify and measure "what direct damage the atomic bombing has caused and how it has affected the lives of the victims after the bombing, what kind of suffering the victims have gone through, and what kind of opinions and attitudes they have toward the victims' relief movement and the campaign against atomic and hydrogen bombs."[101] This last reference to opinions was Kubo's contribution. *Hibakusha* suffering was separated by types of injuries (keloids, physical trauma, etc., and also Hiroshima disease, *genbaku byō*, which amounted to 14.8 percent of complaints), as well as by levels of suffering (*kurushimi*, still experienced by 79.1 percent). The suffering was then separated further into health concerns, loss of income, family issues, etc., and "other." It was only under "other" that the issue of "mental anxiety" (*seishinteki fuan*) was tackled. The report stated that "the problem of 'other' is also a serious problem, although the number is still small. The 'other' category includes [feelings] of loss and mental anxiety. Some of these sufferings have been resolved, but most of them continue to remain unresolved. It was painful for the subjects to talk about this suffering."[102]

The report then asked what kind of emotional support people had, stating that "the source of the victim's emotional support is found inside the mind. It is found in the social aspects of the victim's life, such as inside the home."[103] But then it quickly went on to discuss *hibakusha* religious faith and political opinions. Such cavalier treatment of mental issues continued when Kubo presented the report on 10 August 1956, in Nagasaki. The meeting was held for a packed room of delegates, and was one of four topical meetings (the other reports included a report on nuclear power, of which the movement was quite supportive). Unlike in efforts in the early Fifties to research the problem, the leading delegates in this meeting presented their work not as complementing the ABCC, but as a response in opposition to American research. Much of this hostility can be traced to anger over American handling of the Bikini incident. For instance, Kusano Nobuo, a Tokyo University professor, stated, "According to US surveys, there is no significant damage to the human body, but the reality is that we really need to conduct a scientific survey on a large scale [on our own]. Rather than relying on the US investigation, as the only country affected by the disaster, Japan's own investigation is a matter of necessity." Kusano was followed by Kubo, who emphasized the limited nature of the research: "We conducted this survey in the hope of grasping the psychological and economic aspects of A-bomb survivors in Hiroshima. Social surveys look at general trends, and the problems of individual *hibakusha* may not come out as strongly as they should. In fact, we should address each person individually, and so, I think some of the [survivors] are dissatisfied."[104]

Kubo was indeed facing much dissatisfaction from the audience. He was peppered with questions, most of which he was not qualified to answer, on the problems of in utero exposure, microcephalic children, A-bomb fatigue, and residual radiation. Kubo's colleagues answered most of the questions, but Kubo also avoided answering questions on psychology. When asked by the representative of Iwate prefecture about the connection between "neuroses . . . and to what extents fatigue and radiation affected these," he simply skipped the question and talked about A-bomb orphans and marriage discrimination instead.[105] What Kubo was not asked about was his own contribution to the survey, concerning *hibakusha* political beliefs. Indeed, from the mid-Fifties onward there seems to have been almost no interest in conducting the kind of public opinion surveys Kubo

KUBO AND THE PSYCHOLOGY OF PEACE

215

was engaged in. The *gensuikyō* kept employing Kubo, but for the purpose of surveys on social and medical issues. In the late Fifties he was engaged yet again in a large-scale survey that tried to ascertain *hibakusha's* reluctance to get treatment. His research showed "*hibakusha's* deep-seated anxiety over A-bomb disease." Kubo found that *hibakusha* were afraid of the diagnosis they would receive, and were convinced that the "A-bomb disease could not be cured." Employing the tone of an enlightened educator, not unlike that of the ABCC's Kodama Aki, Kubo told the press that he "was able to fully grasp the complex psychology of the *hibakusha*. . . . We have to make them understand that A-bomb diseases can be cured with early treatment."[106]

Kubo's self-assurance notwithstanding, this piece of research was the last large-scale survey he engaged in. Lacking funds to pursue it further, Kubo turned to the ABCC in search for financial and logistical support. In May 1959 he met with Scott Matsumoto and asked for help with his survey. Matsumoto reported to his superiors that Kubo "spent a great deal of time in relating his past research experiences, probably to convey the great difficulty involved in any attempt to undertake a psychological research program in Hiroshima."[107] This was not the first time Kubo worked with the ABCC. The ABCC, you may recall, was supposed to be involved in the 1956 report, but "according to his account of the research, midway through the project, Dr. [Grant] Taylor called Prof. Kubo in and asked him to be 'cautious' with the use of the material. Later, says Prof. Kubo, some members of the gensui-kyo 'warned' him not 'to be used' by the ABCC. The work, I gather, then came to a standstill."[108] The 1959 project, which was supposedly a survey of ten thousand *hibakusha* "as to health status, family conditions, anxieties, etc. for the local gentai-kyo," was also stalled. City hall was "unenthusiastic," and, though Kubo had the support of Morito and the university, he could not secure enough funding. He got World Brotherhood funding, and asked the ABCC for help with applying for Asia Foundation money. Both organizations, again, were connected with the CIA (Asia Foundation was a CIA front organization), which might explain the enthusiastic support Kubo received from the ABCC.[109] Gilbert Beebe wrote to George Darling, "Professor Kubo's visit presents us with an opportunity that I believe we should grasp provided we have reasonable assurance that he is an honest investigator " Beebe wanted to task Matsumoto to work jointly with Kubo, and said he would "be glad to offer methodological advice and occasional IBM tabulating service" for the project.[110] But although the ABCC was positive about the prospects of

Kubo's research and granted him technical support, nothing much came out of this effort. One would assume that the same political problems that plagued the 1956 effort, also prevented cooperation between *gensuikyō* and the ABCC this time.

This 1959 setback was the beginning of the end of Kubo's involvement with nuclear issues. Kubo did publish a number of other articles, but none was based on new research; and, unlike Konuma, he seemed to be working almost alone in the field of psychology, with very little impact. In the mid-1960's, Kubo changed research tracks and left *hibakusha* research behind. His quest to work for democracy and peace, which had guided his career from the days of the occupation, was at an end. Much of it had to do with his affiliation with the United States. While he was well within the consensus of the first generation of transwar social scientists, the "men of one age," his ideas were increasingly at odds with his colleagues in the antinuclear movement, who positioned themselves in opposition to the United States. With Kubo gone, sociologists were the only psychological experts still involved in the white paper movement. Yamate Shigeru, Nakano Seiichi, and others continued to promote *hibakusha* research, together with Tokyo-based sociologists like Hamatani, Itō Takeshi, and, most notably, Ishida Tadashi. We will return to their work in the last chapter. Here it should suffice to note that without any input from psychologists and psychiatrists, the long-term mental damage of the A-bomb received only marginal attention.

This was not the case in work with Holocaust survivors. Psychologists and psychiatrists led the struggle for recognition of survivors' long-term mental damage. Holocaust survivors, like the *hibakusha*, received little compensation or special care in the first decade after the war. Whether they resided in West Germany, the United States, or even Israel, survivors were facing a hostile state and medical apparatus that, very much like the Japanese state, sought to evade and deny compensation and restitution. As in Japan, the situation led to a campaign on behalf of survivors. In 1956, West Germany passed a law that afforded compensation for "survivors whose capacity to be economically self-supporting has been damaged by at least 25 percent due to persecution and violence experienced in the Third Reich in flight and hiding, in ghettos, or in camps."[111] This was, as Dagmar Herzog has noted, the "law for little people who had no property."[112] Unlike the Japanese law of the same year, the German law allowed for compensation for mental as well as physical damages. This was the result of international pressure and negotiations with Israel and West European countries, as well as a campaign by a dedicated group of

KUBO AND THE PSYCHOLOGY OF PEACE

German activists. Those in charge of evaluating damages, however, were German or German trained psychiatrists, in West Germany itself as well as in its embassies and consulates, or those licensed to do so by the various states that entered into agreements with West Germany. As we have already seen, the profession was quite hostile to the notion of long-term damage and, as Christian Pross aptly put it, German doctors engaged "in a running battle with victims within the framework of the evaluation proceedings."[113]

German doctors, and the legal system as a whole, still subscribed to the 1926 definition of mental damage, which was designed based on the pension neurotics doctrine. They were also operating well within international medical consensus about long-term mental damage. Negative evaluations were the norm, and the "blame" for patients' current problems, as we saw in the last chapter, often was found within their "problematic" personalities. In Israel, psychiatrists, like their Japanese peers, saw themselves as "guardians of the state's treasury" and were mostly suspicious of victims' claims.[114] Thus, Kurt Blumenthal, who like most Israeli doctors was German-trained, wrote to a colleague, combining suspicion of both workers and survivors, "Please consider . . . the special situation of our 'damaged neurotics' [*nivrotikaiim she' me'habala*]. They have no professional education due to the war. They have no mental connection to their [current] jobs, which were often assigned to them and were not of their choosing. . . . So, it is a small wonder that that this situation 'trips a fuse' [*ketzer*] and leads to neurosis, through which one can get the prize [of a better job] conveniently." Blumenthal diagnosed the patient with *Zweckneurose* (purpose-oriented neurosis; German in original).[115] Julius Baumetz, again a German-born psychologist, also toed the German line, writing, "In cases where there is a background of psychopathic personality [in the survivors] and there is a possibility to investigate the pre-damaged personality (*ishiut trom habalatit*), it is often found that these people have always been a social problem. They reacted impulsively to external stimuli, did not consider others, were unable to learn from the past, became entangled with the law, and always demanded pensions. . . . The damage gives such cases an opportunity to cover up such conflicts and demand a legal status for a disease that was supposedly caused by an external factor."[116]

German doctors were even more blatant. Patients were considered hypochondriac and greedy. One Auschwitz survivor was evaluated in 1960 with a "psychopathic personality with a tendency towards abnormal processing of experience and an inability to deal with life." A "normal person," the evaluator wrote, "would have recovered already."[117] The problem was mainly one of causation. While in the Japanese case radiation and social discrimination were ever present and still impacted survivors, in the Holocaust case and at the ABCC, doctors claimed that the event was supposedly over and, thus, those who still complained were suspect. Almost from the start, more sympathetic psychiatrists were pushing back. Hans Strauss, a Jewish émigré who was an examiner for the West German consulate in New York, directly challenged German psychiatry and its "difficulties" with "the evaluation of the causal relationship between the present disorders and acts of persecution," condemning their attitudes as "unbearable for those who rightfully filed such claims."[118] Hillel Klein wrote that he was "ashamed to read" the evaluation of his German colleagues who were "perpetuating 'Freudian paradoxes' in order to reject claims."[119] Indeed, as Dagmar Herzog has insightfully noted, the rejectionist doctors were deploying Freudian orthodoxy and relating trauma to childhood experiences in order to reject claims (a rather ironic development, given establishment hostility to psychoanalysis—"the Jewish science").[120]

The problem, however, was not just one of bias. Even sympathetic doctors struggled with the inadequate psychological categories available to them. Klein, writing in 1963, observed that survivors and soldiers had different experiences: "Whereas in traumatic neurosis there is a single traumatic experience which destroys the defense against excitation [*Reizschutzdurchbruch*], oppression is a long series of traumatic experiences."[121] What sympathizers were grappling with was the issue of comparability between combat, POWs, and camp experience. The Holocaust case had to be differentiated. And, as in the Hiroshima case, "an argument about uniqueness of what we now call the Holocaust began to take shape."[122] Already in 1957 Hans Strauss emphasized the "singularity of the psychic experience" (*das Eigenartige der psychischen Erfahrung*) of the survivors.[123] The work of Strauss, Eitinger, and others led to the emergence of a unique "concentration camp syndrome" to explain the unique gaps between events and syndromes. Here, Bettelheim's and Frankl's work and the view of the camps as a unique "psychiatric mass experiment" was crucial.[124] As I have examined at length elsewhere, the political climate after the Eichmann and Auschwitz trial and the rising status of Holocaust survivors helped to gain recognition to survivors' claims.[125]

These struggles take us beyond 1962 and the Kubo-Lifton meeting. For our purposes we should note that, first, Lifton, who was close to the sympathizers' circles, was aware of "survivor syndrome" and connected it to *hibakusha* symptoms in his work (figure 10).[126] Second, the arguments of

FIGURE 10. Robert Jay Lifton. Photo by Richard Sandler; courtesy of Robert Jay Lifton.

the sympathizers differed significantly from those of the Japanese compensation movement. While in Japan, scientists purported to be *more objective and scientific* than the ABCC, and deplored emotional appeal as unscientific and insufficient, in the Holocaust case the campaign took the opposite approach. Kurt Eisseler, who worked with the US Army and contrasted combat veterans with survivors, condemned the "perverted psychiatry of the Germans," and argued that "its inability to *'feel'* for victims of the Nazis was a *'defect' of objectivity"* (my emphasis).[127] Indeed, rejectionists often, as with the ABCC and Japanese sympathizers, condemned activist doctors as emotional and lacking in objectivity. The very idea of getting any kind of compensation for neurosis "was declared by the lead researcher in Germany, Ernst Kretschmar, 'scientifically insupportable' [*wissenschaftlich unhaltbar*]."[128]

Reacting to such stances, the French psychiatrist Eugene Minkowski argued, "Everything must be evaluated solely from a human standpoint; the state of the soul *cannot be objectified* in any [and all] cases" (My emphasis).[129] Kurt Eisseler, likewise, did not mince words when he wrote in 1963, "The murder of how many of one's children must one be able to survive asymptomatically in order to be deemed to have a normal constitution?"[130] These were forceful and compelling words. But there was a significant difference between French, Israeli, and American experts fighting an increasingly unpopular German establishment that was staffed by former Nazis, and the Japanese social scientists operating in an American-dominated world, who were trained in American methods and who looked up to their peers at the ABCC. Power, and the hierarchies of American, German, and Japanese science, impacted what and who was considered objective, and who got to decide the nature of objectivity and its "defects." Furthermore, Kubo and his peers did not even engage in a debate with the ABCC, not on the psychological front. Their struggle was against the Japanese government. Again, it was what the ABCC did not do, rather than what it did, that mattered. But Kubo and Japanese psychological experts did not fill this gap. Their concerns were elsewhere.

Conclusion: The Curse of Objectivity II

Looking back on his career in 1977, Kubo Yoshitoshi wrote, somewhat cryptically, that he "felt [in the late 1950s] that the campaign against atomic and hydrogen bombs itself was somewhat different from my own research from the psychological perspective, and it has been nearly twenty years since I withdrew from psychological research on A-bomb victims."[131] Indeed, by the late 1950s the movement had moved away from the ideals of Kubo and the immediate postwar generation. Kubo and his peers had seen the role of the social scientist in guarding and guiding the democratic mind. They had allied themselves with the occupation's reformist, if cautious, agenda and set out to help prevent the return of war and fascism. Whether psychologists worked on *hibakusha* or on Holocaust research, they saw it through the lens of this bigger project of promoting democracy and peace. Reconciliation with the United States and its attendant benefits, first and foremost the entry of Japanese science on the (Western) world stage, structured their research goals and methodology. Objective and data-based scientific research of the kind produced by the ABCC was the entry ticket to this world. As the Kanai Tashirō quote above demonstrates, the white paper movement, of which Kubo and Kanai were founding members, had looked for science to redeem what science had wrought. Its methods were to be as "cold and detached" as those which produced the bomb. Appealing to their rivals' humanity, pointing out their "defects" in objectivity, and drawing on the raw emotional power of testimony, strategies were employed with significant success in the case of the Holocaust, were roads not taken by Kubo and his peers.

Thus, though Kubo cherished *hibakusha* opinions and thought it was important for the world to hear them, those voices and stories of survival did not possess an inherent special truth. On the contrary, the experience of trauma made them suspect, emotional, fragmentary, and unobjective. It was the psychologist's role to mediate and properly objectify them. This was very different from today's understanding of survivor testimonies by trauma scholars and activists. But, while Kubo held onto objectivity, the greater compensation movement was moving in the direction of more emotional politics. This pushed people like Kubo away, and also had its own peculiar consequences. As a result, and coupled with the dominance of sociologists and the emphasis on the survivors' political role, psychological trauma was sidelined. Not being unique to Hiroshima, and being shared with "regular" victims of bombing, psychological trauma was just not useful for such an appeal. Kubo's inability to maneuver the stormy politics of survivor politics and, perhaps even more, his continued attachment to the occupation era's American-inspired methods and goals had a large role in this development.

Such criticism notwithstanding, it is important to acknowledge Kubo's importance for the compensation movement. Kubo was important in pushing for the publication of the white paper and other reports, and these were instrumental in bringing about the medical relief laws for the *hibakusha*. Still, he failed to push for any kind of compensation for mental injuries, and his impact on the field of psychology in Japan or elsewhere was quite limited. *Hibakusha* suffering was acknowledged by Kubo and his peers; he tied *hibakusha* anxiety and other disorders to the psychological impact of the bomb, and emphasized their importance for democratic discourse and the cause of peace. Nevertheless, he was interested not in proposing a cure, but in trying to prevent the next war. He thus saw survivors' suffering as a given and did not seek to remedy it. His insistence on the "scientific method" and "finding objective patterns," and his disdain for individual stories and "exaggerations," point to a particular view of social science that aimed at solving social problems, but also neglected individual suffering.

CHAPTER EIGHT

Social Workers, Nuclear Sociology, and the Road to PTSD

"At that time there was no guidebook, no proper manuals. There was no place to receive such training.... [Thus,] Lifton's (1971) translation was like a bible to me." — Yokoyama Teruko[1]

In his 2011 autobiography *Witness to an Extreme Century*, Robert Jay Lifton returned to his 1962 meeting with Kubo Yoshitoshi and his decision to embark on his Hiroshima research. Lifton connected "the moment of [his] decision," to stay in the city, "with the completion of an interview with a psychologist at Hiroshima University." He further recalled that "what struck me most forcibly was that seventeen years after such a tragic turning point in human history, no one had attempted a comprehensive psychological study of what had occurred in Hiroshima."[2] It should be clear to the reader by now that Lifton was not entirely correct on this point. The seventeen years between 1945 and 1962 saw multiple research initiatives that focused on Hiroshima. Lifton, who was not impressed by Kubo (one may note that he did not mention Kubo's name in his memoir), did not know about his and other Japanese researchers' work, and, though aware of the research by Janis and others, he was not heavily involved in civil defense debates.

But Lifton was not simply uninformed. It is easy to see why he saw the seventeen years prior to the 1962 meeting as a gap in research. Lifton's focus and political sensitivities were fundamentally different from those of most who had come before him. While his research focused on the victims and the long-term psychological damage they suffered, almost all the research examined in this book has looked beyond the victims and their psychological suffering. Whether, like Kubo, the researchers sought to use victims' voices, properly objectified and cleared of any embellishments, to

SOCIAL WORKERS AND NUCLEAR SOCIOLOGY

sway public opinion toward peace and democracy, or sought biological explanations like Konuma—or if, like the USSBS, the ABCC, and nuclear defense intellectuals like Janis, they aimed to protect Americans, get *hibakusha* cooperation, or were interested in abstract concepts like morale— the many researchers who embarked on nuclear psychological research across the Pacific did not focus on long-term psychological trauma. And most researchers, even sympathetic ones like Kubo, saw the *hibakusha* as a resource, and as means to achieve a different end.

Lifton was a catalyst toward a focus on the victims of war. He was the right man at the right time, and his meeting with Kubo came at an opportune moment. The year 1962 saw the conclusion of the Eichmann trial and the coming of the Cuban Missile Crisis. In Japan and in the Cold War West, this resulted in a heightened awareness to both Hiroshima and the Holocaust. The rise of antinuclear politics and survivor advocacy in the early 1960s continued to impact psychological research beyond 1962. In the United States and Europe, and to a lesser extent in Japan, these struggles were obscured by the Vietnam War. But, as I argue in this chapter, the heightened awareness (in which Lifton played an important role) toward Hiroshima and the Holocaust had a significant impact in Japan and the West. In both contexts, antinuclear psychology was important in raising awareness to the plight of victims and creating what Lifton called an "openness to survivor trauma" that led directly to the revolt of the psychological professions against the "malignant normality" of ever-present war.[3]

These developments require a book of their own. One cannot really do justice to the rich tapestry of research, activism, and international connections that impacted research on nuclear trauma from the mid-1960s to the 1980s and the rise of PTSD in the limited space of this chapter. What I am aiming at here is merely to paint with wide strokes the evolution of nuclear psychology after Lifton's May 1962 meeting with Kubo in both Japan and the West, and to show the radical shifts but also many continuities of later developments from the 1945–62 era. The first section continues developments discussed in chapter 8. The chapter concludes by looking at the work of sociologists and social workers and how, much like Holocaust survivor advocates, they organized to provide care and advocate for better provisions for *hibakusha*. It is in this context that we examine the reception of Lifton's work among researchers, activists, and care associations. The second part of the chapter focuses on antinuclear activists in the West and connects Lifton's own radicalization with the bigger shifts in the professions as antinuclear activists moved to anti–Vietnam War activism

CHAPTER EIGHT

and rejected the military-academic complex. Here we explore continuities with and departures from the American developments explored in part 1 of this book, and how Japanese and American developments fed into the global flows of knowledge that led to the rise of PTSD.

A-Bomb Social Work, Sociology, and Trauma in Hiroshima and Nagasaki

Until the 1970s, the Lifton-Kubo meeting and Lifton's subsequent work had limited impact in Japan. Kubo retired from nuclear psychology in the early 1960s. With his departure, any momentum for the recognition of psychological damage, in any clinical sense—if there ever had been one—was gone. This did not mean the topic was completely neglected. The mantle of the psychological experts was taken up by sociologists and the compensation movement. Yet the focus was on the breakdown of social relations and the destruction of community. A major emphasis, as in the American movement, was on the A-bomb's power of dehumanization and how the bombing experience and the ongoing struggle with radiation and other effects robbed *hibakusha* of their ability to live a full life. The solution to this, according to sociologists, was through social action and restoring the conditions, both communal and interpersonal, that allowed for dignified living. The focus on politics and struggle was an important part of the grassroots movements of mostly female social workers, who worked with the sociologists and started to form their own associations in the late 1970s. Psychological damage was at best a marginal concern for the movement, on both the grassroots and the academic levels. Furthermore, due to Japanese government policies and other reasons, *hibakusha* uniqueness was emphasized, especially vis-à-vis that of "regular" bombing victims. Thus, psychological damage, which all victims shared, was not pursued. In addition, the historical stigma attached to mental damage persisted and was not tackled by the movement. Quite the contrary: the rise of the status of the *hibakusha* as witnesses made "tarring" them with such a stigma difficult. These considerations impacted the reception of Lifton's work, which was quite hostile overall, but nevertheless had an important and surprising impact especially on Ishida Tadashi and his understanding of *hibakusha* psychology.

Consciously or not, the compensation movement was aiming to undo the work of the USAAF and the USSBS. While the bombing campaign had aimed to destroy social bonds, communities, and minds, the compensation movement sought to rehabilitate them. While the USAAF had bombed abstractions like cities, target zones, and morale, and not human beings, the movement aimed at restoring human dignity. Finally, while the USSBS and civil defense experts did whatever they could to erase differences between nuclear and conventional bombing, the compensation movement emphasized the uniqueness of the *hibakusha* vis-à-vis bombing victims, and the role of chronic radiation effects in the latter's continued suffering. The struggle against the ABCC, then, was an important impetuous for activism. Like the Holocaust redress movement, the Japanese movement developed mostly in reaction to denial and obstruction by government bureaucrats. It was marked by cycles of lobbying, inadequate government response, and reaction. Japanese activists did not directly draw on the example of Holocaust activism, but the rising impact of Holocaust work, especially in relation to Lifton's work, was important.

As in the Holocaust debates, social scientists in Japan mobilized due to what they saw as an inadequate reaction of the government to the white papers. Significantly, these debates were taking place in the increasingly charged atmosphere of the struggle against the US-Japan security treaty (ANPO), which radicalized many scientists. Thus, in November 1959 the scholars' society issued a call for "scientists, artists, and people of culture in Hiroshima" to resist ANPO.[4] Another call came out in June 1960. Just a few weeks later, society members and others protested the inadequacy of the amended A-bomb relief law. Critics of the amendment, including many scientists, saw the need to go beyond "mere welfare," which they also saw as inadequate, and to press for American as well as Japanese state acknowledgment of their responsibility for *hibakusha* suffering. This anti-American stance, which had been unthinkable just a few years earlier, was a direct consequence of the parallel struggle against ANPO. Government representatives acknowledged that "the state has a responsibility to compensate victims of war," but emphasized that "there are limits and an appropriate order to the [implementation of that] responsibility. For the time being, the A-bomb survivors, who are suffering the most, should be given the first helping hand."[5]

Government emphasis on "suffering" was, again, insufficient on political grounds. But more immediately, activists were concerned with the government's lumping together of *hibakusha* and other victims. State compensation was initially directed to military and other state employees, whom the state saw as its responsibility to compensate. Political pressure also saw landlords and others who were hurt by the occupation's land and other reforms added to this group. The state was reluctant to expand this list. Acknowledging responsibility for *hibakusha,* it was feared, would open the gate to victims of firebombing and others requesting support. The *hibakusha* movement, as Naono Akiko has shown, was determined to have the state acknowledge its broad responsibility for the war.[6] But at the same time, the movement, and especially the scientists, emphasized the *hibakusha's* unique situation. Thus, in another round-table in 1961, Scholar Society member Imahori Seiji accused "the ABCC . . . the US Congress and other organizations [of] greatly underestimating the damage caused by nuclear attacks." The purpose of the ongoing surveys, he argued, was twofold: to "reveal the tragic extent of A-bomb damage," and to "reveal the nature of *hibakusha* suffering." Kubo Yoshitoshi elaborated further: "I think it is necessary to clarify the difference between A-bomb survivors who are exposed to radiation, and who are the worst victims [*mottomo hidoi*], and those who are victims of war in a broader sense. The survey of the *hibakusha* should also include the [survivors'] complex anxieties and what can be done to alleviate them."[7]

Kubo's emphasis on "complex anxieties," again, did not survive his departure from the movement. Itō Takeshi, Yamate Shigeru, Nakano Seiichi, and others took on the movement's social science aspect. When the Welfare and Health Ministry launched another survey of the *hibakusha's* situation, it scored a significant victory with the inclusion of Keio University sociologist Chūbashi Masayoshi in the 1965 "Atomic Bomb Victims Health and Welfare Survey" (Kōsei genshi bakudan hibakusha jittai chōsa). Chūbashi was the first social scientist to be included in the government body that advised on *hibakusha* issues. The survey resulted in a new law in 1966 that for the first time provided special welfare and social security measures to *hibakusha.* However, Chūbashi and other sociologists who worked with him, such as Hitsubashi University's Ishida Tadashi, and Chūbashi's Keio colleagues Yoneyama Keizō, Kawai Takeo, and Harada Katsuhiro, felt that the survey and the law based on it were far from sufficient, and were more window dressing than a real admission of responsibility. Thus, they launched their own surveys in Hiroshima and Nagasaki in 1965–68.[8] The surveys were conducted with the help of social workers, who were just beginning to get organized at the time, especially around womens' and survivors' reading groups.

Dissatisfaction with the law was widespread. *Gensuikyō* and others protested it and the surveys as insufficient and unreliable. "From now on,

SOCIAL WORKERS AND NUCLEAR SOCIOLOGY

we will analyze the data ourselves," a survivor group representative stated, calling on more surveys by the city of Hiroshima and others. Imahori Seiji protested that "the conclusion was predictable. The survey is inconclusive because it is incomplete. From the beginning, I had doubts about the survey method itself, and I thought we would not get any significant results."[9] Medical groups and other scientists also criticized the medical portion of the survey, with much of the anger aimed at the dismissal of A-bomb fatigue. However, the purveyors of this critique were themselves wary of the stigma of psychological damage. The letter of protest submitted to the ministry by twelve medical and social scientists in December 1967 stated that "no research has been done on 'A-bomb fatigue,' which implicitly gives the impression that the disease does not exist and that it is based on psychological factors."[10] Thus, reflecting the biological bias of scientists, for A-bomb fatigue to be a "real" disease it could not be the result of simple psychological factors. The social surveys were more accommodating to psychological damage, but not by much. This was not by design, but simply because the focus of sociologists was on society and community, and less on individual psychology.

The first surveys, significantly, challenged the government and the ABCC "concentric circle model" (which was also widely used by survivor groups), and showed that the social and psychological impact of the A-bomb was much wider.[11] The surveys assessed the "deeper impact of the A-bomb" by integrating data on "social disorganization, personality disorganization, family disorganization, and community disorganization."[12] Continuing the anti-ABCC trend of the early 1960s, researchers stretched that "unlike the ABCC, we write from the side of the *hibakusha.*"[13] But many of the researchers, like Shimizu Kiyoshi, who conducted a survey in 1966–67, kept working with the ABCC, Shimizu even replacing Matsumoto as the head of Medical Sociology at the ABCC. Shimizu was censured by Hiroshima University and senior colleagues for coming out publicly against the ABCC, and the university forced him to apologize to the ABCC (this was in the context of Beebe rebuking Shimizu for his sentimentality).[14] This episode demonstrated just how controversial the surveys were, and how difficult it still was to come out against the ABCC and the scientific establishment. Indeed, most of the sociologists were younger than the Kubo generation, except for Chūbashi, who had not been conscripted, and Shimizu. They had not experienced the war as adults, and were far closer to the current student movement than to the postwar generation who worked with and were inspired by occupation reformers.

There were many continuities with the earlier generation of research. The surveys were heavily reliant on data, and differed little from the earlier white paper surveys in terms of methods, data collection, and so on. Researchers also again emphasized their unique position as Japanese. But here they parted ways from Kubo and his peers, who had been always looking for Western work to validate their own work. In their "Atomic Bomb and Social Change," Yoneyama and Kawai argued that Western work was of little use to them, as "we must always consider the limitation of Western scholars . . . who have never faced the primordial state of social change that we experienced in Hiroshima."[15] Ishida Tadashi, the most noted researcher that came out of the surveys, however, was of a different mind. Western work, and particularly work on the Holocaust was especially important for Ishida. He was also less reliant on data and worked on collecting narrative-based "life histories" from *hibakusha.* Ishida worked closely with survivor groups, and was especially connected to social workers in Nagasaki, many of whom helped him in his surveys.[16]

Ishida was the keynote speaker in a 1976 meeting of social workers, where many shared their work and their own life surveys of *hibakusha.* Ishida elaborated in his lecture on his 1973 work "Against the A-bomb" (*hangenbaku*). Ishida's main paradigm was the move from "drifting to resistance (*hyōryū* to *teikō*). For Ishida, recording life histories and enabling *hibakusha* to tell their stories had a transformational effect on both researcher and survivor. "Life histories are not only the history of material life, but also the history of the mind," he argued. . . . These [surveys] are not just [my] methodology; I feel they have a qualitative implication for *hibakusha* life."[17] For Ishida, the *hibakusha* survived but suffered both physically and mentally. As a result, their position in society was of "bystanders" to "human beings" and "society" as a whole. By telling their story and coming out publicly against the bomb, *hibakusha* turned into resisters. Resisters "reacquire the connection with the world" when they position themselves publicly as "A-bomb survivors."[18] The mental journey from "drifting to resistance" comes through an understanding of the *hibakusha* experience and its role in the struggle against nuclear bombs. Ishida connected this to his own war experience and his reading of Frankl's *Man's Search for Meaning.*

Ishida quoted in his 1976 speech a long passage from the book where Frankl manages to escape the daily, degrading, and dehumanizing struggle for survival by imagining himself to be in a cozy lecture room, giving a lecture about Auschwitz to a group of students. Frankl quoted Baruch Spi-

SOCIAL WORKERS AND NUCLEAR SOCIOLOGY

noza: "A suffering ceases to be suffering as soon as we form a clear and precise picture of it."[19] Through this mind manipulation (*toriku*), Ishida claimed, Frankl could overcome his desperate situation in Auschwitz. Frankl's technique was "an extremely objective way to get a sense of your own struggles," Ishida told the social workers. "This is something that all of you will experience in your case studies. If the subject is convinced that what you are saying is true, he or she will be able to gain a certain spiritual ground ... which will give him or her a certain insight into how to live, act, and think in the future." This move, however, was directly connected to the struggle against the A-bomb. Ishida emphasized the ideological aspect of the victim's transformation into a survivor. "The subject itself has been able to contribute to the spiritual work of trying to convert its various experiences into ideas," he continued. "By going through such ideological work, the subject can be prevented from being carried away by the suffering ... and able to confront the affliction and establish himself or herself as a subject who can overcome it."[20]

If ideology was one pillar of this process, objectivity was another. "I think that grasping the meaning of one's own life history is the basic activity in objectifying one's own suffering," Ishida told the audience.[21] Suffering had to be objectified by the survivors themselves. Here Ishida was democratizing Kubo's ideas of objective science and entrusting the action to the *hibakusha* and social worker, and not to the psychology expert in an ivory tower. Such insights were already present in Kido and Shimizu's reading of Bettelheim, but they concerned themselves not with the victims, but with the problem of totalitarianism, and what they admired was Bettelheim's ability as scientist. Like earlier experts, Ishida was using the insights of Holocaust psychology in a consciously political way, but his theories were much more connected to the healing and recovery of *hibakusha*. This again was the undoing of what the American bombing campaign and USSBS dehumanization of the victims had aimed at. Ishida was making this exact argument in 1977 when he argued that "the atomic bomb is essentially a weapon for the destruction of 'community.' ... This becomes a terminal station of the indiscriminate bombings of cities so greatly increased through World War II."[22] Ishida was aiming at restoring community and human relations by giving *hibakusha* voices and agency. His reading of Lifton was important in bringing the Holocaust into focus. According to Hamaya Masaharu, who took over Ishida's research, Ishida was one of the "few people who correctly understood [Lifton's] concepts when his book was translated into Japanese" in 1971.[23]

230   CHAPTER EIGHT

And, indeed, Lifton's ideas of "reformulation" are not very different from Ishida's process of transition into resistance (if far less ideological). Also, as we have seen, Lifton had a similar view of survivors as "divine prophets." But for Ishida it was Lifton's knowledge of the Holocaust that made his work important. In his speech he told the audience: "It was a shock to us that an American could conduct such a study before us Japanese, but the reason he was able to conduct such a worthy study was because of his experience of Auschwitz." Ishida noted, "Lifton himself is Jewish," and claimed that although the Holocaust chapter was the last chapter in *Death in Life*, Lifton had written it first. "I tried to confirm this the last time I met Lifton," Ishida added. "I asked him if he had written this last chapter first, and he admitted that he had."[24] Lifton, in fact, never had any exchange with Ishida, and had not written the Holocaust chapter before the others.[25] But the more important point is that Ishida felt a need to emphasize the role of Holocaust insights in his own understanding of *hibakusha*.

Ishida's work had vital consequences for *hibakusha* care. Again, breaking with the precedent of Konuma, Kubo and others, he actively worked with social workers to supply care for *hibakusha*. The 1976 meeting where he gave his speech was one of the important stepping stones in the formation of the A-Bomb Victims Counselors Association (*Genbaku higaisha sōdanin no kai*). Unlike all organizations and institutions examined above, the association was composed and led mostly by women. Among those care workers, not all of whom were trained MSW, many were either young survivors or from *hibakusha* families. Yokoyama Teruko, who worked in Nagasaki, "had become counselor because I am an atomic bomb survivor and my family had been suffering from the aftereffects of the bombing for a long time."[26] Yokoyama's parents were active in survivor circles and were counseling community members. Most such activities were informal. Activists traced their association to early 1950s survivor circles, self-help groups, and local testimony collections efforts.[27] Women groups like the "Yamashita group" were especially important in this regard. The group was led by the writer Inazawa Junko, and was named after the activist-survivor Yamashita Asayo, who died of A-bomb–related liver cancer. Sagura Kayo, who worked in Hiroshima, came to work with *hibakusha* through this group, which shared testimonies and heard lectures. The A-bomb poet Kurihara Sadako and the historian Funabashi Yoshie were also involved in that circle. Another member, Wakabayashi Setsuko, who was a MSW at the Red Cross Hospital, was the one who "recruited" Sagura as a volunteer counselor.[28]

Other women, however, came from outside the A-bombed cities, and their trajectory was more closely tied with the student movement. Many were trained in welfare studies programs set up by the older generation of social workers like Fusa Asaka and Kodama Aki. But their ideas and motivations were radically different than those of their teachers. With ANPO and later anti-Vietnam protest movement raging outside their classrooms, many of them were radicalized. As Chelsea Schieder has argued, "Young women in particular often found that New Left activism offered them opportunities to formulate a revolutionary sensibility," and many social care workers found their calling in pairing *hibakusha* care with antinuclear activity.[29] Sagura participated in the big demonstrations outside the Diet and in Haneda airport in 1960. Sagura was attacked by right-wing counterprotesters and was wounded in the protests. She recalled, "It was lots of fun . . . [but] I was really shocked by the death of this young woman [Kanba Michiko]. . . . The whole era left a deep impression on me."[30] Nakamura Sumio in Nagasaki was also involved in the anti–Vietnam War and student movement, which already as a student in Tokyo she connected to *hibakusha* care. In 1965 she worked as a student for Ishida and other sociologists in their surveys.[31]

For many social workers and students, working with the surveys was an important gateway to activism. For many working MSW it filled a gap in knowledge and organization that had hindered their work. Yokoyama recalled that in the early Seventies "there was no guidebook, no proper manuals. . . . There was no place to receive such training, and I had to develop and study on my own . . . based on my own and my family's experiences of the atomic bombing." This was the context for Yokoyama's aforementioned reference to the 1971 translation of Lifton's work as a "bible." She was also impressed by Ishida, with whom she also worked: "I became friends with [him] and he taught me how to take life histories."[32] Indeed, Ishida's methodology was, as Mimura Masahiro, the current chair of the association recalled, "the theoretical pillar of the movement, which enabled us to capture the full extent of A-bomb damage on *hibakusha* lives."[33] In the 1976 meeting, counselors conveyed their need for guidance, as when social workers came together and "actually started to compile the case studies, they found themselves in a real panic. Most of the workers had no experience in reporting full-fledged cases."[34] Outside the ABCC, there seemed to be little standardization of practices and no developed body of knowledge that counselors could consult.

The impact of the survey movement was quite evident in the case files shared in the 1976 meeting. These could not be more different than the ones collected by Kodama in 1968. The A-bomb is present in every page and almost every line of the files. The case files are also infused with ideological language and even fervor. Katō Reiko's casework, for instance, was titled "A Life Stolen by the A-Bomb: An Abnormal Life," and it called "the atomic bombing of Hiroshima, the greatest tragedy in the history of mankind, [which] destroyed the city in an instant and plunged the people of Hiroshima into ruin." The bomb and subsequent neglect by the state, for Katō, "left survivors in a vicious cycle of atomic bomb sickness and poverty."[35] Social workers emphasized the interconnection of radiation sickness, discrimination ,and other social problems, and the mental anxiety that plagued the *hibakusha*. Significantly, one finds in the case files a fair number of references to "traumatic head injury sequelae" (*Gaishōseitōbu dabokukōishō*), as in the case of Hirokawa Tarō, analyzed by Katō but also by Nakamura, who mentioned "mental disorders caused by head trauma during the atomic bombing."[36] Kato, significantly, quoted Konuma Masuho, and emphasized that *hibakusha* symptoms "should be understood as an intraneuronal syndrome rather than a direct effect of radiation on the brain ... [but] the neurological complaints of the *hibakusha should not be dismissed as psychosomatic, like neurosis*" (my emphasis)."[37]

Thus, yet again, though these symptoms were widely acknowledged as having been caused by the A-bomb, and were not seen as "inferiority complex" and the like, having a "mere" neurosis was seen negatively. This negative view of psychological damage was both a reflection of earlier psychological research and the new (or, rather, invigorated) view of the *hibakusha* as resisters who had supposedly overcome their suffering. In 1977, at a major gathering of NGOs and researchers in Hiroshima which was also attended by many social workers, Ishida and his team presented their work to an international audience. It was the first time Japanese social and psychological surveys connected with their foreign peers on such a scale. The meeting was as much about politics, with the participants vowing to raise awareness to the plight of the *hibakusha,* as about science per se. The reports were a curious mix of social science and ideological treatises. In his opening remarks, Yukimune Hajime of *Hidankyō* told the audience, "Our 370,000 *hibakusha* must become like Christ ... as the Christ bore the sins of the people of the world when crucified on Golgotha, so our 370,000 *hibakusha* must let their experiences appeal to humanity so that the tragedy may never be repeated."[38] Such language, as we have seen, was also present at Holocaust debates. And psychologist-advocates often highlighted their patients' role as witnesses. Thus, Paul Chodoff, who had written an influential piece denouncing German denial of Jewish survivors' rights for compensation, compared his patients to the "*Lamedvov*, the thirty-six just men who take upon themselves the suffering of the world."[39]

Crucially, however, unlike with Chodoff and his peers, the recognition of psychological harm served only as background for the transformation of the "drifting" and suffering *hibakusha* into a survivor-hero who resisted the A-bomb's hold on her soul and found meaning in the struggle for peace. Hamatani Masaharu made a clear connection between "the shock suffered at the time of the bombing and the mental anguish which the [*hibakusha*] have suffered in their later history of struggle with diseases, difficulty in living, and social discrimination, [which] have eaten into the lives and minds of the *hibakusha* and have seriously affected their ability to earn a living." Demonstrating the integrative and interdisciplinary nature of A-bomb sociology, as well as social workers' input, Hamatani spoke of "the shadow of the A-bomb" that impacted "every aspect of the 'life' of every *hibakusha*."[40] This was a unique situation, as "the conditions of victims of air raids and evacuees who lost their homes, assets, or places of work were similar, except that *hibakusha* suffered a loss and decline of ability to live normally, resulting from acute diseases and lingering chronic affects."[41]

The "shadow of the A-bomb" was physical and not mental. Hamatani and his peers rejected any notion of guilt as a negative factor, a central pillar in Lifton's understanding of trauma, arguing that "this guilt consciousness does not link the survivors with those who died, but in the process of pursuing their own moral rehabilitation, it leads them to opposition to nuclear weapons which deprived human beings of the possibility of responsible moral behavior. Thus, the deaths . . . are given some meaning."[42] Those who did not accept this position were subject to nihilism and despair, "standing always on the border between life and death."[43] The only way for *hibakusha to* overcome their suffering was through resistance, as "only if they reject war and A-bombs and identify themselves completely with those who are opposing their development and use can they establish human and moral relations with the dead."[44] In another instance of such emotional mobilization of guilt and hurt for the cause, the general report stated "the anguish of the *hibakusha* has not lessened. Rather, it has been intensified by the increased arms race and the repeated A-bomb tests which have made the *hibakusha* feel that their appeals have not been heard and their experience has been in vain." *Hibakusha* also supposedly suffered from historical research that denied the American assertion that the A-bomb ended the war, as it denied *hibakusha* noble "sacrifices for peace," and made them "feel they were merely objects whose suffering and death were without meaning."[45] This curious adaptation of American justifications for the A-bomb was another instance in which A-bomb sociology mirrored the ABCC position. Both the ABCC and the movement emphasized the *hibakusha*'s uniqueness. Although their motivations were dissimilar, they both considered the *hibakusha* a unique resource, which they used for the purpose of defending American lives or abolishing nuclear weapons. In both the ABCC and the compensation movement, such attitudes also led to distortion of evidence. For instance, though most *hibakusha* in Ishida's 1977 survey stated that they found meaning in family and their children, and only a small number spoke of politics, Ishida completely ignored his own findings and argued for a political awakening of *hibakusha*, as "however small in number, it is important when [we] consider [the] A-bombs from the angle of humanity."[46]

The emphasis on the political role of *hibakusha* and their sanctification as martyrs for the A-bomb cause was the main reason for the rejection of Lifton's theories. Lifton's title, *Death in Life*, was peculiarly translated as "Life within Death" (*Shi no uchinaru seimei*), which led many critics to believe that he was treating *hibakusha* as the walking dead. His intent was quite the opposite. The "death" in *Death in Life* referred to the ever-present imprint of the bomb on survivors' lives, which continued but nevertheless were connected to "that day." Criticism of Lifton had a strong impact on social workers' circles. All major figures who criticized him were involved with *hibakusha* care. Kurihara Sadako and Funabashi Yoshie were both in the Yamashita group, and Funabashi later headed the counselors' association. Ishida Tadashi and, later, Hiroshima's Mayor Akiba Tadatoshi were also noted critics. The first to critique the book was Kurihara Sadako, in two essays in 1975 and 1982. Kurihara accused Lifton of conducting "ABCC-like research" by interviewing survivors and not offering treatment.[47] She argued that Lifton was "allergic" to the antinuclear movement and had "negative attitudes" toward politically active" survivors, that Lifton was "ambiguous" about American responsibility, and that although his work "appears to be neutral in its academic writing style, eventually, it draws only negative conclusions about the state of A-bomb survivors."[48]

Although he did acknowledge his debt to Lifton, Ishida was also critical of Lifton's attitudes toward the ideologically committed survivors. As

Yagi Yasuhiro has argued, Ishida's main critique of Lifton was on ideological grounds, as Lifton had not "recognized *hibakusha* '"resistance' and the 'ideological leap' into resistance."[49] Funabashi, who wrote the most extensive critique of Lifton, focused on the issue of *hibakusha* uniqueness. For her, the comparison with the Holocaust, plague victims, and the like "watered down the particularity of the Hiroshima situation."[50] Foreshadowing the *Historikerstreit* debates in Germany about the uniqueness of the Holocaust, Funahashi claimed that the comparison "relativized and by extension trivialized the A-bomb experience . . . which thus lost its uniqueness."[51] Funabashi, unlike Ishida and Kurihara, did not take issue with Lifton's distancing of his work from the antinuclear movement, and pointed out that the *hibakusha* themselves probably were taking this stance at the time (this was the time of splits and ideological rancor in the movement).[52] Funahashi had actually interviewed Lifton's research subjects, when in 1980 she and Akiba had assembled a "Lifton study group"[53] composed mostly of social workers who located all of Lifton's interviewees and those who had worked with him. Members were allocated individual chapters. Lifton's work was well known but not widely read. Most social workers had not read the book, which was out of print. Sagura Kayo said, "We only could get one copy and photocopied the chapters on an old machine." The group was, Sagura recalled, "all Mayor Akiba's idea, who really did not like Lifton."[54] Akiba, indeed, had the most vociferous criticism of Lifton. For him, Lifton's description of survivors was akin to treating them like "living corpses . . . eaten by guilt with no exit."[55]

Akiba's criticism was basically similar to that vice by Ishida and Kurihara, and was aimed mostly at what activists saw as Lifton's dismissal of antinuclear activism as a way out of psychological misery. Lifton's attitudes to activism, however, were not so different from Ishida's. Lifton had a more nuanced and multilayered understanding of what he called "reformulation"—survivors' search for meaning—than Ishida. He saw more than one way out of the shadow of the A-bomb; but even then he indeed was more pessimistic and did not quite believe that survivors ever left the experience completely behind them. This nuanced approach did not fare well in the ideologically charged atmosphere of the social worker and care community. Lifton's ideas were not rejected uniformly; some MSW welcomed his input. Most, however, either seemed not to have read him or knew very little about his work apart from what they had heard via his critics (*Death in Life* was not retranslated until 2009, with the very different title *Surviving Hiroshima / Hiroshima o ikinuku*). The

Lifton working group was quickly disbanded after Akiba pulled out due to his election campaign.[56] Thus, Lifton's ideas on psychic trauma were poorly understood at best, or completely unknown until much later. As a result, and especially with the persistent lack of involvement by Japanese psychological experts, social workers had very little guidance on how to deal with psychologically hurt individuals.

The social workers. group did set up monthly counseling sessions at the Hiroshima YMCA, and filled a very important gap in care, especially among minority *hibakusha* and other unrecognized *hibakusha* who received little care or acknowledgment prior to the late 1970s. But the counselors were not trained or had little access to psychologists. Thus, in one case among many, Sagura recalled that when she consulted a clinical psychologist at a hospital, "[the doctor] told me that it was hysteria, and that it would be dangerous if I got involved any further." The survivor, however, refused to go to the hospital. Indeed, for many in Japan the perceived choice was between institutionalization and no treatment at all. Even in the 1970s there were other ways the survivor could get treatment through outpatient clinics and the like. But we must remember that until the early 1950s it was still legal for families to lock mental patients in cages. Sagura commented, "We do not have this culture here, you know; if someone goes crazy, or is thrown into a hospital . . . we see him as such (crazy; *ki ga kurutta*) and have a bad image of him. This is the last option."[57] Other social workers commented similarly on the lack of guidance and their own unfamiliarity with psychological issues. Social workers did not neglect psychological issues; they were and still are dedicated advocates for survivors' health and well-being. *Hibakusha* care was definitely important for the movement, but the emphasis was mostly on social and medical issues, and the political work of bearing witness. Lifton's ideas and, by extension, PTSD were just not part of the lexicon of social and care workers in Japan. The case was different in the contemporary West.

Activism, Psychological Experts, and the Road to PTSD

In February 1974, a NAS committee submitted its recommendation to Congress on its work in Vietnam. The committee shared much with many of the research initiatives examined in these pages. It examined the effects of substances like "Agent Orange" and other herbicides on the local population. The chair of the committee, biochemist Philip Handler, ac-

SOCIAL WORKERS AND NUCLEAR SOCIOLOGY

knowledged such connections when he noted that the committee had less time than "the Atomic Bomb Casualty Commission in Japan, the work of which pursued objectives comparable to . . . our study; it took one year of organization and five years of actual work to obtain major data, and work is still continuing."[58] Handler also connected concerns over radiation and chemical warfare: "It is the difficulty in thus containing the effective dimensions of nuclear weapons which has rendered their use so abhorrent that they have become weapons of last resort. And it was such concerns, inter alia, that led to the present study."[59] Like the USSBS, the committee was sent to Vietnam to clarify and assess the facts about Agent Orange amid what was perceived as public hysteria. The American "public [showed] concern that the extensive use of herbicides in the Vietnam War *may have had* serious adverse effects" (my emphasis). Meanwhile, for the Vietnamese, it "achieved symbolic and emotional significance which sometimes outweighed the actual facts."[60]

Indeed, the Committee on the Effects of Herbicides in Vietnam shared more than just an institutional home and an ideological affinity with the ABCC, the USSBS, and similar research initiatives. In many ways, the committee was a continuation of World War II mobilization of social science in the service of America's wars. It featured many of the same research methods, modalities, and aims, including an emphasis on psychology and morale (referred to here as "attitudes towards the war . . . and their assessment").[61] The commission also used local Vietnamese social scientists and students, many of whom were trained in the United States and were thereby continuing the BSR model. But perhaps the most direct connection was the presence of Alexander Leighton on the commission. It is hard to see why Leighton, by that point a chair in Harvard, would join this difficult and dangerous mission. It is true that he was no stranger to such work But working in the increasingly unstable country was difficult and controversial. What may explain his presence was the resistance of his younger colleagues to join the mission. Handler noted that "formation of the Committee was significantly delayed when anthropologists indicated their reluctance to be associated with this effort because the supporting funds were to be provided through the Department of Defense."[62] Vietnam was not Japan, and many younger researchers abhorred working with the military. But Leighton seemed to have had no such compunctions.

The exact role and details of Leighton's endeavors in Vietnam are beyond the scope of this study. We should note, however, that his presence on the committee did not mean he was toeing the Pentagon's line. This was a significant departure from the earlier entanglement of Leighton and other psychological experts with the defense establishment. Although the report minimized the impact of herbicide on the population, Leighton and two other scientists publicly dissented and disassociated themselves from parts of the report.[63] The psychological experts on the committee included, besides Leighton, the noted psychiatric epidemiologist Jane M. Murphy; the wonderfully named anthropologist Terry Rambo, who had extensive Vietnamese experience; and an unnamed Vietnamese sociologist who had been trained at Ohio University.[64] The behavioral scientists, as they called themselves, wrote a scathing report on the impact of herbicide on rural Vietnamese. Examining the "beliefs, attitude, and behavior of lowland Vietnamese," the committee paid particular attention to the accumulating stress that had led to long-lasting psychological effects. Even at this later date, the committee, with one exception, still did not use the word "trauma," but opted to talk of stress and scars, concluding that "the stress related to the spraying of herbicides played a discernible role among the correlates of psychological strain, and . . . herbicide stress in conjunction with stress from other sources of war activity should be considered as possible causes of the psychological scars sustained by those who were at Operation Cedar Falls."[65] Breaking with the precedent of the USSBS and the ABCC, and with the rest of the report, which was much more positive, the social science report did not try to minimize or instrumentalize mental damage, but concluded, with its one reference to psychological trauma: "Five years after the traumatic upheaval of Cedar Falls, the Binh Hoa refugees still appear to be suffering a psychological aftermath which is not only important in the moment but which may continue into the future."[66]

This shift in attitudes toward war and the long-lasting damage to the affected civilian population can be explained by the radically changed circumstances surrounding Vietnam in general, and the use of herbicide and nonconventional weapons in particular. Such attitudes, and especially the greater awareness to the environmental and psychological price of war, had their origins in nuclear research and antinuclear activism. The turning point in the relationship of both scientists and the public to nuclear weapons came with the 1954 Bikini tests and the grave concerns over radiation poisoning across the Pacific. While the *Lucky Dragon 5* incident intensified efforts by nuclear supporters to neutralize opposition to nuclear weapons and convince the public of the merits of the atom, for others the advent of thermonuclear weapons exposed the absurdity of such efforts. Concerns over radiation in particular raised awareness of the environmental dam-

SOCIAL WORKERS AND NUCLEAR SOCIOLOGY

age of nuclear tests, an awareness that had strong connections to the rise of the environmental movement. The tests were, as Robert Jacobs argued, a sort of limited nuclear war that caused real damage to populations from the Marshall Islands to Nevada, but also led to increasing anxiety in many beyond the affected areas concerning genetic and other damage.[67] Works like Rachel Carson's *Silent Spring,* which condemned the indiscriminate use of pesticide by the very same corporations that were heavily involved in the military-industrial complex, fed into such concerns.[68]

The institutions established by postwar American psychiatrists were an important arena for such debates. Starting in the mid-Fifties, the GAP engaged in several debates on nuclear weapons and civil defense, culminating in two seminars in Asbury Park, New Jersey, in 1958 and 1959, on "the psychological and social aspects of the use of nuclear energy." These seminars revealed that an overwhelming majority within GAP supported a clear antinuclear stance, and they resulted in a major report by GAP's Committee on Social Issues that was decisively antinuclear in its tone and conclusions. These developments can be attributed in large part to the work of Jerome D. Frank, who in 1957 sent an open letter to GAP members challenging current thinking on nuclear issues, a summary of which he also published in the *Atlantic Monthly.*[69] Frank had served in the Philippines as a military psychiatrist. During his service in Asia, he became staunchly antinuclear and, according to Lifton, was the first major psychiatrist to be active in the anti-bomb movement. He formed a lifetime friendship with Lifton, and the two often participated in nuclear conferences as the lone dissenters in rooms full of nuclear and military researchers.[70] Frank's letter ignited quite a controversy. Sixty-seven GAP members submitted their opinions of Frank's letter to the society.[71] Many of these opinions were along the lines of the research presented above, warning of the dangers of "denial, apathy, projection and other uses by individuals of techniques of adaptation to threats and perhaps to the reality of atomic warfare."[72] Frank's argument, however, was radically different. Rather than trying to help people adjust to the "reality of atomic warfare," he was aiming to avoid this reality altogether. This was exactly the stance taken by Lifton and other antinuclear activists. (Lifton had already been part of an antinuclear group led by David Riesman before 1962, called the "committee of correspondence"—a name taken from the American Revolution–era groups of the same name.)[73]

Such activism did not mean a complete break from earlier movements. Frank and his supporters were using language very similar to that of Chisholm and others. The basic assumptions of the role of psychiatry were, at least initially, also very similar. "The nuclear arms race poses a mortal and increasingly pressing danger to civilization," Frank wrote. "It is obvious that the *chief source of peril lies not in the nuclear weapons but in the human beings behind them*, and that therefore the danger can only be resolved by changes in human attitudes" (my emphasis).[74] Like his predecessors, Frank saw a special place for psychiatrists, as experts on human relations, in dealing with the dangers of paranoia and stereotypical thinking that led to the nuclear arms race. He also saw parallels between the behavior of nuclear-armed nations and that of psychiatric patients. For Frank, however, nuclear reality was distorted. Words like "defense" or "balance of power" had lost their meaning. There was no defense, or possibility of a "defensive shield," against the hydrogen bomb. Taking aim at the likes of Janis and the Rand Corporation, Frank wrote, "We seem to have slipped into George Orwell's world of doublethink without knowing it."[75]

Frank's argument was taken up by Franklin McLean, keynote speaker at the first GAP nuclear seminar. Like Frank, McLean pointed to the futility of nuclear defense in a thermonuclear world. Reviewing the objections of psychiatrists, he opposed seeing the arms race as "a natural phenomenon."[76] He preferred to see it "as man-made, and to concentrate my attention on the build-up that has led us into the situation in which we find ourselves today. I would prefer to examine the possibility of [the] reversibility of some of the trends that have produced the threats with which we have to deal rather than regard the arms race as something which cannot be helped."[77] The break with earlier debates, however, was not yet complete. McLean added, "This is a problem of human behavior with which psychiatrists are most familiar and best equipped to deal."[78] He summarized his position using almost the same exact words Chisholm used a decade earlier: "The world is sick, and the nuclear arms race is only one symptom—a symptom that, it is true, may lead to the death of a patient."[79]

Beyond GAP, other medical groups were also coming to a similar conclusion. Perhaps the most important was Physicians for Social Responsibility (PSR), which in 1962 commissioned a report, *The Fallen Sky*, on the possible results of a nuclear attack on Massachusetts.[80] The report was issued after the breakdown of the first partial nuclear test moratorium in the late 1950s, and concerns over fallout were at an all-time high. The PSR was founded by a group of antinuclear physicians in 1961, with, according to its official history, "one major goal: to educate the medical profession and the world about the dangers of nuclear weapons."[81] It was markedly

SOCIAL WORKERS AND NUCLEAR SOCIOLOGY   241

more radical than earlier associations, and had a clear left-of-center political stance, which became even more pronounced through the 1960s. Although there were no psychiatrists in the initial founding group, Lester Grinspoon (a rather prominent psychiatrist) and others became strongly involved in the movement very early on.[82] Both Chisholm and Karl Menninger were among the list of PSR's prominent sponsors appearing on its official letterhead. Roy Menninger, William Menninger's son and Karl's nephew, was also a prominent member and a frequent contributor to PSR newsletters. Frank also became a member, and the presence of such important figures of postwar psychiatry in PSR, as well as Frank's use of language very similar to that of Chisholm and others, point to the difficulty in demarcating clear transitions between one era and the next in psychiatric activism or lines of political allegiances. Especially with figures like Chisholm, traditional definitions of left or right just do not apply. The Sixties campaigners, indeed, showed both continuities with and clear departures from what had come before them.

PSR's early campaigns questioned the very possibility that humanity could deal with nuclear catastrophe in a way that resembled any past experiences. *Fallen Sky* presented a devastating critique of the defense establishment, with essays like "The Illusion of Civil Defence." Using measured and detached language, PSR authors revealed the sheer devastation and nightmarish quality of the aftermath of a nuclear attack. The report emphasized "the human and ecological aspects . . . of an assumed thermonuclear attack," and connected destruction of life with destruction of the environment. The section written by the psychiatrists Herbert Leiderman and Jack Mendelson relied not only on USSBS and European materials but mostly on reports by the Japanese victims.[83] Furthermore, the authors used such firsthand accounts to demonstrate the absurdity of earlier social scientists' attempts to offer solutions. This was plainly exposed by a reference to Margaret Mead's suggestion, at an American Association for the Advancement of Science (AAAS) symposium in Denver in 1961, "that an international program be developed where certain recently married couples be provided their honeymoon underground in a blast proof shelter," so that "at any given time, a reasonable number of the breeding population would be protected from annihilation in event of an attack." Mendelson and Leiderman were quite reserved in their critique, writing, "The serious introduction of such a possibility by an eminent anthropologist points up to the magnitude of some of the issues of even planning a defence shelter program."[84] They unequivocally concluded however, that psychiatric and social issues resulting from even planning for a nuclear exchange "are of a magnitude and complexity that make it advisable to concentrate on eliminating the need for such a program."[85]

Robert Jay Lifton joined PSR in 1963 after reading *Fallen Sky*. He was "recruited" by PSR founder Victor Sidel, who sent him a PSR "propaganda packet." Lifton sent the group an early draft of his Hiroshima research, and told Sidel that reading PSR reports "create[d] a reassuring sense that like-minded people from our profession were giving serious thought to this extraordinary horror that confronts us all."[86] The impact of PSR and Lifton's work was almost immediate. A 1964 GAP report by a group of leading psychiatrists, including Frank, Lifton, and other PSR members, stated that "a nuclear war cannot be won in the conventional sense of the world. A psychiatric follow-up study by Lifton of Hiroshima victims illustrates some of the new meanings that nuclear war involves."[87] The report was staunchly antinuclear and very much along the lines of the objections by Frank and others to normalizing nuclear reality while emphasizing the political role of psychiatrists. This was a complete reversal from GAP's early-Fifties stance. One of the major themes of the report was dehumanization and the other mechanisms that might lead to warfare. In a continuation of earlier themes, the authors argued that dehumanization was one of "the psychological effects of industrialization, specialization, collectivization, urbanization and automation."[88] They went a step further, arguing that these forces were increasingly making industrial killing easier, as killing became "as mechanized and impersonal as pulling a lever to start a production chain belt."[89]

In this context, the authors used a significant number of references to the Holocaust. Regarding nuclear war, the authors of the report wrote, "A foretaste of what the short life of survivors of such an attack could be like is suggested by Bettelheim's graphic description of what happened to the inmates of the Nazi concentration camps when they were reduced to desperation by conditions of extreme starvation and misery."[90] This was a very different reading than the ones by Kido and Shimizu, and even Bettelheim himself, focusing not on the issue of totalitarianism but on the victims themselves. If the victims of nuclear warfare were seen as comparable to concentration camp inmates, the perpetrators of nuclear war were akin to the Nazis and other hate groups. The report stated "It is not only an Eichmann who acquires such distorted self-image. The complacency of the Northern whites vis-a-vis lynching in the South" are a similar example.[91] When talking about the treatment of people as "subhuman," the

SOCIAL WORKERS AND NUCLEAR SOCIOLOGY   243

authors also added, "Examples [of victims] are Jews, Negros, Orientals, and so forth."[92] Thus, a critique of nuclear warfare expanded to a larger critique of the structures of racism and discrimination, contemporary and historical, in both the US and abroad.

The report's universalization and conflation of the categories of nuclear and Holocaust victimhood, as well as their emphasis on dehumanization and the emotional distancing that allowed killing foreshadowed much of Lifton's later work. This was tied to both a challenge of nuclear normality and to psychiatry's role in it. Lifton was part of a new generation in psychiatry that started to forcibly question and challenge old assumptions about social sciences' role in society. His critique of his colleagues' politics was interwoven with a critique of orthodox psychiatry and the older generations' very concept of reason. In a 1962 article, Lifton criticized conservatives' labeling of leftist students and antinuclear activists as "irrational." Directly challenging the entire enterprise of labelling resistance to nuclear power and weapons as irrational anxieties, Lifton argued that the very real fear of personal annihilation in a nuclear world is neither "unreasonable nor irrational." The conservatives' position was, Lifton argued, an "expression of a general tendency, in political and military thinking throughout the world, to distort the fundamental concept of reason."[93]

The influence of Erik Erikson, Lifton's close friend and mentor, made Lifton wary of Freud's insistence on the importance and finality of childhood for personality formation, which consequently made it easier for him to accept that trauma experienced later in life could alter adult personality. This was important in the context of the struggle against German psychiatrists' denial of survivors' compensation. Lifton's views were shared by a number of young researchers who criticized the over-determinism of Freudianism, along with their older colleagues' entanglement with the defence establishment and attendant reluctance to engage in politics.[94] Lifton's contemporaries, including Anne Parsons, Talcott Parsons' daughter and a trained psychoanalyst, similarly criticized psychiatrists' obsession with childhood and their hostility toward those who were maladjusted to the nuclear world. In a letter to her father, written in November 1963 from the Yale Psychiatric Hospital where she was hospitalized following what was seen as her extreme anxiety over nuclear issues, Parsons explained, "This is what an ... important part of my conflict with Dr A [her analyst at the Boston Psychoanalytic Institute] ... was about, since when I was in such a panic about nuclear war and the possibility of American fascism, he simply could not or did not see that people ever have strong emotions about anything but their immediate personal relationships or whatever it is that happens before one is six years old."[95] Lifton's research on *hibakusha* was similarly as motivated by his politics as it was by his resistance to Freudian dogma. He wrote to Riesman from Hiroshima, "The project is as much directed at the preventable future as at the irrevocle [*sic*] past.... [This is] one of the most fundamental events of our age ... and nobody has really probed it with direct study and psychological depth."[96]

Lifton, again, made the long-term effects of the trauma of the A-bomb a central part of his research. In a 1963 report he found the *hibakusha* "not only to have experienced the atomic disaster, but to have inhabited it and incorporated it into their beings, including all of its elements of horror, evil, and particularly of death."[97] Lifton noted that survivors experienced "psychic closure," by which he meant strong feelings of shame and guilt toward the dying and for being alive, and a feeling of being marked by death—being contaminated, and possessing "an inner sense of being doomed for posterity."[98] All of this, and especially the persistence of the little understood condition of *genbaku byō*—A-bomb disease (which Lifton saw as "as much a spiritual as a physical condition"), caused even seemingly healthy *hibakusha* to be "plagued by underlying anxieties."[99] It is in these observations that the shift in psychiatrists' attitudes toward nuclear issues had the most direct influence on the history of the concept of adult trauma. An antinuclear stance also meant more openness to the victims' voices and long-term suffering, and a greater awareness than had been present in earlier research of the long-term impact of violence on the mind. It meant moving away from concentrating on the role of childhood in creating mentally defective adults who could not adjust to warfare and the modern world, and toward an acknowledgment that trauma experienced by adults could have profound and shattering effects on the soul.

Hiroshima also had an important and understudied impact on the anti–Vietnam War movement in general, and Lifton's involvement in particular. PSR communications show an increasing awareness of and involvement in antiwar activities. The conduit for the shift from antinuclear to antiwar activism was concerns over the use of poison gas in Vietnam by the US military. In March 1965 the PSR executive committee sent a letter of protest to the US government over the supply of tear gas to South Vietnam.[100] This action caused some controversy as some members thought the action expanded PSR mandate beyond opposition to nuclear war. In an exchange between Frank and Bernard Lowen, Frank argued that "the use of chemical agents in Vietnam ... was inevitable and flowed from U.S

SOCIAL WORKERS AND NUCLEAR SOCIOLOGY

international policies." Frank further argued, in a direct reproach of the likes of Chisholm, that limiting activism "to searching into deep psychologic causes contributing to human aggression . . . is not enough. Such a course when it is divorced from social action becomes progressively more sterile and ends up as esoteric phrase-mongering."[101] A series of protests and letters regarding "gas warfare" in Vietnam ensued. From 1965 on PSR moved more and more toward an antiwar stance. Significantly, by the late 1960s and early 1970s this also included increased criticism of the contribution of medicine to the war effort. In 1971, leading members called on physicians to prevent their colleagues from "participating in the war effort."[102]

Lifton as well was increasingly vocal in his opposition to established psychiatry support of the war. In *Home from War*, Lifton singled out two articles in the *American Journal of Psychiatry* for special criticism. Both articles' authors took some pride of military psychiatry's effectiveness in containing war neurosis and of returning mentally wounded soldiers quickly to their units. "Especially contemptible," Lifton argued, "was the stance of military Psychiatry as an advocate of the military's interest rather than that of the soldier patient."[103] Lifton argued that psychiatrists were "partak[ing] of the passive complicity which is the mark of guilt in our time."[104] He was not alone in this criticism. In here the impact of GAP and PSR critique of dehumanization is discernible. Critiques singled out "Managerial technicism," that was leading "reasonably decent practitioners into 'ethical corruption.'" In these debates, comparisons were often made with the Nazi doctors and nuclear researchers. Reflecting this mood, in May 1971, the APA passed a motion "add[ing] its voice to the great masses of the American people who have so firmly expressed their agony concerning the war in Southeast Asia and voiced concerns about its effects on morale and on the rate of alienation, dehumanization and divisiveness among the American people."[105] This was the context for Leighton's and the other social scientists' dissent in the 1974 report.

Lifton, together with colleagues like Chaim Shatan, also worked with veterans who returned mentally wounded from the war. Their work on Post-Vietnam Syndrome, was influenced greatly by Lifton's Hiroshima experience. "Whenever we pooled results," Lifton said, "I invoked Hiroshima."[106] Lifton saw in survivors a special kind of people. He grouped veterans, with Holocaust, and Hiroshima survivors, calling them "prophetic survivors" whose "inspiration derives not from the Divinity, but from the holocausts they survived . . . who have managed to emerge from their holocaust with special regenerative insight."[107] As with work with Holocaust survivors, this stance was taken vis-à-vis others in the profession who saw traumatized individuals as malingering and lazy. This stance was controversial, yet Lifton and Shatan's campaign directly led to the APA adding of PTSD to the DSM in 1980. In a recent interview, Lifton recalled that when Shatan, "who was the one who wrote to the APA people, was making the case for inserting the diagnosis of post-traumatic stress disorder. I'm quite sure he mentioned my work in Hiroshima. [I] definitely remember talking to him about it and perhaps writing out something for him as we worked on all this together. And so my work on Hiroshima was very much involved in my sense of traumatized people whom I interviewed [in the 1970s]."[108] The history that led from Vietnam to PTSD was complex and also included other figures and movements (women activists like Mardi J. Horowitz being especially important in this regard).[109] But, Hiroshima's impact, although by no means front and center of their appeal (Vietnam and the Holocaust taking center stage by then), has reverberated far beyond the antinuclear discourse.

Conclusion: Roads not Taken

The entry of PTSD into DSM III was a monumental decision on part of the APA. The acceptance of PTSD and trauma had implications beyond the medical world. The concept changed the way Western societies dealt with the price of war and violence as a whole. In Japan, however, the rise of PTSD had limited consequences. This is not because Japan was an outlier. Quite the contrary. As demonstrated above, both in Japan and in the West the rise of the status of the survivor as a bearer of testimony, and the wider politics of trauma were an important part of the cultural, social, and academic conversation. Where Japan differed was on the complete lack of psychological professionals among those who advocated for survivors' mental health, and the very different meanings ascribed to the rise of the survivor by both leading figures like Ishida and the social workers who dealt with the *hibakusha* on a daily basis. In the West the rise of the survivor enabled a coming together of work on nuclear trauma, activism on behalf of Vietnam War veterans, and other groups. The politicization of the medical debates during the Vietnam War and later, which antinuclear activism was an important precursor to, enabled the coming together of such diverse groups of victims and campaigners. Similar developments enabled

SOCIAL WORKERS AND NUCLEAR SOCIOLOGY

advocates for Holocaust survivor rights to win the debates against the German psychiatrists who argued against concentration camp syndrome. The changed political atmosphere was a direct result also of activism within North American psychiatry and psychology that challenged the role of the professions in promoting war and enabled research initiatives from the USSBS to the Committee on the Effects of Herbicides in Vietnam. Though not directly related, it is no surprise that Homosexuality was de-pathologized and thrown out of the DSM only a few years earlier and by basically the same group of progressive physicians who were advocating for acknowledgment of PTSD. Both moves were part of a much wider progressive turn and a focus on victims of systemic violence, inequality, and discrimination that came out of the 1960s.

Japan also had its 1960s moment, and the social worker movement was an especially important outcome. In Japan the move was away from big ideas and theories and toward a focus on individual victims and their welfare. However, the particular historical circumstances of Hiroshima and Nagasaki led not to universalization of nuclear survivorhood and trauma, but to an emphasis on uniqueness. The suffering and struggle of *hibakusha* was widely recognized and advocated for, but it was understood mostly through a political and sociological rather than a psychological lens. The stigma attached to mental illness made activists hesitant to label the "victim-heroes" of the movement, to use James Orr's astute phrase, as trauma victims.[110] Ishida had democratized scientific know-how and the pursuit of objective knowledge, and entrusted it with the survivor herself, but the move was still away from suffering and victimization. The survivor was to be a figure who overcame her suffering through political action and the act of testimony. Mental hurt was to be left behind. Thus, politicization of trauma had a result almost exactly opposite to how the struggle over trauma victim rights in the West had turned out. This did not mean that trauma research had no impact. As we have seen, Lifton's work was an important influence on Ishida. His work was also important for many social workers. The movement was not a monolith, and reactions were varied. But by and large, Lifton's work in particular and trauma in general were not an accepted explanations, nor were they very well known in Hiroshima and Nagasaki. It would take another twenty years and another major disaster, the 1995 Kobe earthquake, to change this, and for PTSD, or wounds of heart (*kokoro no kizu*) to enter the medical and social conversation about trauma in Japan.

Conclusion

In 2004 the city of Nagasaki, following surveys by a group of researchers from Nagasaki University, set up the the Investigative Commission for Studies on Mental Damages to People Who Experienced the Bombing. The committee advocated for expanding the definition of survivors to include those who had experienced the A-bomb (*hibaku taikensha*), but significantly, it did not designate them as *hibakusha* per se. The decision was meant to include those who suffered from psychiatric damage and the long-term impact of trauma, and it enabled them to receive benefits. It mostly included areas beyond the initial geographical radius acknowledged by existing laws. But the decision was met with vehement protest by activists and survivors who wished to be recognized as radiation victims. As a result, in April 2009, "memory of the bombing experience was excluded from the criteria for psychiatric care beneficiaries."[1] This episode demonstrated how persistent resistance is among the survivor community to the idea of trauma and PTSD as a legitimate syndrome. This is very much a result of the long trajectory of denial and resistance to trauma by the medical establishments in both the United States and Japan, and among survivor activists. The very different reactions to Lifton's work in Japan and the United States, and the paradoxical impact of Holocaust psychology in Japan, served to highlight the ideological role of *hibakusha*. This focus on ideology and struggle led to the fundamental rejection of trauma and mental damage as wholly legitimate. Thus, even as late as 2009, PTSD had still not found acceptance in Hiroshima and Nagasaki as a legitimate stand-alone prognosis.

But, while survivors themselves are reluctant to accept the categories of trauma and PTSD, within academia, trauma is ubiquitous. Trauma often serves scholars as an explanatory deus ex machina, which supposedly

CONCLUSION   249

explains a community reaction to disaster along lines similar to those of an individual. PTSD has been used extensively to explain both survivors' individual reactions and the communities that surround them. This is true for Hiroshima, as in Naono Akiko's astute yet historically misconstrued work on trauma, or Saitō Hiro's notion of "nationalization of trauma," as well as in many other cases.[2] In a classic example of such use, drawing on Vamik Volkan's idea of "chosen trauma," Irit Keynan wrote that "the impact of trauma on a nation is similar to the process in which traumatic memory impacts the individual. . . . One may see collective trauma as a kind of societal PTSD that strikes an entire community and affects all its members."[3] This is a fundamental misunderstanding of both the history of trauma, seen here as an unchanging eternal disorder, and collective memory. What Keynan is doing here is projecting contemporary notions about individual trauma into collective and historical societies. Societies are not organic bodies, and the mechanisms of collective memory are fundamentally different from individual ones. Furthermore, for societies to "choose" trauma, they need to be aware of the existence of the phenomenon. As I argue throughout this book, trauma was not a significant category and was virtually nonexistent as an interpretive category in both Japan and the West prior to the late 1960s, and thus neither individuals nor communities could experience disaster and the reaction to it as trauma. Even beyond the 1960s, in activist circles as well as among psychiatrists and psychologists, there was widespread resistance to trauma, albeit for different reasons. Survivors themselves had varied reactions. They mostly either wanted to integrate and leave the experience behind, or, if they made survivorship a part of their identity, they understood their experience through the prism of ideology—or had other reactions in between these positions.

This does not mean that Hiroshima and Nagasaki did not have an important role in the history of trauma and psychiatry. Quite the contrary. Humanity's encounter with the atom played a significant role in the reaction of established psychiatry to World War II. This had a profound if unrecognized impact on the history of psychiatry, albeit a history both complex and nonlinear. Humanity's encounter with the atom started well before 1945, with the advent of the theories on, and then the praxis of, mass bombing. The second major argument I have made concerns the question of the origins of nuclear psychology. I argue that the encounter with the A-bomb should be seen as part of a wider field that concerned the targeting of civilians during war. Parallel to the history of combat trauma, the invention of "civilian morale" and the advent of categories like "shell shock" converged the minds of bombing theorists and the praxis of bomber commands, and led to the targeting of civilian minds. The hope (or fear) of mass psychic damage and mental shocks leading to another 1919-style German collapse was a major driver of bombing and civil defense praxis. Even after such mass psychosis did not materialize in the United Kingdom following the Blitz, air commanders kept bombing enemy minds, while combatants kept fearing the "war of vegetative neurosis" and the creeping hidden enemy crippling civilians' will to resist. The increasing involvement of psychological experts in bombing, and even more importantly, the evaluation of bombing at the USSBS, did not lead to any developed theory of trauma, a word that barely existed in their manuals. The main lens researchers employed was that of group psychology and the idea of morale. After the war, the surveys, drawing on battlefield psychiatry together with notions like national character, justified the bombing campaign ex post facto as a successful operation against enemy morale. What Atsuko Shigesawa called the "denial of awe" was a major impetus in the continuation of such ideas into the nuclear age, as the atomic bombings were not seen as separate in character or intent from the fire raids.[4]

In the United States, the impact of work in Hiroshima and Nagasaki work led both to political activism by USSBS and other veterans and to a growing field of civil defense psychology. The problem of scientific objectivity and politics came into clear focus in the immediate postwar period. Following the USSBS, psychologists began to act politically against the danger of war while at the same time launching major research initiatives like Janis's efforts at "psychological inoculation." The perceived success of combat psychiatry, and what psychiatrists perceived as a lack of mass psychosis after conventional bombing, was a crucial factor in building up psychological experts' confidence in their ability to manage the atom and its dangers. It was in this nexus of political activism and debates about civil defense that provided crucial context for Lifton's Hiroshima research. Most of the early research was conservative in nature, but it prepared the way for the next generation of anti–Vietnam War and antinuclear researchers. The generation that worked with Vietnam vets, Holocaust survivors, and other victims of mass violence used the "grand analogy" of disaster studies but focused on victims' long-term symptoms rather than group psychology and panic. This was the result of the challenging of nuclear normality, and of established psychiatry's role in the academic-military complex.

CONCLUSION

However, there was no clear move from "domesticating" the atom to opposing it and advocating for its victims. Major figures were active in both arenas. The language they used was similar, and there was much consensus about the role, indeed the duty, of psychiatrists to educate and be active in the community. Nevertheless, change was evident. Although Chisholm and others were certain that their goal was to cure a sick "world" and "society," the emphasis was on neurotic individuals' defective psychology, their unreasonable fear of atomic energy, and their failure to adjust to the changing world around them. To put it simply, it was not that the world was "sick," but that individuals were ill-prepared for it. Men like Chisholm, Leighton, and Kubo did acknowledge that something was wrong with their world. They saw themselves as being on the liberal side of the map, and were driven by an intense concern for peace and the survival of democracy. But for many of the early postwar psychiatrists who engaged with nuclear weapons and energy, nuclear reality was a given; it was simply a question of how humans as a species would adapt to it. This was the crux of the American denial of long-term mental suffering from the A-bomb. Denial in Hiroshima was not a cover-up in the simple sense of the world. Researchers just could not see the causal connection between the bomb and the current state of survivors.

In Japan, USSBS personnel and ideas fed into both the ABCC and the occupation's efforts of reforming Japanese minds. Here the question of objectivity and its relation to race and gender, ideas on transcultural psychiatry (or lack thereof), and the gendering of care all played a role. This had its own peculiar imprint on the issue of denial. The long trajectory that took Leighton and Matsumoto from the internment camps to psychological warfare and then Hiroshima in 1945 also led Matsumoto to work for SCAP and then Medical Sociology at Hiroshima, and finally led Leighton to Vietnam. In those journeys, questions of race and power, impacted the praxis of psychology and the way both researchers viewed long-term mental damage. The question of objectivity and causation was central in the ABCC relationship to survivors and the Japanese medical community, and in the debates on compensation for Holocaust survivors. In both cases, supporters of survivor rights were accused of being unobjective and emotional, and the cause-and-effect relationship between the traumatic event and long-term damage was challenged. Kubo's mistrust of survivor's voices, and his insistence on the superiority of a scientific and objective telling of the events of 6 August 1945, attested to how radically different were 1950s psychologists' views of survivors' testimony in comparison to what we now call trauma and our current understanding of trauma studies.

This was very much the result of the historical circumstances and power relations between Japanese and American science. Matsumoto, as well as Konuma and Kubo, had to prove they were more objective than the Americans. Kodama Aki, being a woman and Japanese, felt even more obliged to do so. Konuma's reasons for downplaying psychological damage, however, were different. Psychiatry, indeed, was a stand-alone field. Psychiatrists did not concern themselves with social activism, were hardly involved in any care schemes, and were less affected by US developments. Japanese psychiatry's inability to recognize long-term mental damage had its own genealogy. In psychiatry one sees more continuity with the profession's wartime past, and with its practice in other locales where German influence was strong, such as Israel and, of course, Germany itself. The bias toward somatic explanations and the difficult issue of radiation damage and its exact relation to patient symptoms made isolating mental damage from other somatic factors difficult. Added to this was the traditionally cautious attitude of researchers, and their desire, as in other fields, to be as objective or even more objective than their peers at the ABCC. It is easy to see why Konuma and his peers had little impact on *hibakusha* research, and even more so on care. This "curse of objectivity" also meant that no one in Japan has tried to delve into cultural factors that might have impacted trauma. The rejection of the Imperial Army's insistence on Japan's unique spirit, as well as the demise of American wartime psychologically infused racism, meant that there was little incentive to view Japanese as different from Americans or anyone else in their psychological reactions, and no work was done on transcultural trauma. Only the ABCC, and to a lesser extent Lifton's critiques (Funahashi being especially prominent in this regard), made any gestures in this direction.[5]

Perhaps even more so than their male counterparts, the women examined on these pages had to keep their distance from culture and emotion. Kodama Aki, for instance, was even more at a disadvantage than Konuma or Kubo, and had to be even more scientific and objective than either the Americans or her male counterparts. Women, as a whole, were assigned a subordinate role as "caregivers" while the men conducted research. It was only with the rise of the social workers' movement, to which Kodama was an important precursor, that women came to the front of the stage. But for Kodama and her generation as well, social work was an avenue for scientific work and a contribution to social change, which had not been available to them before the war, and was opened to them by the Ameri-

CONCLUSION 253

can occupation. American-inspired ideas about survivors' need for adaptation and self-sufficiency was part of this package. The rise of women-led movements was in part a reaction in part to this embrace by the generation of Kodama and Kubo of American ideas on science and politics. This was only one part of the Japanese picture. While psychologists like Kubo changed their methodologies and focus during the early postwar period, Japanese psychiatrists mostly remained ensconced within the German tradition with its emphasis on biological explanations and its suspicion of trauma. This was true also beyond Japan. The ABCC and the German psychiatric establishment were not alone in their resistance to trauma. Similar trends could be observed in Israel and other sites. Konuma and the other Japanese psychiatrists were not exceptional, continuing their German-influenced tradition and the Imperial Military's denial of psychic trauma, and searching for organic causes for survivor symptoms instead.

These early Japanese trajectories, as well as the intense politicization of the issue by sociologists and the greater movement that took over with the exit of Konuma and Kubo, was what eventually led to the absence of psychic trauma as a category of interpretation in Japan. However, ironically, the Japanese model of bearing witness, which Lifton recognized in his work, and the idea of the survivor's "special truth," which also came about around the time of the Eichmann trial in the Holocaust context, did have an important impact on the history of trauma. Lifton formulated his ideas at the time the survivor-witness model was developing in Japan. He carried it back to the United States with him. And it was the convergence of the Hiroshima and Holocaust experience, as well as the Vietnam War and other experiences, that led to the rise of PTSD and its entry into the APA's *DSM III* manual. This shift would not have been possible without a rethinking of the impact of the atom and technology on the modern psyche, nor without the radicalization of a generation of psychiatrists who tackled the impact of nuclear energy head on.

Robert Lifton and Kubo Yoshitoshi's encounter was an important point of convergence on these trajectories of change and resistance. This work tried to make some sense of this encounter and emphasize its importance in the history of psychiatry and of Hiroshima. In uncovering the multiple entangled histories that led to and from the 1962 encounter, many strands of research have been left only partially developed. This is true mostly in relation to the post-1962 part of this book. The rise of the social workers' movement, and its relation to A-bomb sociology as well as the generation that came before it, was a complex and multilayered process. Not all social workers agreed with Ishida and his peers many worked closely with the ABCC, and others were completely apolitical (the counselors' association, for instance, never expanded to Nagasaki). There were many, like Nakamura Sumio, who worked specifically with Korean and other minority *hibakusha*, or concentrated on women issues. Furthermore, before 1962, the exact role and impact of psychological experts on the fire raids, especially after the German surrender, was considerable but remained to be examined in full. The USSBS as a whole, and especially its impact and connection to postwar research, deserves much more scholarly attention than it has enjoyed so far. One could write a whole book just on Scott Matsumoto and Alexander Leighton's journey from the camps to Hiroshima, through SCAP and the ABCC, and finally to Vietnam.

But what is perhaps the most important matter on which this work has shed light is the necessity to uncover and examine more case files and tell the story of the survivors' mental health and struggles through their own eyes. In doing research for this book, I have encountered time and time again reluctance by archivists and hospitals to preserve and make available historical case files. Even when such files exist, the current laws that regulate archival materials in Japan require that 70 years, and in some cases 140 years, should pass before sensitive medical records can be released. Even when records could be released, a general mistrust of researchers has led to reluctance and refusal by institutional archives to let us even see the files that we know to exist. The result of these policies is that much of this book has been written on the basis of researchers' reports, with only a scattering of survivors' voices. Perhaps no episode demonstrates this clearer than Konuma's draft article in which survivors' "subjective" complaints were crossed out. That draft was preserved by Nakazawa Masao, but most of Konuma's case files and archival materials were destroyed by the hospital where they were stored. Kubo's files exist, but the archive where they are stored would not make them public. Thus, I have often had to rely on ABCC and other American materials, and have felt that the Japanese and other victims' stories are not being adequately told. I have tried to counter this with oral histories and other methods, but I still feel that such methods are far from sufficient. One can hardly capture in an interview the psychological state of survivors, and any psychological enquiry (which I am neither trained to do nor wish to conduct) would only capture the present.

This is regrettable, as what has constantly been missing in all histories of research examined here is a focus on the victims, their needs, and their stories. The *hibakusha*, to go back to the ABCC's designation, were

CONCLUSION

a unique resource. Their suffering and lives were not their own. They were too important. Much denial of psychological suffering has been done by people with the best of intentions—sometimes by people who are survivors themselves. What no one has acknowledged is their wish to just forget, and to live their life. As an anonymous *hibakusha* told Ōe Kenzaburō:

> People in Hiroshima prefer to remain silent until they face death. They want to have their own life and death. They do not like to display their misery for use as "data" in the movement against atomic bombs or in other political struggles. Nor do they like to be regarded as beggars, even though they were in fact victimized by the atomic bomb.... Almost all thinkers and writers have said that it is not good for the A-bomb victims to remain silent; they encourage us to speak out. I detest those who fail to appreciate our feeling about silence. We cannot celebrate 6 August; we can only let it pass away with the dead.[6]

This book ends with these words. Not with words of struggle, peace, or scientific triumph, but with the silence of those who faced too much to bear.

Acknowledgments

This book was written mostly during the 2020–21 COVID-19 lockdowns, which we spent first in our home in Pennsylvania and then in faculty housing in Japan. Throughout this time, like so many others, my wife and I have juggled childcare and work commitments while trying to keep safe, healthy, and sane. I would not have been able to write this book without her support. This book is dedicated to her. Two other extraordinary women were also indispensable to this book's research and writing: Kubota Akiko in Hiroshima, and Hashiba Noriko in Nagasaki. Both Kubota sensei, an archivist and scholar, and Hashiba san, a journalist and an emerging scholar herself, and were generous with their time and expertise, and were immensely helpful in locating materials and interviews, and in introducing me to the many people, groups, and document collections mentioned on these pages. Two other colleagues, Oleg Benesch in the United Kingdom and Nathan Hopson in Japan and then Norway, deserve special thanks. Both Oleg and Nathan kindly read through the manuscript, and gave valuable advice throughout the process. Their insights and experience dramatically improved the quality of the writing, and the clarity and delivery of ideas. As much of the subject matter of this book falls outside their immediate expertise (Oleg, a historian of Japan, collaborated with me on a book about castles, and Nathan is an expert on Tohoku and food history), I doubly appreciated their commitment and keen eye as readers.

The list of thank-yous is long and illustrious. Dozens of people and institutions made this book possible. Robert Jacobs, whose book *Nuclear Bodies: The Global Hibakusha* was published in 2021, was generous with his time, connections, and knowledge of American nuclear archives (we have often joked that we should do a "double nuclear feature" on minds and bodies). Susan Lindee, likewise, gave crucial advice and access to materials, and was supportive of the project from early on. Naoko Wake, Robert Hegwood, and Eiichiro Azuma guided me through the unfamiliar history of the relationship of Japanese Americans with Japan, American sociology, and the A-bomb. Aaron Moore, Nakao Maika, and Sheldon Garon taught me much about the history of bombing and the way it has intersected with intimate life histories, futuristic fantasies, and transnational learning. Michal Shapira and Rakefet Zelshik helped in locating Israeli sources and kindly advised me on Israeli and German psychiatry (and the odd Hebrew transliterations of German psychiatric terms by immigrant doctors). Likewise, Rotem Kowner, Nakamura Eri, and Harry Wu advised me in various times on Japanese and cross-cultural psychiatry. The book has also benefited greatly from Sarah Neal's keen eye for detail and her patience with my many nonnative mistakes in English. The Matsumoto family were generous with their time, and kindly shared family documents with me. Kikuraku Shinobu and Nakagawa Toshikuni, in this as in other projects, shared their incredible knowledge of Hiroshima and Nagasaki's history and archival sources. Kanazaki Yumi and Morita Hiromi at the *Chūgoku Shinbun* helped with pictures and introductions. Janice Goldblum at the NAS archives in Washington, Eric Van Slander at the American National archives, Miles Levy at the Smithsonian, Daniel Pick at Birkbeck, and Koike Yoshiko at Hiroshima University all deserve many, many thanks for their help. Sandra Yates, Mathew Richardson, and the McGovern library staff in Houston, which houses the ABCC materials, were extremely helpful going in above and beyond what was expected. Likewise, the staff at the University of Colorado Archives at Boulder Libraries deserve special mention. And then there are the many, many librarians and amateur historians in Hiroshima, Nagasaki, and other places who are rarely acknowledged for their work in preserving and telling local history, often done in small local documents rooms (*kyōdo shiryo shitsu*) and with minimal resources, and who deserve a mention and thanks here. Anton Schweizer and the IMAP crew at Kyushu University hosted me in Japan, and still provide an academic home away from home. On a more official note, first, portions of chapters 3, 4, and 8 have been published in the journals *Medical History* and *History Workshop*. I thank the journal editors for giving me the space to air my early ideas, and for letting me use these texts here. Second, the research in this book was made possible by the support of the Japan Foundation; the National Endowment for Humanities; and the Pennsylvania State University Center for Global

ACKNOWLEDGMENTS

Studies, Asian Studies, and Jewish Studies Department. I truly apologize if I have neglected to mention anyone. This book was aided by dozens of people who all deserve thanks, however big or small their contribution.

Finally, a few words on failure and success. This project, like so many other things in academic life, had its origin in a failure. When I was still a postdoctoral student at Yale, I aimed probably a bit too high and submitted an early version of this work to one of the more prestigious US journals in the field of history. The result was a lesson in the contradictions and pitfalls, but also wonderful camaraderie, one may encounter in our line of work. Having gone through several review cycles, I received six different opinions of the article, which ranged from the bad to the wonderful. Finally, the journal's editor, a senior scholar, very kindly reached out to me and explained why they could not proceed. I was ready to give up on the article and the topic, but both my graduate school adviser, Dagmar Herzog—whose advice was indispensable in several other crucial junctions in this and other projects—and my cohort of young colleagues at the center convinced me to continue with the project. It would take another five years, two "trial" articles, and another book in between for me to be able to get over the failure and, well, "trauma" of my initial foray into medical history, so that I could dive head-on into the project. I do hope younger colleagues can take heart in reading the "origin story" of this work and be reminded that, as cliché as it is, failure is often only the first step in the long journey of making one's research into a book.

Ran Zwigenberg, Tel Aviv, 2022

Notes

Introduction

1. Amiram Ezov, *Hakhraa: Mi nitzekh bemilkhemt yom ha'kippurim* (Tel Aviv: Kineret, 2020), p. 6.

2. Robert Jay Lifton to David Riesman, 10 April 1962, Robert Jay Lifton papers, box 15, folder 8 (1962), Manuscripts and Archives Division, New York Public Library, Astor, Lenox, and Tilden Foundations (hereafter NYPL-MSA).

3. Robert Jay Lifton, *Death in Life: Survivors of Hiroshima* (Chapel Hill and London: University of North Carolina Press, 1968, 1991).

4. Author's interviews with Dr. Tomonaga Masao, 19 February 2015, and Dr. Nakane Yoshibumi, 18 February 2015. Both physicians were pioneers in supplying mental health care for hibakusha. See also Nakazawa Masao, "Genshibakudan tōka ni yoru seishin shōgaisha: Shimin no higai," in Yasuo Okada, ed., *Mō hitotsu no senjō: senō no naka no seishin shōgaisha / shimin* (Tokyo: Rikka Shuppan, 2019), pp. 123–24.

5. Allan Young, *The Harmony of Illusions: Inventing Post-Traumatic Stress Disorder* (Princeton, NJ: Princeton University Press, 2001). pp. 107–10; Ben Shepard, *A War of Nerves: Soldiers and Psychiatrists in the Twentieth Century* (Cambridge, MA: Harvard University Press, 2001). pp. 356, 361–62.

6. Ran Zwigenberg, *Hiroshima: The Origins of Global Memory Culture* (Cambridge, UK: Cambridge University Press, 2014).

7. Ibid., pp. 154–62.

8. Dagmar Herzog, "The Obscenity of Objectivity: Post-Holocaust Antisemitism and the Invention-Discovery of Post-Traumatic Stress Disorder," in Nitzan Lebkovic and Andreas Killen, eds., *Catastrophes: A History and Theory of an Operative Concept* (Berlin: De Gruyter Oldenbourg, 2014), pp. 128–55.

9. For details on recent developments see Hiromitsu Kikuchi, "Waga kuni ni okeru shintekigaishō gainen no uketomekata no rekishi," *Hokkaido daigakuin kyōikugaku kenkyuinkyō*, no. 119 (December 2013): 105–38; Yoshibumi Nakane,

262   NOTES TO THE INTRODUCTION

Progress in Social Psychiatry in Japan: An Approach to Psychiatric Epidemiology
(Tokyo: Springer, 2012), pp. 109–29.

10. As late as 1989, psychologists drew on the Holocaust to explain the nuclear
arms race. See John E. Mack, "Discussion: Psychoanalysis in Germany 1933–1945:
Are There Lessons for the Nuclear Age?" *Political Psychology* 10, no. 1 (1989): 53–61.

11. See, for instance, Aiko Sawada, Julia Chaitin, and Dan Bar-On, "Surviving
Hiroshima and Nagasaki Experiences and Psychosocial Meanings," *Psychiatry: Interpersonal and Biological Processes* 67, no. 1 (2004): 43–60.

12. Svenja Goltermann, "The Imagination of Disaster: Death and Survival in
Postwar West Germany," in Alon Confino, Paul Betts, and Dirk Schumann, eds., *Between Mass Death and Individual Loss: The Place of the Dead in Twentieth-Century
Germany* (New York: Berghahn Books, 2011), p. 264.

13. Yuka Kamite, Hitomi Igawa, and Russell S. Kabir, "A Review of the Long-
Term Psychological Effects of Radiation Exposure in the Cases of the Atomic Bombings of Hiroshima and Nagasaki and the Chernobyl nuclear accident." *Hiroshima
daigaku shinrigakukenkyu,* Vol. 16. (2016), p. 51. See also Yasuyuki Ohta, Mariko
Mine, Masako Wakasugi, Etsuko Yoshimine, Yachiyo Himuro, Megumi Yoneda,
Sayuri Yamaguchi, Akemi Mikita, and Tomoko Morikawa, "Psychological Effect of
the Nagasaki atomic Bombing on Survivors after Half a Century." *Psychiatry and
Clinical Neurosciences* 54, no. 1 (2000): 97–103.

14. Yagi Yoshihiro, "Genbaku mondai to hibakusha no jinsei ni kansuru kenkyū
no kanōsei R. J. rifuton no Hiroshima kenkyū to sore ni taisuru samazamana han'nō
o megutte." Hama Hideo, Arisue Ken, and Takemura Hideki, eds., *Hibakusha chosa
o yomu: Hiroshima nagasaki no keisho* (Tokyo: Keio gijuku daigaku shuppankai,
2013), p. 160.

15. Svenja Goltermann, *The War in Their Minds: German Soldiers and Their
Violent Pasts in West Germany,* trans. Philip Schmitz (Ann Arbor: University of Michigan Press, 2017), p. 283.

16. Ibid., p. 7.

17. Audra Wolfe, *Freedom's Laboratory: The Cold War Struggle for the Soul of
Science* (Baltimore: Johns Hopkins University Press, 2020), p. 3.

18. Ran Zwigenberg, " 'Wounds of the Heart': Psychiatric Trauma and Denial in
Hiroshima," *History Workshop Journal* 84 (Fall 2017): 71; Herzog, "The Obscenity
of Objectivity," p. 130.

19. Miriam K. Kadia, *Into the Field: Human Scientists of Transwar Japan* (Stanford, CA: Stanford University Press, 2020), p. 3.

20. Harry Yi-Jui Wu. *Mad by the Millions: Mental Disorders and the Early Years
of the World Health Organization* (Cambridge, MA: MIT Press, 2021), pp. 55–57.

21. Ran Zwigenberg, "Healing a Sick World: Psychiatric Medicine and the Atomic
Age," *Medical History* 62, no. 1 (2018): 27.

22. Nakazawa, "genshibakudan seishin shōgaisha," p. 118.

23. Paul F. Lerner, *Hysterical Men: War, Psychiatry, and the politics of Trauma in
Germany, 1890–1930* (Ithaca, NY: Cornell University Press, 2003), p. 20.

NOTES TO THE INTRODUCTION

24. Robert Jay Lifton, *Home from the War: Learning from Vietnam Veterans* (Boston: Beacon Press, 1992), p. 412.

25. Quoted in Goltermann, "The Imagination of Disaster," p. 261.

26. Wu, *Mad by the Millions*, p. 11.

27. Ibid.

28. Ben Shepard, *War of Nerves: Soldiers and Psychiatrists in the Twentieth Century* (Cambridge, MA: Harvard University Press), p. 84.

29. Ibid., p. 120.

30. Allan Young, *The Harmony of Illusions: Inventing Post-Traumatic Stress Disorder* (Princeton, NJ: Princeton University Press, 2001), p. 44.

31. Ibid., p. 46.

32. Ibid.; Omnia S. El Shakry, *The Arabic Freud: Psychoanalysis and Islam in Modern Egypt* (Princeton, NJ, Princeton University Press, 2017). Much of this new work centered on colonial psychiatry. See Erik Linstrum, *Ruling Minds: Psychology in the British Empire* (Cambridge, MA: Harvard University Press, 2016); and Richard C. Keller, *Colonial Madness: Psychiatry in French North Africa* (Chicago: University of Chicago Press, 2007).

33. Jun T. Yoo, *It's Madness: the Politics of Mental Health in Colonial Korea* (Oakland, CA: University of California Press, 2016); Emily Baum, *The Invention of Madness: State, Society, and the Insane in Modern China* (Chicago: University of Chicago Press, 2018); Claire E. Edington, *Beyond the Asylum: Mental Illness in French Colonial Vietnam* (Ithaca, NY: Cornell University Press, 2019); Li Zhang, *Anxious China Inner Revolution and Politics of Psychotherapy* (Oakland: University of California Press, 2020).

34. Mark S. Micale and Hans Pols, eds., *Traumatic Pasts in Asia: History, Psychiatry and Trauma from the 1930s to the Present* (New York: Berghahn Books, 2021), forthcoming

35. Among other works, see Nakamura Eri, *Sensō to torauma: Fukashikasareta nihonhei no sensō shinkeishō* (Tokyo: Yoshikawa kōbunkan, 2018); and Janice Matsumura, "State Propaganda and Mental Disorders: The Issue of Psychiatric Casualties among Japanese Soldiers during the Asia-Pacific War," *Bulletin of the History of Medicine* 78, no. 4 (Winter 2004): 804–35.

36. See notes 10 and 12, as well as, among others, Kim Yoshiharu, Kawamura Noriyuki, and Tsutsumi Atsurō, "Hibaku taiken no motarasu shinriteki eikyō ni tsuite," *Seishin shinkei-gaku zasshi/ nihonseishinshinkeigakkai [hen]* 111, no. 4 (2009): 400–404.

37. Nakazawa Masao, *Hibakusha no kokoro no kizu o otte* (Tokyo: Iwanami Shoten, 2007).

38. See note 12.

39. Aritsuka Ryōji, *Okinawa-sen to kokoro no kizu: torauma shinryō no genba kara* (Tokyo: Ōtsuki shoten, 2014).

40. Paul Boyer, *By the Bomb's Early Light: American Thought and Culture at the Dawn of the Atomic Age* (New York: Pantheon, 1985); Spencer R. Weart, *Nuclear*

Fear: A History of Images (Cambridge, MA: Harvard University Press, 1988); Rosemary Mariner and Kurt Piehler, *The Atomic Bomb and American Society: New Perspectives* (Knoxville: University of Tennessee Press, 2009); Joseph Masco, "Atomic Health, or How the Bomb Altered American Notions of Death," in J. Metzl and A. Kirkland, eds., *Against Health: How Health Became the New Morality* (New York: New York University Press, 2010), pp. 133–56.

41. Guy Oakes, "The Cold War System of Emotion Management: Mobilizing the Home Front for World War III," in Robert Jackall, ed, *The Age of Propaganda* (New York: New York University Press, 1995), pp. 275–96.

42. Andrea Tone, *The Age of Anxiety: A History of America's Turbulent Affair with Tranquilizers* (New York: Basic Books, 2009); Jackie Orr, *Panic Diaries: A Genealogy of Panic Disorder* (Durham, NC: Duke University Press, 2006); and Gerald N. Grob, *The Mad among Us: A History of the Care of America's Mentally Ill* (New York: Free Press, 1994).

43. Susan L. Burns, *Kingdom of the Sick: A History of Leprosy and Japan* (Honolulu: University of Hawai'i Press, 2019); Junko Kitanaka, *Depression in Japan: Psychiatric Cures for a Society in Distress* (Princeton, NJ: Princeton University Press, 2012); Suzuki Akihito and Kitanaka Junko, *Seishin igaku no rekishi to jinruigaku* (Tokyo: Tokyo Daigaku Shuppankai, 2016).

44. Kikuchi, "Waga kuni ni okeru shintekigaishō," p. 105.

45. Paul Frederick Lerner and Mark S. Micale, *Traumatic Pasts: History, Psychiatry, and Trauma in the Modern Age, 1870–1930* (Cambridge, UK: Cambridge University Press, 2001), p. 10.

46. Dagmar Herzog, *Cold War Freud: Psychoanalysis in an Age of Catastrophes* (Cambridge, UK: Cambridge University Press, 2018), p. 93.

47. Dagmar Herzog made a similar case in relation to debates about compensation for Holocaust survivors. I have related such debates to nuclear issues in my own recent article. See Herzog, "The Obscenity of Objectivity," p. 31, and Zwigenberg, "Wounds of the Heart."

48. Allan V. Horwitz, *PTSD: A Short History* (Baltimore: Johns Hopkins University Press, 2018), p. 12.

49. Ibid., p. 41.

50. Lerner and Micale, *Traumatic Pasts*, p. 11.

51. Young, *Harmony of Illusions*, p. 93.

52. Horwitz, *PTSD*, p. 84.

53. Ruth Leys, *Trauma: A Genealogy* (Chicago: University of Chicago Press, 2000).

54. Tuomas Vesterinen, "Identifying the Explanatory Domain of the Looping Effect: Congruent and Incongruent Feedback Mechanisms of Interactive Kinds," *Journal of Social Ontology* 6, no. 2 (2020): 159. I thank one of the anonymous reviewers for pointing out this distinction.

55. Young, *Harmony of Illusions*, p. 5.

NOTES TO CHAPTER ONE

56. Author interview with Robert Jay Lifton, 28 May 2020.

57. Ibid.

58. Ibid.

59. Zwigenberg, *Hiroshima*, pp. 144–75.

60. Zwigenberg, "Wounds of the Heart," p. 82.

61. Quoted in Zwigenberg, *Hiroshima*, p. 4.

Chapter One

1. US Strategic Bombing Survey (hereafter USSBS), *The Effects of Strategic Bombing on German Morale* (Washington: 1946), p. 7.

2. USSBS, *The Effects of Strategic Bombing on Japanese Morale* (Washington:. 1947), p. 165

3. David Fedman and Cary Karacas, "A Cartographic Fade to Black: Mapping the Destruction of Urban Japan during World War II," *Journal of Historical Geography* 38, no. 3 (2012): 314.

4. https://www.nationalarchives.gov.uk/education/leaders-and-controversies/tran script/g5cs2s1t.htm. Accessed 29 July 2020.

5. Evaluation Board For Operation Crossroads, "The Evaluation of the Atomic Bomb as a Military Weapon: The Final Report of the Joint Chiefs of Staff" (30 June 1947), pp. 35–36 (hereafter Crossroads Report), https://www.trumanlibrary.gov/lib rary/research-files/evaluation-atomic-bomb-military-weapon, accessed 15 June 2020.

6. Sophia Dafinger, "Die Vermessung der Kriegsgesellschaft Sozialwissenschaft-liche Luftkriegsexpertise in den USA vom Zweiten Weltkrieg bis Vietnam," unpub-lished PhD dissertation, University of Augsburg, 2018, p. 8.

7. James H. Capshew, *Psychologists on the March: Science, Practice, and Professional Identity in America, 1929–1969* (New York: Cambridge University Press, 1999), p. 3.

8. Ibid., p. 5.

9. Ellen Herman, The *Romance of American Psychology: Political Culture in the Age of Experts* (Berkeley: University of California Press, 1996), p. 5.

10. Ibid , p. 17.

11. Ibid., p. 42.

12. Ibid.

13. Capshew, p. 130; Herman, p. 49.

14. Dafinger, p. 218.

15. Herman, p. 52.

16. Ibid.

17. Capshew, p. 121.

18. Hayashi, p. 24.

19. Ellen, pp. 65–66.

20. H. G. Wells, *The War in the Air*, https://www.gutenberg.org/files/780/780-h/780-h.htm, accessed 10 August 2020.

21. Ibid., p. 209.

22. Ibid.

23. Ibid.

24. Sheldon Garon, "On the Transnational Destruction of Cities: What Japan and the United States Learned from the Bombing of Britain and Germany in the Second World War," *Past & Present* 247, no. 1 (May 2020): 279.

25. Dafinger, p. 42.

26. Garon, p. 243.

27. Shepard, *War of Nerves,* pp. 302–3.

28. Ibid., p. 303.

29. Price, p. 178.

30. Dower, *War without Mercy: Race and Power in Pacific War* (New York: Pantheon Books, 2006), p. 101.

31. Conrad C. Crane, *Bombs, Cities, and Civilians: American Airpower Strategy in World War II* (Lawrence: University Press of Kansas, 1993), p. 8; Ronald Schaffer, *Wings of Judgment: American Bombing in World War II* (New York: Oxford University Press, 1988), p. 8.

32. Schaffer, p. 153.

33. Matthew Jones, *After Hiroshima: The United States, Race and Nuclear Weapons in Asia, 1945* (London: Cambridge University Press, 2012).

34. I thank my anonymous reviewers for pointing this important distinction.

35. Garon, p. 238.

36. Ibid., 244.

37. Crane, p. 17.

38. Susan R. Grayzel, *At Home and under Fire: Air Raids and Culture in Britain from the Great War to the Blitz* (Cambridge, UK: Cambridge University Press, 2014), p. 3.

39. Paul K. Saint-Amour, "Air War Prophecy and Interwar Modernism," *Comparative Literature Studies* 42, no. 2 (2005): 130–61.

40. Nakao Maika, *Kaku no yūwaku: Senzen nihon no kagaku bunka to genshiryoku yutopia no shutsugen* (Tokyo: Keisoshobo, 2015), pp. 131–34.

41. Owen Griffiths, "Militarizing Japan: Patriotism, Profit, and Children's Print Media, 1894–1925," *Asia-Pacific Journal: Japan Focus* 5, no. 9 (2007).

42. Maika Nakao, "The Image of the Atomic Bomb in Japan before Hiroshima," *Historia Scientiarum* 19, no. 2 (2009): 124.

43. Nakao, *Kaku no yūwaku*, p. 152.

44. Garon, pp. 24–25.

45. Ibid., p. 25.

46. Janet Borland, "Capitalising on Catastrophe: Reinvigorating the Japanese State with Moral Values through Education Following the 1923 Great Kantô Earthquake," *Modern Asian Studies* 40, no. 4 (2006): 906.

NOTES TO CHAPTER ONE

47. Conrad, p. 16.

48. USSBS, *German Morale*, vol. 1. p. 25.

49. Shepard, *War of Nerves,* p. 175.

50. Thomas Harnett Harrison, *Living through the Blitz* (London: Faber and Faber, 2010), p. 41.

51. Garon, p. 11.

52. Crane, p. 23.

53. David MacIsaac, *Strategic Bombing in World War II* (New York: Garland Publishing, 1976), p. 13.

54. Conrad Crane writes, for instance, that "Curtis LeMay made the decision to firebomb Japan essentially without any direction from Washington." Crane, p. 7.

55. Fedman and Karacas, p. 314.

56. Ibid, p. 318.

57. MacIsaac, p. 7.

58. Schaffer, p. 151.

59. Ibid, p. 157.

60. Ibid., p. 162.

61. Ibid., p. 90.

62. Ibid., p. 91.

63. Garon, p. 235.

64. USSBS, *Japanese Morale* (no page number).

65. USSBS, *German Morale*, vol. 1., p. 2.

66. Ibid., p. 1.

67. Dafinger, p. 92.

68. Ibid., p. 91.

69. USSBS, *German Morale*, ol. 1., p. 1.

70. Ibid.. p. 12.

71. Ibid., p. 42.

72. USSBS, *German Morale*, vol. 2, p. 32.

73. Jennifer M. Kapczynski, *The German Patient: Crisis and Recovery in Postwar Culture* (Ann Arbor: University of Michigan Press, 2011), p. 30.

74. Herman, p. 95.

75. USSBS, *German Morale*, vol. 1., p. 20.

76. Ibid., p. 19.

77. Ibid , p. 24.

78. Ibid , p. 35.

79. Ibid.

80. Ibid.

81. Herman, p. 11.

82. Irving L. Janis, "Problems Related to the Control of Fear in Combat," in Samuel A. Stouffer et al., eds., *The American Soldier: Combat and Its Aftermath* (Princeton, NJ: Princeton University Press, 1949), p. 194.

83. US Strategic Air Forces in Europe, Deputy Commanding General for

268   NOTES TO CHAPTER TWO

Administration, Office of the Surgeon (10 June 1944), "Bombing Assessment Project: Medical Organization." RG 243, box 20, folder 300.6-T., National Archives and Research Administration, College Park, MD (hereafter NARA archives).

84. U S Strategic Air Forces in Europe, Deputy Commanding General for Administration, Office of the Surgeon, "Summary Medical Studies of the Morale Division" (17 September 1945), RG 243, box 20, folder 300.6-T., NARA archives.

85. US Strategic Air Forces in Europe, Deputy Commanding General for Administration, Office of the Surgeon, "Interview with Dr. Leonardo Conti: State Secretary for Health, Ministry of Interior of the German Government (3 and 4 July 1945), RG 243, box 26 (no folder name), NARA archives.

86. See Irving Janis's survey of the professional literature covering the London Blitz and the Spanish Civil War in chapter 2 of Irving L. Janis, *Air War and Emotional Stress: Psychological Studies of Bombing and Civilian Defense; The Rand Corporation* (New York: McGraw-Hill, 1951).

87. USSBS, *German Morale*, vol. 1, p. 23.

88. Ibid., p. 19.

89. Ibid.

90. Ibid.

91. Ibid. p. 20.

92. Peri G. Gentile, "Advocacy or Assessment? The United States Strategic Bombing Survey of Germany and Japan, *Pacific Historical Review* 66, no. 1 (1997): 59.

Chapter Two

1. USSBS, *Japanese Morale*, p. 33.

2. Ibid., p. 186.

3. Ibid.

4. Dower, *War without Mercy*, p. 260.

5. Brian M. Hayashi, *Democratizing the Enemy: The Japanese American Internment* (Princeton, NJ: Princeton University Press, 2008), p. 1.

6. Alexander H. Leighton and Dorothea Cross Leighton, *Gregorio, the Handtrembler: A Psychobiological Personality Study of a Navaho Indian* (Cambridge, MA: Peabody Museum of American Archaeology and Ethnology, 1949).

7. Peter Suzuki, "Anthropologists in the Wartime Camps for Japanese Americans: A Documentary Study," *Dialectical Anthropology* 6, no. 1 (1981): 23.

8. http://encyclopedia.densho.org/Bureau_of_Sociological_Research,_Poston/#cite_note-ftnt_ref3–3. Accessed 27 May, 2020.

9. http://www.westerncounties.ca/isaiah/aleighton.html, Accessed 20 May 2020.

10. http://encyclopedia.densho.org/Bureau_of_Sociological_Research,_Poston/#cite_note-ftnt_ref3–3. Accessed 27 May 2020.

NOTES TO CHAPTER TWO

11. Hayashi, p. 23.

12. Alexander H. Leighton, "Training Social Scientists for Post-War Conditions," *Human Organization* 1, no. 4 (1942): 26.

13. Ibid., p. 28.

14. Ibid., p. 29.

15. Hayashi, p. 106.

16. Jennifer M. Miller, *Cold War Democracy: The United States and Japan* (Cambridge, MA: Harvard University Press, 2019), 2.

17. Leighton, "Training Social Scientists," p. 26.

18. Japanese American World War II Evacuation Oral History Project, Part III: Analysts, California State University, Fullerton, http://www.oac.cdlib.org/view?docId=ft0p30025h&brand=oac4&doc.view=entire_text. Accessed 15 July 2020.

19. Ibid.

20. Ibid.

21. Cited in David H. Price, *Anthropological Intelligence: The Deployment and Neglect of American Anthropology in the Second World War* (Durham, NC: Duke University Press, 2008), p. 151.

22. Leighton, "Training Social Scientists," p. 29.

23. Hayashi, p. 3.

24. Dower, *War Without Mercy,* p. 80.

25. Ibid.

26. "Japs Are Human." *Times Magazine*, 25 June 1945.

27. Karen M. Inouye, "Changing History: Competing Notions of Japanese American Experience, 1942–2006." unpublished PhD dissertation, Brown University, 2008, p. 78.

28. Inouye, p. 93.

29. Herman, p. 28.

30. Inouye, p. 93.

31. Cited in ibid., p. 98.

32. Ibid., pp. 112–13.

33. Alexander H. Leighton, *Human Relations in a Changing World: Observations on the Use of the Social Sciences* (New York: Dutton, 1949), p. 44.

34. Price, p. 172.

35. Herman, p. 33.

36. Cited in ibid., p. 29.

37. Daniel Pick, *The Pursuit of the Nazi Mind: Hitler, Hess, and the Analysts* (Oxford, UK: Oxford University Press, 2014), p. 18.

38. Herman, p. 34.

39. Ibid., p. 58.

40. Leighton, *Human Relations*, p. 49.

41. Alexander H. Leighton and Morris Edward Opler, "Psychiatry and Applied Anthropology in Psychological Warfare against Japan," *American Journal of Psychoanalysis* 6, no. 1 (1946):. 20.

42. Alexander H. Leighton, *Governing of Man: General Principles and Recommendations* (Princeton, NJ: Princeton University Press, 1948), p. 56.

43. Cited in Pauline Kent, "Ruth Benedict's Original Wartime Study of the Japanese," *International Journal of Japanese Sociology* 3, no. 1 (1994): p. 85.

44. Leighton and Opler, p. 20.

45. Ranjana Khanna, *Dark Continents: Psychoanalysis and Colonialism* (Durham, NC: Duke University Press, 2003), p. 2.

46. Erik Linstrum, "Specters of Dependency: Psychoanalysis in the Age of Decolonization," in *Psychoanalysis in the Age of Totalitarianism* (London: Routledge, 2016), pp. 181, 184.

47. Price, p. 155.

48. Ibid., p. 156.

49. Peter Mandler, *Return from the Natives: How Margaret Mead Won the Second World War and Lost the Cold War* (New Haven, CT: Yale University Press, 2013), p. 134.

50. Ibid, p. 135.

51. Kent, p. 92.

52. Ibid., p. 85.

53. Mandler, p. 165.

54. James Beveridge, *History of the United States Strategic Bombing Survey (Pacific), 1945–1946* (Washington: US Government Printing Office, 1946), pp. 1–15. https://www.worldcat.org/title/86131972.

55. Ibid., p. 38.

56. Dafinger, p. 196.

57. Atsuko Shigesawa, "Encountering the Atomic Bomb: the USSBS in Hiroshima and Nagasaki," in David Marples, ed., *Hiroshima-75: Nuclear Issues in Global Contexts* (Stuttgart: Ibidem-Verlag, 2020), p. 26.

58. Garon, p. 235.

59. Ibid., p. 265.

60. Shigesawa, p. 35.

61. "Verbatim Transcript: Medical History," RG 243, box 26, folder: Military Histories / Morale Division (4 December 1945), NARA archives.

62. Quoted in Shigesawa, p. 36.

63. Shigesawa, p. 22.

64. Beveridge, p. 252.

65. USSBS, *Japanese Morale*, p. 1.

66. Ibid.

67. Ibid., p. 2.

68. Ibid., p. 3

69. Shigesawa, p. 36.

70. Quoted in ibid.

71. Beveridge, p. 206.

NOTES TO CHAPTER TWO

72. Alexander Leighton, "The Sown Wind (on Hiroshima)," unpublished manuscript, folder 11, box 1, Lawrence C. Vincent Collection, University of Colorado Archives at Boulder Libraries, Colorado (hereafter Leighton Memoir), p. 1.

73. Ibid., p. 6.

74. Beveridge, p. 79.

75. Ibid.

76. Leighton Memoir, p. 9.

77. Ibid.

78. Hiroshima shi, ed., *Hiroshima Shinshi: Rekishi hen* (Hiroshima: Hiroshima shi, 1984), p. 16.

79. Michihiko Hachiya, *Hiroshima Diary: The Journal of a Japanese Physician, August 6–September 30, 1945* (Chapel Hill: University of North Carolina Press, 1995), p. 16.

80. USSBS, *Japanese Morale*, p. 212.

81. Ran Zwigenberg, "The Atomic City: Military Tourism and Urban Identity in Postwar Hiroshima," *American Quarterly* 68, no. 3 (2016): 617.

82. Leighton Memoir, p. 9.

83. For more on the rise of witness culture, see Zwigenberg, *Hiroshima*, pp. 65–93.

84. USSBS, *Japanese Morale*, p. 189.

85. Ibid., pp. 165–66.

86. Ibid., p. 187.

87. Ibid., p. 177.

88. Ibid., pp. 202–3.

89. Ibid., p. 35.

90. "Preliminary Composite Report on the Atomic Bomb," RG 243, box 23 (no folder name), NARA archives.

91. Ibid.

92. USSBS, *Japanese Morale*, p. 150.

93. Ibid., p. 192.

94. Ibid., p. 150.

95. Leighton Memoir, p. 21.

96. Ibid., p. 22.

97. Ibid., p. 24.

98. Capshew, pp. 124–25.

99. USSBS, *Japanese Morale*, p. 80.

100. Leighton Memoir, p. 6.

101. Ibid., p. 24.

102. Ibid., p. 25.

103. Leighton, *Human Relation,* pp. 38–39.

104. David Bradley, *No Place to Hide* (London: Hodder & Stoughton, 1949), p. 114.

105. Crossroads Report, p. 266.

106. Ibid., p. 291.

107. Ibid., pp. 35–36.

108. Ibid., p. 35.

109. Ibid., pp. 35–36.

110. Zwigenberg, "Wounds of the Heart," p. 76.

111. Crossroads Report, p. 38.

112. Jill Morawski and Sharon Goldstein, "Psychology and Nuclear War: A Chapter in our Legacy of Social Responsibility," *American Psychologist* 40, no. 3 (March 1985): 276.

Chapter Three

1. *United States Congressional Record: Proceedings and Debates of the 79th Congress*, vol. 92, part 10, 11 March to 6 May 1946 (Washington: Government Printing Office, 1946), A1748. Voorhis was quoting a poem by Hermann Hagedorn.

2. Weston La Barre, "Religions, Rorschachs, and Tranquilizers," *American Journal of Orthopsychiatry* 29, no. 4 (October 1959): 688.

3. John Farley, *Brock Chisholm, the World Health Organization, and the Cold War* (Vancouver: University of British Columbia Press, 2008), p. 17.

4. For the Santa Claus reference, see ibid., p. 182.

5. Michael E. Staub, *Madness Is Civilization: When the Diagnosis Was Social, 1948–1980* (Chicago: University of Chicago Press, 2011), p. 18.

6. Ibid.

7. Ian Dowbiggin, *The Quest for Mental Health: A Tale of Science, Medicine, Scandal, Sorrow, and Mass Society* (New York: Cambridge University Press, 2011), p. 139. It should be noted that the Menninger group was actively working to blur the lines between psychology and psychiatry. See Rebecca J. Plant, "William Menninger's Campaign to Reform American Psychoanalysis, 1946–48," *History of Psychiatry* 16, no. 2 (2005): 182.

8. Staub, *Madness Is Civilization*, p. 37.

9. Ibid.

10. See, for instance, John Hersey, "A Short Talk with Erlanger," *Life Magazine*, 29 October 1945, pp. 108–22.

11. Staub, *Madness Is Civilization*, p. 20.

12. Farley, *Chisholm*, pp. 3, 213–19.

13. Ibid., p. 17.

14. Dowbiggin, *The Quest for Mental Health*, p. 138.

15. William C. Menninger, *Psychiatry in a Troubled World: Yesterday's War and Today's Challenge* (New York: MacMillan, 1948), p. 3.

16. George Brock Chisholm, *The Reestablishment of Peacetime Society: Responsibility of Psychiatry, Responsibility of Psychiatrists; Panel Discussion of the First Lecture* (Baltimore: William Alanson White Psychiatric Foundation, 1946), pp. 1, 5–6.

NOTES TO CHAPTER THREE

17. Frank Fremont-Smith, "The Mental Health Aspects of the Peaceful Use of Atomic Energy," *American Journal of Orthopsychiatry* 28, no. 3 (1958), p. 456.

18. Ibid., p. 467.

19. Robert A. Jacobs, *The Dragon's Tail: Americans Face the Atomic Age* (Amherst: University of Massachusetts Press, 2010), p. 42.

20. Boyer, *By the Bomb's Early Light*. pp. 76–81.

21. Ibid., pp. 45, 368.

22. Jamie Cohen-Cole, "Cold War Salons, Social Science, and the Cure for Modern Society," *Isis: An International Review Devoted to the History of Science and Its Cultural Influences* 100, no. 2 (2009): 228.

23. Plant, "William Menninger's Campaign," p. 184.

24. Chisholm, *Peacetime Society*, p. 13.

25. Michal Shapira, *The War Inside: Psychoanalysis, Total War, and the Making of the Democratic Self in Postwar Britain* (London: Cambridge University Press, 2015), p. 197.

26. Ibid.

27. Pick, *The Pursuit of the Nazi Mind*, p. 22.

28. Chisholm, *Peacetime Society*, p. 17.

29. Staub, *Madness Is Civilization*, p. 16.

30. Ibid.

31. Ibid.

32. Ibid., pp. 22–23.

33. Tsuchiya Yuka, "Amerika jōhō shimoniinkai to shinrigakusha Maku A. May," *Intelligence*, no. 13 (2013): 19.

34. Jules H. Maserman, "Mental Hygiene in a World Crisis: Address to the General Conference of the Women's Auxiliary of the American Medical Association, Chicago, 7 November 1947. Papers of the Bulletin of the Atomic Scientists, box 29, folder 9, Special Collections Research Center, University of Chicago Library, Chicago (hereafter BAS papers).

35. Ibid.

36. La Barre" Religions, Rorschachs, and Tranquilizers," p. 688.

37. Quoted in Morawski and Goldstein, p. 276.

38. Committee on International Peace, "Psychology and Atomic Energy," Atomic Scientists' Printed and Near-Print Material, box 3, folder 5, Special Collections Research Center, University of Chicago Library, Chicago (hereafter Atomic Scientists papers).

39. Herman, p. 77.

40. Leighton, *Human Relations in a Changing World*, p. 11.

41. Herman, p. 76.

42. Clem Adelman, "Kurt Lewin and the Origins of Action Research." *Educational Action Research* 1, no. 1 (1993): 7–24.

43. Herman, p. 78.

44. Committee on International Peace, "Psychology and Atomic Energy." Atomic

Scientists' Printed and Near-Print Material, box 3, folder 5, Special Collections Research Center, University of Chicago Library, Chicago (hereafter Krech Report).

45. Ibid.

46. Ibid.

47. Tsuchiya, "Maku A. May," pp. 15–16.

48. Staub, *Madness Is Civilization*, p. 15.

49. Cohen-Cole, "Cold War Salons," p. 228.

50. Dowbiggin, *The Quest for Mental Health*, p. 139.

51. David Riesman, *The Lonely Crowd: A Study of the Changing American Character* (New Haven, CT: Yale University Press, 1950).

52. Chisholm, *Peacetime Society,* p. 7.

53. Morawski and Goldstein, p. 277.

54. Krech Report.

55. For a full review of "Atoms for Peace" and its place in American diplomacy and propaganda, see chapter 5 of Kenneth Osgood, *Total Cold War: Eisenhower's Secret Propaganda Battle at Home and Abroad* (Lawrence: University of Kansas Press, 2006).

56. See "Expert Meeting on the Social and Moral Implications of the Peaceful Uses of Atomic Energy" (UNESCO House 15–19 September 1958), UNESCO/SS/26 620.992/3A06 (44), UNESCO Archives, Paris, France; and A. Zvorkine, "Social and Moral Problems of the Scientific and Technical Revolution of Our Time," in Otto Klineberg, ed., *Social Implications of the Peaceful Uses of Nuclear Energy* (Paris: UNESCO, 1964).

57. Paul Josephson, *Red Atom: Russia's Nuclear Power Program from Stalin to Today* (Pittsburgh: University of Pittsburgh Press, 2005).

58. "Report by the Director General on the Expert Meeting on the Social and Moral Implications of the Peaceful Uses of Atomic Energy" (September 1958), UNESCO/SS/26 620.992/3A06 (44), UNESCO Archives, Paris (hereafter UNESCO Report).

59. Mandler, p. 135.

60. Ibid., p. 1.

61. Hans Hoff, "Mental Health Implications in the Peaceful uses of Nuclear Energy," in Otto Klineberg, ed., *Social Implications of the Peaceful Uses of Nuclear Energy* (Paris: UNESCO, 1964), p. 100.

62. UNESCO Report, p. 5.

63. World Health Organization, "Mental Health Aspects of the Peaceful Uses of Atomic Energy: A Report of a Study Group" (Geneva, 21–26 October 1957), in WHO/ MH/ AE 1–2 (1957–1958), WHO archives, Geneva, 3. I thank Harry Wu for this reference (hereafter WHO Report).

64. Otto Klineberg, introduction to *Social Implications of the Peaceful Uses of Nuclear Energy*, pp. 10–11.

65. WHO Report, p. 6.

NOTES TO CHAPTER FOUR

66. Ibid., p. 24.

67. Ibid., p. 34.

68. Ibid., p. 33.

69. Ibid., p. 6.

70. Ibid., p. 4.

71. Ibid., p. 16.

72. Ibid., p. 17.

73. Ibid., p. 40.

74. Ibid., p. 44.

75. Frank Fremont-Smith, "The Mental Health Aspects of the Peaceful Use of Atomic Energy," *American Journal of Orthopsychiatry* 28, no. 3 (1958): 456.

76. WHO Report, p. 21.

77. Ibid., p. 16.

78. Ibid., p. 41.

79. UNESCO Press Division, "UNESCO and Atomic Energy," *IAEA Bulletin* 2, no. 1 (1960) 21.

80. Ibid.

81. David Serlin, *Replaceable You: Engineering the Body in Postwar America* (Chicago: University of Chicago Press, 2004), p. 182.

82. Franz Alexander, "The Psychiatric Aspects of War and Peace," *American Journal of Sociology* 46, no. 4 (1941): 504.

83. Morawski and Goldstein, p. 279.

Chapter Four

1. Janis, *Air War and Emotional Stress*, p. 153.

2. http://conelrad.blogspot.com/2010/12/atomic-cheesecake-alert-america-convoy .html. Accessed 6 October 2020.

3. *Los Angeles Times*, 22 May 1952.

4. Ibid.

5. Naoko Wake, "Surviving the Bomb in America: Silent Memories and the Rise of Cross-National Identity," *Pacific Historical Review* 86, no. 3 (2017): 489.

6. Oakes, "Emotion Management," p. 275.

7. Mathew Farish, "Panic, Civility and the Homeland," in Deborah Cowen and Emily Gilbert, eds., *War, Citizenship, Territory* (New York: Routledge, 2008), p. 101.

8. Group for the Advancement of Psychiatry (GAP), Committee on Cooperation with Governmental (Federal) Agencies, "An Introduction to the Psychiatric Aspects of Civil Defense," *Group for the Advancement of Psychiatry, Published Reports* 19 (April 1951): 1.

9. Joseph E. McLean, "Project East River: Survival in the Atomic Age," *Bulletin of the Atomic Scientists* 9, no. 7 (1953): 247.

NOTES TO CHAPTER FOUR

10. Staub, *Madness Is Civilization*, p. 20.

11. Gerald N. Grob, *From Asylum to Community: Mental Health Policy in Modern America* (Princeton, NJ: Princeton University Press, 1991), p. 5.

12. Quoted in Staub, *Madness Is Civilization*, p. 33.

13. Rebecca J. Plant, "The Veteran, His Wife, and Their Mothers: Prescriptions for Psychological Rehabilitation after World War II," in Oostdijk Diederik and Markha Valenta, eds., *Tales of the Great American Victory: World War II in Politics and Poetics* (Amsterdam: VU University Press, 2006), pp. 95–105.

14. Ian Dowbiggin, "Prescription for Survival: Brock Chisholm, Sterilization and Mental Health in the Cold War Era," in David Wright and James Moran, eds., *Mental Health and Canadian Society: Historical Perspectives* (Montreal, QC, and Kingston, ON: McGill-Queen's University Press, 2006), pp. 179–82.

15. Chisholm, *The Reestablishment of Peacetime Society*, p. 17.

16. Gerald N. Grob, "World War II and American Psychiatry," *Psychohistory Review* 19 (1990): 53.

17. Author's interview with Robert Jay Lifton, 6 December 2013.

18. Boyer, *By the Bomb's Early Light*, p. 331.

19. Andrea Tone, *The Age of Anxiety: A History of America's Turbulent Affair with Tranquilizers* (New York: Basic Books, 2009), p. 94.

20. *New Yorker*, 3 May 1958. Quoted in ibid., p. 102.

21. Ibid., p. 95.

22. Project "East River" was undertaken by a consortium of Ivy League universities known as "Associated Universities, Inc." It was similar to Project Troy and other government-academy initiatives in the early Cold War. See Allan Needell, "'Truth Is Our Weapon': Project TROY, Political Warfare, and Government-Academic Relations in the National Security State," *Diplomatic History* 17, no. 3 (1993): 399–420.

23. Oakes, "Emotion Management," p. 275.

24. Orr, *Panic Diaries*, p. 87.

25. Dale Cameron, "Psychiatric Implications for Civil Defence." Read at the American Psychiatric Association, Montreal, Quebec, 23–27 May 1949. Reproduced in the *American Journal of Psychiatry* 106, no. 8 (February 1950): 588.

26. Ibid., p. 587.

27. Ibid, p. 588.

28. Ibid.

29. Ibid.

30. Dale Cameron, "Panic Prevention and Control," in Associated Universities Inc., *Report of Project East River* (New York: Associated Universities, 1952), vol. 9: "Information and Training for Civil Defense," p. 55.

31. Ibid., p. 56.

32. Ibid.

33. Ibid., p. 59.

34. Ibid., p. 64.

NOTES TO CHAPTER FOUR

35. Ibid.

36. GAP, "Psychiatric Aspects of Civil Defense," p. 3.

37. Philip Wylie, "Panic, Psychology, and the Bomb," *Bulletin of the Atomic Scientists* 10, no. 2 (February 1954): 40.

38. GAP, "Psychiatric Aspects of Civil Defense," p. 1.

39. Ibid.

40. Edward Geist, *Armageddon Insurance: Civil Defense in the United States and Soviet Union, 1945–1991* (Chapel Hill: University of North Carolina Press, 2019), p. 67.

41. Ibid.

42. Ibid.

43. Ibid., p. 66.

44. GAP, "Psychiatric Aspects of Civil Defense," p. 2.

45. Ibid., p. 4.

46. Ibid.

47. Ibid.

48. James S. Tyhurst, "Individual Reactions to Community Disaster: The Natural History of Psychiatric Phenomena," *American Journal of Psychiatry* 107, no. 10 (April 1951): 764–69.

49. Donald N. Michael, "Civilian Behavior under Atomic Bombardment," *Bulletin of the Atomic Scientists* 11, no. 5 (1955): 175.

50. Ibid., 175.

51. Ibid., 175–76. Michael quotes R. Fraser, I. Leslie, and D. Phelps, "Psychiatric Effects of Severe Personal Experiences during Bombing," *Proceedings of the Royal Society of Medicine*, no. 36 (1943): 119–23.

52. Orr, *Panic Diaries*, p. 103.

53. Ibid.

54. Ibid., p. 104.

55. Jerome D. Frank to Robert Jay Lifton, 16 April 1968, box 6, folder 1, Robert Jay Lifton papers, Manuscripts and Archives Division, New York Public Library. Astor, Lenox, and Tilden Foundations (NYPL- MSA).

56. Joost Abraham Meerloo, *The Rape of the Mind* (New York: World Pub. Co., 1956).

57. Shepard, *War of Nerves*, pp. 45–46.

58. Joost A. Meerloo, "People's Reaction to Danger," in Iago Galdston, ed., *Panic and Morale: Conference Transactions* (New York: International Universities Press, 1958), p. 174.

59. Ibid.

60. Ibid, p. 175.

61. Ibid, p. 177.

62. *New York Times*, 26 November 1976.

63. Dwight Chapman, John Gillin, Irving Janis, and John Spiegel, "The Problem of Panic," *Federal Civil Defense Bulletin* TB-19-2 (June 1955): 1–8.

64. Dwight Chapman, "Some Psychological Problems in Civil Defense," *Bulletin of the Atomic Scientists* 9, no. 7 (September 1953): 280.

65. Ibid.

66. Michael, "Civilian Behavior," p. 174.

67. Guy Oakes and Andrew Grossman. "Managing Nuclear Terror: The Genesis of American Civil Defense Strategy," *International Journal of Politics, Culture, and Society* 5, no. 3 (1992): 364.

68. Chapman, "Psychological Problems," p. 282.

69. Michael, "Civilian Behavior," p. 176.

70. Ibid., p. 173.

71. Ibid.

72. "Community Resources for Morale," in Galdston, p. 241.

73. Irving L. Janis, *Victims of Groupthink: A Psychological Study of Foreign-Policy Decisions and Fiascoes* (Boston: Houghton-Mifflin, 1972).

74. Oaks and Grossman, p. 380; Sharon Ghamari-Tabrizi, "Death and Resurrection in the Early Cold War: The Grand Analogy of the Disaster Researchers," in Leon Hempel, Marie Bartels, and Thomas Markwart, eds., *Aufbruch ins Unversicherbare Zum Katastrophendiskurs der Gegenwart* (Bielefeld, Germany: Transcript Verlag, 2013), p. 369.

75. https://history.state.gov/milestones/1945–1952/NSC68. Accessed 7 October 2020.

76. Carlton Savage to Paul H. Nitze, Memorandum for the Record, 24 October 1951. RG 273, box 5 (no folder number), NARA archives.

77. Ibid.

78. Ibid.

79. Quoted in Farish, "Panic, Civility and the Homeland," p. 109.

80. Ghamari-Tabrizi, p. 354.

81. Ibid., pp. 354–55.

82. Ibid., p. 364.

83. Ibid.

84. Ibid.

85. Ibid

86. Irving L. Janis, "Psychological Effect of Atomic Bombing," Industrial College of the Armed Forces, 14 May 1954, box 3, folder 5, Atomic Scientists papers.

87. Ibid. p. 7.

88. Ibid. pp. 7–8.

89. Ibid., p. 8.

90. Ibid.

91. Ibid., p. 4.

92. Irving L. Janis, "Psychological Aspects of Vulnerability to Atomic Bomb Attacks," RAND Crisis and Disaster Study, 1949, box 3, folder 6, Atomic Scientists papers, p. 45.

93. Janis, *Air War and Emotional Stress*, p. 75.

NOTES TO CHAPTER FOUR

94. Ibid.

95. Ibid. pp. 75–76.

96. Shepard, *War of Nerves*, p. 181.

97. Ibid., p. 300.

98. Goltermann, *The War in Their Minds*, p. 107.

99. Lothar Kalinowsky, "Problems of War Neuroses in the Light of Experiences in Other Countries," *American Journal of Psychiatry* 107, no. 5 (November 1950): 340.

100. Ibid.

101. Ibid. p. 343.

102. Ibid., p. 344.

103. Ibid, p. 343. For Hosokoshi Masaichi, see Nakamura Eri, Sensō to otoko no 'histeri': Jū go nen sensō to nihon rikugunheishi no 'otokorashisa,'" *Rikyō daigaku jenda foramu nenbyō* 16 (2014): 36–37.

104. Eri Nakamura, "'Invisible' War Trauma in Japan: Medicine, Society and Military Psychiatric Casualties," *Historia Scientiarium* 25, no. 2 (2016): 158.

105. Janis, *Air War and Emotional Stress*, pp. 79, 83.

106. Ibid p. 83.

107. Ibid., p. 45.

108. Ibid., p. 18.

109. Ibid. p. 52.

110. Ibid.

111. Ibid., p. 18.

112. Ibid., p. 103.

113. Ibid., pp. 9–10.

114. Ibid., p. 84.

115. Ibid., p. 101.

116. Geist, p. 65.

117. Janis, *Air War and Emotional Stress*, p. 220.

118. Ibid., p. 190.

119. Ibid., p. 258.

120. Jacobs, *The Dragon's Tail*, p. 56.

121. Joseph Masco, "'Survival Is Your Business': Engineering Ruins and Affect in Nuclear America," *Cultural Anthropology* 23, no. 2 (2008): 361–98.

122. H. P. Rand, "Mental Conditioning of the Soldier for Nuclear War," *Military Medicine* 125, no. 2 (1960): 116–19.

123. Speech by Colonel James P. Coney, chief radiological branch division of military application, before the American Public Health Association, Boston, 12 November 1948. Papers of Federation of American Scientists, box 324, folder 2, Chicago Library, Chicago.

124. Ibid.

125. US Department of Energy Openness Project, "Human Radiation Experiments: Roadmap to the Project; ACHRE Report," note 17. https://ehss.energy.gov/ohre/roadmap/achre/chap10_1.html. Accessed 9 October 2020.

126. Ibid.

127. Robert A. Jacobs, "Imagining a Nuclear World War Two in Europe: Preparing US Troops for the Battlefield Use of Nuclear Weapons," *Estonian Yearbook of Military History* 1 (2018): 172.

128. Albert J. Glass, "Psychological Problems in Nuclear Warfare," *American Journal of Nursing* 57, no. 11 (November 1957): 1428–1430.

129. US Army, "Management of Psychological Casualties," T.F. 8/ 2712 (1959). https://www.youtube.com/watch?v=s0rYbkAKVqY accessed 2 February 2021.

130. The US government acknowledged the harm done to these soldiers with the passage of the Atomic Veterans Relief Act (H.R. 1613) in 1985, and with the Justice for Atomic Veterans Act of 1998. On the impact of the tests on the soldiers and others, see the US Department of Energy ACHRE Report, as well as Kate Brown, *Plutopia: Nuclear Families, Atomic Cities, and the Great Soviet and American Plutonium Disasters* (Oxford, UK: Oxford University Press, 2015); Sarah A. Fox, *Downwind: A People's History of the Nuclear West* (Lincoln, NE: Bison Books, 2018).

Chapter Five

1. Gilbert W. Beebe to Dr. Darling, 13 March 1967, series 5, box 43, folder "Dr. Kiyoshi Shimizu," National Academy of Sciences Archives (hereafter NAS archives).

2. HumRRO, "Desert Rock IV: Reactions of an Armored Infantry Battalion to an Atomic Bomb Maneuver," Technical Report 2 (TR-2), (Washington, August 1953), p. 129.

3. Ibid., p. 130.

4. Susan M. Lindee, "Atonement: Understanding the No-Treatment Policy of the Atomic Bomb Casualty Commission," *Bulletin of the History of Medicine* 68, no. 4 (1994): 455.

5. Ibid., p. 461.

6. Ibid., p. 462.

7. Ibid., p. 459.

8. Susan M. Lindee, *Suffering Made Real: American Science and the Survivors at Hiroshima* (Chicago: University of Chicago Press, 1997), p. 35.

9. Austin M. Brues, "With the Atomic Bomb Casualty Commission in Japan," *Bulletin of the Atomic Scientists* 3, no. 6 (1947): 143–67.

10. ABCC General Report (January 1947), series 8, box 63, folder 1947, NAS archives.

11. Ibid., p. 2.

12. Brues, "With the ABCC," p. 144.

13. ABCC General Report (January 1947), p. 8.

14. Hayashi, p. 2.

NOTES TO CHAPTER FIVE

15. Brues, "With the ABCC," p. 144.

16. ABCC General Report (January 1947), p. 4.

17. Gerald O'Malley, "The Grave Is Wide: The Hibakusha of Hiroshima and Nagasaki and the Legacy of the Atomic Bomb Casualty Commission and the Radiation Effects Research Foundation," *Clinical Toxicology* 54, no. 6 (2016): 527.

18. ABCC General Report (January 1947), p. 4.

19. Brues, "With the ABCC," p. 167.

20. "Atomic Bomb Casualty Commission," *New England Journal of Medicine* 247, no. 23 (1952): 912.

21. Edgar Jones and Simone Wessely, "'Forward Psychiatry' in the Military: Its Origins and Effectiveness," *Journal of Traumatic Stress* 16, no. 4 (2003): 414.

22. Fredrick R. Hanson to Edward A. Strecker, 12 August 1947, series 12, box 77, folder "CAC the Conference on 'Psychological Aspects of Radiation Hazards.'" NAS archives.

23. John C. Rensmeir to Strecker, 3 September 1947, series 12, box 77, folder "CAC the Conference on 'Psychological Aspects of Radiation Hazards,'" NAS archives.

24. John C. Rensmeir to Thomas M. Rivers, 3 September 1947, series 12, box 77, folder "CAC the Conference on 'Psychological Aspects of Radiation Hazards,'" NAS archives.

25. Charles Dollard to Lewis Weed, October 17, 1947, series 12, box 77, folder "CAC the Conference on 'Psychological Aspects of Radiation Hazards,'" NAS archives.

26. Thomas M. Rivers to Lewis Weed, 22 October 1947, series 12, box 77, folder "CAC the Conference on 'Psychological Aspects of Radiation Hazards,'" NAS archives.

27. Carroll L. Wilson to Lewis Weed, 5 December 1947, series 12, box 77, folder "CAC the Conference on 'Psychological Aspects of Radiation Hazards,'" NAS archives.

28. Charles Dollard: Report to the Chairman, Division of Medical Sciences, NRC, 12 April 1948, 22 October 1947, series 12, box 77, folder "CAC the Conference on 'Psychological Aspects of Radiation Hazards,'" NAS archives.

29. Ibid.

30. Ibid.

31. Ibid.

32. Lindee, *Suffering,* p. 110.

33. Ibid., p. 113.

34. Grant Taylor to Robert Livingstone, 8 January 1952, series 1, box 9, folder: ABCC-NAS Office Correspondence, 1947–75, NAS archives.

35. Ibid.

36. Robert Livingstone to Grant Taylor, 27 March 1952, series 1, box 9, folder ABCC-NAS Office Correspondence, 1947–75, NAS archives.

37. Grant Taylor to James Neel, undated, series 1, box 9, folder ABCC-NAS Office Correspondence, 1947–75, NAS archives.

38. Ibid.

39. Pediatricians Wataru Sutow and James Yamasaki were two other noted Nisei at the ABCC. Both, like Matsumoto, encountered racial discrimination, but achieved leadership roles. See https://www.rerf.or.jp/en/about/history_e/psnacount_e/yamazaki-en/. Accessed 1 May 2021.

40. Henry Yu, *Thinking Orientals: Migration, Contact, and Exoticism in Modern America* (Oxford, UK: Oxford University Press, 2002), p. 94.

41. Ibid., p. vii.

42. Eiichiro Azuma, "Brokering Race, Culture, and Citizenship: Japanese Americans in Occupied Japan and Postwar National Inclusion," *Journal of American-East Asian Relations* 16, no. 3 (2009): 190.

43. Y. Scott Matsumoto, ""Evacuation in U.S.A. 1942, (8 February 1943)," Matsumoto family papers. I thank Anne Stewart Matsumoto for giving me access to her father's papers.

44. Hirabayashi, *The Politics of Fieldwork*, p. 135.

45. Yu, *Thinking Orientals*, p. 93.

46. War Department, History of USSBS (Pacific), RG 243, box 25, 314.7: Military histories, NARA archives.

47. Order, officers, civilian, and EM concerned, USSBS, (24 November 1945), in RG 243, box 25, 314.7: Military histories, NARA archives.

48. The field reports can be found in "Hiroshima: Special Interviews." Report No. 14f (9)(a), USSBS Index Section 2, Diet Library, Tokyo, Japan. I thank Shigesawa Atsuko for informing me about this source.

49. Author's interview with Anne and Michael Matsumoto, 7 March 2021.

50. "Irene N. Taeuber Report on Scotty Y. Matsumoto Application for the Asian and Near Eastern Studies Program," 11 December 1955, Irene Taeuber papers, collection C2158, folder 171, State Historical Society of Missouri, Columbia, MO (hereafter SHSMO archives).

51. Author's interview with Hashizume Bun and Hanabusa Aya, 27 June 2019, Yokohama, Japan.

52. Naoko Wake, "Atomic Bomb Survivors, Medical Experts, and the Endlessness of Radiation Illness," in Brinda Sarathy, Janet Brodie, and Vivien Hamilton, eds., *Inevitably Toxic: Historical Perspectives on Contamination, Exposure and Expertise* (Pittsburgh: University of Pittsburgh Press, 2018), p. 245.

53. Sagara Kayo, "Hibakusha to ABCC," *IPSHU kenkyū hōkoku shirīzu kenkyū hōkoku*, no. 23 (March 1996): 44.

54. Department of Patient Contacting (ABCC), "Minutes of Contractors Meeting, 2 April 1952," box 13, folder 10, Watauru W. Sutow papers, Texas Medical Library, Houston. I thank Mathew Richardson for this quotation.

55. Y. Scott Matsumoto, "Exit Interviews of Clinic Patients for Research Project

NOTES TO CHAPTER FIVE

ME-47," 17 June 1950, series 8, box 66, folder: unpublished reports Matsumoto, NAS archives.

56. Ibid.

57. Lindee, "Atonement," p. 458.

58. Y. Scott Matsumoto, "Patient Rapport in a Foreign Country," (1952), series 9, box 68, folder: Reprints, NAS archives, p. 3.

59. Irene N. Taeuber, "Report on Scotty Y. Matsumoto Application for the Asian and Near Eastern Studies Program," 17 December 1955, Irene Taeuber papers, collection C2158, folder 171, SHSMO archives.

60. Ibid.

61. Naoko Wake, personal communication with author, 3 March 2021.

62. Author's interview with Anne and Michael Matsumoto, 7 March 2021. I thank Michael Matsumoto for the flight manifest.

63. Y. Scott Matsumoto to Dr. George B. Darling, director; memorandum for the record, consultation with doctor Irene B. Taeuber office population research Princeton University, 16 December 1957, series 5, box 23, folder: Medical Sociology 1967, NAS archives.

64. Ibid.

65. Ibid.

66. Y. Scott Matsumoto to Irene Taeuber, 3 February 1958, Irene Taeuber papers, collection C2158, folder 207, SHSMO archives.

67. C. Segwick to Mr. Morgan and Mr. Hackle, Dr. Holmes, 20 June 1955, RG 34, box 187, folder 3, NARA archives.

68. Y. Scott Matsumoto to George B. Darling, 19 September 1958, series 5, box 23, folder: Medical Sociology 1967, NAS archives.

69. Gilbert W. Beebe to George Darling, 5 November 1958, series 5, box 23, folder: Medical Sociology 1967, NAS archives.

70. "Department of Medical Sociology" (undated), series 5, box 23, folder: Medical Sociology 1967, NAS archives.

71. Y. Scott Matsumoto to George B. Darling, March 13, 1961, series 5, box 23, folder: Medical Sociology 1967, NAS archives.

72. Y. Scott Matsumoto, *Social Impact on Atomic Bomb Survivors, Hiroshima and Nagasaki* (Hiroshima: ABCC, 1969), p. 16.

73. Ibid.

74. Ibid., p. 12.

75. DASA, *Proceedings of the First Interdisciplinary Conference on Selected Effects of a General War* (Santa Barbara, CA: DASA Information and Analysis Center, 1968), p. 321.

76. Robert Jay Lifton to David Riesman, 10 April 1962, Robert Jay Lifton papers, box 15, folder 8 (1962), NYPL-MSA.

77. George Darling to Herbert Gardner, 1 July 1968, series 5, box 41, folder: Dr. Lifton: 1963–1968. NAS archives.

284   NOTES TO CHAPTER FIVE

78. Ibid.

79. Lindee, *Suffering,* p. 154.

80. Ibid., p. 41.

81. Y. Scott Matsumoto to Hiroshi Maki, 23 January 1969, series 5, box 23, folder: Medical Sociology 1969, NAS archives.

82. Lindee, *Suffering,* p. 155.

83. Mire Koikari, *Cold War Encounters in US-Occupied Okinawa: Women, Militarized Domesticity and Transnationalism in East Asia* (Cambridge, UK: Cambridge University Press, 2017), p. 8.

84. Aki Kodama, *Report on Medical Social Work at ABCC Hiroshima, August 1960–July 1964* (Hiroshima, Japan: Atomic Bomb Casualty Commission, 1968), pp. iii–iv).

85. See *Chūgoku Shinbun,* 1 January 1948, 13 March 1948, and 24 March 1948.

86. Katsunobu Kihara, "History of Social Welfare at Doshisha University: A Case Study," presented at NACSW convention, November 2014, Annapolis, MD. https://www.nacsw.org/Convention/KiharaKAHistoryFINAL.pdf. Accessed 5 May 2020.

87. Nishimura Kiyoto, "Mizu no yō ni, semento no yō ni, sono yakuwari o, ABCC/RERF no iryō sōshā wōkā (MSW) toshite," 24 November 2016, RERF Library, Hiroshima, Japan. The English title is "Minutes of the Seventh ABCC/RERF History Forum."

88. "Third Human Relations Seminar: Seminar Group on Problems of Anxiety among A-Bomb Survivors," 3–4 October 1959), Medical Sociology study room report no. 1, 20 October 20 1959, series 5, box 23, folder: Medical Sociology 1967, NAS archives (hereafter Seminar Group on Anxiety).

89. Ibid.

90. Ibid.

91. Kodama, "Report on Medical Social Work," pp. iii–iv. Because Kodama was not fluent in English, and thus in all probability wrote the report in Japanese, I have relied here on the Japanese original and altered the translation done by the ABCC.

92. Nishimura, "Mizu no yō na," p. 1.

93. Kodama, "Report on Medical Social Work," p. 12.

94. Ibid.

95. Ibid., p. 14.

96. Ibid., p. 15.

97. Ibid., p. 27.

98. Ibid., p. 29.

99. Ibid., p. 23.

100. Ibid., p. 69.

101. Ibid., pp. 69–71.

102. Mastumoto, "Social Impact," p. 16.

103. Hatanaka Kunizō, "Hata-chū, 'katasumi no kiroku,' " in Kinoko no kai, ed.,

NOTES TO CHAPTER SIX   285

Genbaku ga nokoshita kora: Dainai hibaku kogashira-shō no kiroku (Tokyo: Nihon tosho sentā, 1984), pp. 399–400.

104. Minoru Ōmuta, "The Microcephalic Children of Hiroshima," *Japan Quarterly* 8, no. 3 (July–September 1966), p. 378.

105. Gilbert W. Beebe to George Darling, 30 November 1966, series 5, box 23, folder "Medical Sociology 1967," NAS archives.

106. George Darling to Y. Scott Matsumoto, 18 February 1967, series 5, box 23, folder "Medical Sociology 1967," NAS archives.

107. Y. Scott Matsumoto to George Darling. 7 March 1967, series 5, box 23, folder "Medical Sociology 1967," NAS archives.

108. Y. Scott Matsumoto to Dr. J. W. Hollingsworth, 15 February 1960, series 5, box 23, folder "Medical Sociology 1967," NAS archives.

109. Ibid.

110. Ibid.

111. Gilbert W. Beebe to George Darling, 13 March 1967, series 5, box 43, folder: Dr. Kiyoshi Shimizu, NAS archives.

112. Ibid.

113. Kaori Iida, "Peaceful Atoms in Japan: Radioisotopes as Shared Technical and Sociopolitical Resources for the Atomic Bomb Casualty Commission and the Japanese Scientific Community in the 1950s," *Studies in History and Philosophy of Biological and Biomedical Sciences* 80 (2020): 1.

Chapter Six

1. Quoted in Yoshikuni Igarashi, *Homecomings: The Belated Return of Japan's Lost Soldiers* (New York: Columbia University Press, 2020), p. 140.

2. Y. Scott Matsumoto to Irene Taeuber, February 3, 1958, Irene Taeuber papers, collection C2158, folder 207, SHSMO archives.

3. Svenja Goltermann, *The War in Their Minds: German soldiers and Their Violent Pasts in West Germany*, trans. Philip Schmitz (Ann Arbor: University of Michigan Press, 2017), p. 7.

4. Ibid., p. 283.

5. Kadia Kingsberg, *Into the Field*, p. 1.

6. Konuma Masuho CV in Hiroshima daigaku igakubu shinkei seishin igaku kyōshitsu, ed., *Kyōshitsu kenkyū gyōseki mokuroku: Konuma Masuho kyōju kaikō 20 shūnen narabini teinen taiken kinen* (Hiroshima: Hiroshima daigaku igakubu shinkei seishin igaku kyōshitsu, 1970), no page numbers.

7. Hiroshima daigaku igakubu shinkei seishin igaku kyōshitsu, ed., *Kyōshitsu kenkyū gyōsekishū: Konuma kyōju kaikō 15 shūnen kinen* (Hiroshima: Hiroshima daigaku igakubu shinkei seishin igaku kyōshitsu, 1964), no page numbers.

8. Ibid., p. 7.

9. Ibid., p. 8.

10. Akihito Suzuki, "Global Theory, Local Practice: Psychiatric Therapeutics in Japan in the Twentieth Century," in Ernst Waltraud and Thomas Mueller, eds., *Transnational Psychiatries: Social and Cultural Histories of Psychiatry in Comparative Perspective c. 1800–2000* (Newcastle, UK: Cambridge Scholars, 2010), p. 118.

11. Kikuchi Hiromitsu, "Wagakuni ni okeru shinteki gaishō gainen no uketome-kata no rekishi," *Hokkaidō daigaku daigakuin kyōiku-gaku kenkyū-in kiyō*, no. 119 (2013): 120.

12. Moriyama Nariakira, "Gaishōgosutoresushōgai no rekishi to tenbō (ichi)," *Nihon iji shinpō*, no. 3444 (1990): 60.

13. Kikuchi, p. 127.

14. Ibid.

15. Ibid.

16. Eri Nakamura, "'Invisible' War Trauma in Japan: Medicine, Society and Military Psychiatric Casualties," *Historia Scientiarium* 25, no. 2 (2016): 144.

17. Sabine Frühstück, "Male Anxieties: Nerve Force, Nation, and the Power of Sexual Knowledge." In Morris Low, ed., *Building a Modern Japan: Science, Technology, and Medicine in the Meiji Era and Beyond* (London: Palgrave Macmillan, 2005), p. 42.

18. Ibid., p. 43.

19. Nakamura Eri, "Nihon teikoku rikugun to sensōshinkeibyō: Senshōbyōsha o meguru shakai kūkan ni okeru 'kokoro no kaze,'" *Sensō sekinin kenkyu* 81 (2013): 52–61.

20. Janice Matsumura, "State Propaganda and Mental Disorders: The Issue of Psychiatric Casualties among Japanese Soldiers during the Asia-Pacific War," *Bulletin of the History of Medicine* 78, no. 4 (Winter 2004): 828.

21. Nakamura, "'Invisible' War Trauma," p. 154.

22. Shepard, *War of Nerves*, pp. 299–301.

23. US Naval Technical Mission to Japan, *References from the Committee for the Technical and Scientific Survey of Japanese Activities in Medical Sciences* (San Francisco: US Naval Technical Mission to Japan, 1945), p. 5.

24. Ibid., p. 133.

25. Janice Matsumura and Diana Wright, "Japanese Military Suicides during the Asia-Pacific War: Studies of the Unauthorized Self-Killings of Soldiers," *Asia-Pacific Journal* 13, issue 25, no. 2 (2015): 14.

26. US Naval Technical Mission to Japan, p. 134.

27. Eri Nakamura, "Psychiatrists as Gatekeepers of War Expenditure: Diagnosis and Distribution of Military Pensions in Japan during the Asia-Pacific War," *East Asian Science, Technology and Society: An International Journal* 13, no. 1 (2019): 57.

28. Nakamura, "'Invisible' War Trauma," p. 154.

29. Ibid., p. 157.

30. US Naval Technical Mission to Japan, p. 133.

NOTES TO CHAPTER SIX

31. Matsumura and Wright, p. 5.

32. US Naval Technical Mission to Japan, p. 134.

33. Ibid., p. 20.

34. Ibid., p. 7.

35. Nakamura, "'Invisible' War Trauma," p. 154.

36. Nakamura Eri, *Sensō to torauma: Fukashikasareta nihonhei no sensō shinkeishō* (Tokyo: Yoshikawakōbunkan, 2018), p. 58.

37. US Naval Technical Mission to Japan, p. 23.

38. Uchimura Yūshi, *Waga ayumishi seishin igaku no michi* (Tokyo: Misuzu Shobo, 1968), p. 220.

39. Ibid. p. 221.

40. US Naval Technical Mission to Japan, p. 22.

41. Uchimura, p. 251.

42. Ibid., p. 240.

43. Ibid., pp. 243–44.

44. Ibid., 244.

45. Nakamura Eri, "Nihon teikoku rikugun to sensōshinkeityō: Senshōbyōsha o meguru shakai kūkan ni okeru 'kokoro no kizu,'" *Sensō sekinin kenkyu* 81, no. 1 (2013): 58.

46. Korumaru Masashiro, "Kaigun no seishin iryō: Kuromaru Masashirō sensei ni kiku," *Seishin iryō*, no. 12 (1982): 83.

47. Konuma Masuho, "Kokuritsu shimofusa ryōyōsho ni okeru sagyō ryōhō ni tsuite (yōshi)," *Iryō*, no. 7 (1948): p. 22.

48. Ibid., p. 24.

49. Okada Yasuo, "Sensō to seishinka iryō, seishin igaku, soshite seishin igakusha," *15-Nen sensō to Nihon no igaku iryō kenkyūkai kaishi* 3, no. 2 (2003): 10.

50. Katō Masaaki, *Noirōze: Shinkeishō to wa nanika* (Tokyo: Sōgen-sha, 1955), pp. 42–43.

51. Okada, p. 9.

52. Korumaru, p. 85.

53. Uchimura, p. 255.

54. Okumura Nikichi and Hitsuda Heizaburo, "Genbakuden hisai kanja seishinkei byōgakuteki chōsa seiseki," *Kyushu shinkeiseishin igaku* 1, no. 50 (1949): 50.

55. Ibid., p. 51.

56. Ibid., p. 52.

57. Tsuiki Shirō et al., "Shūsen go 5 ka nen kan no Nagasaki idai seishinka kyōshitsu ni okeru keiken," *Seishinshi* 50, no. 6 (1951): 10.

58. Ibid.

59. Nishikawa Taneo et al., "Genshi bakudan hisai sha ni tsuite no seishin igakuteki chōsa," *Nagasaki igakkai* 36, no. 11 (1960): 717.

60. Ibid., p. 718.

61. Zwigenberg, "Wounds of the Heart," pp. 67–88.

62. Hiroshima-shi ishi-kai, *Hiroshima ishi no karute* (Hiroshima: Hiroshima-shi ishi-kai, 1989), p. 26.

63. Ibid., pp. 26–27.

64. Ibid., p. 30.

65. Konuma Masuho, "Genbakushō kōishō seishinshinekei kagaku no mondai," in T. Koyama, A. Tabuchi, and S. Watanabe, *Genshi igaku* (Tokyo: Kanehara Shuppan, 1963), p. 388.

66. Konuma Masuho, "'Sasameyuki' ni egaka reta mono no kokoro inron (shōron)," *Kikan ningen kagaku*, no. 4 (1949): 93–94.

67. Meguro Katsumi, "Sensō shinkeishō," *Iryō* 21, no. 2 (1967): 176.

68. Konuma Masuho, "Studies on the After-Effects of Brain Traumata Observed during the Last Three Warfares Implying Japan [*sic*]," *Psychiatry and Clinical Neurosciences* 4, no. 4 (1951): 362–70.

69. M. Konuma and S. Koshiba, "Cases of Accessory Nerve Paresis as the After-Effect of Shot Traumata in Battlefield," *Psychiatry and Clinical Neurosciences* 7, no. 3 (December 1953): 202–8; Konuma Masuho, "Keibu senshō ni tuite," *Seishin keigaku zashi* 50, no. 6 (1949): 1–3.

70. Yoshida Yutaka, *Nihongun heishi: Ajia, Taiheiyō Sensō no genjitsu* (Tokyo: Chūō Kōron Shinsha, 2017); Igarashi, *Homecomings*. p. 2.

71. Konuma, "Studies on the After-Effects of Brain Traumata," p. 364.

72. Hiroshima daigaku igakubu, *Konuma kyōju kaikou juugoshuunen kinen*, p. 12.

73. Konuma, "Studies on the After-Effects of Brain Traumata," p. 369.

74. Konuma Masuho, "Genbakushō narabi ni sono kōishō to shinkei seishin igaku," in Yuya Sato, ed., *Hiroshima daigaku: "Seishi no hi"; Gakujutsu-hen* (Hiroshima: Hiroshima daigaku sōgō hakubutsukan, 2012), p. 96.

75. Hiroshima daigaku igakubu, *Konuma kyōju kaikou juugoshuunen kinen*, p. 13.

76. M. Konuma et al., "Neuropsychiatric Case Studies on the Atomic Bomb Casualties at Hiroshima," in Committee for Compilation of Report on Research in the Effects of Radioactivity, ed., *Research on the Effects and Influences of the Nuclear Bomb Test Explosions* (Tokyo: Japan Society for the Promotion of Science, 1956), p. 1716.

77. Ibid., p. 1717.

78. Ibid., p. 1719.

79. Konuma Masuho, "Genbakushō ato ishō no kannōshō seikuhashiku narabi ni shōkō rikai ni osamute," *Nagasaki igaku zashi*, no. 3 (1961): 158.

80. Ibid., 167. *Noxe* is German for "noxa," something that exerts a harmful effect on the body.

81. Konuma, "Genbakushō kōishō seishinshinekei kakgaku no mondai," p. 389.

82. Ibid., p. 395.

83. Konuma Masuho, "Seishin shinkei kagaku no matome," *Hiroshima genshibakudan ato shogai kenkyukai kōenhen*, no. 7 (1965): 232.

84. Ibid., p. 232.

NOTES TO CHAPTER SIX 289

85. Ibid., p. 239.

86. Jolande Withuis, introduction to *The Politics of War Trauma: The Aftermath of World War II in Eleven European Countries*, ed. Jolande Withuis and Annet Mooij (Amsterdam: Aksant Academic Publishers, 2010), p. 2.

87. "Seminar Group on Anxiety," p. 12.

88. Ibid., p. 13.

89. Masao Nakazawa, "On Neuro-Psychiatric Symptoms of Hibakusha," (name of journal not given), 1985; in Nakazawa Masao, ed., "Genshi bakudan hisai-sha ni kansuru seishin igaku kenkyū bunken-shū," in Yokoyama Teruko papers p. 103. The collection of articles was prepared for a meeting of practitioners and academics in 1999.

90. Goltermann, *War in their Minds,* p. 103.

91. Shepard, *War of Nerves,* p. 312.

92. Ibid., p. 303.

93. Ruth Kloocke, Heinz-Peter Schmiedebach, and Stefan Priebe, "Psychological Injury in the Two World Wars: Changing Concepts and Terms in German Psychiatry," *History of Psychiatry* 16, no. 1 (2005): 51.

94. Peter Riedesser and Axel Verderber, *"Maschinengewehre hinter der Front": Zur Geschichte der deutschen Militärpsychiatrie* (Frankfurt: Mabuse-Verlag, 2011), p. 57.

95. Klocke et al., p. 55.

96. Goltermann, *The War in Their Minds*, p. 143.

97. Frank Biess, *Homecomings: Returning POWs and the Legacies of Defeat in Postwar Germany* (Princeton, NJ: Princeton University Press, 2009), p. 77.

98. Ibid.

99. Ibid., p. 75.

100. Goltermann, *The War in Their Minds*, p. 139.

101. Biess, p. 81.

102. Goltermann, *The War in Their Minds*, p. 127.

103. Ibid., p. 128.

104. Ibid., p. 129.

105. Goltermann, *The War in Their Minds,* p. 172.

106. Nakamura, "Nihon teikoku rikugun to sensōshinkeibyō," p. 59.

107. Tetsuya Fujiwara, "'Japan's Other Forgotten Soldiers," in Christopher Gerteis and Timothy S. George, eds., *Japan since 1945: From Postwar to Post Bubble* (London: Bloomsbury Academic, 2013), p. 134.

108. For examples, see Tetsuya Fujiwara, "Restoring Honor: Japanese Pacific War Disabled War Veterans from 1945 to 1963," unpublished PhD dissertation, University of Iowa, 2011, p. 158.

109. Fujiwara, "Japan's Other Forgotten Soldiers," pp. 135–36.

110. Nadav Davidovitch and Rakefet Zalashik, "Measuring Adaptability: Psychological Examinations of Jewish Detainees in Cyprus Internment Camps," *Science in Context.* 19 (2006)" 438.

290   NOTES TO CHAPTER SIX

111. Nadav Davidovitch and Rakefet Zalashik, "Recalling the Survivors: Between Memory and Forgetfulness of Hospitalized Holocaust Survivors in Israel," *Israel Studies* 12, no. 2 (Summer 2007): 147.

112. Rakefet Zalashik, *Ad nafesh: Mehagrim, olim, pelitim veha-mimsad ha-psikhi'atri be-Yisrael* (Tel Aviv: Ha-kibutz ha-mehuhad, 2008), p. 114.

113. See Dagmar Herzog, "The Obscenity of Objectivity: Post-Holocaust Anti-semitism and the Invention-Discovery of Post-Traumatic Stress Disorder," in Nit-zan Lebkovic and Andreas Killen, eds., *Catastrophes: A History and Theory of an Operative Concept* (Berlin: De Gruyter Oldenbourg, 2014), pp. 128–55.

114. Quoted in Goltermann, *War in Their Minds*, p. 181.

115. Judith Stern, "The Eichmann Trial and Its Influence on Psychiatry and Psy-chology," *Theoretical Inquiries in Law* 1, no. 2 (2000): 400.

116. Davidovitch and Zalashik, "Recalling the Survivors," pp. 145–63.

117. Zalashik, *Ad nafesh*, p. 439.

118. Stern, p. 403.

119. Hillel Klein et al., "Former Concentration Camp Inmates on a Psychiatric Ward: Observations," *Archives of General Psychiatry Archives of General Psychia-try* 8, no. 4 (1963): 334.

120. Stern, p. 403.

121. Zalashik, *Ad nafesh*, p. 172.

122. Leo Eitinger, "Pathology of the Concentration Camp Syndrome Prelimi-nary Report," *Archives of General Psychiatry* 5, no. 4 (1961): 371.

123. Ibid. p. 378.

124. Irit Keynan, *Ke'ilu hi petza' nistar: Traumat milḥamah baḥevrah hayiśraeliyt* (Tel Aviv: Am oved, 2012), p. 36.

125. Rakefet Zalashik, "Institutional, Political, and Military Factors Shaping the Recognition and Treatment of Combat Trauma during the Israeli War of Indepen-dence (1948)," working paper submitted to the open access, University of Edin-burgh research database, PURE, p. 1. I thank Rakefet Zalashik for this source.

126. Benjamin Wolman, "Me'beayot hihigiyena harukhanit ve'ha' psychiatriya ha'tzvait," *Harefuah* 35 (1948): 41.

127. Ibid., p. 41.

128. Quoted in Zalashik, "Institutional, Political, and Military Factors," p. 5.

129. Letz Healpern, "Tazpiot Nevero-p'saikhiatriot be'milkhemt yerushaliim," *Harefuah* 36. (1949): 14.

130. Ernst Kalmus, "Al nivroza milkhamtit," *Harefuah* 36 (1949): 44.

131. Ibid.

132. Amikhai Levy et al., "Tguvot ha'krav be'milkhamot yisrael 1948–1982 (leket pirkei historia mtokh ktav ha'et sikhot)," Mifkedet ktzin refuah rashi, makhleket b'riut ha'nefesh, mador kherum, 1993, p. 11.

133. Ibid., p. 9.

134. Ibid., p. 10.

NOTES TO CHAPTER SEVEN

135. Ibid., p. 12.

136. Konuma Masuho,"Genbaku hibakusha no shinrigakuteki chōsha," in Nakazawa, *Genshi bakudan hisai-sha*, p. 1.

137. Nakazawa, "On Neuro-Psychiatric Symptoms of Hibakusha," p. 97.

138. Zwigenberg, *Hiroshima*, p. 151.

139. Iida. "Peaceful Atoms in Japan," p. 2.

Chapter Seven

1. "Hiroshima to Kanai Tashirō," http://www.hiroshimapeacemedia.jp/peacemu seum_d/jp/text/voice018.html. Accessed 12 July 2021.

2. Cited in Zwigenberg, "The Atomic City," p. 619.

3. United States War Department, Our Job in Japan, (Washington: National Audio-Visual Center, 2015 [1945]). See also Dower, *Embracing Defeat*, p. 215.

4. Miller, *Cold War Democracy*, p. 2.

5. Ibid., p. 26.

6. Herman, p. 37.

7. Kingsberg Kadia, *Into the Field*, p. 78.

8. Ibid., p. 83.

9. Y. Scott Matsumoto to Irene Taeuber, 26 March 1957. C2158, folder 191, SHSMO archives.

10. Kingsberg Kadia, *Into the Field*, p. 75.

11. Ibid., p. 4.

12. Tsuruta Shōichi,"Kaigun ni okeru shinri gakuteki kenkyu," *Shinrigaku kenkyū*, no. 5 (1980), p. 31.

13. Brian McVeigh, *The History of Japanese Psychology: Global Perspectives, 1875–1950* (New York: Bloomsbury Academic, 2018), p. 169.

14. Ibid., p. 171.

15. Tsuruta, p. 27.

16. McVeigh, p. 60.

17. Ibid., p. 156.

18. Osaka Eiko,"Senryō Nihon shinrigaku," *Surugadai Daigaku kyuyō kenkyū-sho* 1 (2011): 181.

19. Ibid., pp. 177, 186.

20. Harry Wray,"Change and Continuity in Modern Japanese Educational History: Allied Occupational Reforms Forty Years Later," *Comparative Education Review* 53, no. 3 (August 1991): 252.

21. McVeigh, 174.

22. Ibid.

23. Osaka, p. 185.

24. Ibid., p.185.

25. Makita Minoru, "Seronchōsa koto hajime: Man 20-shūnen no yoron kagaku kyōkai," *Nihon seronchōsa kyōkaihō*, no. 4 (1966): 68.

26. Ibid., p. 69.

27. Ibid., p. 68.

28. Ibid., p. 70.

29. Ibid.

30. "CIE ni okeru shakai chōsa no tenkai," *Minzokugaku kenkyū* 17, no. 1 (1952): 68.

31. Osaka, p. 187.

32. Kubo Yoshitoshi, "Hibaku shita hitobito to no," *Heiwa bunka*, no. 5 (May 1977): 6.

33. Ibid.

34. *Chūgoku Shinbun*, 2 June 1950.

35. Ibid.

36. Henry Greenspan, Sara R. Horowitz, Éva Kovács, Berel Lang, Dori Laub, Kenneth Waltzer, and Annette Wieviorka, "Engaging Survivors: Assessing 'Testimony' and 'Trauma' as Foundational Concepts," *Dapim: Studies on the Holocaust* 28, no. 3 (2014): 190–226.

37. Kubo Yoshitoshi, "Genshi bakudan oyobi genshiryoku ni taisuru shakai shinrigakuteki kenkyū" (Genshi bakudan hibakusha no kōdō ni kansuru chōsa, no. 1), *Hiroshima daigaku Yoron kagaku kyōkai*, April 1950, p. 2.

38. Kubo Yoshitoshi, "Hiroshima hibaku chokugo no ningen kōdō no kenkyū," *Shinrigaku kenkyū*, 22, no. 2 (1952): 103.

39. Kubo, "'Genshi bakudan," p. 3.

40. Kubo, "Hiroshima hibaku chokugo," p. 103.

41. Ibid.

42. Kubo, "Genshi bakudan," p. 10.

43. Ibid., p. 14.

44. Kubo, "Hiroshima hibaku chokugo," p. 109.

45. Kubo, "Genshi bakudan," p. 16. This reflects the common belief that these who did not die peacefully haunt the living.

46. Ibid.

47. Ogura Kaoru to Robert Jungk, 2 July 1957, Ogura Keiko papers. The letters are reproduced also in Ogura Kaoru, Wakao Yūji, Ogura Keiko, and Kawaguchi Yūko, *Sengo Hiroshima no kiroku to kioku: Ogura kaoru no āru yunku ate shokan (shita)* (Nagoya, Japan: Nagoya daigaku shuppankai, 2018), pp. 64–70.

48. Ogura Kaoru to Robert Jungk, 9 July 1957, Ogura Keiko papers.

49. Heiwa no Tame no Shinrigakusha Kondankai, *Heiwa shinrigaku no ibuki* (Kyoto: Hōsei shuppan, 1990), p. 1.

50. Ibid., p. 2.

51. Ibid., p. 12.

52. Hadley Cantril, *Tensions That Cause Wars* (Urbana: University of Illinois Press, 1950), pp. 299–303.

NOTES TO CHAPTER SEVEN 293

53. Glenn D. Hook, "Sengonihon no heiwa no shisō no genryū: Heiwamondai danwakai o cāūshin ni," *Kokusai seiji* 10 (1981), p. 58.

54. Rachel M. MacNair, "The Interweaving Threads of Peace Psychology," *History of Peace Psychology and Division* 48, http://peacepsychology.org/history-of-division-48. Accessed 28 July 2021.

55. Shinrigakusha Kondankai, *Heiwa shinrigaku*, p. 2.

56. Shimizu Ikutarō, "Jinkaku no Kuzure jō ni kō shite ichi ichi Nachisu shūchū shūyōsho no hitobito," *Nihon hyōron* 25, no. 12 (1950): 32.

57. Miller, *Cold War Democracy*, p. 90.

58. Shimizu, "Jinkaku no Kuzure," p. 34.

59. Ibid., p. 42; Bruno Bettelheim, "Individual and Mass Behavior in Extreme Situations," *Journal of Abnormal and Social Psychology*, no. 38 (1943): 417–52.

60. Shimizu, "Jinkaku no Kuzure," p. 42.

61. Bruno Bettelheim, "Eichmann; the System; the Victims," *New Republic* 40, no. 24 (15 June 1963): 22.

62. Kido Kōtarō, "Tamashī no satsujin ichi ichi kyōseishūyōshc to ningen," *Gendai shinri-gaku*, no. 6 (1955): 59.

63. Ibid.

64. Ibid , p. 64.

65. Ibid.

66. Ibid., p. 55.

67. Introduction to Viktor E. Frankl, *Yoru to kiri: Doitsu kyōseishūyōsho no taiken kiroku* (Man's Search for Meaning), translated into Japanese by Shimoyama Tokuji (Tokyo: Misuzushobō, 1956), p. 2.

68. Ibid., p. 3.

69. Ibid., p. 4.

70. Shomoyama Tokuji, "Atogaki," postscript to Viktor E. Frankl, *Yoru to kiri: Doitsu kyōseishūyōsho no taiken kiroku* (Man's Search for Meaning), translated into Japanese by Shimoyama Tokuji (Tokyo: Misuzushobō, 1955), p. 209.

71. Shinrigakusha Kondankai, *Heiwa shinrigaku*, p. 3.

72. Ibid.

73. Miyagi Otoya, "Shi ni masaru kyōfu hibakusha no kokuhaku," *Kaizō* 17, no. 33 (1952): 196, 198.

74. Ibid.

75. Ibid., p. 196.

76. Nemoto Masaya, *Hiroshima paradokusu: Sengo Nihon no hankaku to jindō ishiki* (Tokyo: Bensei Shuppan, 2018), p. 4.

77. Morito Tastuo, "Hiroshima the Peace City" (c. 1958), MYH09593300. Morito Collection, Hiroshima University Archives, Saijo, Japan.

78. "World Brotherhood" (1956), MYH 09990100. Morito Collection, Hiroshima University Archives, Saijo, Japan.

79. Martin Erdmann, *Building the Kingdom of God on Earth: The Churches' Contribution to Marshal* (Eugene, OR: Wipf & Stock, 2005), p. 142.

80. Personal communication with the author, July 2, 2021.

81. Kubo Yoshitoshi to Everett R. Clinchy (c. 1951), MYH 09990100. Morito Collection, Hiroshima University Archives, Saijo, Japan.

82. *Chūgoku Shinbun*, 5 August 1950.

83. *Chūgoku Shinbun*, 7 August 1950.

84. *Chūgoku Shinbun*, 21 March 1953.

85. *Chūgoku Shinbun*, 15 May 1953.

86. Kubo Yoshitoshi, "Gensuibaku e no taido," *Genbaku to Hiroshima* 16 (1954): 13.

87. Ibid., p. 15.

88. Ibid., p. 16.

89. Ibid., p. 24.

90. Ibid., p. 23.

91. Ibid., p. 27.

92. Kingsberg Kadia, *Into the Field*, p. 68.

93. Hamatani Masaharu, "Genbaku higaisha mondai chōsa kenkyū no rekishi to hōhō," *Hitotsubashi kenkyū*, no. 21 (1971): 56.

94. Ibid., p. 62.

95. Zwigenberg, *Hiroshima*, p. 3.

96. Akiko Naono, "'Ban the Bomb! Redress the Damage!': The History of the Contentious Politics of Atomic Bomb Sufferers in Japan," *Asian Journal of Peacebuilding* 6, no. 2 (2018): 235.

97. Cited in ibid., p. 237.

98. *Chūgoku Shinbun*, 25 January 1956.

99. *Chūgoku Shinbun*, 30 June 1956.

100. Kubo Yoshitoshi and Nakano Seiichi, foreword to Gensuibakukinshi Hiroshima kyōgikai genbaku higaisha kyūen iinkai, eds., *Genbaku higaisha jitai chōsa hōkoku* (Hiroshima, 1956).

101. Gensuibakukinshi Hiroshima kyōgikai genbaku higaisha kyūen iinkai, eds., *Genbaku higaisha jitai chōsa hōkoku* (Hiroshima, 1956), p. 1.

102. Ibid., p. 6.

103. Ibid., pp. 6–7.

104. Kobayashi Tōru, ed., *Gensuibaku kinshiundō shiryōshū*, vol. 3 (Tokyo: Ryokuin shobō, 1995), p. 174.

105. Ibid., p. 175.

106. *Chūgoku Shinbun*, 1 August 1958.

107. Scott Matsumoto to George Darling, 20 May 1959, box 23, folder: Medical Sociology, NAS archives.

108. Ibid.

109. Wolfe, *Freedom's Laboratory*, p. 157.

110. Gilbert W. Beebe to George Darling, 26 May 1959. Folder: Medical Sociology, NAS archives.

NOTES TO CHAPTER EIGHT

111. Herzog, *Cold War Freud,* p. 94.

112. Ibid.

113. Quoted in Goltermann, *The War in Their Minds,* p. 15.

114. Ra Zalashik, *Ad nafesh,* p. 176.

115. Ibid., p. 177.

116. Ibid.

117. Herzog, *Cold War Freud,* p. 98.

118. Goltermann, *The War in Their Minds,* p. 189.

119. Herzog, *Cold War Freud,* p. 102.

120. Ibid., p. 101.

121. Klein, "Former Concentration Camp," p. 342.

122. Herzog, *Cold War Freud,* p. 104.

123. Ibid.

124. Ibid.

125. Zwigenberg, *Hiroshima,* pp. 92–93, 146.

126. Ibid., p. 170.

127. Herzog, *Cold War Freud,* p. 97.

128. Ibid., p. 100.

129. Goltermann, *The War in Their Minds,* p. 201.

130. Cited in Zwigenberg, *Hiroshima,* p. 161.

131. Kubo, "Hibaku shita hitobito," p. 6.

Chapter Eight

1. Author's interview with Yokoyama Teruko, 13 January 2021.

2. Robert Jay Lifton, *Witness to an Extreme Century: A Memoir* (New York: Free Press, 2011), p. 96.

3. Author's interview with Robert Jay Lifton, 28 May 2020.

4. *Chūgoku Shinbun,* 14 November 1959.

5. *Chūgoku Shinbun,* 4 June 1960.

6. Naono, "Ban the Bomb!" p. 223.

7. *Chūgoku Shinbun,* 9 January 1961.

8. Arisue Ken, "Sengo hibakusha chōsa no shakai chōsashi," in Hama et al., *Hibakusha chosa o yomu,* p. 17.

9. *Chūgoku Shinbun,* 2 November 1967.

10. *Chūgoku Shinbun,* 15 December 1967.

11. Arisue, "Sengo hibakusha chōsa," p. 17.

12. Ibid., p. 13.

13. Ibid., p. 14.

14. Shimizu Kiyoshi to George Darling, 19 September 1967, box 43, folder: Dr. Kiyoshi Shimizu, NAS archives.

15. Cited in Arisue, "Sengo hibakusha chōsa," p. 13.

16. Author's interview with Yokoyama Teruko, 13 January 2021.

17. Ito Naoko, ed. *Genbaku higai ni kan suru jirei hōkoku: iki tsudzuketa 31-nen* (Hiroshima: Genbaku higaisha mondai kēsuwāka kondankai, 1976), p. 55.

18. Yagi Yoshihiro, "Genbaku mondai to hibakusha no jinsei ni kansuru kenkyū no kanōsei R. J. Rifuton no Hiroshima kenkyū to sore ni taisuru samazamana han'nō o megutte," in Hama et al., *Hibakusha chosa o yomu*, p. 154.

19. Frankl, *Yoru to kiri*, p. 180.

20. Ito, *Iki tsudzuketa 31nen*, p. 56.

21. Ibid., p. 57.

22. International Symposium on the Damage and After-Effects of the Atomic Bombing of Hiroshima and Nagasaki, and Shoichirō Kawasaki, *A Call from Hibakusha of Hiroshima and Nagasaki: Proceedings International Symposium on the Damage and After-Effects of the Atomic Bombing of Hiroshima and Nagasaki, July 21–August 9, 1977, Tokyo*. (Tokyo: Asahi Evening News, 1978), p. 127.

23. Takahara Kōhei, "Rifuton o Nihonjin ha dōno yō ni yonde kitaka," *Metafuyushika* 47 (December 2016): 69.

24. Ito, *Iki tsudzuketa 31nen*, p. 60.

25. Author's communication with Robert Jay Lifton, 20 July 2021.

26. Author's interview with Yokoyama Teruko, 13 January 2021.

27. Naono Akiko, "Hibakusha o hikiukeru dōhansha toshite no sōdan'in no kai kara keishōsha toshite no 'sōdanin no kai' e," in Genbaku Higaisha Sodan'in No Kai, *Hiroshima no sosharu wākā: Fujori no zesei to iu honshitsu ni semaru* (Hiroshima: Kamogawa shuppan, 2019), p. 67.

28. Author's interview with Sagura Kayo, 15 June 2021.

29. Chelsea Schieder, *Co-Ed Revolution: The Female Student in the Japanese New Left* (Durham, NC: Duke University Press, 2021), p. 2.

30. Author's interview with Sagura Kayo, 15 June 2021.

31. Author's interview with Nakamura Sumio, 16 June 2021.

32. Author's interview with Yokoyama Teruko, 13 January 2021.

33. Mimura Masahiro, introduction to *Hiroshima no sosharu waku*, p. 1.

34. Ito, *Iki tsudzuketa 31nen*, p. 3.

35. Ibid., p. 5.

36. Ibid., pp. 9, 26.

37. Ibid., p. 9.

38. International Symposium, *A Call from Hibakusha*, p. 47.

39. Cited in Zwigenberg, *Hiroshima*, p. 162.

40. International Symposium, *A Call from Hibakusha*, p. 26.

41. Ibid., p. 113.

42. Ibid., p. 28.

43. Ibid., p. 71.

44. Ibid., p. 70.

NOTES TO CHAPTER EIGHT

45. Ibid.

46. Ibid., p. 225.

47. Yagi, "Genbaku mondai," p. 155.

48. Cited in Takahara, "Rifuton," p. 67.

49. Yagi, "Genbaku mondai," p. 154.

50. Ibid., p. 162.

51. Ibid., p. 152.

52. Takhara, "Rifuton," p. 68.

53. Author's interview with Sagura Kayo, 15 June 2021.

54. Ibid.

55. Yagi, "Genbaku mondai," p. 159.

56. Author's interview with Sagura Kayo, 15 June 2021.

57. Ibid.

58. Committee on the Effects of Herbicides in Vietnam, *The Effects of Herbicides in South Vietnam* (Springfield, VA: National Technical Information Service, 1974), section 1, p. 5.

59. Ibid., section 5, p. 1.

60. Ibid., p. S-16.

61. Ibid.

62. Ibid.

63. Ibid., part B, p. 20.

64. Rambo discusses his name (which is actually Swedish) and his work in Vietnam in an oral history interview with the East-West Center in Hawaii: https://www .eastwestcenter.org/research/research-information-services/oral-history-project /terry-rambo. Accessed 17 September 2021.

65. Ibid., section 3, p. 44.

66. Ibid., section 3, p. 45.

67. Robert A. Jacobs, *Nuclear Bodies: The Global Hibakusha* (New Haven, CT: Yale University Press, 2022), p. 103.

68. See, for instance, Barry Weisberg, *Ecocide in Indochina: The Ecology of War* (San Francisco: Canfield Press, 1970). I thank Jon Mitchel for this reference.

69. GAP, *The Psychological and Medical Aspects of the Use of Nuclear Energy: The Meetings of the Group for the Advancement of Psychiatry, Held at the Berkeley-Carteret Hotel, Asbury Park, New Jersey on Sunday November 9, 1958, and on Sunday April 5 1959* (New York: Group for the Advancement of Psychiatry, 1960), p. 205.

70. Author's communication with Robert Jay Lifton, 8 January 2014.

71. GAP, *Psychological and Medical Aspects*, p. 209.

72. Ibid.

73. Lifton, *Extreme Century*, p. 92.

74. Jerome D. Frank, "The Great Antagonism," *Atlantic Monthly*, November 1958, p. 21.

75. Ibid., p. 24.

76. GAP, *Psychological and Medical Aspects*, p. 209.

77. Ibid.

78. Ibid., p. 218.

79. Ibid., p. 215.

80. Saul Aronow, ed., *The Fallen Sky: Medical Consequences of Thermonuclear War*. New York: Hill and Wang, 1963.

81. Physicians for Social Responsibility, *A History of Accomplishments* (Boston: Physicians for Social Responsibility, 2000), p. 1.

82. Author's communication with Robert Jay Lifton, 8 January 2014.

83. Aronow, *Fallen Sky*, pp. 45–46.

84. Ibid., p. 45.

85. Ibid., p. 54.

86. Robert Jay Lifton to Victor Sidel, 27 July 1963, box 14, folder: Physicians for Social Responsibility, NYPL-MSA.

87. GAP, Committee on Social Issues, *Psychiatric Aspects of the Prevention of Nuclear War* (New York: Group for the Advancement of Psychiatry, 1964), p. 224.

88. Ibid., p. 245.

89. Ibid., p. 235.

90. Ibid., p. 278.

91. Ibid., p. 247.

92. Ibid., p. 246.

93. Robert Jay Lifton, "Reason, Rearmament, and Peace: Japan's Struggles with a Universal Dilemma," *Asian Survey* 11, no. 1 (1 January 1962): 15.

94. Author's interview with Robert Jay Lifton, 6 December 2013.

95. Orr, *Panic Diaries*, p. 157. As Orr points out, Parsons' critique of psychiatry also contained a strong gender element.

96. Robert Jay Lifton to David Riesman, 9 April 1962, box 15, folder 8 (1962), Robert Jay Lifton papers, NYPL-MSA.

97. Robert Jay Lifton, "Psychological Effects of the Atomic Bomb in Hiroshima: The Theme of Death," *Daedalus* 3, no. 92 (Summer 1963): 482.

98. Ibid., p. 476.

99. Ibid., pp. 476, 478.

100. *PSR Newsletter*, March 1965, p. 2. Box 14, folder: Physicians for Social Responsibility, NYPL-MSA.

101. *PSR Newsletter*, May 1965, p. 1. Box 14, folder: Physicians for Social Responsibility, NYPL-MSA.

102. Richard Feinbbloom, MD, to PSR members, 5 March 1971. Box 14, folder: Physicians for Social Responsibility, NYPL-MSA.

103. Young, *The Harmony of Illusions*, p. 109.

104. Shepard, *War of Nerves*, p. 348.

105. Ibid.

106. Author's interview with Robert Jay Lifton, 28 May 2020.

NOTES TO THE CONCLUSION

107. Shepard, *War of Nerves*, p. 361.

108. Author's interview with Robert Jay Lifton, 28 May 2020.

109. Shepard, *War of Nerves*, p. 367.

110. James Orr, *The Victim as Hero: Ideologies of Peace and National Identity in Postwar Japan* (Honolulu: University of Hawai'i Press, 2005).

Conclusion

1. Nakane, *Progress in Social Psychiatry*, pp. 114–15.

2. Naono Akiko, *Genbaku taiken to sengo nihon: Kioku no keisei to keishō* (Tokyo: Iwanami shoten, 2015); Hiro Saito, "Reiterated Commemoration: Hiroshima as National Trauma," *Sociological Theory* 24, no. 4 (2006): 353–76.

3. Irit Keynan, "The Memory of the Holocaust and Israel's Attitude toward War Trauma, 1948–1973: The Collective vs. the Individual," *Israel Studies* 23, no. 2 (2018): 99.

4. Shigesawa, p. 36.

5. Yagi, "Genbaku mondai," p. 62. Funahashi wrote that Japanese were "too close" to the *hibakusha*, while at the same time implying that only a Japanese researcher could truly understand them.

6. Cited in Zwigenberg, *Hiroshima*, p. 87.

Index

A-bomb hospital, 146–47
A-Bomb Museum, 1
A-Bomb Victims Counselors Association, 230
Academy of Medicine, Lasker Award, 77
Adenauer, Konrad, 208
Adorno, Theodor, 84
Affektstupor, 169
Africa, 14, 61
AIDS, 13
air wars. *See* bombing
Akiba Tadatoshi, 234–36
Akihito Suzuki, 15, 161–62
Akita (Japan), 132
Aktion T4 euthanasia program, 43, 111–12
Allport, Gordon, 31–33, 41, 81–82, 128, 203
American Association for the Advancement of Science (AAAS), 241
American Civil War, 16
American Council on Education, 84
American Medical Association, Women's Auxiliary, 80–81
American Psychiatric Association (APA), 33, 77, 82, 90, 245–46, 253; Committee on the Implications of Atomic Energy, 81; and post-traumatic stress disorder (PTSD), 2
anthropology, 13
antinuclear movement, 211
antiracism, 9, 61, 71
anti-Semitism, 177, 204
Appel, Kenneth, 85
Arendt, Hannah, 204
arms race, 233, 262n10; as natural phenomenon, 240

Arnsberg, Conrad B., 63
Asada Shigeyo, 174–75, 186
Asbury Park (New Jersey), 239
Asia, 14, 20, 61, 239, 245
Asia Foundation, 215
Asia-Pacific War, 162–63
Associated Universities, Inc., 276n22
Association for the Scientific Study of Public Opinion (*Yoron kagaku kyōkai*), 196–97
atomic age, 78
atomic bomb, 7, 10, 23, 27, 43–50, 67–68, 74, 76, 81–83, 91, 132, 133, 136, 141, 149, 157, 187, 197, 198, 202, 203, 210–11, 220; A-bomb disease, 6, 9, 146, 170, 173–74, 215, 244; A-bomb fatigue, 173, 175, 207, 214, 227; A-bomb neurosis, 171, 175, 182; A-bomb psychiatry, 159, 168; A-bomb psychology, 191, 205; and absenteeism, 43, 65–66, 110, 137; American justification for, 234; and atom, as force for good, 86; and "atomic bomb neurosis," as term, 175; and capacity of equilibrium, 179; choice of targets for, 35–36; and dehumanization, power of, 224; demystification of, 64–66, 73, 115, 121, 208; devastation of, 212; distinctive impact of, 213; effects of, 206, 209; fear of, as dangerous and unscientific, 110; firebombing, connected to, 73; and inferiority complex, 232; and long-term suffering, American denial of, 251; mass reactions to, 95; medical impact of, 127; and mental anguish, 122–23; and mental damage, and declining morale, 65–66;

INDEX

atomic bomb (cont.)
mental impact of, 124, 159–60, 216; and microcephaly, 150; minimizing effects of, 116, 118; normalizing of, 53; and panic, 110–11, 114, 130–31, 200–201; physical and mental price of, 207; psychiatric effects of, 173; and psychic damage, 158–59; and psychogenic psychosis, 174; psychological effects of, and morale, 6; psychological impact of, 9, 29, 94, 96, 105–6, 108, 118, 124, 126, 131, 137, 154–55, 159, 221; as psychological weapon, 8, 29–30, 72; radiation, 64, 66, 69, 71–72, 75, 94, 105–6, 108, 113, 115, 117, 128, 153–54, 170, 174, 224, 226, 248; radiation, minimization of, 118; rational management of, 122; relief law, 225; researchers, effect on, 70; secrecy surrounding, 64; and sexual potency, 121; shadow of, 233; shelters, effectiveness of, 66, 93; shock of, 200–201; and silence, 255; social effects of, 78–79; social work, 143–45, 253; strategic bombing, as ultimate expression of, 72; and suffering, denial of, 123, 178–79; and suffering, recognition of, 178, 205; and suicide attempts, 174; and survivor guilt, 113–14; as symptom of wider disease, 90; trauma of, as main threat, 114; trauma of, long-term effects of, 244; as unprecedented, 198–99; and urbicide, 29–30. See also atomic bomb survivors
Atomic Bomb Casualty Commission (ABCC), 23, 55, 72, 86, 113, 122, 125–31, 133–48, 154, 156, 158, 169–70, 172, 187, 189–90, 192–93, 197, 208–9, 212–16, 218–20, 222–23, 225, 231, 234, 236–38, 251–54; anxiety, stance on, 150; "concentric circle model," 227; and denial, 155; establishing of, 124; female survivors, treatment of, 151–53; Medical Sociology department, 123, 150; mental health, neglect of, 129; patient and social work, by women, 155; psychiatric issues, lack of attention to, 169, 173; Social Welfare Funding, 149; social work, 150, 180–81; social work, as buying survivors' silence, 151; somatic issues, focus on, 123; survivors, concern with, 124; trauma, inability to tackle, 155; and women and Japanese-Americans, marginal status of, 155

atomic bomb survivors, 1, 3–4, 12, 122, 129, 147, 148, 175, 228, 233, 253; anxiety of, 2, 146; emotional and psychological problems of, as unscientific, 149; and emotional stability, regaining of, 154; mental health of, 254; "psychic closure" of, 244; re-adaptation of, 147; and self-confidence, problems with, 148; special truth of, 253; suffering of, denial of, 154; uplifting of, 149; as victimized and neglected, 154; women survivors, 230–31; women survivors, emotional instability of, 148–49; Yamashita group, 230
Atomic Bomb Victims Relief Committee, 212
atomic bura-bura disease: as hypochondria, 175; as laziness, 170–71, 175
atomic energy, 85, 88; anxieties about, 89; domestication of, 89; irrational pathological fear of, 86; mental health, effects on, 88; peaceful uses of, 87
Atomic Energy Commission (AEC), 117, 124, 127, 129, 143
Atomic Veterans Relief Act, 280n130
Atoms for Peace program, 86, 138
Auschwitz, 205–6, 217–18, 228–29
authoritarianism, 84, 125
automation, 87, 142
Azuma, Eiichiro, 131

Baldwin, Stanley, 37
Ballachey, Egerton L., 63
Battle of Guadalcanal, 109
Battle of the Bulge, 109
Baumetz, Julius, 217
Beard, George, 162
Beebe, Gilbert W., 121, 138–40, 150–51, 153–55, 215, 227
behavioralism, 101
behavioral theory, 101–2, 109
Benedict, Ruth, 20, 31, 52, 62–63, 194
Benton, William, 208
Berning, Heinrich, 176–77
Bettelheim, Bruno, 60, 80, 193, 203–5, 218, 229, 242; and national character, 61
Biess, Frank, 178
Bikini Atoll, 71, 105–6, 117, 126–28, 138, 214, 238
biodynamics, 83
Blumenthal, Kurt, 217

INDEX

Boasian anthropology, 52, 61, 132
bombing, 59; aerial, impact of on human psyche, 98; and anticipatory anxiety, 36–37; of civilians, 33–35, 37, 39, 45, 49; colonial, 34; and depersonalization, 166; morality of, 41; and "other," 34; price of, 49; psychologization of, 38–39, 41–43, 46, 48, 54; psychology, language of, 49; and race, 33–35; and racism, 35, 39; rationalization and quantification of, 40, 48–49; research analyst, 30–31; surveys, and psychological experts, 31; theory, 48; theory, American, 45–46; as transnational, 37, 41, 48; as "war of vegetative neuroses," 45–46
Bonhoeffer, Karl, 178–79
Boyer, Paul, 15, 98
Britain, 38, 111, 182; and Blitz, 250
Brues, Austin M., 72, 86, 125–26, 128, 136, 140
Buchenwald, 60, 204
Bureau of Sociological Research (BSR), 54–55, 58–59, 131–32, 193–94, 197, 237
Burma, 167
Burns, Susan, 15
Bush, Vannevar, 127
Byrnes, James, 193

Cameron, Dale, 101, 110, 115; antiracism of, 100; on group behavior, and McCarthyism, 100; on panic, 99–100; and Project East River, 98–99
Canton (China), 39
Cantril, Hadley, 200, 203, 210
capitalism, 87, 210
Capra, Frank, 189
care workers, 11–12; care workers' associations, 11; as female, 11. *See also* social work
Carson, Rachel, 239
Caruth, Cathy, 199
Central Intelligence Agency (CIA), 24, 208, 215
Chapman, Dwight, 103, 105–6, 109
Charcot, Jean-Martin, 17, 104, 162
Chernobyl (Ukraine), 15, 75–76
China, 14, 165; and "thought reform," 20
Chisholm, George Brock, 10, 22, 74–75, 77–80, 82–83, 85–86, 88, 91, 97, 239–41, 245, 251

Chodoff, Paul, 232–33
Chūbashi Masayoshi, 226
Civil Affairs Training Schools, 62
civil defense studies, 97, 116–18, 140
Clinchy, Everett R., 208
Cohen, Bruce, 13
Cohen, Gerald, 185
Cohen, Norman, 185
Cohen-Cole, Jamie, 84
Cold War, 4, 6, 30, 55, 75, 80, 83, 90–91, 94–95, 98, 100–101, 109, 128–29, 190, 195, 276n22; Cold War Asia, 52; Cold War West, 8, 223; "duck and cover" exercises, 116; "duck and cover" exercises, and "active shooter" exercises, 117; fearmongering, 84; and NSC 68 (policy paper), 107–8; science, 7, 192; social science, 79, 84
Collier, John, 54
colonialism, 9, 13–14, 16
Columbia University, 40, 86, 107, 195
combat psychiatry, 18, 43–44, 58, 114, 250; and "healthy fear," 45
Committee for National Morale (CNM), 31, 41, 83
Committee of Operations Analysts (COA), 40
Committee on the Effects of Herbicides in Vietnam, 237–38, 247
communism, 80, 84, 100, 105
compensation neurosis, 163
Compton, Arthur H., 208
concentration camps, 176–79, 182, 242; concentration camp syndrome 218, 246–47
Coney, James P., 117
conservatism, 84; as psychiatric disorder, 85
Conti, Leonardo, 45–46
Crane, Conrad, 35
Cross, Dorothea, 54
Cuban Missile Crisis, 223

Dachau, 60, 204
Dafinger, Sophia, 30, 42
Dairiki, Jack, 93
Darling, George, 136–38, 140–43, 150–51, 154–55, 213, 215
Death in Life (Lifton), 230, 234–35
Defense Atomic Support Agency (DASA), 140
dehumanization, 27, 229, 245; A-bomb's power of, 224; and emotional distancing,

INDEX

dehumanization (*cont.*)
243; of enemy "others," 34; industrialization, as psychological effect of, 242; and technology, 34
Desert Rock exercises, 95, 117, 121, 128, 157–58
Dessau, Dorothy, 145–46
DeWitt, John, 57
Dickerson, George W., 118
disaster neurosis, 159
disaster studies, 110; grand analogy of, 250; and panic, 115–16
Docus, Roy M., 129
Doi Takeo, 20
Dollard, Charles, 127
Dollard, John, 45
Douhet, Giulio, 34–38
Dower, John, 35, 57
Dresden (Germany), 48
Dulles, Allen W., 208
Dulles, John Foster, 208
Dunn, Halbert L., 43–44
Dyke, Kermit R., 195–96
dystrophy, 178

East Asia, 14, 16, 33, 56
Edo period, 196
Eichmann, Adolf, 242; trial of, 218, 223, 253
Eichmann in Jerusalem (Arendt), 204
Einstein, Albert, 90
Eisenhower, Dwight D., "Atoms for Peace" address, 86
Eisseler, Kurt R., 219–20
Eitinger, Leo, 176, 182, 218
electric shock, 167
electrotherapy, 104
elite men: in Eurocentric and male-centric world, 11; as researchers, 10–11
Embree, John, 58–59, 61, 63
Emergency Committee on Psychology, 31
"emotional management," 15, 95, 98, 107–8
emotional overload, 169
emotional turmoil, 169
enemy morale, as military target, 48
English, Horace B., 41, 63, 81
Eniwetok Atoll, 117
Enloe, Curtis, 64
entangled histories, 22
Erichsen, John Eric, 16–17
Erikson, Erik, 21, 31, 97, 243

ethnography, 62
Europe, 7, 16, 31, 35, 37, 39, 56–57, 59, 112, 166, 181, 183, 195, 223; imperialism of, 61; political prisoners in, 182
Ezov, Amiram, 1

Fallen Sky, The (PSR), 240–42
Farish, Mathew, 95
fascism, 9, 60–61, 84, 91, 203, 205, 220, 243
Fassin, Didier, 15
Federal Civil Defense Administration (FCDA), 101, 105; "Alert America" convoy, 92–93; and tranquilizers in fallout shelters, stocking of, 98
Federal Republic of Germany, 179. *See also* Germany
Federation of American Scientists (FSA), 82
Fedman, David, 29, 39–40
Felix, Robert H., 80
Finch, Glen, 108–9
firebombing, 35, 36, 65, 71, 73, 165–66, 190, 213, 226
Fleischhacker, H. H., 181
Folley, Jarrett, 130
Ford Foundation, 101, 108–9
Foucault, Michel, 13
France, 34
Frank, Jerome D., 103, 140–41, 239–41, 244–45
Frank, Lawrence K., 76, 78
Frankl, Viktor, 176, 181, 205, 218, 228–29
Fremont-Smith, Frank, 78, 88–89, 103, 140
Frenkel-Brunswik, Else, 84
Freud, Sigmund, 17, 21, 60, 62, 74, 90, 161, 195, 202, 243–44
Fromm, Erich, 31
Fukushima (Japan), 15, 75–76
Fukuzawa Yukichi, 161
Funabashi Yoshie, 230, 234–35, 252
Fusa Asaka, 145–46, 231

Garon, Sheldon, 36, 64
Geisel, Theodor S., 189
Geist, Edward, 101
gendered politics, 10
gensuikyō (Japan Council against Atomic and Hydrogen Bombs), 212, 215–16, 226
gentaikyō (Hiroshima City Atomic Bomb Casualty Treatment Council), 211–12, 215

INDEX

George Washington University, Human Resources Research Office (HumRRO), 117
Gerard, Ralph, 142
German Association of Returnees (VdH), 178–79
Germany, 15, 18, 21, 23–24, 30, 35, 38, 41, 45, 65, 68–70, 180–83, 204, 235, 252; authority of, acceptance of, 60; morale of, and shell shock, 177; national character of, 193; and "neurosis," prohibition of term, 177; and psychiatry, 111–12, 160, 176, 218; and "stab in the back" myth, 34; and trauma, 176. *See also* West Germany
Gerstaecker, Wilhelm, 179
Gestalt psychology, 82
Gestapo, 204–5
Ghamari-Tabrizi, Sharon, 109
Glass, Albert, 103–4, 118
Glazer, Nathan, 85
Glover, Edward, 111
Goldstein, Sharon, 85, 91
Goltermann, Svenja, 4, 7, 15, 176, 178
Gorer, Geoffrey, 31, 60, 62–63, 194
Graham, Henry, 195
Grayzel, Susan, 37
Great Kanto Earthquake, 37–38
Greenberg, Gary, 13
Grinker, Roy, 44, 97, 103–4, 106–7, 109, 185
Grinspoon, Lester, 241
Grob, Gerald, 96
Group for the Advancement of Psychiatry (GAP), 77–78, 81–82, 86, 95, 103, 239, 240, 245; Committee on Social Issues, 239; and mental hygiene campaign, advocating of, 101; and "post-traumatic" period, 102; and racism, as mental illness, 100

Habuto Eiji, 163
Hacking, Ian, 19
Hagedorn, Hermann, 90
Hagi (Japan), 132
Haifa (Israel), 185
Hall, Robert, 129–30
Halpern, Letz, 184
Hamatani Masaharu, 211, 216, 233
Hamaya Masaharu, 229
Hamburg (Germany), 29, 64
Handler, Philip, 236, 237
Hansen, Arthur, 56
Hanson, Fredrick R., 126–27, 130

Harada Katsuhiro, 226
Harada Tomin, 170
Hardie, George A., 143
Hashizume Bun, 133
Hatanaka Yuriko, 150–51
Hatano Kanji, 196
Hayashi, Brian, 55
Henshaw, Paul S., 125–26, 136
Herman, Ellen, 31–32, 59, 83
Hersey, John, 96–97, 105, 113
Herzog, Dagmar, 16, 216, 218, 264n47
hibakusha (A-bomb survivors), 1, 11, 15, 20, 21–24, 50, 52–53, 73, 76, 86, 94, 116, 122, 133, 147, 154–56, 160, 167–68, 180, 186, 198, 209, 248, 261n4; A-bomb's impact on, 126, 211; agency of, 229; and American censorship, 169; as anxious, 170, 215, 221; brain damage, research on, 88; care of, 211, 230–31, 234, 236; and cause of peace, 211; and compensation movement, 211, 213, 218–19, 221, 225; complaints, as legitimate, 171; cooperation of, 131, 222–23; cooperation of, concern over, 123–24; and denial, 6, 10; discrimination toward, 10; distrust of, 199, 201; emotional reaction of, 68–69; female, and maintaining steady jobs, 146; female, poor health of, 149; and ghosts, 207; healing and recovery of, 229; as heroes, 10; and "Hiroshima disease," 170–71; interviewees, as guinea pigs, 143; "life histories" from, 228; living conditions of, as poor, 173–74; and medical relief laws, 221; mental anxiety, 213–14; mental damage to, 93, 171; mental health, 95, 137, 174, 232; mental health, neglect of, 5; mental suffering, 159, 212; and "morale index," 68; and objectivity, impact on research, 8; and "overcoming suffering," concept of, 212; and panic, 201; peace movement, role in, 212; political role of, as martyrs, 234; and "press code," 5; problems of, as own making, 149–50; as prophetic survivors, 245–46; psychiatric examination of, 158; psychological and social damage to, 210–11, 214; psychology, 171; reactions of, 200–201; relief, 192; relief bill, 169; religious faith, 214; research, 172–73, 176, 188, 197, 216, 220, 244; resistance, 233, 235; as resource,

hibakusha (A-bomb survivors) *(cont.)*
223; responsibility for, 226; social impact
on, 140; sociological impact on, 211; and
special medical care, need for, 212; special nature of, 212–13; suffering of, 118,
134–37, 175–76, 211–14, 221, 225–26, 228,
233–34, 247, 255; as "suicide squad," 201;
and supernatural images, 206; survey of,
27, 29, 67–70; and survivor guilt, 113–14;
as survivor-hero, 233; and survivor syndrome, 218; testimonies of, 199–202, 207,
211, 221; trauma, 14; as trauma victims,
247; uniqueness of, 224–26, 234–35, 247,
254–55; as unreliable, 200; as victim-
heroes, 213, 247; wish to forget, 255.
See also Hiroshima (Japan); Nagasaki
(Japan)
hibaku taikensha (people who experienced
the A-bomb), 248
Hidankyō (Japan Confederation of A- and
H-Bomb Sufferers Organizations), 169–
70, 211–12, 232
Hijiyama (Japan), 124, 158
Hilgard, Ernest, 73
Himmler, Heinrich, 27, 41
Hiroshima (Japan), 1–7, 9, 20–24, 27, 39,
49–50, 52–53, 58, 64–65, 68, 71, 74–76,
82, 83, 86, 90–93, 96, 104, 106–7, 117–18,
122–24, 126, 128, 130, 132–34, 137–38,
141, 146, 153–54, 160, 168–70, 172–73,
176–78, 187, 192, 197–98, 200–201, 203,
209, 218, 225–28, 247, 248–50, 254; and
anti–Vietnam War movement, impact
on, 244–46; Auschwitz, as equivalent to,
206; bouncing back, as capable of, 66;
denial in, 251; destruction of, 66, 70, 73,
202, 232; heightened awareness to, 223;
and Holocaust, convergence of, 253;
and Japanese stoicism, 105; and killing
of civilians, as breaking morale, 29; as
military-worthy target, 29; as "preview
of next war," 70; psychic trauma in, 155;
psychological aspects of bombing of,
142; research, 188, 222, 242; researchers' gaze, turning away from, 73; and
silence, 255; and social workers, 145; and
survivor guilt, 113–14; typhoon in, 67;
victimization of, 207; victim status of, as
unique, 208
Hiroshima City Atomic Bomb Casualty
Treatment Council, 211–12

"Hiroshima Paradox," 208
Hiroshima Peace Museum, 138
Hiroshima University, 139, 141, 197–98,
207–8, 227
Hitler, Adolf, 60, 204
Hitsuda Heizaburō, 169
Hmong, 56
Hoff, Hans, 86
Hoffmann, Eva, 159
Hofstadter, Richard, 85
Holocaust, 4, 13, 15, 21, 104, 109, 118, 159,
192, 199, 204, 221, 228, 230, 232, 242; and
authoritarianism, connection to, 205;
heightened awareness to, 223; and Hiroshima, convergence of, 253; psychology,
229; redress movement, 225; research,
188, 220; trauma, 3, 22; uniqueness of,
218, 235; victimhood, 243
Holocaust survivors, 2–4, 7, 10–11, 15, 19–21,
24, 141, 172, 176, 184, 223, 250; and anxiety, 180; and compensation movement,
24, 192, 211, 213, 216, 218–19, 221, 224–
25, 234, 251, 264n47; and concentration
camp syndrome, 246–47; dehumanization of, 243; mental damage to, 216–18;
and Nazi defect of objectivity, 219; and
pension neurotics doctrine, 217; as potential burden, 181; as prophetic survivors, 245–46; psychological suffering of,
recognition for, 180–81; and repatriation
neurosis, 182; and trauma, 159; as unreliable soldiers, 183; unsympathetic to, 177,
181–82
Home from War (Lifton), 245
homosexuality, 163, 247
Hong Kong (China), 20
Hopkins, William, 56–57
Horowitz, Mardi J., 246
Horwitz, Allan, 16
Hosokoshi Masaichi, 112
Hovland, Carl, 107
Human Resources Research Office
(HumRRO), 117, 121
Huyssen, Andreas, 13
hysteria, 16–17, 38, 112, 161, 164

Imahori Seiji, 226–27
Imperial Navy Technological Research
Institute, 194, 196
Inazawa Junko, 230
industrialization, 162

INDEX

Inouye, Karen M., 57–58, 242
Institute for Educational Leadership (IFEL), 195
International Atomic Energy Agency (IAEA), 88
Invasion from Mars (Cantril), 200
Iron Curtain, 88
Ishida Tadashi, 205, 216, 224, 226, 228–31, 234–35, 246–47, 253–54
Ishihara Yoshirō, 157, 172
Ishino, Iwao, 55
Israel, 3, 15, 21, 24, 176, 185, 187, 216, 252; and Holocaust survivors, 182; and Holocaust survivors, fault of, 181; and mental illness, 180–81; and war trauma, attitude toward, 183
Israeli Defense Forces (IDF), 184; and "battle shock," 183, 185
Israel-Lebanon war, 183
Italy, 34, 185
Itō Takeshi, 216, 226
Iwakuni (Japan), 150–51, 202

Jacobs, Robert, 116, 239
Jaffa (Israel), 185
Janet, Pierre, 104, 162
Janis, Irving, 22–23, 32, 45, 92, 99, 101–2, 104–5, 109, 112–13, 116–17, 137, 193, 200–201, 213, 222–23, 240, 250; on absenteeism, 110; and defense planning, impact on, 107–8, 115; on "emotional inoculation," 108, 117; on emotion management, 107; grand analogy, as proponent of, 109, 118; on "groupthink," 107; on "near-miss" reactions, 114; panic, as critic of, 95, 110–11; and "psychological inoculation," 250; on traumatic neurosis, 110–11, 114
Janz, Hans-Werner, 179
Japan, 1, 3, 6, 10–11, 15, 18, 20, 22, 30, 34, 36–38, 40, 48, 50, 52, 60, 65–66, 68, 73, 75, 77, 84, 94, 121–22, 126, 128, 131–32, 136, 176, 179, 181, 185, 187, 189, 201–2, 214, 216, 221, 223–25, 236, 248–49, 251, 254; and A-bomb, "denial of awe" from, 64; applied psychology in, 194; authoritarianism in, 125; and bearing witness, model of, 253; and compensation movement, 218–19; concentration camp, as akin to, 205; and "democratic mind," creating of, 192–94, 196–97; and Great Kanto Earthquake,

37; and Imperial Army, 14, 112, 162–63, 167–68, 177, 252; and Japanese military, homosocial setting of, 163; and Japanese minds, policing of, 53; and Japanese people, as subhuman, 35; and Japanese veteran organizations, and "white gown soldiers," 180; Korean War's effect on, 203; mental issues in, and Westernized lifestyle, 166; military and civilian victims in, connection between, 160; national character of, 193; as "other," 53; post-traumatic stress disorder (PTSD) in, rise of, 246; postwar transformation of, 190–91; and psychic trauma, absence of, 253; psychology of, 55, 59, 61–63; psychology of, and imperial state, 194–95; racial hatred toward, 35; racialized notion of, 53; racism toward, 35, 39, 49, 59, 64; social worker movement in, 247; survivor-witness model of, 253; trauma, as rare term in, 159; and trauma, politics of, 246; and traumatic neurosis, research into, 160; unique spirit of, 252; and United States, reconciliation with, 220
Japanese Americans, 71, 155, 191, 258; and internment camps, 33, 61, 132, 251; internment of, 53, 56; internment of, stress on, 57–58; as model minority, 136; Nisei, 56, 59, 64, 69, 93, 131–32, 141, 193–94, 196, 282n39; and psychic trauma, 58; seizure of, 100
Japanese Disabled Veterans Association (JDVA), 180
Japanese military psychiatry, 160, 163, 175; and "bad" and "good" suicides, 165; and nervous breakdowns, 166; in Reboul, 165–66; and self-discipline, 165
Japanese psychiatry, 158–62, 167, 176, 186–87; and Westernized lifestyle, and mental issues, 166
Japanese Psychological Association (JPA), 202, 206
Japanese Psychologists for Peace (JPP), 202–3, 206–7
Japanese psychology, 5–6, 53, 55, 194–95, 202
Japan Public Opinion Research Association (*Nihon yoron chōsa kenkyūkai*), 196
Japan Special Higher Police, 196
Johns Hopkins University Operations Research Office (ORO), 117

308 INDEX

Joint Panel on Medical Aspects of Atomic
Warfare, 117
Josephson, Paul, 86
Joshua Macy Jr. Foundation, 103
Jungk, Robert, 201–2
Justice for Atomic Veterans Act of 1998,
280n130
Juza Unno, 37

Kadia, Miriam Kingsberg, 9, 193–94, 210
Kalinowsky, Lothar, 111–12, 187
Kalmus, Ernst, 184
Kamata Shirabe, 162–63
kamikaze, 37, 80
Kanai Tashirō, 189, 220–21
Kanba Michiko, 231
Kaneko Hiroshi, 196
Kaori, Iida, 155, 187
Karacas, Cary, 29, 39–40
Kardiner, Abraham, 18, 20–21, 102, 114–15
Kasamtsu Akira, 164–65
Katō Fusajirō, 167
Katō Masaaki, 167–68, 171
Katō Reiko, 232
Katsunuma Seizō, 166
Kawai Takeo, 226, 228
Kawasaki (Japan), 40
Kawashima Takefumi, 195
Keio University, 161, 226
Kent, Pauline, 62–63
Keynan, Irit, 183–84, 249
Khartoum (Sudan), 34
Kido Kōtarō, 203–6, 242
Kikkawa Kiyoshi, 146, 175
Kinoko no kai (Mushroom Cloud Organiza-
tion), 150
Kitanaka, Junko, 15
Klein, Hillel, 218
Klineberg, Otto, 52, 81, 86, 88, 90, 107
Kluckhohn, Clyde, 193–94
Kobe (Japan), 40, 64–65; earthquake, 247
Kocka, Jürgen, 22
Kodama Aki, 124, 145–50, 153, 155, 171, 175,
178, 215, 231–32, 252–53, 284n91
Koikari, Mire, 145
Konuma Masuho, 22, 24, 123–24, 141, 156,
167–69, 173–75, 181–82, 185–88, 222–23,
230, 232, 252–54; as elitist, 160; and
Freud's work, translation of, 161; and
incest, 157; and military veterans, follow-
up research on, 171–72; as nonwhite sci-
entist in white world, 160; and Oedipus
complex, interest in, 171; and psychoanalysis, and errant sexuality, 158, 171;
and psychosomatic medicine, interest in,
157, 171–72; and sexuality, darker side of,
157; as unorthodox figure, 159, 161
Korean War, 104, 129, 203, 211
Korumaru Masahiro, 167
Krech, David, 70, 81–82, 90, 203; Krech
report, 83–87
Kretschmar, Ernst, 219
Kristallnacht, 204
Kubo Yoshihide, 191–92, 195, 197
Kubo Yoshitoshi, 1–2, 4–6, 20–22, 24, 123–24,
133, 156, 160, 191, 193–97, 199, 201–2, 211–
15, 218, 220, 222, 228, 230, 253; and compensation movement, importance to, 221;
and complex anxieties, emphasis on, 226;
and fictional Mars invasion, as reference
for tackling A-bomb experience, 200; and
Lifton, meeting with, 223–24; and mistrust
of survivor's voices, 251–52; objectivity
of, 221, 229; and "peace psychology," 192,
210; and social science, ideal of, 209, 221;
on survivor experience, and peace, 198;
and United States, affiliation with, 216
Kurihara Sadako, 230, 234–35
Kuromaru Shoshiro, 168
Kusano Nobuo, 214
Kyoto (Japan), 145, 195
Kyushu University, 169

La Barre, Weston, 62, 74, 81, 90
Lambros, Jeanne, 92
Laub, Dori, 199
Lebanon War (1982), 183
Leible, Samuel, 92
Leiderman, Herbert, 241
Leighton, Alexander, 13, 22–23, 31, 52, 54–
56, 59–61, 63, 65–67, 71–72, 76, 86, 90–91,
99, 100, 103–4, 123, 131–33, 136, 191,
197, 237–38, 251, 254; and "behavioral
weather stations," 82, 88; as guilt-ridden,
70; on individual psychology and group
psychology, 53; on Japanese "other," 53;
on psychic trauma, 58; and race, rejection of, 57; on "walking death," 69; on
"walking death," and mental stress, 58
Leighton, Dorothea Cross, 54, 59

INDEX

Leighton, Jane Murphy, 54
LeMay, Curtis, 39, 267n54
Lerner, Paul, 16–17
Levinson, Daniel, 84
Lévi-Strauss, Claude, 86
Lewin, Kurt, 31, 82
Leys, Ruth, 15, 19
Lifton, Betty Jean, 1
Lifton, Robert Jay, 1–6, 9–10, 12–13, 19–24, 31, 58, 97, 103–4, 107, 109, 123, 140–43, 153–54, 187, 193, 205, 213, 222, 225, 229, 233, 242–47, 250; and bearing witness, 236, 253; criticism of, 234–35; and Kubo, meeting with, 223–24; and military-academic complex, rejection of, 223–24; radicalization of, 223–24; and "reformulation," ideas of, 230, 235; and survivor syndrome, 218; and survivor trauma, openness to, 223; and victims of war, 223
Likely, Wadsworth, 129
Likert, Rensis, 42, 63, 81, 127–28, 139, 196; interview techniques and public opinion surveys, as pioneer of, 32
Lindee, Susan, 122, 124, 134
Livingstone, Robert, 130
London (England), 34, 37, 166; and Blitz, 7–8, 10–11, 102, 111, 250
Lonely Crowd, The (Riesman), 85
Los Angeles (California), 92, 129
Lowen, Bernard, 244–45
Luce, Henry R., 208
Lucky Dragon 5 incident, 86, 138, 211, 238
lynching, 67, 100

MacArthur, Douglas, 63
Maco, Joseph, 15
Madagascar, 61–62
Malinowski, Bronisław, 203–4
Manhattan Project, 71, 127–28
Mannoni, Octave, 61–62
Man's Search for Meaning (Frankl), 205, 228
Marcuse, Herbert, 42
Marshall, S. L. A., 95, 100
Marshall Islands, 239
Masaharu Hamatani, 211
Masaya, Abe, 206–7
Masco, Joseph, 116–17
Maslow, Abraham, 75
Massachusetts, 240
Masserman, Jules, 80–81, 83

Matsumoto, Nobue, 135
Matsumoto, Y. Scott, 22–24, 55, 123–24, 131–32, 134, 138–40, 142–46, 148, 151–54, 158–59, 171–74, 187, 193–94, 197, 215, 227, 251–52, 254; as bi-cultural, 135; empiricism of, 137; and incest, 157; as model Japanese-American, 136; as nonwhite scientist in white world, 160; and psychosomatic medicine, interest in, 157; racial straitjacket, placed in, 155; skepticism of, 141
Matsumoto Matataró, 194
Matsumura, Janice, 14–15, 165
Matsumura Shūitsu 206–7
Mauthausen, 176–77
May, Mark, 80, 84
McCarthyism, and mob behavior, 100
McDougall, William, 14
McIntyre, Ross, 56
McLean, Franklin, 240
McLean, Joseph, 95–96
McNally, Richard, 159
McVeigh, Brian, 194–95
Mead, Margaret, 31, 78, 86, 241
Meerloo, Joost, 103–5
Meguro Katsumi, 171
Meiji era, 162–63
Mendelson, Jack, 241
Menninger, Karl, 31, 77, 241
Menninger, Roy, 241
Menninger, William, 75, 77–80, 82–83, 91, 99, 241
Menninger group, 272n7
"mental hygiene," 79–80, 83
mental illness, 32, 80, 102, 157, 157, 180–81; as physiological susceptibility, 57–58; racism as, 100; and social environment, 157; stigma of, 10, 178, 247
mental injuries, 183
Meyer, Adolf, 31, 53–54, 57–58
Micale, Mark S., 14, 16–17
Michael, Donald, 102–3, 105–7, 109
Middle East, 14
militarism, 84
military-academic complex, 7, 52–53, 100, 103, 223–24; psychiatry's role in, 250
military-industrial complex, 239
military psychiatry, 7, 18–19, 22, 95, 98, 105, 110, 116, 175, 182–83, 185, 187, 245; German, 21; and "hotbeds of hysteria," 112;

military psychiatry (*cont.*)
  Japanese, 24, 163; United States, 111; and wartime research, 94
Miller, Jennifer, 56, 190, 203
Miller, Louise, 185
Mills, China, 13
Mimura Masahiro, 231
Minkowski, Eugene, 219–20
Mitchell, Billy, 37
Miyagi Otoya, 206–7
Miyazaki Ichiu, 37
modernity, 16, 90; and mechanized mass killing, 206
Moore, Felix, 136
"Morale and Prevention of Panic" conference, 103–4
morale studies, 29, 30, 32, 48–49, 56, 82–84, 110, 197; and mental stress and social health, 80
Morawski, Jil, 85, 91
Mori Michiko, 207
Moritaki Ichirō, 209
Morito Tatsuo, 207–8
Morocco, 34
Motora Yūjirō, 195
Mumford, Lewis, 37
Murphy, Jane M., 238
Myers, Charles, 13–14, 17–18

Nagai, Takashi, 113–14
Nagasaki (Japan), 3–6, 9, 15, 21–23, 29, 41, 49–50, 64–65, 75, 83, 91, 96, 106–7, 114, 118, 122, 126, 128, 137, 142, 173, 187, 202, 206, 212, 214, 226, 230–31, 249–50, 253–54; bouncing back, as capable of, 66; Investigative Commission for Studies on Mental Damages to People Who Experienced the Bombing, 248; and mental suffering, 159; psychological aspects of bombing of, 142; survivors, 20–21, 88, 116, 159–60, 169, 209, 247; survivors, uniqueness of, 247
Nagasaki Medical School, and "atomic bomb neurosis," 175
Nagasaki University, 248; and neurotic cases, 169–70
Nagino Iwao, 164
Nagoya (Japan), 40
Nakamura Eri, 14–15, 164
Nakamura Sumio, 231–32, 254

Nakamura Tsuyoshi, 167
Nakane Yoshibumi, 261n4
Nakano Seiichi, 209–11, 216, 226
Nakao Maika, 37
Nakayama Hiromi, 170
Nakazawa Masao, 5, 14–15, 175–76, 186, 254
Nanking incident, 205–6
Naono Akiko, 226, 249
napalm, 30
National Academy of Sciences (NAS), 127, 142, 236
national character studies, 84
National Committee against Mental Illness, 77
National Conference of Christians and Jews, 208
National Eugenics Law, 168
National Foundation of Psychiatric Research, 80–81
National Institute of Mental Health (NIMH), 80, 98–99
National Research Council (NRC), 31, 110, 126; Committee on Atomic Casualties, 127; Committee on Disaster Studies, 108–9; Disaster Research Committee, 107
National Science Foundation, 78
Native Americans, 23, 56
Navajo, 54
Nazis, 34, 41, 59, 168, 179, 182, 199, 219–20, 242, 245; health, obsessed with, 43; mental health, attitudes to, 45–46
Neel, James, 130
Nemoto Masaya, 208
Neumann, Franz, 42
neurasthenia, 161–62, 183
Nevada, 117–18, 239
Newall, Cyril, 36
New Deal, 32, 132, 196
New Guinea, 14
New York, 33, 63, 77, 103, 140, 218
New York Academy of Medicine, 103
New York Academy of Science, 140
Night and Fog (film), 205
Nimitz, Chester, 35
Nishikawa Taneo, 169, 187
Nishimura Kiyoto, 148, 172
Nitze, Paul H., 107–8
Noma Hiroshi, 205
North Africa, 183
North America, 74, 76

INDEX

North Korea, 14
nuclear age, 34, 71, 75, 90, 250
nuclear anxiety, 98
nuclear energy, 74, 88, 90–91, 239; embrace of, 75; mental health aspects of, 76
nuclear psychology, 7, 19, 223, 249
nuclear war, 30, 97–98, 100, 109, 116–17, 242–43
nuclear weapons, 7–8, 35, 53, 70–71, 83, 90, 92–93, 116, 140–41, 233–34, 237–40, 251; demystifying of, 121; psychological reactions to, as temporary, 110
Nuremberg trials, 111–12

Oakes, Guy, on "emotional management," 15, 95
Obonai Torao, 194
Ōe Kenzaburō, 255
Office of Indian Affairs (OIA), 54–55
Office of Strategic Services (OSS), 42, 63
Office of War Information (OWI), 31–32, 42, 60, 62–63, 69, 72, 193; Far East Division, 59; Foreign Morale Analysis Division, 35–36, 52, 59, 62–63
Ogura Kaoru, 201–2
Oho Gensaku, 170, 172–73, 187
Ōhori, Joe, 134
Okada Kei, 168
Okada Yasuo, 168
Okinawa (Japan), 15, 145
Okumura Nikichi, 169
Omura Hospital, 169
Ōmuta Minoru, 150
Ōnishi Yoshie, 165
Operation Cedar Falls, 238
Operation Crossroads, 71–73, 106, 128
Opler, Morris, 59
Oppenheim, Hermann, 16–17, 162
Orr, Jackie, 15
Orr, James, 247
Orwell, George, and doublethink, 240
Osaka (Japan), 40, 64–65, 154
Osaka Eiko, 195, 197
Our Job in Japan (film), 189, 193

Paris (France), 34, 208
Parsons, Anne, 243
Parsons, Talcott, 243
Parsons, William S., 71, 128
Passen, Friedrich, 177

Passin, Herbert, 193–94, 196–97
Paul, Helmut, 181
Peace Study Group, 203
Pearl Harbor (Hawaii), 62
peer groups, and vulnerability to demagogues, 85
Peking (China), 34
pesticide, 239
Philippines, 239
Physicians for Social Responsibility (PSR), 240–42, 244–45
Pick, Daniel, 79
"PIE principles," 17–18
politics of memory, 10
Pols, Hans, 14
Porter, Roy, 76
Poston (Arizona), 54, 56–59, 69, 131–32
post-traumatic stress disorder (PTSD), 2–7, 12–13, 15–17, 94, 102, 142, 159–60, 177, 236, 248–49; acknowledgment of, 247; in *DSM I*, 18–19; in *DSM II*, 18; in *DSM III*, 24, 246, 253; as legitimate syndrome, 248; rise of, 223–24, 253
Post-Vietnam Syndrome, 245
Price, David, 35–36
Princeton University, 86
prisoners of war (POWs), 20, 176–77, 218; victim status of, 178
Project East River, 98, 108, 276n22
Project Troy, 276n22
Pross, Christian, 217
psychiatry, 14–15, 21–24, 31, 71, 77–78, 80–83, 90, 97, 99, 142, 167, 172, 195, 240, 247, 251, 253, 272n7; and academic-military complex, role in, 250; and atomic bomb, 249; combat, 250; and defense, role in, 98; and democracy, 33; expansion of, 79; and nuclear normality, role in, 243; popularity of, 76; as social critique, 76; as stand-alone field, 252; transcultural, 20; transnational nature of, 185; World War II's paradoxical influence on, 96
psychic damage, 130, 164, 179, 250; by atomic bombs, 158–59
psychoanalysis, 79, 158, 186 as "Jewish science," 218
psychological defense studies, 106
psychological warfare, 39
psychology, 31, 48, 71, 78, 81, 83, 90–91, 97, 99, 195, 198, 247, 249, 272n7; and atomic

psychology (*cont.*)
bomb crisis, 82; and colonial racial hierarchies, justifying of, 52, 61–62; role of, 87; as social critique, 76; and world, attempt to save, 75
Public Opinion Research Division, 196
Pyle, Ernie, 57

race, 57, 131; debunking of, 52; and "race war" between United States and Japan, 52; and trauma, 54
racism, 27, 35, 39, 49, 55, 59, 84, 132, 136, 194, 243, 252; as mental illness, 100; psychological language, clothed in, 62
Rambo, Terry, 238, 297n64
RAND Corporation, 23, 99, 101, 107–8, 193, 240
Rechtman, Richard, 15
Reich Air Defense League (RLB), 43; on *Stimmung* (mood) and *Haltung* (attitude), distinction between, 43
Rensmeir, John C., 127
Resnais, Alain, 205
Reynolds, Earl, 153
Riesman, David, 1, 85, 239, 244
Rivers, Thomas, 127
Rivers, W. H. R., 13–14, 104
Rockefeller Foundation, 103, 127
Royal Air Force (RAF), 39
Russia, 183. *See also* Soviet Union
Russo-Japanese War, 171

Sagura Kayo, 230–31, 235–36
Saito Hiro, 249
Sakurai Tsunao, 164–65, 167–68
Salmon, Thomas, 17–18
Sanford, Nevitt, 84
Sasaki, Tom, 55, 132
Sassoon, Siegfried, 14
Savage, Carlton, 107–8, 116
Schaffer, Ronald, 35, 40
Schieder, Chelsea, 231
Schlesinger, Arthur, Jr., 85
Schneck, Ernest Gunther, 176–77
Schneider, Kurt, 178
Schull, William J., 140
Seki Keigo, 197
Serlin, David, 89–90
Shapira, Michal, 79
Shatan, Chaim, 20, 245, 246

"shell shock," 13, 38, 172, 174, 177, 249–50; concept of, 17–18
Shepard, Ben, 15, 19, 111
Shigesawa, Atsuko, and "denial of awe," 64, 250
Shimizano Yasuo, 168
Shimizu Ikutarō, 203–6
Shimizu Kiyoshi, 121, 153–55, 187, 227, 242
Shimofusa Sanatorium, 167–68
Shimoyama Tokuji, 205–6
Shneerson, Fishel, 181
Sidel, Victor, 242
Silent Spring (Carson), 239
Sino-Japanese War: First, 171; Second, 39
slavery, 13
social science, 73, 79, 82, 132, 209; and war effort, 55–56
Social Science Research Council (SSRC), 78, 128, 200
social work, 148–55, 230–31, 232, 235–36, 246, 254; and Christianity, 145; and democracy, 145; and self-help, emphasis on, 147; and social change, contribution to, 252–53. *See also* care workers
social workers' movement, 247, 252; and A-bomb sociology, relation to, 253
Society for the Psychological Study of Social Issues (SPSSI), 31, 81, 83, 203; Committee on International Peace, 82; and "Human Nature and Peace," as psychologists' peace manifesto, 82
sociology, 198
Solomon Islands, 14
South Korea, 14
Soviet Union, 18, 91, 96–98, 108, 178; Atoms for Peace programs, 86. *See also* Russia
Spain, 34
Spicer, Edward, 33, 54, 132
Spicer, Rosamond, 33, 54
Spiegel, John, 44, 97, 105, 185
Spinoza, Baruch, 228–29
Srole, Leo, 181
Stalin, Joseph, 36
Stapledon, Olaf, 37
Staub, Michael, 84
Stengel, E., 111; on "air-raid phobia," 102
Stern, Judith, 181
Stirling County Study, 54
Stouffer, Samuel, 107
Strauss, Hans, 218

INDEX

Strecker, Edward, 33, 126–27
Sugita Naoki, 162, 164, 166
Supreme Commander for the Allied Powers
(SCAP), 55, 63, 191, 251, 254; censorship
by, 186; Civil Information and Education
(CIE) unit, 133, 193–97
survey movement, 231
Suwa Keishiro, 164
Swarthmore College, 70–71

Taeuber, Irene N., 135–37, 139–40, 157
Taiwan, 14, 34
Tanaka Tarō, 166
Tanizaki Jun'ichirō, 171
Taylor, George, 59
Taylor, Grant, 229–30, 215
terrorism, 117
Thomas, Dorothy, 132
Toda Teizō, 196
Togawa Yuiko, 196
Tokyo (Japan), 37–40, 64–65, 123–24,
133, 154, 231; bombing raid of, 35;
firebombing of, 165–66, 190
Tokyo Imperial University, 195; Aviation
Research Institute, 194
Tomonaga Masao, 261n4
Tone, Andrea, 75, 98
Topaz internment camp, 62
totalitarianism, 100, 229, 242; and concentration camps, 204; and war, 203–4
tranquilizers, 98
trauma, 2, 15, 20, 24, 45, 52, 55, 58, 61, 95, 96,
118, 143, 159, 176, 206; applied, 8; and
brainwashing, 104; chosen, 249; and civil
defense, intersection with, 97; and civilian morale, 249–50; collective, as societal
post-traumatic stress disorder (PTSD),
249; combat, 249–50; definition of, 12;
discourse of, 13; and "emotional inoculation," 108, 115–16; gendered history of,
16; and historicity, importance of, 19;
hostility toward, 112; long-term impact
of, 248; malingerers, 246; management of,
112–13; and modernity, 16; nationalization of, 249; nuclear, 11, 223; overcoming
of, 154; patients, as problem, 178; and
personality structures, altering of, 97;
politicization of, 247; politics of, 246; psychic, 58, 129–30, 155, 253; as psychogenetic reaction, 164; psychological, 221;

and psychological experts, rise of, 23;
and race, 14, 54; and radiation, 153–54;
resistance to, 178; and self-discipline, 165;
studies, 3–4, 6, 94, 251–52; survivor, 223;
suspicion toward, 97; temporary nature
of, 103–5, 115; as term, 12, 38; theory of,
21, 72; transcultural, 9; and traumatic
memory, 200; and traumatic neurosis, 17–
18, 30, 46, 110–11, 114, 159–62, 170, 186;
and war, 7; "war trauma," 183; as word, 30
Trenchard, Hugh, 36–37
Trotter, Wilfred, 60
Truman, Harry S., 29, 79, 124, 193; and Truman letter, 125
Tsuboi Hayamai, 162
Tsuchiyama, Tamie, 55, 132
Tsuiki Shiro, 169
Tsuno-gun, 132
Tunisia, 105
Tyhurst, James, 102, 111

Uchimura Yūshi, 164–69, 178–79, 181, 187
Uematsu, Shichikuro, 161
Ugaki Kazushige, 37
United Nations (UN), 52–53, 76, 85, 90–91,
210; UNESCO, 9, 86–89, 208
United States, 3, 6, 22–24, 30, 50, 56, 60, 62,
65, 71, 73, 75, 86, 90, 92–94, 96–98, 105–7,
113, 116, 118, 122, 124–26, 129, 136, 140,
170, 182, 186–87, 190–91, 195–97, 201–3,
208, 210, 216, 223, 237, 243, 248, 250, 253;
American society, militarization of, 117;
fascism in, rise of, 84; and Japan, reconciliation with, 220; mass psychological
trauma as threat to, 95; mental health
crisis in, 76, 81; and morale studies, rise
of, 48
University of Hawaii, 55
University Scholars Society for the Preservation of Peace and Scholarship (Heiwa
to gakumon o mamoru daigakujin no
kai), 209–12
urban bombing, 23–24
urbicide, 29–30
US Army Air Force (USAAF), 29, 36, 40,
203, 224–25; terror bombing, turn to, 39
US Army Resources Research Office
(HumRRO), 121
US Army Specialized Training Program, Far
Eastern section, 62

314

US-Japan security treaty (ANPO), 225, 231
USSR. *See* Soviet Union
US Strategic Bombing Survey (USSBS),
  5–6, 23, 27, 29, 31, 36, 38, 40–41, 49, 52–
  55, 70–72, 75–76, 81–83, 85–86, 90–91,
  93–95, 96, 99–100, 109, 111, 113–16, 118,
  121–22, 125, 127–28, 131, 133, 137, 139,
  160, 163, 179, 187, 192, 197, 200, 203, 208,
  213, 222–24, 229, 237–38, 241, 247, 251,
  254; Civil Defense Division (CDD), 63,
  66; database, 209; on Japanese morale,
  50; "little men" argument, 106; Medical
  Division, 63, 66; and mental breakdown,
  as negligible, 30; and mental suffering,
  46; Morale Division, 32, 63–66, 105,
  132; and "morale index," 46; political
  activism by, 250; psychological implications of, as paramount, 73; and psychological morale, 44; and psychological
  morale versus behavioral morale, 43;
  reports of, and morale survey, 42; and
  trauma, definition of, 45; and traumatic
  neuroses, 46; Urban Area Division
  (UAD), 66
US Veterans Administration, 97

Venzlaff, Ulrich, 181
Vietnam War, 18, 56, 83, 141, 250, 253–54;
  and Agent Orange, 10–11, 236–37; anti-
  Vietnam War activism, 223–24, 244–45;
  "gas warfare" in, 245; and medical
  debates, politicization of, 246
Volkan, Vamik, 249
Voorhis, Horace Jeremiah, 74, 90

Wakabayashi Setsuko, 230
Wake, Naoko, 93, 136
War in the Air, The (Wells), 33
war neurosis, 159, 162–64, 167, 170–71; long-
  term impact of, 137; psychogenic cases
  of, 184
War Relocation Authority (WRA), 54
Warren, Shields, 124
Warren, Stafford, 127, 140

wartime psychology, 32
Watanabe Shōji, 211
Waters, Ethan, 13
Weart, Spencer, 15
Weed, Lewis, 127
Wells, H. G., 33, 36
West Germany, 176, 178, 187, 216–17.
  See also Germany
white paper movement, 216, 220–21, 225
Wilson, Carroll L., 127
Windscale plant, 88
Witness to an Extreme Century (Lifton), 222
Wolfe, Audra, 8, 208
Wolman, Benjamin, 183–84
World Brotherhood (WB), 208, 215
World Federation for Mental Health
  (WFMH), 74, 87–89
World Health Organization (WHO), 10, 14,
  74, 76–77, 86–88, 101
World War I, 13, 17–18, 21, 31, 34, 37–38,
  48, 54, 60, 104, 111–12, 162, 163, 176–78,
  182, 184
World War II, 8, 18, 21, 31, 36, 76–77, 84–85,
  93–94, 96, 98, 100, 104–5, 111, 128, 160,
  176, 178, 229, 237, 249
Wright, Diana, 165
Wylie, Philip, 101, 110

Yagi Yasuhiro, 234–35
Yale University, 62
Yamanashi Hanzō, 37–38
Yamashita Asayo, 230
Yamate Shigeru, 211–13, 216, 226
Yokohama (Japan), 40
Yokoyama Teruko, 222, 230–31
Yom Kippur War (1973), 183
Yoneyama Keizō, 226, 228
Young, Allan, 15, 18–20
Yoyogi Psychiatric Hospital, 12
Yu, Henry, 131
Yukimune Hajime, 232

Zalashik, Rakefet, 180, 183
Zanetty, J. Enrique, 40